THE CATHOLIC ANTHOLOGY

THE MACMILLAN COMPANY
NEW YORK · BOSTON · CHICAGO · DALLAS
ATLANTA · SAN FRANCISCO

MACMILLAN & CO., LIMITED
LONDON · BOMBAY · CALCUTTA
MELBOURNE

THE MACMILLAN CO. OF CANADA, LTD.
TORONTO

THE CATHOLIC ANTHOLOGY

BY

THOMAS WALSH, Ph.D., Litt.D.

New York
THE MACMILLAN COMPANY
1927

ARTHUR J. SCANLON, S.T.D.,
Censor Librorum

✠PATRICK CARDINAL HAYES,
Archbishop, New York

New York, March 5, 1927.

PRINTED IN THE UNITED STATES OF AMERICA
BY THE BERWICK & SMITH CO.

PREFACE

In crowning his work with so impressive a title as that of
"The Catholic Anthology," the editor has not been unmindful of
the responsibilities he has assumed. Therefore to state the
purposes he has entertained and the system he has adopted may
not be altogether untimely before releasing his collection to
speak for itself.

The Catholic Anthology is intended primarily as a selection
of Catholic poems written by Catholics and bearing the impress
of Catholic dogma, tradition and life; so that the editor has
purposely chosen the completely Catholic utterances of his poets
in preference, sometimes, to their pieces of general aesthetical
charm. The orthodoxy of the poet has been another considera-
tion, and where that has been found unquestionable the editor
has felt at some liberty to vary the coloring of his selection.
Whenever there is a question of the full orthodoxy of the poet,
care has been taken to represent him only by utterances in his
work that are unmistakably Catholic.

The Catholic Church, in its long history, its world-wide
expansion and its fundamental operation in building our
Christian civilization, our schools and universities of antiquity,
the beginnings of modern languages and literatures, so deeply
permeated European thought that its spirit is to be found inter-
woven throughout all thought, secular as well as religious, of
the past sixteen or seventeen centuries; therefore in the expres-
sions of dissidents, and even enemies of the Church, one dis-
covers the residual traces of its cultural forms, which create,
in a way, a body of Catholic poetry not altogether of its fold
yet definitely and unmistakably to be based on Catholic foundations. The editor, without pretending to cloak much of this
product under the robe of the Church, has endeavored to
recognize this, in arranging a special division of *The Catholic
Anthology* to include some of these masterpieces. He has
striven also to mark a clear distinction between Catholic

poetry and that large and beautiful body of hymnology which arose during the divisions within the Church and since the Protestant Reformation, and which represents the personal aspirations and spiritual longings of poets who cannot in any sense be denominated as Catholic.

It is the privilege of *The Catholic Anthology* to present for the first time in any language the outline of Catholic poetry in chronological order from the beginning of the Church, in the poems of its holy founder, Our Lord and Savior Jesus Christ, His Blessed Mother and the apostles and saints of the New Dispensation. It distinguishes the soulful utterances of faith and mystical love from the rigid declarations of the primitive liturgies of the Syrians, Greeks and Latins. It traces the Catholic lyric spirit down through the first lispings of poetry in Italy, Spain and France, supplemented by the early outbursts of piety in Ireland, England and Germany, which created the vast unbroken harmony of the Ages of Faith, through the disorders of the Lutheran revolts, and, long after, through the Continental centers of Renaissance Catholicity.

The large and cosmopolitan body of literature drawn upon under this system has necessitated a careful reserve in the selection of poets, the individual importance of whom can sometimes be no more than indicated. There have been difficulties in the face of varying excellence of translations, lack of English versions in many instances, which the editor has endeavored to remedy by his own hand and the kindly coöperation of scholarly friends; there have also been some difficulties of copyright due to the misunderstanding of the purpose of *The Catholic Anthology*. As it stands, it will convince our critics that it is not only timely but in a way necessary for the better presentation of Catholic poetry, which in later days has won new recognition in the world of letters as of prime importance in the expression of the modern soul.

The editor would here thank generally and individually the many friends, poets, publishers and correspondents who have helped him in his task of compilation. A special acknowledgement is due to the editors of *The Commonweal,* Michael Williams, George N. Shuster, Helen Walker, Henry Longan Stuart and John F. McCormick; the Reverend John J. Wynne, S.J., of *The Catholic Encyclopedia* and The Universal Knowledge Foundation; the Trustees of The Hispanic Society; Monsignor

H. T. Henry of The Catholic University; Messrs. Wilfrid
Meynell, G. K. Chesterton, Condé B. Pallen, John Bunker,
James J. Daly, S.J., Charles L. O'Donnell, C.S.C., Thomas
Augustine Daly, Theodore Maynard, Miss Katherine Brégy,
Sister Mary Madeleva, C.S.C., and many other friends with
whom he gladly shares any merit that may accrue from the
spread and propagation of *The Catholic Anthology.*

T. W.

CONTENTS

I

AGES OF FAITH

THE CATHOLIC ANTHOLOGY

THE SIBYLLINE PROPHECY

From the *Fourth Eclogue*

PUBLIUS VERGILIUS MARO (B.C. 70-19)

Muses of Sicily, loftier be our song!
—Not to all do humble pastorals and fields give joy;
Thus if we sing of groves, let them be lofty as the Consul's rank.
For now we reach the final epoch foretold by Cumæ's Sibyl;
A new cycle among the ages comes to birth;
The virgin, Astraea, returns; the Saturnian age of peace is
    renewed,
For a new order of generation is sent down from the high
    heavens!
Thou, chaste Lucina, be propitious to the boy new-born,
Through whom the Iron Age will reach its end
And the Golden Age will spread over the entire world;
So may the reign of Apollo begin!——

From the Latin by Roderick Gill.

PRELUDE OF THE NEW TESTAMENT

The Angel of the Lord:

Hail Mary full of grace! The Lord is with thee! Blessed art
    thou among women and blessed is the fruit of thy womb,
    Jesus!

The Blessed Virgin:

Behold the handmaid of the Lord. Be it done unto me accord-
    ing to thy word!

3

The Heavenly Choir:

Fear not; for behold, I bring you tidings of great joy which shall be to all the people.

For unto you is born this day in the City of David a Saviour who is Christ the Lord.

Glory to God in the highest and on earth Peace to men of good will!

THE HYMN OF THE BLESSED VIRGIN

My soul doth magnify the Lord and my spirit hath rejoiced in God my Saviour.

For He hath regarded the lowliness of His handmaiden; for behold, from henceforth all generations shall call me blessed.

For He that is mighty hath done to me great things; and holy is His name!

And His mercy is on them that fear Him from generation to generation.

He hath showed the strength of His arm; he hath scattered the proud in the conceit of their heart.

He hath put down the mighty from their seats and exalteth them of low degree.

He hath filled the hungry with good things; and the rich he hath sent away empty.

He hath holpen His servant Israel in remembrance of His mercy.

As He spake to our fathers, to Abraham and to his seed forever!

THE POEM OF THE OUR FATHER

JESUS CHRIST

Matthew vi.

Our Father in heaven	Hallowed be Thy name
Thy kingdom come	Thy will be done
As in the heavens	So on earth.
Our daily bread	Give us this day;
And forgive us our debts	as we forgive our debtors;
And lead us not into temptation	But deliver us from evil.

POEMS BY THE ROADSIDE

JESUS CHRIST

Luke xii.

Fear not, little flock,
For it pleaseth your Father to give you the kingdom.
Sell your goods, and give alms;
Make yourselves scrips that wax not old,
A treasure in heaven that never faileth,
Where no thief approacheth nor moth corrupteth;
For where your treasure there your heart.
Let your loins be girt, and your lamps burning,
And ye like men awaiting their lord,
When he shall return from the marriage feast;
That coming and knocking at once they may open to him.

Blessed those servants
Whom the lord, when he cometh
Shall find watching.

Matthew xvi.

Blessed thou, Simon thou son of Jonah,
For flesh and blood revealed not to thee,
But My Father Who is in heaven.
And I say unto thee that thou art Peter,
And upon this rock I will build my church,
And the gates of Sheol shall not prevail against it.
I will give thee the keys of the kingdom of heaven
And that thou shalt bind on shall be bound in heaven
earth
And that thou shalt loose on shall be loosed in heaven.
earth

Matthew v.

Ye are the light of the world.
A city cannot be hid
Which is set on the top of a hill.
Neither light they a lamp,
Nor set it beneath a bushel;
But on the lamp-stand set it.
And it lighteth all those in the house.
So shine your light before men,
That they may see your works that are good,
And may glorify your Father who is in heaven.

TO HIS DISCIPLES

JESUS CHRIST

Consider the ravens; for they neither sow nor reap; which
neither have storehouse nor barn; and God feedeth them;
how much more are ye better than the fowls?

And which of you with taking thought can add to his stature
one cubit?

Consider the lilies how they grow; they toil not, neither do they
spin; and yet I say unto you that Solomon in all his glory
was not arrayed like one of these.

If then God so clothe the grass which is today in the field and
tomorrow is cast into the oven; how much more will He
clothe you, O ye of little faith?

REVELATIONS XII

SAINT JOHN THE EVANGELIST

(First Christian Century)

And there appeared a great wonder in heaven, a woman clothed
with the sun and the moon under her heel, and upon her
head a crown of twelve stars.

And she being with child cried, travailing in birth and pained to
be delivered.

And there appeared another wonder in heaven; and behold a
great red dragon having seven heads and ten horns and
seven crowns upon his heads.

And his tail drew the third part of the stars of heaven and did
cast them to earth; and the dragon stood before the woman
who was ready to be delivered for to devour her child as
soon as it was born.

And she brought forth a man child who was to rule all nations
with a rod of iron; and her child was caught up unto God
and to His throne.

And the woman fled into the wilderness, where she hath a place
prepared of God that they should feed her there a thousand
two hundred and threescore days.

And there was war in heaven; Michael and his angels fought
against the dragon; and the dragon fought and his angels.

And prevailed not; neither was their place found any more in heaven.

And the great dragon was cast out, that old serpent called the Devil and Satan, who deceiveth the whole world; he was cast out into the earth and his angels were cast out with him.

And I heard a loud voice saying in heaven, Now is come salvation and strength and the kingdom of our God and the power of His Christ; for the accuser of our brethren is cast down, who accused them before our God day and night.

And they overcame him by the blood of the Lamb and by the word of their testimony; and they loved not their lives unto the death.

Therefore rejoice, ye heavens, and ye that dwell in them! Woe to the inhabitants of the earth and of the sea! for the devil is come down unto you, having great wrath because he knoweth that he hath but a short time.

And when the dragon saw that he was cast unto the earth he persecuted the woman who brought forth the man child.

And to the woman were given two wings of a great eagle that she might fly into the wilderness, into her place where she is nourished for a time and times and half a time, from the face of the serpent.

And the serpent cast out of his mouth water as a flood after the woman, that he might cause her to be carried away of the flood.

And the earth helped the woman, and the earth opened her mouth and swallowed up the flood which the dragon cast out of his mouth.

And the dragon was wroth with the woman and went to make war with the remnant of her seed, which keep the commandments of God and have the testimony of Jesus Christ.

And he stood upon the sand of the sea.

HYMN FOR THE LIGHTING OF THE LAMPS

Attributed to Saint Athenogenes (Martyr of the Second Century)

Hail, gladdening Light, of his pure glory poured
Who is the Immortal Father, heavenly blest,
Holiest of Holies, Jesus Christ, Our Lord.
Now we are come to the sun's hour of rest,

The lights of evening round us shine,
We hymn the Father, Son and Holy Spirit divine.
Worthiest art Thou at all times to be sung
With undefilèd tongue,
Son of our God, giver of life alone.
Therefore in all the world, Thy glories, Lord, they own.

From the Greek by John Keble.

HYMN TO CHRIST THE SAVIOUR

CLEMENT OF ALEXANDRIA (160-215)

Curb for stubborn steed,
Making its will give heed;
Wing that directest right
The wild bird's wandering flight;
Helm for the ships that keep
Their pathway o'er the deep;
Shepherd of sheep that own
Their Master on the throne,
Stir up Thy children meek
With guileless lips to speak
In hymn and song Thy praise,
Guide of their infant ways.
O King of saints, O Lord,
Mighty, all-conquering Word;
Son of the Highest God
Wielding His wisdom's rod;
Our stay when cares annoy,
Giver of endless joy;
Of all our mortal race
Saviour, of boundless grace,
  O Jesus, hear!
Shepherd and Sower, Thou,
Now helm, and bridle now,
Wing for the heavenward flight
Of flocks all pure and bright,
Fisher of men, the blest,
Out of the world's unrest,
Out of Sin's troubled sea
Taking us, Lord to Thee;

Out of the waves of strife
With bait of blissful life,
With choicest fish, good store,
Drawing Thy nets to shore.
Lead us, O Shepherd true,
Thy mystic sheep, we sue,
Lead us, O holy Lord,
Whom from Thy sons dost ward
With all-prevailing charm,
Peril, curse and harm;
O path where Christ has trod,
O way that leads to God,
O Word abiding aye,
O endless Light on high,
Mercy's fresh-springing flood,
Worker of all things good,
O glorious Life of all
That on their Maker call.
    Christ Jesus, hear!
O Milk of Heaven, that prest
From full o'erflowing breast
Of her, the mystic bride,
Thy wisdom hath supplied;
Thine infant children seek
With baby lips all weak,
Filled with the Spirit's dew
From that dear bosom true,
Thy praises pure to sing
Hymns meet for Thee Our King,
    For Thee, the Christ;
Our holy tribute, this,
For wisdom, life and bliss,
Singing in chorus meet,
Singing in concert sweet
    The Almighty Son.
We, heirs of peace unpriced,
We, who are born in Christ,
A people pure from stain,
Praise we our God again,
    Lord of our Peace!
       From the Greek by E. H. Plumtre.

THE LAMENT OF SAINT ANN

From the *Protevangelium of James* (Second or Fifth Century)

Woe is me! what am I like?
I am not like the birds of heaven,
For even the birds of heaven are fruitful before Thee,
O Lord!
Woe is me! what am I like?
I am not like the beasts of the earth,
For the beasts of the earth are fruitful before Thee,
O Lord!
Woe is me! what am I like?
I am not like this earth,
For even this earth bears its fruits in due season and blesses
    Thee,
O Lord!

EPIGRAM ON MARCUS THE GNOSTIC

St. Pothinus of Lyons (Second Century)

Marcus, thou maker of idols, inspector of portents,
Skilled in consulting the stars and deep in the deep arts of magic,
Ever by tricks such as these confirming the doctrines of error,
Furnishing signs unto those involved by thee in deception.
Wonders of power that is utterly severed from God, and
    apostate,
Which Satan thy true father enables thee still to accomplish
By means of Azazel, that fallen yet mighty angel,
Thus making thee the precursor of his own impious actions.

THE CHRISTMAS HYMN

Saint Ephrem (306-373)

Virgin truly full of wonder
Bringing forth God's Son to save us!
My poor lips are all too worthless
And I may not sing thy brightness.

Cherubim with faces fourfold
With such brightness are not hallowed;
Seraphim six wings outstretching
Are not glorified above thee!
Priests, rejoice in her, the blest one
Bearing our great Priest and Victim,
Freeing you from sacrifices.
He Himself, become our Victim,
Reconciles us with the Father.
Mary now for us becometh
As the heavens where God abideth;
For His everlasting Godhead
Deigns to make in her His dwelling;
Made a little Child to lift us,
While His nature never changeth;
In her womb the robe He weaveth
Clad in which He comes to save us;
Wonder that no tongue can utter,
See, her Son the Virgin beareth!
Lo, she gives her milk to feed Him,
Food to Him who feedeth all things;
See, her tender knees support Him,
Him whose power upholdeth all things!
Still a maid and still a mother,
What is there we may not call her?
Fair in soul, in body holy;
Pure her mind and clear her judgment,
And her thoughts exceeding perfect,
She is chaste and she is prudent,
Fair in form and full of beauty.
Hark, with love and gladness glowing
Mary sweetly sings before Him:
"Whence this gift to one so lowly?
That I should conceive and bear Him—
One so little, One so mighty!
All in me, who dwells in all things!
In the hour when Gabriel sought me,
From a servant freed He made me;
Lo, the handmaid of Thy Godhead
Made the mother of Thy manhood!
Thou my Son and Thou my Maker!

Shall I ope these milky fountains,
Giving drink to Thee the Fountain?
Whence is this that I should feed Thee,
Feeding all things from Thy table?
From the Syriac by W. H. Kent, C.S.C.

VENI CREATOR SPIRITUS

(Fourth Century)

Creator Spirit, by whose aid
The world's foundations first were laid,
Come visit every pious mind,
Come pour Thy joys on human kind;
From sin and sorrow set us free
And make Thy temples worthy Thee.
O Source of uncreated light,
The Father's promised Paraclete!
Thrice holy fount, thrice holy fire,
Our hearts with heavenly love inspire;
Come and Thy sacred unction bring
To sanctify us while we sing.
Plenteous of grace, descend from high,
Rich in Thy sevenfold energy!
Thou strength of His almighty hand,
Whose power does heaven and earth command.
Proceeding Spirit, our defense,
Who dost the gifts of tongues dispense,
And crown'st Thy gift with eloquence!
Refine and purge our earthly parts;
But, oh, inflame and fire our hearts!
Our frailties help, our vice control,
Submit the senses to the soul;
And when rebellious they are grown
Then lay Thy hand and hold them down.
Chase from our minds the infernal foe,
And peace, the fruit of love bestow;
And lest our feet should step astray,
Protect and guide us on the way.
Make us eternal truths receive,
And practice all that we believe;

Give us Thyself that we may see
The Father and the Son by Thee.
Immortal honor, endless fame
Attend the Almighty Father's name;
The Saviour Son be glorified,
Who for lost man's redemption died;
And equal adoration be,
Eternal Paraclete, to Thee!

From the Latin by John Dryden.

VERBUM SUPERNUM

Saint Ambrose (340-397)

Eternal Word proceeding from
    The Heavenly Father's breast sublime,
Willing to help us Thou dost come
    In the appointed time.

Illumine now each waiting breast,
    Fill it with flames of Thy dear love,
That in our hearts alone may rest
    Desire of joys above.

That when to flames the Judgment Seat
    Condemns the bad for evil done,
And calls the just in accents sweet
    Unto their Heaven won;

We may not feed the hungry flame
    Tossed in the black and whirling pool,
But rather God's great Presence claim
    In heavenly pastures cool.

Unto the Father and the Son
    And Spirit Paraclete, to Thee
What praise hath been, so be it done
    Through all eternity.

From the Latin by H. T. Henry.

LAUDATE FOR CHRISTMAS

AURELIUS CLEMENS PRUDENTIUS (348-413)

Praise Him, all ye heights of heaven,
Praise Him, ye angelic throng;
Whatsoe'er hath voice or power
Praises to the Lord prolong;
Let no tongue retire in silence
From the universal song
Through the ages evermore!

This is He whom eager singers
Chanted in the days of old;
Whom the Prophets' faithful pages
Witnessing to us foretold;
Lo, the Promised One appeareth—
Praise Him, all ye faithful fold,
Through the ages evermore!

Christ, to Thee—to Thee, O Father,
Holy Spirit, unto Thee—
Hymn and psalm of praise perennial
And of great thanksgiving be;
Honor, power, benediction
Unto God the One and Three
Through the ages evermore!
From the Latin by H. T. Henry.

THE HOLY INNOCENTS

AURELIUS CLEMENS PRUDENTIUS (348-413)

All hail, ye tender martyr-flowers
Whose petals scarce did yet unclose
When the Christ-seeker spoiled your bowers
As tempests through the budding rose.

O first who for the Saviour died,
 O tender flocks whom hirelings slay,
How by the very altar-side
 With your own palms and wreaths ye play!

To Thee, O Jesus, glory meet,
 Who came to us a Virgin's Son,
And Father and the Paraclete,
 The while the endless ages run!
    From the Latin by H. T. Henry.

THE JOYS OF PARADISE

Saint Augustine (354-430)

For the fount of life eternal
 Panteth the enamored soul,
From its bonds the imprisoned spirit
 Seeketh freedom of control,
Exiled here it turns and flutters,
 Struggling for its native goal.

Who can voice the joy surpassing,
 Of that endless peace supreme,
Where the living pearls of beauty
 In the lofty dwellings gleam,
Where the spacious halls and mansions
 With a golden glory stream?

Precious are the gems compacted
 In that palace, stone on stone,
Purest gold like unto crystal
 Is upon the highway strown,
Free of dust and spotless ever,
 For no darkening stain is known.

Verdant are the springing meadows,
 And the honeyed rivers flow,
Odors breathe their sweet aroma,
 As the spicy breezes blow,
In the groves, with fruit unfailing,
 Leafy boughs are bending low.

There no fickle moon appeareth,
    Nor do planets speed their way,
For the Lamb is light undying
    Of that happy land alway,
Night and time are ever banished,
    For 'tis never-ending day.

There the saints in light supernal,
    As a glorious sunburst shine,
Crowned triumphant; then, exulting
    In an ecstasy divine,
They recount their glorious conquests
    With the raging foe in line.

Free from stain, their battle over,
    E'en the flesh is glorified;
Flesh transfigured, with the spirit
    Doth in harmony abide,
Peaceful with a holy stillness,
    Troubled by no sinful tide.

Free from weight of all mutation,
    To their source they swiftly rise,
On the Face of Truth eternal
    Gazing with enraptured eyes,
Thence to draw reviving sweetness
    From the fount of Paradise.

They rejoice in changeless being,
    Glory in a steadfast will,
Lit with vivifying rapture,
    Subject to no passing ill,
Sickness flying, health undying,
    Though eternal, youthful still.

Knowing Him who knoweth all things,
    In all knowledge they delight,
E'en the secret of each bosom,
    Charmeth now each ravished sight,
One in mind, in will, in spirit,
    They in all of good unite.

"Star shall differ," for the glory
  Is apportioned to the pain,
But in bond of sweet communion,
  Charity doth so ordain
That the treasure each possesseth
  Shall enrich the common gain.

To the Body flock the eagles,
  For the royal feast is spread,
Saints and Angels rest together,
  On celestial bounty fed:
Citizens of earth and heaven,
  Seek the one Life-giving Bread.

Songs of melody enchanting
  Their melodious voices raise,
String and psaltery are mingled
  With the jubilee of lays,
Offering to the King eternal
  Homage of the victor's praise.

Happy soul to whom the vision
  Of the Heavenly King is known,
Who hath seen the vast creation
  Circling 'neath His lofty throne,
Sun and moon and sphery splendors
  In their varied beauty shown!

Thou, O Christ, the palm of battle,
  Lead me to Thy land of rest,
When I shall have loosed the sword-belt,
  Cast the buckler from my breast,
Make me sharer in the guerdon
  Thou bestowest on the blest!

Prove the valor of Thy warrior
  When the din of war is rife,
But refuse not sweet refreshment
  To the victor after strife,
Be Thyself, my prize eternal,
  Thou, my everlasting life!
      From the Latin by the Prioress Augustine
        of the Mother of God.

THE DEER'S CRY

SAINT PATRICK OF TARA (377-460)

I arise today
Through a mighty strength, the invocation of the Trinity,
Through a belief in the Threeness,
Through confession of the Oneness
Of the Creator of creation.
I arise today
Through the strength of Christ's birth and His baptism,
Through the strength of His crucifixion and His burial,
Through the strength of His resurrection and His ascension,
Through the strength of His descent for the judgment of doom.
I arise today
Through the strength of the love of cherubim,
In obedience of angels,
In service of archangels,
In the hope of resurrection to meet with reward,
In prayers of patriarchs,
In predictions of prophets,
In preachings of apostles,
In faiths of confessors,
In innocence of virgins,
In deeds of righteous men.
I arise today
Through the strength of heaven;
Light of the sun,
Radiance of the moon,
Splendor of fire,
Speed of lightning,
Swiftness of the wind,
Depth of the sea,
Stability of the earth,
Firmness of the rock.
I arise today
Through God's strength to pilot me;
God's might to uphold me,
God's wisdom to guide me,
God's eye to look before me,
God's ear to hear me,

God's word to speak for me,
God's hand to guard me,
God's way to lie before me,
God's shield to protect me,
God's hosts to save me
From snares of the devil,
From temptations of vices,
Fro mevery one who desires me ill,
Afar or anear,
Alone or in a multitude.
I summon today all these powers between me and evil,
Against every cruel merciless power that opposes my body and
    soul,
Against incantations of false prophets,
Against black laws of pagandom,
Against false laws of heretics,
Against craft of idolatry,
Against spells of women and smiths and wizards,
Against every knowledge that corrupts man's body and soul.
Christ shield me today
Against poison, against burning,
Against drowning, against wounding,
So that reward may come to me in abundance.
Christ with me, Christ before me, Christ behind me,
Christ in me, Christ beneath me, Christ above me,
Christ on my right, Christ on my left,
Christ when I lie down, Christ when I sit down,
Christ when I arise,
Christ in the heart of every man who thinks of me,
Christ in the mouth of every man who speaks of me,
Christ in the eye that sees me,
Christ in the ear that hears me.
I arise today
Through a mighty strength, the invocation of the Trinity,
Through a belief in the Threeness,
Through a confession of the Oneness
Of the Creator of creation.

Anonymous Translation from the Gaelic.

ON A PAPYRUS OF OXYRHYNCHUS
(Fourth Century)

Of the light of the dawn let none be silent
Nor let the bright stars be wanting in praise;
Let all the fountains of the rivers lift up their songs
To the Father and Son and Holy Spirit.
So let all powers on earth cry aloud Amen, Amen.
Might and honor, glory and praise to God,
Only Giver of all that is good. Amen. Amen.

HYMN

Synesius (373-410)

Ah, what are strength and beauty?
What golden store and fame?
And what are kings' poor honors
When thoughts of God make claim?
Let others speed their chariots,
Let others stretch the bow,
Let others pile their riches
And clasp the wealth they know;
Be mine to pass unnoted
Through life remote from care,
Unknown, unmarked by others
But to my God laid bare!

From the Greek by Roderick Gill.

THE BIRDS

Blossius Æmilius Dracontius (Fifth Century)

As they join their various voices
In a melody so bland
To the glory of their Maker,—
They seem worthy of His Hand.

From the Latin by Thomas Walsh.

THE MAGI VISIT HEROD

CAELIUS SEDULIUS (Fifth Century)

Why, cruel Herod, dost thou fear?
The King is God who dwelleth near;
No realms of earth allure His eyes
Who giveth kingdoms in the skies!

The Magi follow still the Star
That marshalled them from lands afar;
And by its light they seek the Light—
The God their gifts confess aright!
From the Latin by H. T. Henry.

THE MIRACLE

CAELIUS SEDULIUS (Fifth Century)

Now Cana sees a wonder new—
The water blushes at His view;
Thus changed by Him with power divine,
It poureth out as purest wine.
From the Latin by H. T. Henry.

GREAT AND MIGHTY WONDER

SAINT ANATOLIUS (Died 458)

A great and mighty wonder!
A full and holy cure!
The Virgin bears the Infant
With Virgin-honor pure!

The Word becomes Incarnate,
And yet remains on high;
And cherubim sing anthems
To shepherds from the sky.

And we with them triumphant
Repeat the hymn again;
"To God on high be glory,
And peace on earth to men!"

While thus they sing your Monarch,
Those bright angelic bands,
Rejoice, ye vales and mountains!
Ye oceans, clap your hands!

Since all He comes to ransom,
By all be He adored,
The Infant born in Bethlehem,
The Saviour and the Lord!

And idol forms shall perish
And error shall decay,
And Christ shall wield His sceptre,
Our Lord and God for aye.
            From the Greek by J. M. Neale.

THE FEAST OF SAINT BRIGID OF KILDARE

(453-523)

I should like a great lake of ale
For the King of kings;
I should like the family of Heaven
To be drinking it through time eternal.
I should like the viands
Of belief and pure piety;
I should like the flails
Of penance at my house;
I should like the men of Heaven
In my own house; I should like kieves
Of peace to be at their disposal;
I should like the vessels
Of charity for distribution;
I should like caves
Of mercy for their company;

I should like cheerfulness
To be in their drinking;
I should like Jesus
Too to be here among them;
I should like the Three
Maries of illustrious renown;
I should like the people of Heaven
There from all parts;
I should like that I should be
A rent-payer to the Lord;
That, should I suffer distress,
He would bestow upon me a good blessing.

From the Irish by Eugene O'Curry.

JESUKIN

SAINT ITA (480-570)

Jesukin
Lives my little cell within;
What were wealth of cleric high—
All is lie but Jesukin.

Nursling nurtured, as 'tis right,
Harbors here no servile spright,
Jesu of the skies, who art
Next my heart through every night.

Jesukin, my good for aye,
Calling and will not have nay,
King of all things, ever true,
He shall have me who will away.

Jesu, more than angel aid,
Fosterling not formed to fade,
Nursed by me in desert wild,
Jesu, Child of Judah's Maid.

Sons of kings and kingly kin
To my land may enter in;
Guest of none I hope to be
Save of Thee, my Jesukin.

Unto heaven's High King confest
Sing a chorus, maidens blest!
He is o'er us, though within
Jesukin is on our breast.
            From the Irish by George Sigerson.

THE PRAISE OF DERRY

SAINT COLUMCILLE (521-597)

Were all the tributes of Scotia mine,
From its midland to its borders,
I would give all for one little cell
In my beautiful Derry.
For its peace and its purity,
For the white angels that go
In crowds from one end to the other,
I love my Derry.

My Derry, my fair oak grove,
My dear little cell and dwelling,—
O God in the heavens above!
Let him who profanes it be cursèd.
Belovèd are Durrow and Derry,
Belovèd is Raphoe the pure,
Belovèd the fertile Drumhome,
Belovèd are Sords and Kells;
But sweeter and fairer to me
The salt sea where the seagulls cry,—
When I come to Derry from afar,
It is sweeter and dearer to me.
            From the Irish by D. P. Conyngham.

ON HIS EXILE TO IONA

SAINT COLUMCILLE

Too swiftly my coracle flies on her way,
    From Derry I mournfully turned her prow,
I grieve on the errand which drives me today
    To the Land of the Ravens, to Alba, now.

How swiftly we travel! There is a gray eye
  Looks back upon Erin, but it no more
Shall see while the stars shall endure in the sky
  Her women, her men, or her stainless shore.

From the plank of the oak where in sorrow I lie
  I am straining my sight through the water and wind,
And large is the tear of the soft gray eye
  Looking back on the land that it leaves behind.

To Erin alone is my memory given,
  To Meath and to Munster my wild thoughts flow,
To the shores of Moy-linny, the slopes of Loch Leven,
  And the beautiful land the Ultonians know.

O bear me my blessing afar to the West,
  For the heart in my bosom is broken; I fail.
Should death of a sudden now pierce my breast
  I should die of the love that I bear the Gael!

From the Irish by Douglas Hyde.

VEXILLA REGIS

VENANTIUS FORTUNATUS (530-600)

The Royal Banners forward go;
The Cross shines forth in mystic glow;
Where He in flesh, our flesh who made,
Our sentence bore, our ransom paid.

Where deep for us the spear was dyed,
Life's torrent rushing from His side,
To wash us in that precious flood
Where mingled water flowed and blood.

Fulfilled is all that David told
In true prophetic song of old;
Amidst the nations God, saith he,
Hath reigned and triumphed from that Tree.

O Tree of Beauty! Tree of Light!
O Tree with royal purple dight!
Elect on whose triumphal breast
Those holy limbs should find their rest!

On whose dear arms, so widely flung,
The weight of this world's ransom hung;
The price of humankind to pay,
And spoil the Spoiler of his prey.

O Cross, our one reliance, hail!
This holy Passiontide, avail
To give fresh merit to the saint,
And pardon to the penitent.

To Thee, eternal Three in One,
Let homage meet by all be done
Whom by the Cross Thou dost restore,
Preserve and govern evermore!
From the Latin by John Mason Neale.

MORNING HYMN

SAINT GREGORY THE GREAT (538-594)

Lo, fainter now lie spread the shades of night,
    And upward spread the trembling gleams of morn;
Suppliant we bend before the Lord of Light,
    And pray at early dawn,
That His sweet charity may all our sin
    Forgive, and make our miseries to cease;
May grant us health, grant us the gift divine
    Of everlasting peace.
Father Supreme, this grace on us confer;
    And Thou, O Son by an eternal birth!
With Thee, coequal spirit, comforter!
    Whose glory fills the earth.
From the Latin by Edward Caswall.

GAELIC FRAGMENT

I am Eve, great Adam's wife,—
'Tis I that outraged Jesus of old;
'Tis I that robbed my children of heaven,
By rights, 'tis I should have gone upon the Cross—

There would be no ice in any place,
There would be no glistening windy winter,
There would be no hell, there would be no sorrow
There would be no fear, if it were not for me—

From THE HYMN OF THE WORLD'S CREATOR

St. Caedmon (Died 680)

Now must we hymn the Maker of heaven,
The might of the Maker, the deeds of the Father,
The thought of His heart! He, Lord everlasting,
Established of old the source of all wonders;
Creator all-holy, He hung the bright heaven,
A roof high upreared o'er the children of men;
The King of mankind then created for mortals
The world in its beauty, the earth spread beneath them,—
He, Lord everlasting, Omnipotent God!

From the Anglo-Saxon.

THE COMING OF PHARAOH

St. Caedmon

Then they saw
Forth and forward faring Pharaoh's war array
Gliding on a grove of spears; glittering hosts!
Fluttered the banners, there the folk the march trod,
Onward surged the war, strode the spears along.
Blickered the broad shields; blew aloud the trumpets;
Wheeling round in gyres yelled the fowls of war
For the battle greedy; hoarsely barked the raven.

Dew upon his feathers, o'er the fallen corpses.
Swart that chooser of the slain! Sang aloud the wolves
At the eve their horrid song, hoping for the carrion.
Kindless were the beasts, cruelly they threaten;
Death did these march-warders all the midnight through
Howl along the hostile trail—hideous slaughter of the host.

From the Anglo-Saxon.

HYMNUM CANENTES MARTYRUM

St. Bede the Venerable (673-735)

The Hymn for conquering Martyrs raise;
The Victor Innocents we praise,
Whom in their woe earth cast away,
But heaven with joy received today.
Whose Angels see the Father's face
World without end, and hymn His Grace;
And while they chant unceasing lays,
The Hymn for conquering Martyrs raise.

By that accursèd monarch slain,
Their loving Maker bade them reign.
With Him they dwell, no more distressed,
In the fair land of light and rest;
He gives them mansions, one and all,
In that His Heavenly Father's Hall;
Thus have they changed their loss for gain,
By that cursèd monarch slain.

A voice from Ramah there was sent,
A voice of weeping and lament;
When Rachel mourned the children's care
Whom for the tyrant's sword she bare.
Triumphal is their glory now
Whom earthly torments could not bow;
What time, both far and near that went,
A voice from Ramah there was sent.

Fear not, O little flock and blest,
The lion that your life oppressed!
To heavenly pastures ever new
The heavenly Shepherd leadeth you;
Who, dwelling now on Sion's hill,
The Lamb's dear footsteps follow still;
By tyrant there no more distressed,
Fear not, O little flock and blest!

And every tear is wiped away
By your dear Father's hands for aye; .
Death hath no power to hurt you more,
Whose own is Life's eternal store,—
Who sow their seed, and sowing, weep,
In everlasting joy shall reap;
What time they shine in heavenly day,
And every tear is wiped away.

O City blest o'er all the earth,
Who gloriest in the Saviour's birth!
Whose are His earliest Martyrs dear,
By kindred and by triumph here.
None from henceforth may call thee small,—
Of rival towns thou passest all;
In whom our Monarch had His Birth,—
O City blest o'er all the earth!

From the Latin by J. M. Neale.

EASTER HYMN

St. John Damascene (Died 754)

Let us rise in early morning,
    And instead of ointments bring
Hymns of praises to our Master,
    And His Resurrection sing;
We shall see the Sun of Justice
    Risen with healing in His wing.

Thy unbounded loving-kindness,
  They that groaned in Hades' chain,
Prisoners, from afar beholding,
  Hasten to the light again,
And to that eternal Pascha
  Wove the dance and raised the strain.

Go ye forth, His Saints, to meet Him!
  Go with lamps in every hand!
From the sepulchre He riseth;
  Ready for the Bridegroom stand;
And the Pascha of salvation
  Hail, with His triumphant band.
                    From the Greek by J. M. Neale.

ART THOU WEARY?

St. Stephen the Sabaite (725-794)

Art thou weary, art thou languid,
  Art thou sore distrest?
"Come to me," saith One, "and coming,
  Be at rest!"
Hath He marks to lead me to Him
  If He be my Guide?
"In His Feet and Hands are Wound-prints,
  And His side."
Is there Diadem, as Monarch,
  That His Brow adorns?
"Yea, a Crown, in very surety,
  But of Thorns!"
If I find Him, if I follow,
  What His guerdon here?
"Many a sorrow, many a labor,
  Many a tear."
If I still hold closely to Him,
  What hath He at last?
"Sorrow vanquished, labor ended,
  Jordan passed!"

If I ask Him to receive me,
  Will He say me nay?
"Not till earth and not till heaven
  Pass away!"
Finding, following, keeping, struggling,
  Is He sure to bless?
"Angels, Martyrs, Prophets, Virgins,
  Answer, Yes!"
          From the Greek by J. M. Neale.

THE DREAM OF THE ROOD

(Eighth Century)

Behold, of dreams   the best will I tell,
That met me at midnight,   the while men rest.
I saw, methought,   a marvelous tree
Lifted aloft,   light illumined;
Of all beams brightest   that beacon was.
Gilded with gold,   agleam with gems
Fairest on the face of earth.   Five there shone
On the shoulder-span.   Stood God's angel,
Fair for all future life;   nor was that now an inglorious
    gallows;
Souls of the saved, men upon earth,   and all earth's creatures
    upon it gazed.

Fair was that victory-tree;   I, foul with vice,
Wounded with wickedness,   witnessed the glory-tree,
Sheathèd in splendor,   wondrously shining
With gems and gold,   garmented nobly, this tree of the
    forest.
Though through that gold   thought might I gather
Of warfare wretched,   when first it began
Sweat from its right side   of blood to shed.
Feared I that sight so fair,   saw I that beacon bright
Change hue and color,   covered with moisture now,
Soiled with sweat streaming   that was sometime gold-
    geared.

I there lying   a long time thus
Beheld, sorrow-stricken,   the tree of my Savior,
Till that I heard how   haply it spoke,
Began with words blessèd,   this best of trees:

"Yet I remember   that slaying of yore,
How I was hewed,   hacked from my stem,
Fast at the forest-edge;   fierce fiends there took me,
Wrought me a spectacle   for wayfarers,
Bade me their wicked ones   aloft to bear.
There they fixed me,   there fastened on me many a fiend.

Then marked I   the Maker of mankind
Hastened with courage high,   me He would mount.
There then I durst not   against the decree of God
Bow nor break.   I beheld tremble
The face of the earth;   at most I might
Slay the fell fiends   where I stood fast.

The young Hero stripped Him there,   He that was mighty
          God,
Strong and stout-hearted,   strode He up to the gallows of
          shame,
Steadfast in sight of all;   man He would save.
I trembled as tenderly this Man touched me   nor dared I
          however to bow to earth.
A rood I was raised;   aloft I lifted the King of rank,
Lord of high heaven,   nor dared to bow.

Dark nails they drove through me;   on me are still the
          scars,
Wide wounds of malice,   nor revenge durst I one of them.
Us both they besmeared;   all with blood was I wet
From that Man's side shed   when His spirit forth He sent.

Death on that mount   have I endured
Through grievous fate.   Saw I the God of hosts
Stretched severely.   Darkness deepened,
Covered with clouds   the corpse of the King;
Shadow shrouded   its splendor bright.
Wrapped in clouds   wept all creation,
Wailed the King's death,   Christ on the cross.

From afar came there   some few eager ones,
Nobly sought Him   in solitude.
As this I saw,   smitten with sorrow,
I must yet bow   to the might of man,
Humbly with tireless zeal.   Then they took thence the
        almighty God,
Lifted Him down from that terrible torment;   there the
        armed ones left me abandoned,
Wet with the welter,   wounded with arrows.

They laid Him, limb-weary, down,   stood at His body's
        head,
Looked they at heaven's Lord   the while He there lay,
Aweary for that   so much He had won them.
Then men of both hands began   building a sepulcher,
Shaped it of shining stone,   shut there the Vanquisher.
Began they a sorrow-song   for Him to sing,
At the dusk, desolate   for that they must depart,
Must leave the best of Lords,   leave Him there lonely.
We there a long while   waited weeping,
Stood in our strength;   our stem they mounted, the soldier
        band.
Cold was the corpse,   Christ's beautiful body.

Forthwith men began   there to fell us,
Even to earth;   that was a fearful fate.
Men us buried   in a deep barrow,
Where found me the friends   of the Lord of freemen.
Me they geared   in gold and silver.

Now mayest thou believe,   my hero beloved,
That bitter woes   had I to bear,
Sorry cares.   Now is happiness come,
As is fitting for me;   far and wide
Men over the earth   and all the elect
Pray by this saving sign.   On me the Son of God
Sometime suffered;   for that I am splendid now,
High under heaven;   and I each one may heal
Of all folk that come   in fear to me.

Formerly I was held   punishment hardest,
To men most hateful,   before that I marked the way
Unto all people,   the path of life.
Lo, me there He honored,   the Prince of heaven,
Over woods of the wold,   the kingdom's Warder,
Even as almighty God   Mary, His mother,
Blessed among women,   before all men honored.

Now I thee bid,   my hero beloved,
That thou of this vision   tell men the glory:
Unravel with words   that this is the wonder-wood
Upon which suffered   the Saviour almighty
For the manifold sins   of all manknid,
And for the ancient   deeds of Adam.

Death He there tasted;   and thereafter the Lord arose,
In His mickle might   men to heal.
He ascended to heaven;   whence He will come again
Here to this mid-earth   mankind to seek
On the day of doom,   the dread Lord Himself,
God almighty   among His angels.
Then will He judge each one,   He that possesses power
Each one alone   as he erstwhile here
In this perishing life   payment has earned.
Nor dare any there   undaunted stand
By the words He will speak,   the Wielder of power;
He will ask of the multitude   where the man may be
Who would for God's sake   taste of sharp death,
As He once did   Who died on the cross;
Then will they be fearful   and scarcely think
What they to Christ   can begin to say:
There need be then   no terror to him
Who bears on his breast   this blessed sign;
But through that cross   shall every soul come
From his sojourn on earth   to Christ's kingdom safe
Who there desires   with his Lord to dwell."

To that cross then I prayed,   happy in heart,
Constant in courage;   as for companions
I was alone.   Always my heart
Desired departure;   many delays it has erstwhile endured,

Weary waiting.   Now my life's longing is
That I may seek   that saving sign
More than all men else,   that I myself
May worship it worthily.   This my wish
Is much in my mind,   and my most help
Rests in that rood.   There now remain to me
Few friends of power,   they have fared far
From the goods of earth,   have sought for themselves the
   King of glory.
They live now in heaven   with their most high Lord,
They dwell in delight; and I desire
That day to come   when Christ's own cross
Which I beheld   before upon earth,
Me shall fetch   from this fleeting life,
And bring me there   where much bliss is.
At heaven's high feast   the Lord's loved folk
Dwell in delight   forever and ever.
There let my place be   where I hereafter may
Live with the holy ones,   happy in heaven, may
Bide in its beauty.   Be the Lord my Friend,
He that suffered   sometime on earth,
For the guilt of men   on the gallows tree;
He has ransomed us,   life restored to us,
A home in heaven.

Thus hope was reborn   with bliss and with blessedness
To them that before   burning endured.
God's Son as a Victor   advanced on that journey,
Mighty and masterful   as with a multitude
Of chosen souls He came   into God's kingdom,
Master almighty,   bliss of the angels
And the holy ones   who from the first had
Inhabited heaven,   when their King
God almighty   came to His home.

From the Old English by Sister M. Madeleva.

NATIVITY ODE

SAINT COSMAS (Died 760)

The Holy Children boldly stand
Against the tyrant's fierce command;
The kindled furnace they defy—
No doom can shake their constancy;
They in the midmost flame confessed,
"God of our Fathers! Thou art blessed!"

The Shepherds keep their flocks by night;
The Heaven glows out with wondrous light;
The glory of the Lord is there,
The Angel-bands their Lord declare:
The watchers of the night confessed,
"God of our Fathers! Thou art blessed!"

The Angel ceased; and suddenly
Seraphic legions filled the sky;
"Glory to God," they cry again;
"Peace upon earth, good will to men;
Christ comes!"—And they that heard confessed.
"God of our Fathers! Thou art blessed!"

What said the Shepherds? "Let us turn
This new-born miracle to learn."
To Bethlehem's gate their footsteps drew;
The Mother with the Child they view;
They knelt, and worshipped and confessed,
"God of our Fathers! Thou art blessed!"

From the Greek by J. M. Neale.

THE GAELIC LITANY TO OUR LADY

(Middle of the Eighth Century)

O Great Mary.
O Mary, greatest of Maries.
O Greatest of Women.
O Queen of Angels.

O Mistress of the Heavens.

O Woman full and replete with the grace of the Holy Ghost.

O Blessed and Most Blessed.

O Mother of Eternal Glory.

O Mother of the heavenly and earthly Church.

O Mother of Love and Indulgence.

O Mother of the Golden Heights.

O Honor of the Sky.

O Sign of Tranquillity.

O Gate of Heaven.

O Golden Casket.

O Couch of Love and Mercy.

O Temple of Divinity.

O Beauty of Virgins.

O Mistress of the Tribes.

O Fountain of the Parterres.

O Cleansing of the Sins.

O Purifying of Souls.

O Mother of Orphans.

O Breast of the Infants.

O Solace of the Wretched.

O Star of the Sea.

O Handmaid of the Lord.

O Mother of Christ.

O Resort of the Lord.

O Graceful like the Dove.

O Serene like the Moon.

O Resplendent like the Sun.

O Cancelling Eve's disgrace.

O Regeneration of Life.

O Beauty of Women.

O Leader of the Virgins.

O Enclosed Garden.

O Closely Locked Fountain.

O Mother of God.

O Perpetual Virgin.

O Holy Virgin.

O Prudent Virgin.

O Serene Virgin.

O Chaste Virgin.

O Temple of the Living God.
O Royal Throne of the Eternal King.
O Sanctuary of the Holy Ghost.
O Virgin of the Root of Jesse.
O Cedar of Mount Lebanon.
O Cypress of Mount Sion.
O Crimson Rose of the Land of Jacob.
O Blooming like the Palm Tree.
O Fruitful like the Olive Tree.
O Glorious Son-bearer.
O Light of Nazareth.
O Glory of Jerusalem.
O Beauty of the World.
O Noblest-Born of the Christian Flock.
O Queen of Life.
O Ladder of heaven.

Translated by Eugene O'Curry.

THE CANON FOR APOCREOS

St. Theodore of the Studium (Died 826)

That fearful day, that day of speechless dread,
When Thou shalt come to judge the quick and dead—
     I shudder to foresee,
     O God! what then shall be!
When Thou shalt come, angelic legions round,
With thousand thousands, and with trumpet sound,
     Christ, grant me in the air
     With saints to meet Thee there!
Weep, O my soul, ere that great hour and day
When God shall shine in manifest array,
     Thy sin, that thou mayst be
     In that strict judgment free!
The terror!—hell-fire fierce and unsufficed;
The bitter worm; the gnashing teeth; O Christ,
     Forgive, remit, protect;
     And set me with the elect!
That I may hear the blessèd voice that calls
The righteous to the joy of heavenly halls;

And, King of Heaven, may reach
The realm that passeth speech!
Enter Thou not in judgment with each deed,
Nor each intent and thought in strictness read;
　Forgive and save me then,
O Thou that lovest men!
Thee, One in Three blest Persons! Lord o'er all!
Essence of essence, Power of power, we call!
　Save us, O Father, Son,
　And Spirit, ever one!

From the Greek by J. M. Neale.

SANCTE CONFESSOR

RHABANUS MAURUS (Died 856)

Holy Confessor, blessèd in thy merit,
See how thy people congregate before thee
Bow in devotion, and a thousand voices
　　Chant of thy glory!

So they rejoice to celebrate thy feast-day,
Thou who didst quell the bitter pain of dying,
Loosed from the thraldom of the flesh, ascending
　　Victor to heaven.

Therefore we pray thee, bending low before thee,
By thy blest prayer destroy the fear of judgment,
That the Creator, of His loving kindness,
　　Hearing, have mercy.

So may He grant us hearts forever faithful,
So may we ever serve Him in thanksgiving,
So may that Saviour grant for every sin-stain
　　Healing and pardon.

This, Holy Father, at Thy servant's pleading,
Grant, and Thy Son who with Thee reigns forever,
With the Blest Spirit, He who filleth all things,
　　Unity Trinal!

From the Latin by Alan G. McDougall.

A CHARM FOR BEES

ANONYMOUS (Ninth Century)

Christ, there is a swarm of bees outside.
Fly hither, my little cattle,
In blest peace, in God's protection,
Come home safe and sound!
Sit down, sit down, Bee,
Saint Mary commanded thee.
Thou shalt not have leave,
Thou shalt not fly to the wood!
Thou shalt not escape me,
Nor go away from me.
Sit very still,
And wait God's will!

From the Old High German.

THE HEAVENLY PILOT

CORMAC, King-Bishop of Cashel (837-903)

Wilt Thou steer my frail black bark
O'er the dark broad ocean's foam?
Wilt Thou come, Lord, to my boat
Where afloat my will would roam?

Thine the mighty; Thine the small;
Thine to mark men fall like rain;
God! wilt Thou grant aid to me
Who come o'er the upheaving main?

From the Irish by George Sigerson.

MEDIA VITA

Attributed to Blessed NOTKER BALBULUS (840-912)

In life still death is here,
There is one common doom.
Oh, how shall we prepare
For a believer's tomb?

Peace is of Thee alone—
Thou only canst atone
The sins we grieve, and from Thy wrath
Make us a path
To heaven.
O holy Lord and God,
Eternal Christ of God,
Hear Thou our faltering breath,
Spare us from endless death,
Kyrie Eleison.

In death the jaws of hell
Against our spirits gape.
Lord God, wilt Thou not save,
And grant us swift escape?
'Tis Thou, dear Lord, didst win
The conquest of our sin,
And pity for our souls obtain;
Else hope were vain
Of heaven.
O holy Lord and God,
Eternal Christ of God,
Hear Thou our bitter cry,
And save us e'er we die!
Kyrie Eleison.

In hell's dark midst, our sin
Would drive us to despair.
Oh, whither shall we fly?
Where is our refuge, where?
Thy blood, O Christ, alone
Can for our sin atone.
'Tis in the holy Rood to give
The grace to live
In heaven.
O holy Lord and God,
Eternal Christ of God,
Grant from Thy faith we all
May never, never fall!
Kyrie Eleison.
    From the Latin by Frederick Rowland Marvin.

CANTEMUS CUNCTI MELODUM

Blessed NOTKER BALBULUS (840-912)

The strains upraise of joy and praise.   Alleluia!
To the glory of their King
Shall ransomed people sing, Alleluia!
And the Choirs that dwell on high
Shall reëcho through the sky, Alleluia!
They on the fields of Paradise that roam,
The Blessèd ones, repeat through that bright home, Alleluia!
The planets glittering on their heavenly way,
The shining constellations, join and say, Alleluia!
Ye clouds that onward sweep,
Ye winds on pinions light,
Ye thunders echoing loud and deep,
Ye lightnings wildly bright,—
In sweet consent unite your Alleluia!
Ye floods and ocean billows,
Ye storms and winter snow,
Ye days of cloudless beauty,
Hoar frost and summer glow,
Ye groves that wave in spring,
And glorious forests, sing Alleluia!
First let the birds with painted plumage gay
Exalt their great Creator's praise, and say Alleluia!
Then let the beasts of earth with varying strain
Join in Creation's Hymn and cry again, Alleluia!
Here let the mountains thunder forth sonorous, Alleluia!
There let the valleys sing in gentler chorus, Alleluia!
Thou jubilant abyss of ocean, cry Alleluia!
Ye tracts of earth and continents, reply Alleluia!
To God who all Creation made,
The frequent hymn be duly paid, Alleluia!
This is the strain, the eternal strain, the Lord of all things loves:
        Alleluia!
This is the song, the heavenly song, that Christ Himself
    approves:
        Alleluia!
Wherefore we sing, both heart and voice awaking, Alleluia!
And children's voices echo, answer making, Alleluia!

Now from all men be outpoured
Alleluia to the Lord!
With Alleluia evermore.
The Son and Spirit we adore!
Praise be done to the Three in One,
      Alleluia! Alleluia!

From the Latin by John Mason Neale.

COMMUNION HYMN OF THE ANCIENT IRISH CHURCH

May the sweet name of Jesus
Be lovingly graven
On my heart's inmost haven.

O Mary, sweet mother,
Be Jesus my brother,
And I Jesus' lover.

A binding of love
That no distance can sever
Be between us for ever;
Yea, O my Saviour, for ever and ever.

Anonymous Translation.

IRISH HYMN TO MARY

ANONYMOUS (Ninth Century)

In alternate measure chanting, daily sing we Mary's praise;
And in strains of glad rejoicing, to the Lord our voices raise.

With a twofold choir repeating Mary's never-dying fame,
Let each ear the praises gather which our grateful tongues
    proclaim.

Judah's ever-glorious daughter—chosen Mother of the Lord—
Who, to weak and fallen manhood, all its ancient worth restored.

From the everlasting Father, Gabriel brought the glad decree,
That, the Word Divine conceiving, she should set poor sinners
    free.

Of all virgins pure, the Purest—ever stainless, ever bright,
Still from grace to grace advancing, fairest Daughter of the
    Light.

Wondrous title—who shall tell it?—whilst the Word Divine
    she bore,
Though in mother's name rejoicing, virgin purer than before!

By a woman's disobedience, eating the forbidden tree,
Was the world betrayed and ruined—was by woman's hand
    set free.

From the Irish by Dr. Potter.

THE GOOD BISHOP

ANONYMOUS (Tenth Century)

Before Saint Anne,
Six were sainted
Of our holy bishops.
Like the seven stars
They shall shine from heaven.
Purer and brighter
Is the light of Anno
Than a hyacinth set in a gold ring!
This darling man
We will have for a pattern;
And those that would grow
In virtue and trustiness
Shall dress by him as at a mirror.
As the sun in the air
Between earth and heaven
Glitters to both—
So went Bishop Anno
Between God and man.
Such was his virtue in the palace
That the emperor obeyed him;
He behaved with honor to both sides
And was counted among the first barons.
In his gestures at worship
He was awful as an angel.

Many a man knew his goodness.
Hear what were his manners—
His words were frank and open;
He spoke truth, fearing no man;
Like a lamb he sat among princes;
Like a lamb he walked among the people;
To the unruly he was sharp;
To the gentle he was mild;
Widows and orphans praised him always.
Preaching and praying
No one could do better.
Happy was Cologne
To be worthy of such a bishop!

From the German by William Taylor.

THE CHRIST-CHILD

Saint Gregory of Narek (951-1011)

The lips of the Christ-child are like to twin leaves;
    They let roses fall when He smiles tenderly.
The tears of the Christ-child are pearls when he grieves;
    The eyes of the Christ-child are deep as the sea.
Like pomegranate grains are the dimples He hath,
And clustering lilies spring up in His path.

From the Armenian by Alice Stone Blackwell.

DEUS MEUS

Mael-Isu (Died in 1038)

Deus meus adjuva me,
Give me Thy love, O Christ, I pray.
Give me Thy love, O Christ, I pray.
Deus meus adjuva me.

In meum cor ut sanum sit,
Pour, loving King, Thy love in it;
Pour, loving King, Thy love in it;
In meum cor ut sanum sit.

Domine, da ut peto a Te,
A pure bright sun give Thou today,
A pure bright sun give Thou today,
Domine, da ut peto a Te.

Hanc spero rem et quaero quam
Thy love to have where'er I am,
Thy love to have where'er I am,
Hanc spero rem et quaero quam.

Tuum amorem sicut vis
Give to me swiftly, strongly, this,
Give to me swiftly, strongly, this,
Tuum amorem sicut vis.

Quaero, postulo, peto a Te.
That I in heaven, dear Christ, may stay,
That I in heaven, dear Christ, may stay,
Quaero, postulo, peto a Te.

Domine, Domine, exaudi me
Fill my soul, Lord, with Thy love's ray,
Fill my soul, Lord, with Thy love's ray,
Domine, Domine, exaudi me.
Deus meus adjuva me.
Deus meus adjuva me.
          From the Irish by George Sigerson.

VICTIMÆ PASCHALI LAUDES

WIPO (Died 1048)

Now comes the Paschal Victim bringing
Sacrifice, while praises singing,
Christians saved through His redeeming,
See the Lamb with lifeblood streaming,—
Christ through Calvary's dread reviling
God and sinners reconciling.
Life and Death by dire contending
Brought man's doom to gracious ending.
Answer, Mary: what glad warning
Met thee on thy way that morning?

Lo! I saw where through night glooming
Christ had risen from His entombing.
Angels then the truth attesting,
And the cloths the Lord investing.
Christ arisen, new hope bestowing,
Back to Galilee is going.
Drawn from death by fond affection,
Well we know Christ's Resurrection:
Victor-King from grave emerging,
Hear the prayers our hearts are urging.

From the Latin by Charles Kent.

TO OUR LORD IN THE SACRAMENT

SAINT ANSELM (1033-1109)

Hail! Christ's pure Body—born of the Holy Virgin—
  Living flesh, and true Man, and perfect Godhead!
Hail! Fount of health, of life—the Way, the world's redemp-
    tion—
  Thy mighty right hand free us from all evil!

Hail! Christ's pure Blood. Hail! hallowed Draught of Heaven,
  Life-giving Wave that cleanseth all offenses!
From Christ's own Heart—while on the Cross He dieth—
  Thou gushest forth! O, hail! Fount of salvation!

From the Latin by Romano Rios, O.S.B.

THE BELL OF THE HERMITAGE

ANONYMOUS

Sweet little bell
That is struck in the windy night,
I had liefer go to a tryst with thee
Than to a tryst with a foolish woman.

From the Old Irish.

DEUS IMMENSA TRINITAS

FROM *The Mozarabic Breviary*

O Glorious Immensity
And One eternal Trinity,
Father and Comforter and Word,
Of all that is, unconquered Lord.

The Saint, for whom our chants of praise
Consenting on this feast we raise,
With princely guerdons Thou didst bless;
Thy crown, Thy palm, Thy happiness.

In tortures great and cruel pain
Thou didst with Thy right hand sustain
Thy servant who with steadfast heart
Bore the tormentor's every art.

Thy gracious ear, O Christ divine,
Unto Thy servant's prayer incline,
To whom Thy fairest gifts are given
Within the glorious halls of heaven.

Thee Prince of Princes we proclaim,
The King that bear'st the mystic Name;
Blot out in Thy great love, we pray,
The sins that mar this holy day.

That so when Thou shalt come again,
O Christ, in light on earth to reign,
Led by Thy martyr, we may dare
To rise to meet Thee in the air.

To God the Father glory be,
And God the Son eternally,
With God the Holy Paraclete
Through endless ages, as is meet.

From the Latin by Alan G. McDougall.

TO GABRIEL OF THE ANNUNCIATION

Peter Abelard (1079-1142)

On with thine embassy;
  Say AVE! say ALL HAIL!
Say THE LORD IS WITH THEE!
  And, that thou mayst avail,
    Say too the words FEAR NOT!

Virginal Lily, nod
  Gently thy jewelled brow
In the soft breath of God;
  Chastely thou'lt keep thy vow
    With never stain or spot.

Heareth She, and believes!
  Now is the message done;
Credits the word, conceives,
  Brings forth her only Son,
    Marvellous in emprise;

Jesus the Counsellor
  Unto the sons of men,
Man-God who shall restore
  Unto the earth again
    Peace by His sacrifice!

Who shall blot out our sin
  With His almighty hand,
Bidding us enter in
  Unto the fatherland
    Over the starry skies!

From the Latin by H. T. Henry.

JESU DULCIS

Saint Bernard of Clairvaux (1090-1153)

Jesus, sweet is love of Thee
Nor may nothing so sweet be;
Nought that man may think or see
Can have sweetness near Thee.

Jesus, no song may be sweeter
Nor thought in heart blissfuller,
Nought may be felt lightsomer
Than Thou, so sweet a Lover.

Jesus, Thy love was to us so free
That it from heaven brought Thee;
For love full dear Thou boughtest me,
For love Thou hung on Roode-tree.

Jesus, for us Thou hung on Rood,
For love Thou gave Thy hearte blood;
Love Thee made our soule's food,
Thy love us brought to alle good.

Jesus, my Lover, Thou art so free
That all Thou diddest for love of me.
What shall I for that yielde Thee?
Thou askest but the love of me.

Jesus my Dear, my Love, my Light,
I will Thee love and that is right;
Make me Thee love with all my might
And for Thee mourn both day and night.

Jesus, forsooth there is no thing
In all this world of such liking
That knows so much of love-longing
As Thou, Jesus, my Dear Sweeting.

Jesus, Thy love is sweet and strong.
All my life for Thee I long.
Teach me, Lord, Thy love song,
With sweet tears ever among.

Jesus, look Thou pity me.
When shall my soul come to Thee?
How long shall it here be
Where I can not my Lover see?

Jesus Lord, my Sweeting,
Hold me ever in Thy keeping:
Make of me Thy darling
That I Thee love over all thing.

Extract from the Vernon MS. fol.cv.b.

THY KINGDOM COME

SAINT BERNARD OF CLAIRVAUX

Thou hope of all the lowly!
  To thirsting souls how kind!
Gracious to all who seek Thee,
  Oh, what to those who find!

My tongue but lisps Thy praises,
  Yet praise be my employ;
Love makes me bold to praise Thee,
  For Thou art all my joy.

In Thee my soul delighting,
  Findeth her only rest;
And so in Thee confiding,
  May all the world be blest!

Dwell with us, and our darkness
  Will flee before Thy light;
Scatter the world's deep midnight,
  And fill it with delight.

O all mankind! behold Him,
  And seek His love to know;
And let your hearts, in seeking,
  Be fired with love and glow!

O come, O come, great Monarch!
  Eternal glory Thine;
The longing world waits for Thee:
  Arise, arise and shine!

Anonymous Translation from the Latin.

THE ASSUMPTION

SAINT NERSES (1098-1173)

Unsullied temple, heavenly light enshrining,
God's Mother true, and still a stainless Maiden;
Prophets of old prefigured and foretold thee:
The Tree of Life in God's fair garden planted.
In Abraham's tent was heard the gladsome tidings
From God's own Word thy motherhood foretelling.
Hail bush of Moses unconsumed by burning!
Hail golden vessel filled with heavenly Manna!
Hail Gideon's Fleece, the gentle dew containing!
Isaias sang of thee, the Maid conceiving;
The lightsome cloud, the book made fast with sealing.
Ezechiel saw the portal barred and bolted;
Daniel, the mount whence the great stone was taken!

From the Armenian by W. H. Kent, O.S.C.

From the MARIALE

BERNARD OF MORLAS (About 1140)

Every day
To Mary pay,
Soul, thy tribute praises high.
All her glory,
All her story
Celebrate and magnify.
Contemplate
Her lofty state,
Thyself with lowly awe possessed.
Mother hail her,
Neither fail her
To salute as Virgin Blest.
Oh, adore her
And implore her
Thee from sin to liberate.
Her to aid thee
When invade thee

Passion's whirlwinds, supplicate.
By this maiden
Bounty-laden
God to earth did once incline.
Queen of Heaven,
She hath given
To her children grace divine.
Eve's offending
Far descending
Barred the Gate of Paradise.
Mary's credence
And obedience
Ope the portals of the skies.
'Twas by reason
Of Eve's treason
Sentence stern on man was passed;
By her holy
Hearkening lowly
Mary leads him home at last.

Anonymous Translation from the Latin.

JERUSALEM THE GOLDEN

BERNARD OF MORLAS

Jerusalem the Golden
  With milk and honey blest,
Beneath thy contemplation
  Sink heart and voice opprest;
I know not, oh, I know not,
  What social joys are there,
What radiancy of glory,
  What light beyond compare.

They stand, those walls of Zion,
  All jubilant with song,
And bright with many an angel,
  And all the martyr throng;

The Prince is ever in them,
The daylight is serene;
The pastures of the blest
Are decked in glorious sheen.

There is the throne of David;
And there, from care released,
The song of them that triumph,
The shout of them that feast;
And they, who with their Leader
Have conquered in the fight
Forever and forever
Are clad in robes of white.

O sweet and blessèd country,
Shall I e'er see thy face?
O sweet and blessèd country,
Shall I e'er win thy grace?
Exult, O dust and ashes:
The Lord shall be thy part;
His only, His forever,
Thou shalt be and thou art!

Anonymous Translation from the Latin.

CRUSADERS' SONG

From the *Chronicle of The Dukes of Normandy* (1145)

Take the good and cast the evil,
Listen, people to my song,
For 'tis God for whom I'm speaking
To the valiant and the strong.
Take the Cross, the Cross He died on,
Oh, repay Him as ye may:
For by dying He redeemed us,
Can we give Him less today?

Counts and princes they may spoil us,
But their spoiling stays at death;
What the treasures of their hoarding
When they give their final breath?

Better far to up and rally
In the good cause I proclaim;
Where at death are earthly honors?
Lost forever, lost in shame.

Cowards! spending time and labor
For your bodies, for a wage;
All shall pass and all shall wither
Soon the youth shall turn to age.
But the guerdons of true virtue
Oh, they live forever more,
Oh, the bitterness of losing
Of their everlasting store!

He to whom the Light is given,
He will up for Holy Land
At the Day of Judgment scathless
When the good from evil stand.
When the world shall mighty tremble
Oh, that soul shall fearless be,
Quailing never such before Him
Coming in His majesty!

Help me, God, in this my pleading!
Tardy have we been to free
That Thy Cross and that Thy country
Where the Infidels mock Thee.
'Tis our sins that have delayed us
Let us cast them and be free,
Leaving everything behind us,
Finding Paradise with Thee.

Such an one will all men honor,
If returning God decrees,
Sweet in absence is his country,
Sweeter if once home he sees.
Living still his lovely lady
As he left her hardly won,
Oh, he jousts for her sweet favor
Now his task for God is done.

Envoy:
O my good knights, may God keep you
  Whom I've loved so evermore,
That in loving you I've almost
  Oft forgot my God of yore!
From the Old French by Walter Clifford Meller.

THE GOLDEN SEQUENCE

INNOCENT III (1161-1216)

Come, Thou Holy Spirit, come,
And from Thy celestial home
  Shed a ray of light divine;
Come, Thou Father of the poor,
Come, Thou source of all our store,
  Come, within our bosoms shine.

Heal our wounds; our strength renew;
On our dryness pour Thy dew;
  Wash the stains of guilt away;
Bend the stubborn heart and will;
Melt the frozen, warm the chill;
  Guide the steps that go astray.
        Anonymous Translation from the Latin.

STABAT MATER DOLOROSA

Ascribed to INNOCENT III (1161-1216) and JACOPONE DA TODI (1230-1306)

Stood the Mother in her anguish
By the Cross whereon did languish,
  Clenched with nails, her Son and Lord;
While her spirit's desolation,
Sorrowing and lamentation
  Felt the piercing of the sword.

Oh, how mournful and distressèd
Stood she there, who was the Blessèd
  Mother of the Promised One;
And her weeping—and her grieving!
And her trembling at perceiving
  There her First-Born's Passion!

Who is he whose eyes are tearless,
Witnessing Christ's Mother peerless,
  Dolorous and so alone?
Who is he who would not share her
Mother pangs, such griefs prepare her
  As she stands and mourns her Own?

For the sins of generations
Christ she sees mid flagellations,
  And the pains He must endure;
Sees the Son her breast did cherish
Desolate and doomed to perish,
  Giving up His spirit pure.

Mother—source of love's affection!
Let me share in thy abjection,
  Let my tears be joined to thine!
Set my heart aglow with burning
Unto Christ my God in yearning
  So to calm thy breast benign!

Blessèd Mother, this, oh, fashion
That the wounds of Cross and Passion
  Be fixed firmly on my heart;
That the scars thy Son is bearing
Find me worthily preparing
  To assume an humble part.

Weeping with thee in affliction
At the direful crucifixion
  All the days I live below,
'Neath the Cross with thee in sorrow
Portion of thy grief to borrow
  In the cataclysmic blow.

Virgin of all Virgins brightest,
Grant the plea thou never slightest—
　　Let me stand with thee and weep;
Grant me Christ to bear as mourner—
In His sufferings, sojourner—
　　Impress of His wounds to keep!

Scars like His for my salvation—
Crosses for inebriation
　　In thy Son, my Jesus' love—
Flamed amid the radiance splendid,
Let me be by thee defended
　　On that Judgment Day above!

May I, by the Cross protected,
Through the death of Christ elected,
　　Be anointed unto grace;
When the body's day is ended
Be my soul by thee attended.
　　To the Paradisial place!

From the Latin by Thomas Walsh.

From THE LIFE OF SAN MILLAN

GONZALO DE BERCEO (1180-1246)

He walked those mountains wild, and lived within that nook
For forty years and more, nor ever comfort took
Of offered food or alms or human speech or look;
No other saint in Spain did such a penance brook.
For many a painful year he passed the seasons there
And many a night consumed in penitence and prayer—
In solitude and cold, with want and evil fare,
His thoughts to God resigned and free from human care.
Oh, sacred is the place, the fountain and the hill,
The rocks where he reposed in meditation still,
The solitary shades through which he roved at will;
His presence all that place with sanctity did fill.

From the Spanish by Hookham Frere.

SAN MIGUEL DE LA TUMBA

GONZALO DE BERCEO

San Miguel de la Tumba is a convent vast and wide;
The sea encircles it around, and groans on every side;
It is a wild and dangerous place, and many woes betide
The monks who in that burial place in penitence abide.
Within those dark monastic walls, amid the ocean flood,
Of pious fasting monks there dwelt a holy brotherhood;
To the Madonna's glory there an altar high was placed
And a rich and costly image the sacred altar graced.
Exalted high upon a throne, the Virgin Mother smiled,
And as the custom is, she held within her arms the Child;
The kings and wisemen of the East were kneeling by her side;
Attended was she like a queen whom God had sanctified.

Descending low before her face a screen of feathers hung,—
A *moscader* or fan for flies, 'tis called in vulgar tongue;
From the feathers of the peacock's wing 'twas fashioned bright
    and fair,
And glistened like the heaven above when all its stars are there.
It chanced that for the people's sins, fell lightning's blasting
    stroke;
Forth from all four sacred walls the flames consuming broke;
The sacred robes were all consumed, missal and holy book;
And hardly with their lives the monks their crumbling walls
    forsook.

But though the desolating flame raged fearfully and wild,
It did not reach the Virgin Queen, it did not reach the Child;
It did not reach the feathery screen before her face that shone,
Nor injured in a farthing's worth the image or the throne.
The image it did not consume, it did not burn the screen;
Even in the value of a hair they were not hurt, I ween;
Not even the smoke did reach them, nor injure more the shrine
Than the bishop, hight Don Tello, has been hurt by hand of
    mine.

From the Spanish by H. W. Longfellow.

THE SONG OF THE CREATURES

Saint Francis of Assisi (1182-1226)

O most high, almighty, good Lord God, to Thee belong praise,
   glory, honor and all blessing!
Praised be my Lord God with all His creatures, and especially
   our brother the sun, who brings us the day and who brings
   us the light; fair is he and shines with very great splendor;
   O Lord, he signifies to us Thee!
Praised be my Lord for our sister the moon, and for the stars,
   the which He has set clear and lovely in heaven.
Praised be my Lord for our brother the wind, and for air and
   cloud calms and all weather by which Thou upholdest life in
   all creatures—
Praised be my Lord for all those who pardon one another, for
   His love's sake, and who endure weakness and tribulation;
   blessèd are they who peaceably shall endure. For Thou, O
   Most Highest, shalt give them a crown!
Praised be my Lord for our sister, the death of the body, from
   which no man escapeth. Woe to him who dieth in mortal
   sin! Blessèd are they who are found walking by Thy most
   holy will, for the second death shall have no power to do
   them harm.
Praise ye and bless the Lord, and give thanks unto Him and
   serve Him with great humility.

From the Italian by Matthew Arnold.

OF ORDER IN OUR LORD CHRIST

Saint Francis of Assisi

Set love in order, thou that lovest Me,
   Never was virtue out of order found;
And though I fill thy heart desirously,
   By thine own virtue I must keep My ground;
When to My love thou dost bring charity,
   Even she must come with order girt and gowned.
Look how the trees are bound

To order, bearing fruit;
And by one thing compute
In all things earthly order's grace and gain.

All earthly things I had the making of
    Were numbered and were measured then by Me;
And each was ordered to its end by Love,
    Each kept, through order, clean for ministry.
Charity most of all, when known enough,
    Is of her very nature orderly.
    Lo, now! what heat in thee,
Soul, can have bred this rout?
Thou put'st all order out,
Even this love's heat must be its curb and rein.
                From the Italian by Dante Gabriel Rossetti.

DEATH-BED HYMN OF SAINT ANTHONY OF PADUA

(1195-1231)

O glorious Lady of the Light
    Whose rays all other stars eclipse;
'Twas thine to give thy breast-milk white
    To thy Creator's lips;

What Eve's sad penalties had cost
    Thy fertile womb in full would pay;
To exiles mid the star-paths lost
    Thy Heavenly Window lights the way.

Thou Threshold of the Highest King,—
    Thou Gateway of a noontide flame!
In her, Life's Virgin heralding,
    O ye, redeemed, acclaim!

Glory, Thou Sovereign Lord, to Thee
    Whom spotless birth to earth did lend,—
Father and Holy Spirit, Three—
    Through ages without end!
                From the Latin by Thomas Walsh.

LUX ADVENIT VENERANDA

ADAM DE ST. VICTOR (Later Twelfth Century)

Thou whose prayer doth vice destroy,
Thou whose name brings only joy,
Thou whose perfume shames the rose,
Thou whose lip with nectar flows
    Sweeter than the honeycomb;
Redder than the rose art thou,
Whiter than the falling snow,
Dewier than the rose dew-strewn,
Brighter than the splendorous moon
    Shinest thou in heaven's dome.
Empress of the host supernal,
Victress over foes infernal,
Pathway leading up to heaven
To be followed as 'twas given;
Call them back who far have wandered,
And, recalled, what they have squandered—
    Show them how it may be won!
To thy clients thee addressing
Grant in fullness every blessing;
Nor the lowly sinner spurning,
But his pleading heart discerning;
And thus all who feel their weakness
And beseech thy loving meekness,
    Place before thy pardoning Son!
                        From the Latin by H. T. Henry.

HOURS OF THE PASSION

WILLIAM OF SHOREHAM (Latter Half of the Twelfth Century)

At Prime Jesus was y-led
    Tofore Sir Pilate,
There witnesses false and fele
Belowen Him for hate.
They to-stake His sweet head
With one thornen crown;
To Calvary His cross He bear
Well reulichy out of the town.

On cross y-nailed was Jesus
At Sixten tide;
Strong thieves hangen they on
Either half His side.
In His pine His strong thirst
Staunched they with gall,
So that God's holy Lamb
Of sin wash us all.
At Nones Jesus Christ
Thane hard death deeled;
He cried Eloi to His Father,
The soul He gan upyield.
A Knight with one sharp spear
Stung Him in the right side.
The earth shoke, the sun dim become,
In thare tide.
Of the cross He was do
At Evesong's hour;
The strength left lotede in God
Of our Saviour.
Such death He under-yede
Of life the medecine,
Alas, He was y-laid adown
The crown of bliss in pine.
At Compline it was y-bore
To the burying,
That noble corpse of Jesus Christ.
Hope of lives coming,
Well richly it was anoint,
Fulfilled His holy book;
I bid, Lord, Thy passion
To mine mend look.

THE RUNE OF HOSPITALITY

I saw a stranger yestereen,
I put food in the eating-place,
Drink in the drinking-place,
Music in the listening-place,
And in the blessed name of the Triune

He blessed myself and my house,
My cattle and my dear ones,
And the lark said in her song,
Often, often, often
Goes the Christ in the stranger's guise.
Often, often, often
Goes the Christ in the stranger's guise.

From the Gaelic.

THE VISION OF MAC CONGLINNE

(Twelfth Century)

In a slumber visional
Wonders apparitional
    Sudden shone on me;
Was it not a miracle?
Built of lard, a coracle
    Swam a sweet milk sea.

. . . . .

Ramparts rose of custard all
Where a castle mustered all
    Forces o'er the lake;
Butter was the bridge of it,
Wheaten meal the ridge of it,
    Bacon every stake.

. . . . .

Old cheese-columns happily,
Pork that pillared sappily,
    Raised their heads aloof;
While curd-rafters mellowly
Crossing cream-beams yellowly
    Held aloft the roof.

From the Old Irish by George Sigerson.

THE LAND OF COKAIGNE

English Folk Poetry (Later Thirteenth Century)

Up a river of sweet milk,
Where is plenty great of silk,
When the summer's day is hot,
The young nunnes taketh a boat
And doth ham forth in that rivere
Both with oares and with steere.

. . . . .

There is a well fair Abbey
Of white monks and of grey:
There beth bowrs and halls;
All of pasties beth the walls;
Of flesh, of fish, and a rich meat
The likefullest that man may eat;
Flouren cakes beth the shingles all
Of church, cloister, bowrs and hall;
The pinnes beth fat puddings
Rich meat to princes and kings.

DIES IRÆ

The Requiem Sequence (Thirteenth Century)

Day of wrath, that day of burning
All shall melt, to ashes turning,
All foretold by seers discerning.

Oh, what fear it shall engender
When the Judge shall come in splendor,
Strict to mark and just to render!

Trumpet-scattered sound of wonder,
Rending sepulchres asunder
Shall resistless summons thunder.

All aghast then Death shall shiver
And great nature's frame shall quiver
When the graves their dead deliver.

Think, O Jesus, for what reason
Thou enduredest earth's spite and treason,
Nor me lose in that dread season!

Seeking me Thy worn feet hasted,
On the cross Thy soul death tasted,
Let such labor not be wasted.

Righteous Judge of retribution,
Grant me perfect absolution
Ere that day of execution!

Culprit-like, I—heart all broken,
On my cheek shame's crimson token—
Plead the pardoning word be spoken.

Mid the sheep a place decide me,
And from goats on left divide me,
Standing on the right beside Thee.

When the accursed away are driven
To eternal burnings given,
Call me with the Blest to heaven.

I beseech Thee, prostrate lying,
Heart as ashes, contrite, sighing,
Care for me when I am dying.

On that awful day of story,
When man, rising, stands before Thee,
Spare the culprit, God of Glory!
                From the Latin by Abraham Coles.

WELCOME YULE

Welcome be Thou, Heavenly King,
Welcome born in on morning,
Welcome for Him we shall syng,
Welcome Yule!

Welcome be ye, Steven and John,
Welcome Innocents everyone,
Welcome Thomas Martyr on,
Welcome Yule!

Welcome be ye, Good New Year,
Welcome Twelfth Day both infer,
Welcome Saintes 'loved and dear,
Welcome Yule!

Welcome be ye Candelmasse
Welcome be ye Queen of Bliss,
Welcome both to more and less,
Welcome Yule!

Welcome be ye that are here,
Welcome alle and make good cheer,
Welcome alle another year,
Welcome Yule!

THE BASQUE SONG

ANONYMOUS (Thirteenth Century)

O little lark, you need not fly
To seek your Master in the sky.
He's near our native sod.
    Why should you sing aloft, apart?
    Sing to the Heaven of my heart,
In me, in me, in me is God.

O travellers, passing in your car,
Ye pity me, who come from far
On dusty feet, rough shod.
    You cannot guess, you cannot know,
    Upon what wings of joy I go
Who travel home with God.

Ships bring from far your curious care.
Earth's richest morsels are your share,
And prize of gun and rod.
 At richer boards I take my seat,
 Have dainties angels may not eat.
In me, in me, in me is God.

O little lark, sing loud and long
To Him who gave you flight and song,
And me a heart of flame.
 He loveth them of low degree,
 And He hath magnifièd me,
And Holy, Holy, Holy is His name.
   Anonymous Translation from the Basque.

THE CRUSADE

RINALDO D'AQUINO (About 1200-1240)

 Never can I forget my woe,
  And comfort naught avails;
 The ships are in the port below,
  Waiting to hoist their sails.
 The men are all for sailing
  To lands beyond the sea,
 And I alone am wailing,
  What will become of me?

 The Cross that saves all living
  Has set my steps astray;
 The Cross such grief is giving,
  To God I cannot pray.
 O Cross of pilgrim faring,
  What of my lonely strife!
 The grief my heart is bearing
  Will waste away my life.
   From the Italian by Moira O'Neill

PRAYER

(Thirteenth Century)

Spirit of Christ my sanctification;
Body of Christ be mine to save;
Blood of Christ my inebriation;
Ooze from Christ's side be mine to lave;
Passion of Christ my consolation;
O gentle Jesus, aid provide
And in Thy wounds so let me hide
That from Thee never shall I go.
Defend me from the evil foe,
And call me in the hour of death
And take to Thee my final breath;
So I may join Thy Chosen then,
And age on ages sing Amen.
From the Spanish by Thomas Walsh.

IN THE HEART OF JESUS

MUIREADACH O'DALY—ALBANACH (About 1215)

That in Jesus' heart should be
One like me is marvellous;
Sin has made my life a loss,
But His Cross shall speak for us.

As of old, O Jesus sweet,
Bless my feet and hands Thine own;
Of Thy bounty, bless to good
These my blood and flesh and bone.

Never now I keep from ill
Since my body will take part;
Make it hallowed by Thy love
From above, in head and heart.

Sweet and Great One, grant relief,
   All my grief take quite away;
So that ere my life be spent
   Thou'lt have sent and cleared my way.
            From the Old Irish by George Sigerson.

ADESTES FIDELES

Ascribed to SAINT BONAVENTURE (1221-1274)

O come, all ye faithful,
Joyful and triumphant,
O come ye, O come ye to Bethlehem;
Come and behold Him
Born, the King of Angels;
O come, let us adore Him,
O come, let us adore Him,
O come, let us adore Him, Christ the Lord.

God of God,
Light of Light,
Lo, He abhors not the Virgin's womb!
Very God,
Begotten not created;
O come, let us adore Him,
O come, let us adore Him,
O come, let us adore Him, Christ the Lord.

Sing, choirs of angels;
Sing in exultation,
Sing, all ye citizens of Heaven above;
"Glory to God,
All glory in the highest!"
O come, let us adore Him,
O come, let us adore Him,
O come, let us adore Him, Christ the Lord.

Yea, Lord, we greet Thee,
Born this happy morning;
Jesu, to Thee be glory given;

Word of the Father
Now in flesh appearing,
O come, let us adore Him,
O come, let us adore Him,
O come, let us adore Him, Christ the Lord.
From the Latin by Frederick Oakeley.

ADORO TE DEVOTE

SAINT THOMAS AQUINAS (1225-1274)

O Godhead hid, devoutly I adore Thee,
Who truly art within the forms before me;
To Thee my heart I bow with bended knee,
As failing quite in contemplating Thee.
Sight, touch and taste in Thee are each deceived;
The ear alone most safely is believed;
I believe all the Son of God has spoken;
Than Truth's own word there is no truer token.
God only on the Cross lay hid from view,
But here lies hid at once the Manhood too;
And I, in both professing my belief,
Make the same prayer as the repentant thief.
Thy wounds, as Thomas saw, I do not see,
Yet Thee confess my Lord and God to be.
Make me believe Thee ever more and more,
In Thee my hope, in Thee my love to store.
O thou Memorial of Our Lord's own dying,
O living Bread to mortals life supplying,
Make thou my soul henceforth on thee to live,
Ever a taste of heavenly sweetness give!
O loving pelican, O Jesu Lord,
Unclean I am, but cleanse me in Thy blood;
Of which a single drop, for sinners spilt,
Can purge the universe from all its guilt.
Jesu, whom for the present veiled I see,
What I so thirst for, oh, vouchsafe to me:
That I may see Thy countenance unfolding
And may be blest Thy glory in beholding!
From the Latin by Dom F. Cabrol, O.S.B.

HYMN

SAINT THOMAS AQUINAS

Sing, my tongue, the Saviour's glory,
  Of His flesh the mystery sing;
Of the blood, all price excelling,
  Shed by our Immortal King.
Destined for the world's redemption
  From a noble womb to spring.

Of a pure and spotless Virgin
  Born for us on earth below,
He, as Man with man conversing,
  Stayed the seeds of truth to sow;
Then He closed in solemn order
  Wondrously His life of woe.

On the night of that Last Supper
  Seated with His chosen band,
He the paschal victim eating,
  First fulfils the Law's command;
Then as food to all His brethren
  Gives Himself with His own Hand.

Word made flesh, the bread of nature
  By His word to Flesh He turns;
Wine into His blood He changes:—
  What though sense no change discerns,
Only be the heart in earnest,
  Faith her lesson quickly learns.

Down in adoration falling,
  Lo! the Sacred Host we hail;
Lo! o'er ancient forms departing,
  Newer rites of grace prevail;
Faith for all defects supplying,
  Where the feeble senses fail.

To the Everlasting Father,
　And the Son who reigns on high,
With the Holy Ghost proceeding
　Forth from each eternally,
Be salvation, honor, blessing,
　Might and endless majesty!
　　　　Anonymous Translation from the Latin.

LATIN LULLABY

(Thirteenth Century)

Dormi, Jesu, mater ridet
Quae tam dulcem somnum videt,
Dormi, Jesu blandule.
Si non dormis mater plorat,
Inter fila cantans orat:
Blande veni somnule.

Slumber, Jesu, o'er Thy dreaming
Here Thy mother's smile is beaming,
Slumber, Jesu fair to see.
She will grieve if Thou art waking
And her distaff croon is making:
"Gentle dreams, steal over Thee."
　　　　Version of Garrett Strange.

STABAT MATER SPECIOSA

Ascribed to FRA JACOPONE DA TODI (About 1228-1306)

Stood the lovely Mother smiling
By the Manger where beguiling
　Lay her little one at rest;
All her soul its gladness voicing,
As the gleam of her rejoicing
　Swept across her gentle breast.
Oh, how joyous she, the Blessèd

And Immaculate, caressèd
  Him that was her only Son!
How her heart exulted for Him—
How she bent enraptured o'er Him,
  Born of her the Holy One!
Who is there that contemplating
Christ's own Mother jubilating
Would not share in such a joy?
Who beholding could be other
Than entranced with Christ's own Mother
  Fondling her Immortal Boy?
Through the sins of man, His creatures,
She beholds the Christ-Child's features
  'Mid the breathing kine and cold;
Sees her darling born deploring;
And the place of His adoring
  But a miserable fold.
"Born is Christ within a stable!"
Hark, the joy immensurable
  Heaven's townfolk sing around!
There anear the Maid the Elder
Stood in silence and beheld her,
  Wondering with her at the sound.
Would, O Mother,—Love-Fount tender!—
Thou to me wouldst ardor render
  So my breast might glow as thine!
Till my heart for love inflaming
Might be also made unblaming
  For His gentle head divine.
Blessèd Mother, thou art playing
Just as though no wounds are staying
  To be fixed upon thy heart;
Of thy Son the heaven-descended
To the Manger unattended—
  Of His sorrows grant me part!
Grant me all my life's full measure
Jesukin that I may treasure,
  Gladly on my breast to strain;
Fervor like to thine to fill me,
Grant thine Infant's arms to thrill me
  While in exile I remain!

Virgin of all Virgins Fairest,—
Nay, withhold not Him thou bearest,—
 Let thy Babe of Paradise
By my arms be soft surrounded—
Him—whose birth hath Death confounded
 At the Final Sacrifice!
Grant, as thine, to slake my yearning
With thy Child in rapture turning
 In the joyful surge of grace;
All inflamed and love-enkindled—
Every mortal impulse dwindled—
 Let me share in such embrace.
Hark ye, all ye Manger-lovers,
Shepherds leave your watchful covers—
 Join the Voices of the Night!
He in taking birth hath heard you;
Chant, and with His Chosen, gird you
 For the Fatherland of Light!
When thy Son hath ta'en and healed me
And the Word of God doth shield me,
 Grant I be confirmed in Grace!
When my body's life is ended,
Be my soul by thee attended
 To the Vision of His Face!
From the Latin by Thomas Walsh.

THE LITTLE ANGELS

Fra Jacopone da Todi

The little angels join their hands
 And dance in holy ring.
 Love-songs they're whispering,
The little angel bands.

Good men and bad they call and greet;
 High glory doffs its crown,
 And has come down,
Low lies there at your feet.

Now, shamefaced boors, why keep
Ye back? Show courtesie.
Hasten and ye will see
The little Jesus sleep.

The earth and all the skiey space
Break into flowery smiles,
So draws and so beguiles
The sweetness of His face.
        From the Italian by Anne Macdonell.

THE HIGHEST WISDOM

Fra Jacopone da Todi

Wisdom 'tis and Courtesy,
Crazed for Jesus Christ to be.

No such learning can be found
In Paris, nor the world around;
In this folly to abound
    Is the best philosophy.

Who by Christ is all possessed,
Seems afflicted and distressed,
Yet is Master of the best
    In Science and Theology.

Who for Christ is all distraught,
Gives his wits, men say, for naught;
Those whom Love hath never taught,
    Deem he erreth utterly.

He who enters in this school,
Learns a new and wondrous rule,—
"Who hath never been a fool,
    Wisdom's scholar cannot be."

He who enters on this dance,
Enters Love's unwalled expanse;
Those who mock and look askance,
    Should do penance certainly.

He that worldly praise achieves,
Jesus Christ his Saviour grieves,
Who Himself, between two thieves,
  On the Cross hung patiently.

He that seeks for shame and pain,
Shall his heart's desire attain;
All Bologna's lore were vain,
  To increase his mastery.
      From the Italian by Mrs. Theodore Beck.

OF IMPATIENCE WHICH BRINGS ALL OUR GAINS TO NOTHING

Fra Jacopone da Todi

I labored long, I strove with might and main;
And yet I cannot keep the good I gain.

Yea, I have been a monk full many a year,
Have suffered much, and wandered far and near,
Have sought and found—yet held not—till I fear
  That nothing can I show for all my pain.

In calm retreats my truest joy I found;
I strove in prayer, with no uncertain sound;
I fed the poor for many miles around;
  In sickness, very patient have I lain.

In uttermost obedience did I dwell,
In suffering and poverty as well;
Yea, I was chaste and happy in my cell,
  So far as my poor powers could attain.

Famished and weak, I fasted many a day;
Dried up by heat and pinched by cold I lay;
I was a pilgrim on a weary way,
  Or so it seemed, in sunshine and in rain.

To pray, I daily rose before the sun;
Mass did I hear before the dark was done;
To tierce and nones and vespers would I run,
    And after compine, still to watch was fain.

And then was said to me a scornful word!—
Deep in my heart the poisoned arrow stirred—
At once my tongue was ready when I heard,
    With fierce and burning fury to complain.

Now see how great and wealthy I must be!
I heap my gains for all the world to see;
Yet one poor word so fiercely angers me,
    That I must strive to pardon it in vain!
            From the Italian by Mrs. Theodore Beck.

CHRIST AND HIS MOTHER AT THE CROSS

Fra Jacopone da Todi

Christ:
Lady, take my broken heart
For thine own to share apart.
John, belovèd as thou art,
Shalt be to thee a son.

John, my mother dear, behold;
Take her tenderly and fold
In thy pity. She is cold
And her heart undone!

Mary:
Son, Thy spirit hath gone forth!
Son of most stupendous worth!
My sight is of its vision dearth
And bloodless is my heart!

Hear me, Son most innocent,
Son of splendor o'er me spent,
Passing to thine element,
With darkness for my part;

Son of whiteness and of rose,
Son unrivalled as the snows,
Son my bosom held so close,—
My heart, why hast Thou gone?

Son of beauty and of gold,
Son, whose eyes all gladness told,
Son, why hath the world so cold,
Thee cast scorn upon!

Son so gentle and so meek,
Son to all the sad and weak,
Oh, how bitterly they wreak
Evil on Thy head!

John, my nephew, look and see;
Dead thy brother now must be;
For I feel the sword through me,
As the Prophets said.

Slain are mother here and Son,
Stricken by this blow as one,
Clasped in final union
On one cross of dread.
          From the Italian by Thomas Walsh.

LADY OF HEAVEN

Guittone d'Arezzo (1230-1294)

Lady of Heaven, the mother glorified
  Of glory, which is Jesus,—He whose death
  Us from the gates of Hell delivereth
And our first parents' error puts aside;
Behold this earthly Love, how his darts glide
  How sharpened—to what fate—throughout this earth!
  Pitiful Mother, partner of our birth,
Win these from following where his flight doth guide.

And O, inspire in me that holy love
 Which leads the soul back to its origin,
  Till of all other love the link doth fail.
This water only can this fire reprove,—
 Only such cure suffice for suchlike sin;
  As nail from out a plank is struck by nail.

From the Italian by Dante Gabriel Rossetti.

DOMINE, QUO VADIS?

ANONYMOUS

Now wend we to the Palmalle—
 Domine, quo vadis? men it call,
Where Peter met with Jesu
And said, "Lord, whither wilt Thou?"
Christ answered to Peter tho.
"Into Rome," he said, "I go,
Eft to die on Rood for thee:
Thou dreadest to die, Peter, for me."
"Lord," he said, "Mercy I cry,
To take my death I am ready."
There is a sign of His foot
On Marblestone where He stood.

From the Old English.

OLD ENGLISH CHARM SONG

Hail be thou, holie hearbe,
 Growing on the ground,
All in the Mount Calvary
 First wert thou found.

Thou art good for manie a sore,
 Thou healest manie a wound;
In the name of sweete Jesus
 I take thee from the ground.

THE TREE OF LOVE

Blessèd Ramon Lull (1235-1315)

The leaves of the Tree of Love are fears and sighs and tears.
The sighs are they that issue from the heart of the Lover who
is full of love, so that it makes him to sigh for the exceeding
great desire that he has for the Belovèd and for the trials
which he bears for love's own sake.
The tears of love are the streams that bathe the eyes, flowing
therefrom because of love, to make the Lover know the
trials, the griefs, the risks and perils that must be his who
serves and honors his Belovèd.
And the fears of love are witnesses that tell the sins the Lover
has committed against love and the Belovèd.
And the afflictions with which they afflict him when his loving
faints.

THE LOVER AND THE BELOVÉD

Blessèd Ramon Lull

"Say, O Fool, hast thou riches?"
He answered: "I have my Belovèd."
"Hast thou lands, castles, cities, provinces or kingdoms?"
He answered: "I have thoughts of love, and tears, and desires,
    and trials and griefs, which are better than kingdoms or
    empire."
"Say, O Fool, which one knows more of love—he that finds joy
    or he that has trials and grief?"
He answered: "There can be no knowledge in love without one
    and the other."
"Say, O Fool, wherefore is thy love so great?"
He answered: "Because far and perilous is the journey I must
    make seeking my Belovèd;
I must seek Him in fullness of faith, and must journey with all
    speed.
Naught of these can be fulfilled if I have not great love."

"Say, O Fool, what is love?"

He answered: "Love is the combining of thought and action
toward one end to which the Lover's will is likewise moved;
and the end is that man may serve and honor his Belovèd."

"Think ye now that the Lover's will is in truer harmony with
this end when he longs for union with his Belovèd, or when
he desires to win for Him many lovers?"

The Lover went one day into a cloister and the monks asked
him if he was a religious.

"Yea," he answered, "of the Order of my Belovèd."

What rule dost thou follow?

He answered: "My Belovèd's."

"To whom art thou vowed?"

"To my Belovèd."

From the Catalan by Garret Strange.

THE CARAVAN

HOVHANNES BLOUZ (1250-1326)

Behold, I gathered mine offenses
  And wept their weighty pack upon;
The caravan is off for heaven
  So I must take them and be gone.
"And whither goest thou so laden?"
  The Angel asks me in disdain;
"Dost think with such unwieldy bundle
  The mart of Paradise to gain?"
From the Armenian by Thomas Walsh.

SONG

KING DINIS (1261-1325)

Friend and lover mine
—Be God our shield!—
See the flower o' the pine
And fare afield.

Friend and lover, ah me!
—Be God our shield!—
See the flower on the tree
And fare afield.

See the flower o' the pine
—Be God our shield!—
Saddle the colt so fine
And fare afield.

See the flower of the tree
—Be God our shield!—
The bay horse fair to see
And fare afield.

Saddle the little bay
—Be God our shield!—
Hasten, my love, away,
And fare afield.

The horse so fair to see
—Be God our shield!—
My friend, come speedily
To fare afield.

From the Portuguese by Aubrey F. G. Bell.

Sonnet from LA VITA NUOVA

DANTE ALIGHIERI (1265-1321)

Ye pilgrims, who with pensive aspect go
    Thinking, perhaps, of bygone things and dear,
    Come you from lands so very far from here
As unto us who watch your port would show
For that you weep not outright, filing slow
    Through the mid-highway of this city dread,
    You even as gentle stranger-folk appear,
Who of the common sorrow nothing know!

Would you but linger, would you but be told,
  Pledge with its thousand sighs my soul doth give
    That you, likewise, should travel on heartbroken;
Ah, we have lost our Beatrice! Behold,
  What least soever word of her be spoken,
    The tears must follow now from all that live.

From the Italian by Louise Imogen Guiney.

THE DIVINE COMEDY

DANTE ALIGHIERI

Inferno, Canto XXVIII.
While I was all absorbed in seeing him,
He looked at me, and opened with his hands
His bosom, saying: "See now I rend me;
How mutilated, see, is Mahomet;
In front of me doth Ali weeping go,
Cleft in the face from forelock unto chin;
And all the others whom thou here beholdest,
Sowers of scandals and of schism have been
While living, and therefore are thus cleft asunder
A devil is behind here, who doth cleave us
Thus cruelly, unto the falchion's edge
Putting again each one of all this ream
When we have gone around the doleful road;
By reason that our wounds are closed again
Ere any one in front of him repass."

.   .   .   .   .   .

I truly saw, and still I seem to see it,
A trunk without a head walk in like manner
As walked the others of the mournful herd.
And by the hair it held the head dissevered,
Hung from the hand in fashion of a lantern,
And that upon us gazed and said: "O me!"
It of itself made to itself a lamp,
And they were two in one and one in two;
How that can be He knows who so ordains it.
When it was come close to the bridge's foot,

It lifted high its arm with all the head,
To bring more closely unto us its words,
Which were: "Behold now the sore penalty,
Thou, who dost breathing go the dead beholding:
Behold if any be as great as this.
And so that thou mayst carry news of me,
Know that Bertram de Born am I, the same
Who gave to the Young King the evil comfort.
I made the father and the son rebellious;
Achitophel not more with Absalom
And David did with his accursèd goadings.
Because I parted persons so united,
Parted do I now bear my brain, alas!
From its beginning, which is in this trunk.
Thus is observed in me the counterpoise."
From the Italian by Henry Wadsworth Longfellow.

THE DIVINE COMEDY

Dante Alighieri

Purgatorio, Canto VIII.
'Twas now the hour that turneth back desire
In those who sail the sea, and melts the heart,
The day they've said to their sweet friends farewell.
And the new pilgrim penetrates with love
If he doth hear from far away a bell
That seemeth to deplore the dying day,
When I began to make of no avail
My hearing, and to watch one of the souls
Uprisen, that begged attention with its hand.
It joined and lifted upward both its palms,
Fixing its eyes upon the Orient,
As if it said to God, "Naught else I care for."
"Te lucis ante" so devoutly issued
Forth from its mouth, and with such dulcet notes
It made me issue forth from my own mind.
And then the others, sweetly and devoutly,
Accompanied it through all the hymn entire,
Having their eyes on the supernal wheels.

Here, Reader, fix thine eyes well on the truth,
For now indeed so subtile is the veil
Surely to penetrate within is easy.
I saw that army of the gentle-born
Thereafterward in silence upward gaze,
As if in expectation, pale and humble;
And from on high come forth and down descend
I saw two Angels with two flaming swords,
Truncated and deprivèd of their points.
Green as the little leaflets just now born
Their garments were, which, by their verdant pinions
Beaten and blown abroad, they trailed behind.
One just above us came to take his station,
And one descended to the opposite bank,
So that the people were contained between them.
Clearly in them discerned I the blond head;
But in their faces was the eye bewildered,
As faculty confounded by excess.
"From Mary's bosom both of them have come,"
Sordello said, "As guardians of the valley
Against the serpent, that will come anon."
Whereupon I, who knew not by what road,
Turned round about, and closely drew myself,
Utterly frozen, to the faithful shoulders.

.   .   .   .   .   .

My greedy eyes still wandered up to heaven,
Still to that point where slowest are the stars,
Even as a wheel the nearest to its axle.
And my Conductor: "Son, what dost thou gaze at
Up there?"   And I to him: "At those three torches
With which this hither pole is all on fire."
And he to me: "The four resplendent stars
Thou sawest this morning are down yonder low,
And these have mounted up to where those were."
As he was speaking, to himself Sordello
Drew him, and said: "Lo, there our Adversary!"
And pointed with his finger to look thither.
Upon the side on which the little valley
No barrier hath, a serpent was; perchance
The same which gave to Eve the bitter food

'Twixt grass and flowers came on the evil streak,
Turning at times its head about, and licking
Its back like to a beast that smoothes itself.
I did not see, and therefore cannot say
How the celestial falcons 'gan to move,—
But well I saw that they were both in motion.
Hearing the air cleft by their verdant wings,
The serpent fled, and round the Angels wheeled,
Up to their stations flying back alike.

Purgatorio, Canto XXX.

                  The veracious people
Turned themselves to the car as to their peace.
And one of them, as if by heaven commissioned,
Singing, *"Veni, sponsa, de Libano,"*
Shouted three times, and all the others after.
Even as the Blessèd at the final summons
Shall rise up quickened each one from his cavern,
Uplifting light the reinvested flesh,
So upon that celestial chariot
A hundred rose *ad vocem tanti senis,*
Ministers and messengers of life eternal.
They all were saying, *"Benedictus qui venis,"*
And scattering flowers above and round about,
"Manibus o date lilia plenis!"

BEING UNDERIVED

Dante Alighieri

Paradiso, Canto I.

                 All things whate'er they be
Have order among themselves, and this is form,
That makes the universe resemble God.
Here do the higher creatures see the footprints
Of the Eternal Power, which is the end
Whereto is made the law already mentioned.
In the order that I speak of are inclined
All natures, by their destinies diverse,
More or less near their origin;

Hence they move onward unto ports diverse
O'er the great sea of being; and each one
With instinct given it which bears it on.
This bears away the fire towards the moon;
This is in mortal hearts the motive power;
This binds together and unites the earth.
Nor only the created things that are
Without intelligence this bow shoots forth,
But those that have both intellect and love.
The Providence that regulates all this
Makes with its light the heaven forever quiet,
Wherein that turns which has the greatest haste.
And thither now, as to a site decreed,
Bears us away the virtue of that cord
Which aims its arrows at a joyous mark.
From the Italian by Henry Wadsworth Longfellow.

THE PRIMAL CAUSE

Dante Alighieri

Paradiso, Canto XXVIII.
A point beheld I, that was raying out
Light so acute, the sight which it enkindles
Must close perforce before such great acuteness.
And whatsoever star seems smallest here
Would seem to be a moon, if placed beside it
As one star with another star is placed.

.   .   .   .   .   .

My Lady, who in my anxiety
Beheld me much perplexed, said: "From that point
Dependent is the heaven and nature all.
Behold that circle most conjoined to it,
And know thou, that its motion is so swift
Through burning love whereby it is spurred on."
. . . Do thou take
What I shall tell thee, if thou wouldst be sated,
And exercise on that thy sublety.
The circles corporal are wide and narrow.

According to the more or less of virtue
Which is distributed through all their parts.
The greater goodness works the greater weal,
The greater weal the greater body holds,
If perfect equally be all its parts.
Therefore this one which sweeps along with it
The universe sublime, doth correspond
Unto the circle which most loves and knows.
On which account if thou unto the virtue
Apply thy measure, not to the appearance
Of substances that unto thee seem round,
Thou wilt behold a marvellous agreement
Of more to greater and of less to smaller,
In every heaven, with its Intelligence."
Even as remaineth splendid and serene
The hemisphere of air, when Boreas
Is blowing from that cheek where he is mildest,
Because is purified and resolved the rack
That erst disturbed it, till the welkin laughs
With all the beauties of its pageantry;
Thus did I likewise, after that my Lady
Had me provided with her clear response,
And like a star in heaven the truth was seen.
    From the Italian by Henry Wadsworth Longfellow.

THE DIVINE COMEDY

Dante Alighieri

Paradiso Canto XXXIII

"Thou Virgin Mother, daughter of thy Son,
Humble and high beyond all other creature,
The limit fixed of the eternal counsel,
Thou art the one who such nobility
To human nature gave, that its Creator
Did not disdain to make Himself its creature.
Within thy womb rekindled was the love
By heat of which in the eternal peace
After such wise this flower has germinated.
Here unto us thou art a noonday torch

Of charity, and below there among mortals
Thou art the living fountain-head of hope,
Lady, thou art so great and so prevailing
That he who wishes grace, nor runs to thee,
His aspirations without wings would fly.
Not only thy benignity gives succor
To him who asketh it, but oftentimes
Forerunneth of its own accord the asking.
In thee compassion is, in thee pity,
In thee magnificence; in thee unites
Whate'er of goodness is in any creature.
        From the Italian by Henry Wadsworth Longfellow.

LOVE IS LIFE

RICHARD ROLLE (1290-1349)

For now, love thou, I rede, Christ, as I thee tell:
And with Angels take thy stead; that joy look thou nought sell!
In earth thou hate, I rede, all that thy love may fell:
For Love is stalworth as the death, Love is hard as hell.

Love is a light burden, Love gladdeth young and old;
Love is without pine, as lovers have me told:
Love is a ghostly wine, that makes men big and bold:
Of Love shall he nothing tyne that it in heart will hold.

But fleshly love shall fare as doth the flower in May
And lasting be no more than one hour of a day,
And sithen sigh full sore their lust, their pride, their play,
When they are cast in care, till pine that lasteth aye.

Jesu is Love that lasteth aye: to Him is our longing:
Jesu the night turneth to day, the dawning into spring.
Jesu, think on us now and aye: for Thee we hold our King;
Jesu, give us grace, as Thou well may, to love Thee without
    ending.

PRAYER TO SANTA MARIA DEL VADE

JUAN RUIZ, Archpriest of Hita (Fourteenth Century)

Behold, O noble Lady, O Mother piteous,—
Thou Light and Brightness shone from Heaven upon us,—
Thy Majesty, I offer my soul and body, thus
Before thee in abasement with singing dolorous.
O Mother of the Saviour, I kneel to thee,—O Queen,
Grant hearing to a sinner, O Virgin pure and clean!
Unto thy praise I proffer my soul and life entire,
Assured that in thy favor there rests my heart's desire.
O Virgin, haste and send me the strength I so require;
To God for me petition—thy Son, my Lord serene!—
Across thy mighty glory and bliss I call to mind
The memories in thy bosom with other days entwined,
The bitterness thy Jesus upon the earth did find—
From out my weary prison, my life of woes so mean!

From the Spanish by Garrett Strange.

THE FLYING LESSON

FRANCESCO PETRARCH (1304-1374)

Sorrow and love did thrust me in the way
   Of bitter words that all too mournful rang
   To her for whom so long I flamed and sang—
And: "Great has been my fault," I humbly say.
For lo! My sorrow goes out at the door—
   And her great glory breaks its waves in foam
   Upon my heart. How well she is at home
With Him, whom, loving, in her breast she bore.

All my scars vanish—hushèd is my cry—
   I would not have her back again, O fates!
No, no. Far rather lonely live and die!
   How plain I see the sapphire-studded gates—
The vaporous angels coaxing her to fly—
   But near the Sacred Feet she sits and waits.

From the Italian by Agnes Tobin.

SONNET

Francesco Petrarch

Father in heaven! after the days misspent
  After the nights of wild tumultuous thought,
In that fierce passion's strong entanglement
  One, for my peace too lovely far, had wrought;
Vouchsafe that by Thy grace, my spirit bent
  On nobler aims, to holier ways be brought;
That so my foe, spreading with dark intent
  His mortal snares, be foiled, and held at nought.

E'en now the eleventh year its course fulfils,
  That I have bowed me to the tyranny
      Relentless most to fealty most tried.
Have mercy, Lord! on my unworthy ills;
  Fix all my thoughts in contemplation high;
      How on the Cross this day a Saviour died.
                    From the Italian by Dacre.

TO THE VIRGIN MARY

Francesco Petrarch

Beautiful Virgin! clothèd with the sun,
Crowned with the stars, who so the Eternal Sun
Well pleasedst that in thine His light He hid;
Love pricks me on to utter speech of thee,
And, feeble to commence without thine aid,
Of Him who on thy bosom rests in love.
Her I invoke who gracious still replies
To all who ask in faith,
Virgin, if ever yet
The misery of man and mortal things
To mercy moved thee, to my prayer incline;
Help me in this my strife,
Though I am but of dust—and thou heaven's radiant Queen!

Bright Virgin! and immutable as bright,
O'er life's tempestuous ocean the sure star
Each trusting mariner that truly guides,
Look down, and see amid this dreadful storm
How I am tost at random and alone,
And how already my last shriek is near,
Yet still in thee, sinful although and vile,
My soul keeps all her trust;
Virgin! I thee implore
Let not thy foe have triumph in my fall;
Remember how our sin made God Himself
To free us from its chain;
Within thy virgin womb our image on Him take!

Virgin! what tears already have I shed,
Cherished what dreams and breathed what prayers in vain,
But for my own worse penance and sure loss;
Since first on Arno's shore I saw the light
Till now, whate'er I sought, wherever turned,
My life has passed in torment and in tears;
For mortal loveliness in air, act, speech,
Has seized and soiled my soul;
O Virgin! pure and good,
Delay not till I reach my life's last year;
Swifter than shaft and shuttle are my days.
Mid misery and sin
Have vanished all and now Death only is behind!

Virgin! benevolent and foe of pride,
Ah! let the love of our one Author win,
Some mercy for a contrite humble heart;
For, if her frail and mortal dust I loved
With loyalty so wonderful and long,
Much more my faith and gratitude for thee
From this my present sad and sunken state
If by thy help I rise,
Virgin! to thy dear name
I consecrate and cleanse my thoughts, speech, pen,
My mind and heart with all its tears and sighs;
Point then that better path,
And with complacence view my changed desires at last.

The day must come, nor distant far its date,
Time flies so swift and sure,
O peerless and alone!
When death my heart, now conscience struck, shall seize;
Commend me, Virgin! then to thy dear Son,
True God and Very Man,
That my last sigh in peace may in His arms, be breathed!

From the Italian by Macgregor.

THE QUEEN OF THE ANGELS

GIOVANNI BOCCACCIO (1313-1375)

Queen of the Angels, Mary, thou whose smile
    Adorns the heavens with their brightest ray;
    Calm star that o'er the sea directs the way
Of wandering barks unto their homing isle;
By all thy glory, Virgin without guile,
    Relieve me of my grievous woes, I pray!
    Protect me, save me from the snares that stay
Beyond to misdirect me and defile!

I trust in thee with that same trust of old,
    Fixed in the ancient love and reverence
Which now I tell as I have always told.
    Guide thou my journey, strengthen my pretense
To reach with thee at last the blessèd fold
    Thy Son prepares His flock in recompense.

From the Italian by Thomas Walsh.

THE LOVE OF GOD

BERNARD RASCAS (Died 1353)

All things that are on earth shall wholly pass away,
Except the love of God, which shall live and last for aye.
The forms of men shall be as they had never been;
The blasted groves shall lose their fresh and tender green;
The birds of the thicket shall end their pleasant song,
And the nightingale shall cease to chant the evening long.

The kine of the pasture shall feel the dart that kills,
And all the fair white flocks shall perish from the hills.
The goat and antlered stag, the wolf and the fox,
The wild boar of the wood, and the chamois of the rocks,
And the strong and fearless bear, in the trodden dust shall lie;
And the dolphin of the sea, and the mighty whale shall die.
And realms shall be dissolved, and empires be no more,
And they shall bow to death, who ruled from shore to shore;
And the great globe itself, so Holy Writings tell,
With the rolling firmament, where starry armies dwell,
Shall melt with fervent heat,—they shall all pass away,
Except the love of God, which shall live and last for aye!
                From the Limousin by William Cullen Bryant.

THE KNIGHTLY CODE

Eustache Deschamps (1340-1410)

You who seek the knightly order
Must begin your life anew;
Watch and pray you most devoutly,
Pride and wicked sin eschew;
Protect the Church, the child, the widow,
Strongly guard the people too;
Valor, loyalty and virtue
From a worthy knight are due.

An humble heart and active body
Chivalry of you demands;
Fight you well and often journey
O'er the seas to other lands;
Joust you for the love of lady
On the tilt-yard's tawny sands;
Tenderly protect your honor
With your soul and with your hands.

Love the lord who calls you vassal,
Guard his fields from enemy;
Liberality and justice
Cherish; seek the company

Of other knights that, from their wisdom,
Yours may grow to like degree;
Thus, a knight like Alexander
May you hope in time to be.
    From the French by Daniel J. McKenna.

THE PALMER

WILLIAM LANGLAND (1330-1400)

From *Piers Plowman*

Apparelled as a Paynim in pilgrim's wise
He bare a bordon bound with a broad list
Like a withe-wind-weed wounden about.
A bowl and a bag he bare by his side,
A hundred phials on his hat sit,
Signs of Syse and shells of Galicia
And many a Cross on his cloak and Keys of Rome,
And the Vernicle before for men should know
And see by his signs whom he had sought.
This folk frayned him first from whence he come?
"From Sinai," he said, "and from our Lord's Sepulchre;
In Bethlehem, in Babylon, I have been in both;
In Armenia, in Alexandria, and in Damask.
Ye may see by my signs that sit on my cap,
I have sought good Saints for my soul's health,
And walked full wide in wet and in dry."

THE VISION OF JESUS

WILLIAM LANGLAND

From *Piers Plowman*

Thus I awakened and wrote what I had dreamed
And dight me dearly and due me to Church
To hear wholly the Mass and be houseled after,
In midst of the Mass tho men geden to offering.
I fell eftsoons asleep and suddenly me mette

That Piers the Plowman was painted all bloody
And came in with a cross before the common people,
And right like in all limbs to our Lord Jesu;
And then called I Conscience to ken me the sooth.
Is this Jesus the jouster, quoth I, that Jews duden to die;
Or is it Piers Plowman? Who painted him so red?
Quoth Conscience and kneeled then: These aren Christ's arms,
His colours and his coat-armour, and he that cometh so bloody
It is Christ with His Cross, conqueror of Christdom.

SONG TO THE VIRGIN MARY

PERO LÓPEZ DE AYALA (1332-1407)

Lady, as I know thy power,
   I place my hopes in thee;
Thy shrine in Guadalupe's tower
   My pilgrim steps shall see.

Thy welcome ever was most sweet
   To those who come in care;
When from this prison I retreat,
   I'll seek thine image there.

Lady, as I know thy power,
   I place my hopes in thee;
Thy shrine in Guadalupe's tower
   My pilgrim steps shall see.

In all my sorrows would I call
   On thee, Sweet Advocate;
My heart adores thee more than all,
   And so my sins seem great.

Lady, as I know thy power,
   I place my hopes in thee;
Thy shrine in Guadalupe's tower
   My pilgrim steps shall see.

Thou art the star that shows the way,
The balm that heals my wrong;
In gentleness be mine today
And lead to heaven along.

Lady, as I know thy power,
I place my hopes in thee;
Thy shrine in Guadalupe's tower
My pilgrim steps shall see.
From the Spanish by Thomas Walsh.

THE QUEEN OF COURTESY

ANONYMOUS

From *Pearl*

"Blissful," quoth I, "may this be true?
    Displeaseth not if I speak error.
Art thou the Queen of Heaven's blue
That all this world shall do honour?
We lieven on Mary of whom Grace grew,
That bore a bairn of virgin flower;
The crown from her who might remew
But she her passed in some favour?
        Now for singleness of her douceur
        We call her Phoenix of Araby
        That freless flew of her fasour
        Like to the Queen of Courtesy."
"Courteous Queen," then said that gay,
Kneeling to ground, enfolden her face,
"Makeless Mother and merriest May,
Blessed beginner of every Grace!"
Then rose she up and did restay,
And spake toward me in that space:
"Sir, many here pourchaseth and fongeth prey,
But supplantereth none within this place.
        That Empress all Heaven hath,
        And Earth and Hell in her baily;
        From heritage yet none will she chase
        For she is Queen of Courtesy.

Of Courtesy, as saith Saint Paul,
All are we members of Jesu Christ;
As head and arm and leg and naul
Serve to his body full true and tryst,
Right so is every Christian soul
Belonging limb to the Master of might.
Then look, what hate or any gall
Is tached or tied thy limbs betwist?
>   Thy head hath neither greme nor grist
>   On arm or finger though thou bear ring.
>   So fare we all with love and list
>   To King and Queen by Courtesy.

From TROILUS AND CRESSIDA

Geoffrey Chaucer (1340-1400)

O younge freshe folkes, he and she,
  In which that love up groweth with your age,
Repair ye home from worldy vanity
  And of your hearts cast upwards the visage
  To thilke God that after His image
You made, and think ye all is but a passing fair
This world, that passeth soon as floures fair.

And love ye Him the which that just for love
  Upon a cross our soules for to buy,
First died, then rose, and sits in heaven above;
  For He will not be false to you, say I,
  If all your heart on Him you wholly lie.
And since He best to love is and most meek,
What need you feigned loves for to seek?

BALLAD OF GOOD COUNSEL

Geoffrey Chaucer

Flee from the press and dwell with soothfastness;
Suffice unto thy good though it be small,
For hoard hath hate and clibing ticklishness,
Press hath envy and weal blent overall;
Savour no more than thee bihoven shall;
Work well thyself that other folk canst rede;
And Truthe shall deliver, it is no dread.

Tempest thee not all crooked to redresse
In trust of her that turneth as a ball:
Great reste stands in little business;
And eke be ware to spurn against an awl:
Strive not, as doth the crocke with the wall.
Daunt thyself that dauntest others deed,
And Truthe shall deliver, it is no dread.

That thee is sent receive in buxomness:
The wrestling for this world asketh a fall.
Here is no home, here is but wilderness;
Forth, pilgrim, forth! Forth, beast, out of thy stall!
Know thy country, look up, thank God of all;
Hold the high way and let thy ghost thee lead
And Truthe shall deliver, it is no dread.

THE POOR PARSON

GEOFFREY CHAUCER

From *Canterbury Tales*

A good man was there of religion,
    And was a poor Parson of a town;
But rich he was of holy thought and work;
He was also a learned man, a clerk,
That Christes Gospel truly woulde preach;
His parishens devoutly would he teach.
Benign he was and wonder diligent,
And in adversity full patient;
And such he was y-proved ofte sythes.
Full loath were him to cursen for his tythes,
But rather would he given out of doubt
Unto his poor parishens about
Of his offering, and eke of his substance;
He could in little thing have sufficance.
Wide was his parish, and houses far a-sunder,
But he left not, for rain nor thunder,
In sickness nor in mischief, to visit
The farthest in his parish, much and lyte,

Upon his feet, and in his hand a staff.
This noble ensample to his sheep he gave,
That first he wrought, and afterward he taught
Out of the gospel he those wordes caught.
And this figure he added eke thereto.
That if gold ruste, what shall iron do?
He sette not his benefice to hire,
And let his sheep encumbered in the mire,
And ran to London, unto Saint Paul's,
To seeken him a chauntery for souls,
Or with a brotherhood to be withhold;
But dwelt at home, and kepte well his fold,
So that the wolf made it not miscarry;
He was a shepherd and no mercenary.
And though he holy were and virtuous,
He was to sinful man not despitous.
Nor of his speeches dangerous nor digne,
But in his teaching discreet and benign.
To drawen folk to Heaven by fairness
By good ensample was his business;
But it were any person obstinate,
Whatso he were, of high or low estate,
Him would he snubben sharply for the nones:
A better priest, I trow that nowhere none is.
He waited after no pomp and reverence,
Nor made him a spiced conscience.
But Christes lore and his apostles twelve
He taught and first he followed it himself.

A PRAYER TO THE BLESSED VIRGIN

GEOFFREY CHAUCER

From *Canterbury Tales*

O mother maid, O maiden mother free!
O bush unbrent brenning in Moses' sight
That ravishedst down from the Deity
Through thine humbless the Ghost that in thee lit,
Of whose vertue when He thine hearte lit,
Conceived was the Father's Sapience;
Help me to tell it in my reverence.

ROSA MYSTICA

An Old English Hymn

There is no rose of such virtue
As is the rose that bare Jesu:
Alleluia!
For in this rose containèd was
Heaven and earth in little space:
Res Miranda!
By that rose we well may see
There be One God in Persons Three:
Pares Forma!
The angels sang, the shepherds too:
Gloria in excelsis Deo!
Gaudeamus!
Leave we all this worldly mirth
And follow we this joyful birth:
Transeamus!

MOTHER MOST POWERFUL

Giovanni Dominici (1356-1420)

That thou so often held Him in thine arms—
    So often pressed His infant lips to thine
And in thy bosom warded off the harms
That came with flesh e'en to the Child Divine—
That thou couldst clothe Him, feel Him cheek to cheek
    In dreams and waking, at thine ear hast known
His first lisped "Mother," watched His soft hands seek
    Thine aid with glances cast on thee alone—
That thou couldst know such countless ecstasies
    Of love through that sweet hidden time of yore—
And yet thy heart held strong through all of these—
    Shows thou wert mortal,—Mother,—yea, and more!
                    From the Italian by Thomas Walsh.

TEMPERANCE

ANONYMOUS

Wine taken with excess,
As Scripture doth express,
Causeth great heaviness
    Unto the mind.

But they that take pleasure
To drink it with measure
No doubt a great treasure
    They shall it find.

Then give not a cherry
For cider nor perry;
Wine maketh man merry,
    Ye know well this.

Then put aside all wrath,
For David shewed us hath;
Vinum laetificat
    Cor hominis.

Now, ye that be present,
Laud God omnipotent,
That hath us given and sent
    Our daily food.

When through sin were slain
He sent His Son again
Us to redeem from pain
    By His sweet blood.

And He is the true Vine
From whom distilled the wine
That bought your souls and mine.
    You know well this.

Then put aside all wrath,
For David shewed us hath;
Vinum laetificat
Cor hominis.

TO THE VIRGIN

JOHN LYDGATE (1370-1451)

Queen of Heaven, of Hell eke Emperess,
Lady of this world, O very lodestar!
To mariners gainst all mortal distress
In their passage that they do not err;
Thy look of mercy cast down from so far
On all thy servants by chaste compassion,
Grant them good peace, save them from mortal war,
To thy five Joys that have devotion.

Celestial Cypress set upon Syon,
Highest Cedar of perfit holiness,
Carbuncle of charity and green emerald stone,
Whole and unbroken by virginal clearness;
O Sapphire, loupe all swelling to repress
On cankered sores and venomous feloun,
In ghostly woundes by their governess,
To thy five Joys that have devotion.

Yard of Aaron, gracious and benign,
Well of all grace and merciful pity,
Where the Holy Ghost list to close and sign
The crystal cloister of thy Virginity;
Balm of Engadi gainst all Infirmity,
Of folk that languish to tribulation,
Preserve and keep from all adversity,
To thy five Joys that have devotion.

THE CHILD JESUS TO MARY THE ROSE

JOHN LYDGATE

My Father above, beholding the meekness
  As dew on roses doth his balm spread,
Sendeth His Ghost most sovereign of cleanness
  Into thy breast, ah, Rose of Womanhood!
  When I for man was born in my manhood—
For which with roses of heavenly influence
I me rejoice to play in thy presence.

O Mother, Mother, of mercy abound,
  Fairest Mother that ever was alive,
Though I for man have many a bloody wound,
  Among them all there be roses five,
  Against whose mercy fiends may not strive;
Mankind to save, best roses of defence,
When they me pray for helpe in thy presence.

HYMN TO THE BLESSÉD VIRGIN

ANONYMOUS

Of on that is so fayr and bright
    Velut maris stella
Brighter than the day is light
    Parens et puella
Ic cry to thee, thou see to me,
Levedy, preye thi Sone for me
    Tam pia
That ic mote come to thee,
    Maria!
Al this world was for-lore
    Eva peccatrice
Tyl our Lord was y-bore
    De te genetrice
With *Ave* it went away
Thuster nyth and comz the day
    Salutis,

The welle springet ut of thee
Virtutis.
Levedy, flower of alle thing,
Rosa sine spina
Thou bere Jhesu, hevene king
Gratia divina;
Of all thou ber'st the pris,
Levedy, quene of paradys
Electa;
Mayde milde, moder es
Effecta.

THE JOYS OF HEAVEN

THOMAS À KEMPIS (1380-1471)

Angel choirs on high are singing,
To the Lord their praises bringing,
Yielding Him in royal beauty
Heart and voice in love and duty;
Waving wings the throne surrounding,
Timbrels, harps and bells are sounding.
See their heavenly vestments glisten,
To their heavenly music listen;
Hear them, by the Godhead staying,
Holy, holy, holy, saying!
None that grieveth or complaineth
In that heavenly land remaineth—
Every voice, in concord joining
Holy praise to God combining.
Holy love their minds disposeth,
Heavenly light to all discloseth
Blessèd Three in God united—
Seraphs worshipping delighted,
Sweet affection overflowing—
Cherubim their reverence showing,
Bowing low, their pinions folding—
God's majestic throne beholding.
Oh, what fair and heavenly region!
Oh, what bright and glorious legion,

Saints and angels, all excelling!—
In that glorious city dwelling.
Which in rest divine reposeth,
And sweet light and peace discloseth!
Every one who there resideth,
Clad in purity abideth,
Charity their spirits joining—
Firm in unity combining—
Toil nor ignorance undergoing—
Trouble nor temptation knowing;
Always health and joy undying,
To them every good supplying.

From the Latin by Erastus C. Benedict.

THE PATER NOSTER

ANONYMOUS

From *The Lay-Folks' Mass Book*

Our Father our all-wielding is,
God let us never His mirthes miss.
Lord, hallowed be Thy name.
In Heaven and earth Thy will
Be done and that is skill
Or else we been to blame.
Our each day's bread give us today
That we may trustily, when we shall away,
To come to Thy Kingdom.
God keep us to our last ending,
Let never the fiend with false fending
Cumber us in no shame.

WHAT GUARDIAN COUNSELS?

AUZIAS MARCH (1397-1459)

What guardian counsels hast thou learned or sought for,
O heart of mine so weary of the earth?
What balm to sooth thy griefs can now be brought for
Thy love of tears, thy dissonance from mirth?

On—toward death!—since he it is awaits thee,
  The more thy tardiness upon the way,
The farther off his final comfort baits thee;
  Wherefore the sweets of death shouldst thou delay?

Out on thy road, with sturdy elbows swinging,
  Joy mid thy weeping while his voice serene
Melodiously the chant divine is singing
  That tells me: *"Friend, leave thou this hovel mean;*
I come to thee with fonder invitation,
  I who to mortals give but bitter fare,
Responding never to their perturbation,
  But seeking him who trusts not to my snare."

Life, with its cheeks of terror and of weepings,
  Its hair all tangled from its fearful dreams,
Would offer me the miserable sweepings
  And the poor promises it ne'er redeems.
Death, too, would come with hideous shouts of terror
  For them that lie disheartened at its feet:
How bland for him whose griefs can read the error,
  Thy voice, O death! thy melody, how sweet!

"I marvel when I gaze upon the power
  That marks so many lovers in their will;
In me alone finds Love its fullest hour,
  Yet far from me they would their quest fulfil!
Blinded they seek the atoms of their treasure
  Until with clearer eyes its void they see,
And when I tell them of my hoard of pleasure
  They shall blaspheme the time they lost from me."

Since none there lives, from whom my love would borrow,
  Compassion only adds to my complaint;
I am a man that should be given sorrow,
  For in my heart the blood runs slack and faint.
All life has left me worn-away and weary
  Amid a melancholy that ne'er dies,
Poisons my hopes, slays me with daylight dreary,
  And leaves me naught save what my fate supplies.

My hour of death already is attended;
 My hapless life has come to final dearth,
For all my hopes below are lost and ended;
 My soul awaits—imprisoned here on earth.
From the Catalan by Thomas Walsh.

HYMN TO MARY

ZEREA JACOB, Emperor of Abyssinia (Fifteenth Century)

Hail, hail to thy blessèd name, O Mary. Thy name which is
 sweeter than all perfumes. Gentle Virgin, may thy love be
 as a refreshing stream flowing into my soul.

Hail to thy abundant hair, O Mary. O great citadel of God,
 leave not thy servant in grief so that my enemies say to
 me: "Where now is the source of all your confidence?"

Hail to thine eyelashes, O Mary. Heavy they were with tears
 that day thy Jesus was dragged before Pilate and Caiaphas.
 Be my support on the Day of Judgement, my advocate on
 that great Day of the Lord!

Hail to thine eyes, O Mary. Like the morning stars they stand
 vigils of the Will of God. Refuge of my soul, in whose
 undisturbed peace is my consolation for days of sadness.
 Let the cords of bitterness never enchain my soul.

Hail to thy hands, O Mary. They have touched the fire of
 Divinity. No need have they of jewelled ornaments. O
 Elect Dove, keep me pure beneath thy wings!

Hail to thy fingers, O Mary. Lovely were the garments they
 fashioned in the village of Nazareth. Thou art as gold to
 poor exiles lost in distant lands. No solicitude is on their
 lives, for art thou not their Viaticum?

Hail to thy lips, O Mary. Red they are and sweet as the rose,
 O thou, redolent of holiness and purity, Virgin Mary, star
 of God to save and shield me from griefs and tears!

Hail to thy mouth, O Mary. Whose lips kissed the fruit of
 thy bosom, that Divine Infant who was the Father of the
 Aged. O sweet Virgin Mary, draw me to thee when sadness
 bows me down!

Hail to thine Assumption into Heaven, O Mary. Thornless art
thou and more fragrant than the rose. Poor and outcast
as I am, oh, bestow thy love on me, be a Mother to me!

O Virgin Mary, thus I stammer in my praises. Were the whole
globe the surface of my parchment, my utterance would still
be unworthy of thee. All the winter rains turned into ink,
all the firmament into paper, could never be sufficient to
praise thee.

O Virgin, thou art the heaven that enshrines the sun, the field
that bears the corn. Refuge of sinners, have pity on me.
Give life to me as thou didst to my fathers, and pardon the
sins of all my people!

From the Abyssinian by Fr. Baetman.

TO OUR LADY

ROBERT HENRYSON (1425-1500)

O Lady leal and lovesomest,
  Thy face most fair and sheen is!
O blossom blithe and buxomest,
From carnal crime that clean is!
This prayer from my spleen is,
That all my works wickedest
Thou put away and make me chaste
From Termagent that teen is
And from his claw that keen is;
And syne till heaven my soul thou hast
Where thy Maker of mightiness most
Is King and thou their Queen is!

CORYDON AND TITYRUS

Carol of the Netherlands (Fifteenth Century)

"See, Corydon, see, here's the stall
Where lies the Babe that's Lord of all."
"Speak, Tityrus, to the Mother mild,
And ask if we may enter to adore her holy Child?"
—"Come, shepherds, come, but softly still;
To sleep, methinks, my Babekin hath a will."

"Hail, Mother, thee with love we greet;
Be welcome, little Boykin sweet;
Heaven's in high holiday for Thee,
And the angels singing say that Thou our Saviour
     art to be."
—"Kneel, shepherds; He that's thus adored,
This little Babekin, is indeed your Lord."

"O Babekin sweet, how comes it then
That Thou lie'st here neglect of men?
Hath Bethlehem that's here hard by
No chamber warm and cosy where securely
     Thou might'st lie?"
—"O shepherds, shepherds, sure you wot
The children of Israel know Him not."

"Fly, angels, haste and let your hymn
Re-echo over Bethlehem;
Her gates shall then be opened wide,
And every house a refuge where Messias may abide."
—"Nay, shepherds, nay, His one desire
Is that the hearts of men be all afire."

"O lovely Child, Jesu divine,
Our love, our lives, our all, be Thine;
Give but a spark from Thine own fire,
And we will forth to kindle hearts to this Thy
     heart's desire."
—"Go, shepherds, hasten; go and call
The neighbors all to this thrice blessèd stall."
                    Translated by Montgomery Carmichael.

HIS MOTHER'S SERVICE TO OUR LADY

François Villon (1431-1484)

Lady of Heaven and earth, and therewithal
     Crowned Empress of the nether clefts of Hell,—
I, thy poor Christian, on thy name do call
     Commending me to thee, with thee to dwell,

Albeit in nought I be commendable.
But all mine undeserving may not mar
Such mercies as thy sovereign mercies are;
    Without the which (as true words testify)
No soul can reach thy Heaven so fair and far.
Even in this faith I choose to live and die.

Unto thy Son say thou that I am His,
    And to me graceless make Him gracious.
Sad Mary of Egypt lacked not of that bliss,
    Nor yet the sorrowful clerk Theophilus,
    Whose bitter sins were set aside even thus
Though to the Fiend his bounden service was.
Oh, help me, lest in vain for me should pass
    (Sweet Virgin that shalt have no loss thereby!)
The blessed Host and sacring of the Mass.
    Even in this faith I choose to live and die.

A pitiful woman, shrunk and old,
    I am, and nothing learned in letter-lore.
Within my parish-cloister I behold
    A painted heaven where harps and lutes adore,
    And eke an Hell whose damned folk seethe full sore:
One bringeth fear, the other joy to me.
That joy, great Goddess, make thou mine to be,—
    Thou of whom all must ask it even as I;
And that which faith desires, that let it see.
    For in this faith I choose to live and die.

O excellent Virgin Princess! thou didst bear
    King Jesus, the most excellent comforter,
Who even of this our weakness craved a share
    And for our sake stooped to us from on high,
Offering to death His young life sweet and fair.
Such as He is, Our Lord, I Him declare,
    And in this faith I choose to live and die.
            From the French by Dante Gabriel Rossetti.

THE BENEDICTINE ULTIMA

Ultima in mortis hora
Filium pro nobis ora
Bonam mortem impetra,
Virgo, Mater, Domina!

When the last dread hour is o'er us,
Pray Thy Son may fashion for us
Death anointed and serene,—
Holy Virgin, Mother, Queen!

HOLY CROSS

ANONYMOUS

Steadfast Cross, among all other
Thou art a tree mickle of price,
In branch and flower such another
I ne wot none in wood nor rys.
Sweet be the nails
And sweet be the tree,
And sweeter be the burden that hangs upon thee.
From the Old English.

BEFORE SLEEPING

Old English Prayer

Matthew, Mark, Luke and John,
Bless the bed that I lie on.
Before I lay me down to sleep,
I give my soul to Christ to keep.
Four corners to my bed,
Four angels there aspread,
Two to foot and two to head,
And four to carry me when I'm dead.
I go by sea, I go by land,
The Lord made me with His right hand.

If any danger come to me,
Sweet Jesus Christ, deliver me.
He's the branch and I'm the flower,
Pray God send me a happy hour,
And if I die before I wake,
I pray that Christ my soul will take.

THE MONKS OF ELY

Merry sang the monks who in Ely fare
When Canute the King came rowing there,
—Row, knights, nearer to the land
And hear we the song of monken band.
                        From the Old English.

TO HOLY JESUS

PHILIPA DE AVIS AND LANCASTER (1437-1497)

I lack in service, lack in love,
    Yet never cease in my desire;
Forever crying Thee above,
    Unresting never from my tire.

O Life and Warmth and Holy Light,
    Boon infinite and all complete,
My Jesus, my true God, in plight
    Who on the Cross my love would meet!—

For all the failure of my heart,
    For all the lacking in my love,
I call on Thee to grant a part,
    Send down the peace Thou holdst above!
            From the Portuguese by Thomas Walsh.

THE COPLAS ON THE DEATH OF HIS FATHER, THE GRANDMASTER OF SANTIAGO

JORGE MANRIQUE (1440-1479)

The Introit

Let from its dream the soul awaken,
    And reason mark with open eyes
        The scene unfolding,—
How lightly life away is taken,
    How cometh Death in stealthy guise,—
        At last beholding;

What swiftness hath the flight of pleasure
    That, once attained, seems nothing more
        Than respite cold;
How fain is memory to measure
    Each latter day inferior
        To those of old.

Beholding how each instant flies
    So swift, that, as we count, 'tis gone
        Beyond recover,
Let us resolve to be more wise
    Than stake our future lot upon
        What soon is over.

Let none be self-deluding, none,—
    Imagining some longer stay
        For his own treasure
Than what today he sees undone;
    For everything must pass away
        In equal measure.

Our lives are fated as the rivers
    That gather downward to the sea
        We know as Death;
And thither every flood delivers
    The pride and pomp of seigniory
        That forfeiteth;

Thither, the rivers in their splendor;
  Thither, the streams of modest worth,—
    The rills beside them;
Till there all equal they surrender;
  And so with those who toil in earth,
    And those who guide them.

The Invocation

I turn me from the praise and singing
  Of panegyrists, and the proud
    Old poets' stories;
I would not have them hither bringing
  Their artful potions that but cloud
    His honest glories;

On Him alone I lay my burden—
  Him only do I now implore
    In my distress,—
Who came on earth and had for guerdon
  The scorn of man that did ignore
    His Godliness.

This world is but a highway going
  Unto that other, the abode
    Without a sorrow;
The wise are they who gird them, knowing
  The guideposts set along that road
    Unto tomorrow.

We start with birth upon that questing;
  We journey all the while we live,
    Our goal attaining
The day alone that brings us resting,
  When Death shall last quietus give
    To all complaining.

This were a hallowed world indeed,
  Did we but give it the employ
    That was intended;
For by the precepts of our Creed
  We earn hereby a life of joy
    When this is ended.

The Son of God Himself on earth
  Came down to raise our lowly race
    Unto the sky;
Here took upon Him human birth;
  Here lived among us for a space;
    And here did die.

Behold what miserable prize—
  What futile task we set upon,
    Whilst greed awakes us!
And what a traitor world of lies
  Is this, whose very gifts are gone
    Ere Death o'ertakes us!

Some through increasing age deprived,
  Some by unhappy turn of fate
    Destroyed and banished,
Some, as with blight inherent rived
  At topmost of their branching state,
    Have failed and vanished.

Yea, tell me shall the lovely blason,
  The gentle freshness and contour
    Of smiling faces,—
The blush and pallor's sweet occasion,—
  Of all—shall one a truce secure
    From Time's grim traces?

The flowing tress, the stature slender,
  The corporal litheness, and the strength
    Of gallant youth,—
All, all,—to weariness surrender
  As o'er them falls the shadow's length
    Of age in truth.

The Visigoths whose lineage kingly,
  Whose feats of war and mighty reign
    Were so exalted,—
What divers ways did all and singly
  Drop down to the obscure again
    And were defaulted!

Some through their worthlessness (How lowly
    And base among the rabble came
        Their estimation!)
Whilst others as a refuge solely
    In offices they only shame
        Maintain their station.

Estate and luxury's providing
    Can leave us pauper—who may doubt?—
        Within an hour;
Let us not count on their abiding,
    Since there is nothing sure about
        Dame Fortune's dower.

Hers are the gifts of one unstable
    Upon her globe as swift as light
        Revolving ever;
Who to be constant is unable,
    Who cannot stay nor rest from flight
        On aught soever.

And though, say I, her highest favor
    Should follow to the tomb and heap
        With wreaths her master;
Let not our solid judgment waver
    Since life is like a dream and sleep
        Flies nothing faster.

The soft occasions of today
    Wherein we find our joy and ease
        Are but diurnal;
Whilst the dread torments that must pay
    The cost of our iniquities
        Shall be eternal.

The pleasures light, the fond evasions
    That life on troubled earth deploys
        For eyes of mortals,
What are they but the fair persuasions
    Of labyrinths where Death decoys
        To trap-like portals?

Where heedless of the doom ensuing
We hasten laughing to the snare
Without suspicion.
Until aghast at our undoing,
We turn to find the bolt is there,
And our perdition.

Could we but have procured the power
To make our faded youth anew
Both fresh and whole,
As now through life's probation hour
'Tis ours to give angelic hue
Unto the soul,—

What ceaseless care we then had taken,
What pains had welcomed, so to bring
A health but human,—
Our summer bloom to re-awaken,
Our stains to clear,—outrivalling
The arts of woman!

The kings whose mighty deeds are spacious
Upon the parchments of the years,
Alas!—the weeping
That overtook their boast audacious.
And swept their thrones to grime and tears
And sorrow's keeping!

Naught else proves any more enduring;
Nor are the popes, nor emperors,
Nor prelatries
A longer stay or truce securing
Than the poor herdsman of the moors
From Death's decrees.

Recount no more of Troy, or foeman
The echo of whose wars is now
But far tradition;
Recount no more how fared the Roman
(His scroll of glories we allow)
Nor his perdition;

Nor here rehearse the homely fable
    Of such as yielded up their sway
        These decades gone,
But let us say what lamentable
    Fate the lords of yesterday
        Have fallen upon.

Of fair Don Juan, the king that ruled us,—
    Of those hight heirs of Aragon,—
        What are the tidings?
Of him whose courtly graces schooled us,
    Whom song and wisdom smiled upon,
        Where the abidings?

The jousts and tourneys where they vaunted
    With trappings, and caparison,
        And armor sheathing,—
Were they but phantasies that taunted,—
    But blades of grass that vanished on
        A summer's breathing?

What of the dames of birth and station,
    Their head-attire, their sweeping trains,
        Their vesture scented?
What of that gallant conflagration
    They made of lovers' hearts whose pains
        Were uncontented?

And what of him, that troubadour
    Whose melting lutany and rime
        Was all their pleasure?
Ah, what of her who danced demure,
    And trailed her robes of olden time
        So fair a measure?

Then Don Enriqué, in succession,
    His brother's heir,—think, to what height
        Was he anointed!
What blandishment and sweet possession
    The world prepared for his delight,
        As seemed appointed!

Yet see what unrelenting foeman,
   What cruel adversary, Fate
      To him became;
A friend befriended as was no man—
   How brief for him endured the state
      His birth might claim.

The golden bounties without stinting,
   The strongholds and the lairs of kings
      With treasure glutted;
The flagons of their wassail glinting,
   The sceptres, orbs, and crowns, and rings
      With which they strutted;

The steeds, the spurs, and bits to rein them,
   The pillions draped unto the ground
      Beneath their paces,—
Ah, whither must we fare to gain them?—
   That were but as the dews around
      The meadow places.

His brother then, the unoffending,
   Who was intruded on his reign
      To act as heir,—
What gallant court was round him bending,
   How many a haughty lord was fain
      To tend him there!

Yet as but mortal was his station,
   Death for his goblet soon distilled
      A draught for draining;
O Thou Divine Predestination!—
   When most his blaze the world had filled
      Thou sent'st the raining!

And then, Don Alvaro, Grand-Master
   And Constable, whom we have known
      When loved and dreaded,—
What need to tell of his disaster,
   Since we behold him overthrown
      And swift beheaded!

His treasures that defied accounting,
His manors and his feudal lands,
His boundless power,—
What more than tears were their amounting?
What more than bonds to tie his hands
At life's last hour?

That other twain, Grand-Masters solely,
Yet with the fortunes as of kings
Fraternal reigning,—
Who brought the high as well as lowly
Submissive to their challenges
And laws' ordaining.

And what of all their power and prize
That touched the very peaks of fame
That none could limit?—
A conflagration 'gainst the skies,
Till at its brightest ruthless came
Death's hand to dim it.

The dukes so many and excelling,
The marquises, and counts, the throng
Of barons splendid,
Speak, Death, where hast thou hid their dwelling?
The sway we saw them wield so strong—
How was it ended?

What fields upon were they engaging,—
What prowess showing us in war
Or its cessation,
When thou, O Death, didst come outraging
Both one and all, and swept them o'er
With desolation.

Their warriors' unnumbered hosting,
The pennon, and the battle-flag,
And bannered splendor,—
The castles with their turrets boasting,
Their walls and barricades to brag
And mock surrender,—

The cavern's ancient crypt of hiding,
　Or secret passage, vault, or stair,—
　　What use affords it?
Since thou upon thy onslaught striding
　Canst send a shaft unerring where
　　No buckler wards it!

O World that givest and destroyest,
　Would that the life which thou hast shown
　　Were worth the living!
But here, as good or ill deployest,
　The parting is with gladness known
　　Or with misgiving.

Thy span is so with griefs encumbered,
　With sighing every breeze so steeped,
　　With wrongs so clouded,
A desert where no boon is numbered,
　The sweetness and allurement reaped
　　And black and shrouded.

Thy highway is the road of weeping;
　Thy long farewells are bitterness
　　Without a morrow;
Adown thy ruts and witches keeping
　The traveller who doth most possess
　　Hath most of sorrow.

Thy chattels are but had with sighing;
　With sweat of brow alone obtained
　　The wage they give;
In myriads thine ills come hieing,
　And once existence they have gained,
　　They longest live.

And he, the shield and knightly pastor
　Of honest folk, beloved by all
　　The unoffending,—
Don Roderic Manrique, Master
　Of Santiago,—Fame shall call
　　Him brave unending!

Not here behooves to chant his praises
Or laud his valor to the skies,
        Since none but knows them;
Nor would I crave a word that raises
His merit higher than the prize
        The world bestows them.

Oh what a comrade comrades found him!
Unto his henchmen what a lord!
        And what a brother!
What foeman for the foes around him!
His peer as Master of the Sword
        There was no other!

What precious counsel mid the knowing!
What grace amid the courtly bower!
        What prudence rare!
What bounty to the vanquished showing!
How 'mid the brave in danger's hour
        A lion there!

In destiny a new Augustus;
A Cæsar for his victories
        And battle forces;
An Africanus in his justice;
A Hannibal for energies
        And deep resources;

A Trajan in his gracious hour;
A Titus for his open hand
        And cheer unfailing;
His arm, a Spartan king's in power;
His voice, a Tully's to command
        The truth's prevailing!

In mildness Antoninus Pius;
A Marc Aurelius in the light
        Of calm attending;
A Hadrian to pacify us;
A Theodosius in his right
        And high intending;

Aurelius Alexander stern
In discipline and laws of war
Among his legions;
A Constantine in faith eterne;
Gamaliel in the love he bore
His native regions.

He left no weighty chests of treasure,
Nor ever unto wealth attained
Nor store excelling;
To fight the Moors was all his pleasure
And thus his fortresses he gained,
Demesne, and dwelling.

Amid the lists where he prevailed
Fell knights and steeds into his hands
Through fierce compression,
Whereby he came to be regaled
With vassals and with feudal lands
In fair possession.

Ask you how in his rank and station
When first he started his career
Himself he righted?
Left orphan and in desolation
His brothers and his henchmen dear
He held united.

And ask you how his course was guided
When once his gallant deeds were famed
And war was ended?
His high contracting so provided
That broader, as his honors claimed,
His lands extended.

And these, the proud exploits narrated
In chronicles to show his youth
And martial force,
With triumphs equal he was fated
To reaffirm in very sooth
As years did course.

Then for the prudence of his ways,
For merit and in high award
Of service knightly,
His dignity they came to raise
Till he was Master of the Sword
Elected rightly.

Finding his father's forts and manors
By false intruders occupied
And sore oppressed,
With siege and onslaught, shouts and banners,
His broad-sword in his hand to guide,
He repossessed.

And for our rightful king how well
He bore the brunt of warfare keen
In siege and action,
Let Portugal's poor monarch tell,
Or those who in Castile have been
Among his faction.

Then having risked his life maintaining
The cause of justice in the fight
For law appointed,
With years in harness spent sustaining
The royal crown of him by right
His lord anointed,

With feats so mighty that Hispania
Can never make account of all
In number mortal,—
Unto his township of Ocaña
Came Death at last to strike and call
Against his portal:

Speaketh Death
"Good Cavalier,"—he cried,—"divest you
Of all this hollow world of lies
And soft devices;
Let your old courage now attest you,
And show a breast of steel that vies
In this hard crisis!

"And since of life and fortune's prizes
  You ever made so small account
    For sake of honor,
Array your soul in virtue's guises
  To undergo this paramount
    Assault upon her!

"For you, are only half its terrors
  And half the battles and the pains
    Your heart perceiveth;
Since here a life devoid of errors
  And glorious for noble pains
    To-day it leaveth;

"A life for such as bravely bear it
  And make its fleeting breath sublime
    In right pursuing,
Untainted, as is theirs who share it
  And put their pleasure in the grime
    Of their undoing.

"The life that is The Everlasting
  Was never yet by aught attained
    Save meed eternal;
And ne'er through soft indulgence casting
  The shadow of its solace stained
    With guilt infernal;

"But in the cloister holy brothers
  Besiege it with unceasing prayer
    And hard denial;
And faithful paladins are others
  Who 'gainst the Moors to win it bear
    With wound and trial.

"And since, O noble and undaunted,
  Your hands the Paynim's blood have shed
    In war and tourney,—
Make ready now to take the vaunted
  High guerdon you have merited
    For this great journey!

"Upon this holy trust confiding,
   And in the faith entire and pure
      You e'er commended,
Away,—unto your new abiding,
   Take up the Life that shall endure
      When this is ended!"

Respondeth the Grand-Master

"Waste we not here the final hours
   This puny life can now afford
      My mortal being;
But let my will in all its powers
   Conformable approach the Lord
      And His decreeing.

"Unto my death I yield, contenting
   My soul to put the body by
      In peace and gladness;
The thought of man to live, preventing
   God's loving will that he should die,
      Is only madness."

The Supplication

O Thou who for our weight of sin
   Descended to a place on earth
      And human feature;
Thou who didst join Thy Godhead in
   A being of such lowly worth
      As man Thy creature;

Thou who amid Thy dire tormenting
   Didst unresistingly endure
      Such pangs to ease us;
Not for my mean deserts relenting,
   But only on a sinner poor,
      Have mercy, Jesus!

The Codicil

And thus, his hopes so nobly founded,
    His senses clear and unimpaired
        So none could doubt him,—
With spouse and offspring fond surrounded,
    His kinsmen and his servants bared
        And knelt around him,—
He gave his soul to Him who gave it,
    (May God in heaven ordain it place
        And share of glory!)
And left our life as balm to save it,
    And dry the tears upon our face,
        His deathless story.

From the Spanish by Thomas Walsh.

LAUDA

Girolamo Beniveni (1453-1542)

Jesus, whoso with Thee
Hangs not in pain and loss,
Pierced on the cruel cross,
    At peace shall never be.
Lord, unto me be kind;
Give me that peace of mind
Which in this world so blind
    And false, dwells but with Thee.
Give me that strife and pain,
Apart from which 'twere vain
Thy love on earth to gain
    Or seek a share with Thee.
If, Lord, with Thee alone
Heart's peace and love be known,
My heart shall be Thine own,
    Ever to rest with Thee.
Here in my heart be lit
Thy fire, to feed on it,
Till, burning bit by bit,

It dies to live with Thee.
Jesus, whoso with Thee
Hangs not in pain and loss,
Pierced on the cruel cross,
At peace shall never be.
From the Italian by John Addington Symonds.

CONSIDER

GIOVANNI PICO DELLA MIRANDOLA (1463-1494)

Consider when thou art movèd to be wroth,
He who that was God and of all men the best,
Seeing Himself scorned and scourgèd both,
And as a thief between two thievès threst,
With all rebuke and shame; yet from His breast
Came never sign of wrath or of disdain,
But patiently endurèd all the pain—

Think on the very lamentable pain,
Think on the piteous cross of woeful Christ,
Think on His blood beat out at every vein,
Think on His precious heart carvèd in twain;
Think how for thy redemption all was wrought,
Let Him not lose what He so dear hath bought.
From the Italian by Blessed Sir Thomas More.

BALLAD OF OUR LADY

WILLIAM DUNBAR (1465-1530)

Hail sterne superne. Hail in eterne
In God is sight to shine!
Lucerne in dern, for to discern
Be glory and grace divine;
Hodiern, modern, sempitern,
Angelical regine!
Our tern inferne for to dispern,
Help royalest rosine.

Ave Maria Gratia plena!
Hail fresh flower feminine.
Yerne us, guberne, virgin matern,
Of ruth both root and rine.
Hail, ying, benign, fresh flourishing!
Hail, Alpha's habitacle!
The dign offspring made us to sing
Before his tabernacle;
All thing malign we down thing
By sight of His signacle;
Which King us bring unto His ring
Fro Death's dark umbracle.
    Ave Maria Gratia plena!
Hail moder and maid but macle!
Bright sign, gladding out languishing,
By might of the miracle
Empress of price, imperatrice,
Bright polished precious stone;
Victrice of vice, high genetrice
Of Jesu, Lord Soverane:
Our wise paviss fro enemies
Again the Fiend's train;
Oratrice, mediatrice, salvatrice
To God great suffragane!
    Ave Maria Gratia plena!
Hail sterne meridiane!
Spice, flower-de-lyce of paradise,
That bare the glorious grain.
Imperial wall, place palestral,
Of peerless pulchritude;
Triumphal hall, high tower royal
Of Godis celsitude;
Hospital royal! the Lord of all
Thy closet did include;
Bright ball crystal, rose virginal
Fulfilled of angel food!
    Ave Maria Gratia plena!
Thy birth has with His blood
Fro fall mortal original
Us ransomed on the Rood.

CANTIGA

GIL VICENTE (1470-1540)

White and crimson, cheek and breast,
O Virgin Blest!
The pledge of love in Bethlehem
A flower was on the rosetree's stem,
O Virgin blest!
In Bethlehem in sign of love
The rosebranch raised a rose above,
O Virgin blest!
In the rose came forth a flower—
Jesus, our high Lord of Power—
O Virgin blest!
The Rose of all the rosetree's span,
God in nature and a Man,—
O Virgin blest!
From the Galician-Castilian by Thomas Walsh.

SONG OF THE THREE ANGELS

GIL VICENTE

From *The Auto of the Bark of Purgatory*

Rowers now are rowing
    A boat of great delight;
The boatman who was steering it
    The Son of God is hight;
And angels were the rowers,
    Rowing with all their might;
Its flag the flag of hope:
    O how fair a sight!
Its mast the mast of fortitude,
    And as crystal bright.
The boat's sail, sewn with faith,
    To all the world gave light.
Upon the waters calm
    No breath of wind may light.
From the Galician-Castilian by Aubrey F. G. Bell.

THE ANGELIC VILANCETE

GIL VICENTE

From *The Auto of the Four Seasons*

Worthy of adoration, Thee,
O Lord our God, we praise;
To Thee our hymn we raise,
"Holy, Holy," ceaselessly.
To laud Thee doth conspire
All earth and honor most
With the angelic host
In their celestial choir.
Worthy of adoration, Thee
We Cherubim do sing,
Archangels' voices ring,
"Holy, Holy," ceaselessly.
From the Galician-Castilian by Aubrey F. G. Bell.

HYMN OF THE ANGELS AND SIBYLS

GIL VICENTE

Full of Grace exceedingly,
And oh, what charm and loveliness!
Speak, thou sailor of the sea,
And, for all thy barque, confess
Never ship nor sail can be
Beautiful as She!

Speak, thou knightly lord of arms
Boasting of thy panoply,—
Are horse and sword and war-alarms
Beautiful as She?

Speak, thou shepherd of the hills
With thy gamboling lambkins free—
Are there peaks or vales or rills
Beautiful as She?
From the Galician-Castilian by Thomas Walsh.

CAN I BELIEVE

Ludovico Ariosto (1474-1533)

Can I believe in heaven they reach Thine ear,
  O Lord benign, my prayers that are so cold—
  When my tongue cries on Thee, to loose the hold
Which yet, Thou seest, my secret heart holds dear?
Thou who dost know the truth, release me here
  And heed not, though my senses, rebels bold,
  Deny Thee; hasten! When my corpse is tolled
Let me not in that barque with Charon steer!

Forgive me all, eternal Lord! too well
  Hath evil custom blinded my clear sight
Till good from ill I scarcely now can tell.
  A heart that's penitent can ask with right
A mortal pardon; to draw hearts from hell
  Against their will Thou only hast the might!
             From the Italian by Moira O'Neill.

PREACHMENT FOR PREACHERS

Alexander Barclay (1475-1552)

From *The Ship of Fools*

Ye clerks that on your shoulders bear the shield
Unto you granted by the University,
How dare ye aventure to fight in Christes field
Against sin without ye clear and guiltless be?

Consider the cock and in him shall ye see
A great example, for with his wings thrice
He betides himself to wake his own body
Before he crow to cause others wake or rise.

STAR OF THE SEA

ALEXANDER BARCLAY

From *The Ship of Fools*

Thou art the Star, blazing with beames bright
Above these worldes waves so violent,
Our sins dark enclearing with thy light,
Man's Mediatrice to God Omnipotent.
Wherefore to thee, O Lady, I present
This simple book, though it unworthy be,
But poor and simple and much ineloquent,
Rudely composed in this tempestuous sea.

PRAYER TO THE BLESSED VIRGIN

RODRÍQUEZ DE PADRÓN (Middle of Fifteenth Century)

Fire of heaven's eternal ray
   Gentle and unscorching flame,
Strength in moments of dismay,
   Grief's redress and sorrow's balm,—
Light thy servant on his way!
Teach him all earth's passing folly,
   All its dazzling art
      To distrust;
And let thoughts profound and holy
   Penetrate his heart
      Low in dust.
Lead him to the realms sublime
   Where thy footsteps tread;
   Teach him, Virgin! so to dread
Judgment's soul-tormenting clime,
That he may harvest for the better time.
                    From the Spanish by John Bowring.

FOR INSPIRATION

Michelangelo Buonarroti (1475-1564)

The prayers I make will then be sweet indeed,
    If Thou the Spirit give by which I pray;
    My unassisted heart is barren clay,
Which of its native self can nothing feed;
Of good and pious works Thou art the seed
    Which quickens where Thou sayst it may;
    Unless Thou show us then Thine own true way,
No man can find it! Father, Thou must lead!

Do Thou, then, breathe those thoughts into my mind
    By which such virtue may in me be bred
    That in Thy holy footsteps I may tread;
The fetters of my tongue do Thou unbind,
    That I may have the power to sing of Thee
    And sound Thy praises everlastingly.
                    From the Italian by William Wordsworth.

THE DEFENCE OF NIGHT

Michelangelo Buonarroti

O night, O sweet thou sombre span of time!
    All things find rest upon their journey's end—
    Whoso hath praised thee well doth apprehend;
And whoso honors thee, hath wisdom's prime.
Our cares thou canst to quietude sublime;
    For dews and darkness are of peace the friend;
    Often by thee in dreams upborne, I wend
From earth to heaven, where yet I hope to climb.

Thou shade of death, through whom the soul at length
    Shuns pain and sadness hostile to the heart,
        Whom mourners find their last and sure relief!
Thou dost restore our suffering flesh to strength,
    Driest our tears, assuagest every smart,
        Purging the spirits of the pure from grief.
                From the Italian by John Addington Symonds.

ON THE CRUCIFIX

MICHELANGELO BUONARROTI

The course of my long life hath reached at last
    In fragile bark o'er a tempestuous sea,
    The common harbor where must rendered be
Account of all the actions of the past.
The impassioned phantasy, that, vague and vast,
    Made art an idol and a king to me,
    Was an illusion, and but vanity
Were the desires that lured me and harassed.

The dreams of love, that were so sweet of yore,
    What are they now, when two deaths may be mine,
        One sure, and one forecasting its alarms?
Painting and sculpture satisfy no more
    The soul now turning to the Love Divine,
        That oped, to embrace us, on the Cross its arms.
From the Italian by Henry Wadsworth Longfellow.

CONSIDER WELL

By BLESSED SIR THOMAS MORE (1478-1535)

Consider well that both by night and day
While we busily provide and care
For our disport, our revel and our play,
For pleasant melody and dainty fare,
Death stealeth on full slily; unaware
He lieth at hand and shall us all surprise,
We wot not when nor where nor in what wise.

When fierce temptations threat thy soul with loss
Think on His Passion and the bitter pain,
Think on the mortal anguish of the Cross,
Think on Christ's blood let out at every vein,
Think of His precious heart all rent in twain;
For thy redemption think all this was wrought,
Nor be that lost which he so dearly bought.

THE SILKWORM

MARCO GIROLAMO VIDA (1480-1566)

Extracts from *De Bombycibus*

Full many a century it crept, the child
    Of distant China or the torrid zone;
Wasted its web upon the woodlands wild
    And spun its golden tissue all alone,
    Clothing no reptile's body but its own.
So crawled a brother-worm o'er mount and glen,
    Uncivilised, uncouth; till, social grown,
He sought the cities and the haunts of men—
Science and Art soon tamed the forest denizen.

Rescued from woods, now under friendly roof
    Fostered and fed, and sheltered from the blast,
Full soon the wondrous wealth of warp and woof—
    Wealth by these puny laborers amassed,
    Repaid the hand that spread their green repast;
Right merrily they plied their jocund toil,
    And from their mouths the silken treasures cast,
Twisting their canny thread in many a coil,
While men looked on and smiled, and hailed the shining spoil.

Methinks that here some gentle maiden begs
    To know how best this genial deed is done:
Some on a napkin strew the little eggs,
    And simply hatch their silkworms in the sun;
    But there's a better plan to fix upon.
Wrapt in a muslin kerchief pure and warm,
    Lay them within thy bosom safe; nor shun
Nature's kind office till the tiny swarm
Begins to creep. Fear not; they cannot do thee harm.

Venus it was who first invented silk—
    Linen had long, by Ceres patronised,
Supplied Olympus; ladies of that ilk
    No better sort of clothing had devised—

Linen alone their *garde de robe* comprised.
Hence at her cambric loom the suitors found
  Penelope, whom hath immortaiised
The blind man eloquent; nor less renowned
Were "Troy's proud dames" whose robes of linen "swept the
    ground."

The good inhabitants of Pekin, when
  They saw the dame in downright *déshabille,*
Were shocked. Such sight was far beyond the ken
  Of their Confucian notions. Full of zeal
  To guard the morals of the commonweal,
They straight deputed Sylk, a mandarin,
  Humbly before the visitant to kneel
With downcast eye, and offer Beauty's queen
A rich resplendent robe of gorgeous bombazine.

Venus received the vesture nothing loath,
  And much its gloss, its softness, much admired,
And praised that specimen of foreign growth,
  So splendid, and so cheaply too acquired.
  Quick in the robe her graceful limbs attired,
She seeks a mirror—there delighted dallies;
  So rich a dress was all could be desired.
How she rejoiced to disappoint the malice
Of her unfeeling foe, the vile, vindictive Pallas!

But while she praised the gift and thanked the giver
  Of spinner-worms she sued for a supply.
Forthwith the good Chinese filled Cupid's quiver
  With the cocoons in which each worm doth lie
  Snug, until changed into a butterfly.
The light cocoons wild Cupid showered o'er Greece,
  And o'er the Isles and over Italy,
Into the lap of industry and peace;
And the glad nations hailed the long-sought "Golden Fleece."
    From the Latin by Francis S. Mahony (Father Prout).

CHANT OF THE NINTH ORDER OF SERAPHIM

Fray Íñigo de Mendoza (About 1482)

Joy is everywhere on earth,
  Gladness throughout Limbo waking;
Feasts in honor of the birth
  Of Maria they are making;
Sorrow can no haven find;
  Noon's without a cloud attended,
For today doth humankind
  Hail the Son of God descended
Virgin body to assume,
  Our salvation to restore,
Wiping out the stains and gloom
  With the power of Love once more!

From the Spanish by Roderick Gill.

THE PALMER

John Heywood (1497-1580)

From *The Play of the Four P. P.*

St. Uncumber and St. Trumnion
At St. Botolph and St. Anne of Buxton,
On the hills of Armenia where I saw Noe's Ark
With holy Job and St. George in Southwark;
At Waltham and at Walsingham;
And at the good road at Dagenham
At St. Cornelys; at St. James in Gales,
And at St. Winifred's well in Wales;
At our Lady of Boston; at St. Edmundsbury
And straight to St. Patrick's Purgatory;
At Redburne and at the Blood of Hales
Where pilgrims' pains right much avails;
At St. David's and at St. Denis,
At St. Matthew and St. Mark in Venice,
At Master John Shorn at Canterbury,
The great God of Catwade, at King Henry,

At St. Saviour's, at our Lady of Southwell,
At Crome, at Willesden and at Muswell;
At St. Richard and at St. Rock;
And at Our Lady that standeth in the Oak.

CAROL TO OUR LADY

I sing of a maiden
That is makeless,
King of all kings
To her son she chose.
He came all so still
There his mother was,
As dew in April
That falleth on the grass.
He came all so still
To his mother's bower,
As dew in April
That falleth on the flower.
He came all so still
There his mother lay,
As dew in April
That falleth on the spray.
Mother and maiden
Was never none but she;
Well may such a lady
God's mother be.

From the Old English.

EVERYMAN

An Old English Morality

Eternal God!
Oh! Beatific Vision! Road of Truth,
And heavenly Light! Here at my final hour
I cry to Thee, and wailing fills this mouth!
O Saviour dear, pray my Creator now
That He be merciful unto the end,

When the dark Enemy draws near from Hell
And Death's appalling clutch is at my throat!
Pray that He take my soul above, that I
Through Thy sweeet intercession may approach,
O Christ, Thy seat at His right hand, and go
With Him in glory! Let this be my prayer,
For Thou upon the Cross hast saved our souls!

From the Old English by George Sterling.

I SAW THREE SHIPS

ANONYMOUS

As I sat under a sycamore tree,
A sycamore tree, a sycamore tree,
I looked me out upon the sea
On Christ's Sunday at morn.

I saw three ships a-sailing there,
A-sailing there, a-sailing there,
Jesu, Mary and Joseph they bare
On Christ's Sunday at morn.

Joseph did whistle and Mary did sing,
Mary did sing, Mary did sing,
And all the bells on earth did ring
For joy our Lord was born.

O they sailed into Bethlehem!
To Bethlehem, to Bethlehem;
Saint Michael was the steersman,
Saint John sat in the horn.

And all the bells on earth did ring,
On earth did ring, on earth did ring:
"Welcome be thou, Heaven's King,
On Christ's Sunday at morn!"

PRAYER TO THE CRUCIFIX

MOSSÉN JUAN TALLANTE (End of Fifteenth Century)

Almighty God, unchangeable,
    Who framed the universe entire
        Thy truth to see;
Thou who for loving us so well
    Didst in Thine agony expire
        On Calvary;
Since with such suffering didst deign
    To make amend for our transgression,
        O Agnus Dei.
Placed with the thief let us obtain
    Salvation in his grief's confession:
        Memento mei.
                From the Spanish by Thomas Walsh.

THE HARROWING OF HELL

An Old English Miracle

Jesus:

> *Principes portas tollite,*
> Undo your gates, ye Princes of pride,
> *Et introibit rex gloriæ;*
> The King of Bliss comes in this tide.

> (Jesus enters Hell)

Satan:

> Out, harrow.   What hirelot is he
> That says his Kingdom shall be cried?

David (in Limbo):

> That may thou in my Psalter see,
> For of this Prince I prophesied.
> I said that he should break
> Your bars and bands by name,
> And of your works take wreck:
> Now shalt thou see the same.

Jesus:

>   This stead shall stand no longer stoken:
>   Open up and let my people pass.

Diabolus:

>   Out behold our bailey broken
>   And bursten are all our bands of brass!

Beelzebub:

>   What then, is Limbo lorn? Alas!

Jesus:

>   *Attolite portas principes, vestras et*
>   *elevamini portæ eternales et*
>   *introibit Rex Gloriæ.*

Ribald:

>   Out, harrow, out! What devil is he
>   That calls him king over us all?
>   Hark, Beelzebub, come nigh,
>   For hideously I heard him call.

Beelzebub:

>   Honour? Heard'st thou, hirelot, for what deed
>   All earthly men to me are thrall?
>   The Lad that thou callest Lord-in-lede
>   He never had herborough, house, nor hall.

Jesus:

>   *Attollite portas principes,*
>   Open up, ye Princes of pains sere,
>   *Et elevamini eternales*
>   Your endless gates that ye have here.

Satan:

>   What page is there that makes press
>   And calls him King of us in fere?

Ribald:

>   Of Him cometh all this light
>   That shineth in this bower,
>   He is full fierce in fight,
>   Worthy to win honour.

Jesus:

> Ye Princes of Hell, open your gate
> And let my folk further gone:
> A Prince of Peace shall enter thereat
> Whither ye will or none.

Ribald:

> What art thou that speakest thus?

Jesus:

> A King of Bliss that hight Jesus.

THE SNARES

NAHAB KOUTCHAK (Early Sixteenth Century)

> With those proud birds that feed not
> Upon the grains of earth,
> I winged my flight to heed not
> What snares of love were worth.
>
> But through the skies elated
> Love spreads celestial strings;
> On earth man's feet are baited,
> In heaven He caught my wings.
>> *From the Armenian by Thomas Walsh.*

"O FELIX CULPA!"

> Adam lay inbounden
> Bounden in a bond;
> Four thousand winter
> Thought he not too long;
> And all was for an apple,
> An apple that he took
> As clerics finden
> Written in their book;
> Nor had the apple taken been,
> The apple taken been,

Nor had never Our Lady
Been of Heaven Queen.
Blessed be the time
That apple taken was.
Therefore we must singen
Deo Gratias.

From the Old English.

MY GOD, I LOVE THEE

SAINT FRANCIS XAVIER (1506-1552)

My God, I love Thee! not because
  I hope for heaven thereby;
Nor because those who love Thee not
  Must burn eternally.

Thus, O my Jesus, thou didst me
  Upon the cross embrace!
For me didst bear the nails and spear
  And manifold disgrace.

And griefs and torments numberless
  And sweat of agony,
Yea, death itself—and all for one
  That was Thy enemy.

Then why, O blessèd Jesus Christ,
  Should I not love Thee well!
Not for the hope of winning heaven
  Nor of escaping hell!

Not with the hope of gaining aught,
  Not seeking a reward;
But as Thyself hast lovèd me
  O everlasting Lord!

E'en so I love Thee and will love
  And in Thy praise will sing—
Solely because Thou art my God
  And my eternal King!
              From the Latin by Edward Caswell.

THE MARIGOLD

WILLIAM FORREST (1510-1565)

To Mary our Queen, that flower so sweet,
This Marigold I do apply,
For that the name doth serve so meet
And properly in each party;
For her enduring patiently
The storms of such as list to scold
At her doings, with cause why
Loth to see spring this Marigold.

Christ save her in her high estate
Therein in rest long to endure:
Christ so all wrongs here mitigate
That all may be to His pleasure:
The high, the low, in due measure
As members true with her to hold,
So each to be the other's treasure
In cherishing the Marigold.

Be Thou, O God, so good as thus
Thy perfect faith to see take place,
Thy peace Thou plant here among us
That error may go hide his face:
So to concord us in each case
As in Thy court it is enrolled,
We all as one to love Her Grace
That is our Queen, the Marigold.

IF LORD THY LOVE FOR ME IS STRONG

SAINT TERESA OF AVILA (1515-1582)

If, Lord, Thy love for me is strong
As this which binds me unto Thee,
What holds me from Thee, Lord, so long,
What holds Thee, Lord, so long from me?

O soul, what then desirest thou?
—Lord, I would see Thee, who thus choose Thee.
What fears can yet assail thee now?
—All that I fear is but to lose Thee.

Love's whole possession I entreat,
Lord, make my soul Thine own abode,
And I will build a nest so sweet
It may not be too poor for God.

A soul in God hidden from sin
What more desires for thee remain,
Save but to love, and love again,
And, all on flame with love within,
Love on, and turn to love again?

From the Spanish by Arthur Symons.

LET MINE EYES SEE THEE

SAINT TERESA OF AVILA

Let mine eyes see Thee,
Sweet Jesus of Nazareth,
Let mine eyes see Thee,
And then see death.

Let them see that care
Roses and jessamine;
Seeing Thy face most fair
All blossoms are therein.

Flower of seraphin,
Sweet Jesus of Nazareth,
Let mine eyes see Thee,
And then see death.

Nothing I require
Where my Jesus is;
Anguish all desire,
Saving only this;
All my help is His,
He only succoreth.

Let mine eyes see Thee,
Sweet Jesus of Nazareth,
Let mine eyes see Thee and then see death.
                From the Spanish by Arthur Symons.

LINES WRITTEN IN HER BREVIARY

SAINT TERESA OF AVILA

Let nothing disturb thee,
Nothing affright thee;
All things are passing;
God never changeth;
Patient endurance
Attaineth to all things;
Who God possesseth
In nothing is wanting;
Alone God sufficeth.
From the Spanish by Henry Wadsworth Longfellow.

SHEPHERD, SHEPHERD, HARK

SAINT TERESA OF AVILA

Shepherd, shepherd, hark that calling!
Angels they are, and the day is dawning.

What is this ding-dong,
Or loud singing is it?
Come, Bras, now the day is here,
The shepherdess we'll visit.

Shepherd, shepherd, hark that calling!
Angels they are and the day is dawning.

Oh, is this the Alcalde's daughter,
Or some lady come from far?
She is the daughter of God the Father,
And she shines like a star.

Shepherd, shepherd, hark that calling!
Angels they are, and the day is dawning.

From the Spanish by Arthur Symons.

SONNET

JOACHIM DU BELLAY (1524-1560)

If life on earth be less than is a day
Hereafter, if the year in its swift flight
Chases our days for ever out of sight,
If all things having birth must know decay,
O prisoned soul o' mine, why still delay?
Why art thou so contented with this night,
When for thy voyage to untroubled light,
Thine are strong wings accordant for the way?

There, is the good that every soul desires,
There, is the peace to which the world aspires,
And there, are love and joy for evermore.

There, O my soul, brought to the highest skies,
Ideal beauty thou wilt recognise—
Beauty that in this dim world, I adore.

From the French by Armel O'Connor.

SONNET

Luis Vaz de Camoens (1524-1579)

Leave me, all sweet refrains my lip hath made;
  Leave me, all instruments attuned for song;
  Leave me, all fountains pleasant meads among;
Leave me, all charms of garden and of glade;
Leave me, all melodies the pipe hath played;
  Leave me, all rural feast and sportive throng;
  Leave me, all flocks the reed beguiles along;
Leave me, all shepherds happy in the shade.

Sun, moon and stars, for me no longer glow;
  Night would I have, to wail for vanished peace;
Let me from pole to pole no pleasure know;
  Let all that I have loved and cherished, cease;
But see that thou forsake me not, my Woe,
  Who wilt, by killing, finally release.

From the Portuguese by Richard Garnett.

AT THE ASCENSION

Fray Luis de Leon (1528-1591)

And wouldst Thou, Holy Shepherd, leave
  Thy flock within this vale of woe
And solitude to grieve,
  Whilst Thou through ambient skies aglow
  Ascendst where death and sorrow cannot go!

But they—so blessèd in the past,
  Yet now with hearts afflicted sore—
Thy little ones, outcast,
  Bereft of Thee their guide of yore—
  Whither shall turn they when Thou leadst no more?

What now remains to glad the eyes
    That once Thy comeliness have known?
What longer can they prize?
    What voices, but discordant grown
    To them who harkened to Thy loving tone?

The waves of yon perturbèd deep,
    Whose hand shall curb?—Who now assuage
The blasts and bid them sleep?
    In Thine eclipse,—what star presage
    For our benighted bark the harborage?

Alas! swift cloud unpitying
    That bidst our joys no more endure,—
Whither thy silvery wing?
    How rich the bliss thou dost secure!—
    How beggared wilt thou leave us, how obscure!—
            From the Spanish by Thomas Walsh.

AT THE ASSUMPTION

Fray Luis de Leon

As unto heaven thou'rt soaring,
    O Queen, to blissful lays,
Take thou my soul imploring
    Thy mantle's hem, and raise
    Me to those Hills of Praise!

The choiring angels round thee
    Attend as from thy birth;
With stars their hands have crowned thee
    Of more than queenly worth—
    Thou treadst the moon as earth!

But turn thine eyes, O Tender,
    O Loving,—ere dost leave
This vale whose flowery splendor
    Masks but a waste where grieve
    Thine exiled sons of Eve.

So when thy gentle vision
  Hath marked our dismal plight,
Thou on thy way elysian
  Mayst trail us in thy flight—
    Heaven's lode-star to the Light!
        From the Spanish by Thomas Walsh.

THE VALLEY OF THE HEAVENS

FRAY LUIS DE LEON

Resplendent precinct of the skies,
  Fair sward of gladness neither snow
Nor parching breath of noonday tries,
  Domain whose sacred uplands show
    Its peace ungarnered deathlessly aglow!

His brows in white and azure crowned
  Athwart its pastures softly wends,
O flock endeared with thee around,
  The Holy Shepherd; thee He tends
    Unarmed with staff or sling where naught offends.

He leads, and happy sheep o'erflow
  Around Him in a loving feud,
Where the immortal roses blow
  And verdure ever is renewed,
    Howe'er the flock may graze, in plenitude.

And now upon the mountain ways
  Of Bliss He guides; now by the stream
To bathe them in His grace He strays;
  Now grants them banqueting agleam—
    Himself the Giver and the Gift Supreme.

And when the eye of noon attains
  The zenith of its fiery powers,
Amid His fondlings He remains
  To drowse away the torrid hours
    And cheer with voice serene the holy bowers.

He wakes the viol's melting tone
  And sweetness trembles through the soul
Unto such golden joy unknown;
  Enraptured then beyond control
  It casts itself on Him, its only goal.

O Breath! O Voice!—mightst Thou ordain
  Some little echo for my breast
That—self-surrendering in that strain
  To Thee—of Thee 'twould be possest,
  O Love, and on Thy shoulder finds its rest!

Where Thou dost linger at the noon,
  Sweet Spouse, oh, would my spirit knew!—
And breaking from this prison swoon,
  Of Thy far flocks might come in view
  And stray no more, save paths Thou leadst them through.
              From the Spanish by Thomas Walsh.

THE NIGHT SERENE

FRAY LUIS DE LEON

When I contemplate o'er me
  The heaven of stars profound
And mark the earth before me
  In darkness swathed around—
  In careless slumber and oblivion bound—

Then love and longing waken
  The anguish of my breast;
Mine eyes with tears are taken
  Like founts beyond control,
  My soul sighs forth at last its voice of dole!

O Temple-Seat of Glory,
  Of Beauteousness and Light,
To thy calm promontory
  My soul was born! What blight
  Holds it endungeoned here from such a height?

What mortal aberration
  Hath so estranged mankind
That from God's destination
  He turns, abandoned, blind,
    To follow mocking shade and empty rind?

No thought amid his slumber
  He grants impending fate,
While nights and dawns keep number
  In step apportionate,
    And life is filched away—his poor estate.

Alas!—arise, weak mortals,
  And measure all your loss;
Begirt for deathless portals,
  Can souls their birthright toss
    Aside and live on shadows vain and dross?

Oh, let your eyes beholding
  Yon pure celestial sphere,
Unmask the wiles enfolding
  The life that flatters here—
    The little day of mingled hope and fear!

What more can base earth render
  Than one poor moment's pause,
Compared with that far splendor
  Where in its primal cause
    Lives all that is—that shall be—and that was!

Who on that constellation
  Eternal can set gaze—
Its silvery gradation,
  Its majesty of ways,
    The concord and proportion it displays—

In argent wonder turning,
  The moon doth nightly rove,
Squired by the Star of Learning
  And melting Star of Love,
    She trails with gentle retinue above—

And lo! through outer spaces
  Where Mars is rolled aflame!
Where Jupiter retraces
  The calmed horizon's frame
  And all the heavens his ray beloved acclaim!

Beyond swings Saturn, father
  Of the fabled Age of Gold;
And o'er his shoulders gather
  Night's chantries manifold,
  In their proportioned grade and lustre stoled!—

Who can behold such vision—
  And still earth's baubles prize?
Nor sob the last decision
  To rend the bond that ties
  His soul a captive from such blissful skies?

For there Content hath dwelling;
  And Peace, her realm; and there
'Mid joys and glories swelling
  Lifts up the dais fair
  With Sacred Love enthroned beyond compare.

Immensurable Beauty
  Shows cloudless to that light;
And there a Sun doth duty
  That knows no stain of night;
  There Spring Eternal blossoms without blight.

O fields of Truth Abiding!
  Green pasturelands and rills!
And mines of treasures hiding!
  O joyous-breasted hills!
  Re-echoing vales where every balm distils!
          From the Spanish by Thomas Walsh.

LINES ON THE WALL OF HIS PRISON CELL

Fray Luis de Leon

Lo, where enviousness and lies
  Held me in this prison cell;
Blessèd is the sage to dwell
  Humble in his hermit guise,
Bidding the false world farewell.

With his thatch and homely fare
  Down his chosen paths forgot;
Lone with God contented there,
Uncompanioned, without care,
  Envying none and envied not.

From the Spanish by Thomas Walsh.

II

AGE OF TRANSITION

SONNET

Pedro Malon de Chaide (1530-1589)

O patience, that dost wait eternally!
  O heart of mine so hard, that cannot love!
  How am I wearied as from Thee I rove!
How dost Thou, never wearying, pardon me!
O Face Divine, how often did I see
  Thy grieving gaze toward me sadly turned,
  While I, my Lord, Thy laws have basely spurned,
And Thou hast loved and suffered silently.

Guardian of all men, turn Thy wrath away
  From this Thy child of earth, oh, turn again!
See, Thine own child am I: raise me, I pray,
For 'tis not pleasure now that makes me stray,
  But habits fought and striven against in vain:
I hate the sin, and yet I sin alway.
          From the Spanish by E. Allison Peers.

Lines from THE CONVERSION OF THE MAGDALENE

Pedro Malon de Chaide

Encircling Thee Thy holy brides,
  With loveliest of garlands crowned
In rose and jasmine's glowing prides,
  Amid the measured chanting sound,
  O gentle Shepherd, on Thy way are bound.

And when at midday by the streams
  Thou takest Thy siesta fair
Where soft the cooling water gleams,
  Impatient of the love they bear
  They loiter round the fountains in their care.

Thou walkest with them where they throng
  With holy radiance agleam—
A Sun the blinded stars among;
  And higher as the mountains teem,
  Thou light'st the peaks with Thine eternal beam.
                From the Spanish by Thomas Walsh.

IDEAL BEAUTY

Fernando de Herrera (1534-1594)

O light serene! present in him who breathes
  That love divine, which kindles yet restrains
  The high-born soul—that in its mortal chains
Heavenward aspires for love's immortal wreaths!
Rich golden locks, within whose clustered curls
  Celestial and eternal treasures lie!
  A voice that breathes angelic harmony
Among bright coral and unspotted pearls!

What marvelous beauty! Of the high estate
  Of immortality, within this light
    Transparent veil of flesh, a glimpse is given;
And in the glorious form I contemplate
  (Although its brightness blinds my feeble sight)
    The immortal still I seek and follow on to Heaven!
From the Spanish by Henry Wadsworth Longfellow.

RELIGION

Vauquelin de la Fresnaye (1536-1606)

Who art thou, girl, in such mean garb arrayed?
I am Religion, God's own serving maid.
Why dost thou wear such raiment? Since for me
A richer one would seem but vanity.
What book hast thou? God's gift it is, and there
I find His Holy Testament writ fair.

Why is thy breast uncovered? 'Tis, she saith,
Because I keep there an unspotted faith.
Why dost thou lean on that rude Cross? Its shade
Eternal solace for my soul hath made.
Why art thou fledged thus? It is that I
May teach men far above these clouds to fly.
Why art thou set about with flame? My fire
Beats off the shadow from God's holy choir.
Why art thou bridled? Better so to hold
Thy fervent soul within the heavenly fold.
Why dost thou tread down Death? It is that I
Am Death's own slayer, who can never die.

From the French by Wilfrid Thorley.

TO OUR SAVIOUR

Frei Agostinho da Cruz (1540-1619)

When shall I, Lord, this mortal load untied,
  Be joined to Thee in union entire,
  Binding my soul in Thee whom I desire,
Beholding all for which in Thee I sighed?
Wherefore should I upon such glory bide
  Who never felt the valorous battle fire;
  Enough, if but my weakness but aspire
In love for Thee along the battle-side.

This is the strength so potent for my needs;
  This is the fortifying of my sighs,
That he who loves the most the most succeeds;
  Whatever pains I know, what insufficiency
Or what unworthiness my step impedes,
  Loving, I shall attain Love's perfect fee.

From the Portuguese by Thomas Walsh.

PRAYER BEFORE EXECUTION

Mary Queen of Scots (1542-1587)

O Domine Deus! Speravi in Te,
O care mi Jesus, nunc libera me!
In dura catena, in misera poena,
Desidero Te!
Languendo, gemendo, et genuflectendo,
Adoro, imploro ut liberes me!

. . . . . .

O merciful Father, my hope is in Thee!
O gracious Redeemer, deliver Thou me!
My bondage bemoaning, with sorrowful groaning,
I long to be free;
Lamenting, relenting, and humbly repenting,
O Jesu, my Saviour, I languish for Thee.

Version of John Fawcett, 1782.

THE FRIAR OF ORDERS GREY

Anonymous (Sixteenth Century)

It was a Friar of Orders Grey
  Walked forth to tell his beads;
And he met with a lady fair
  Clad in a pilgrim's weeds.

"Now Christ thee save, thou reverend Friar,
  I pray thee tell to me,
If ever at yon holy shrine
  My true love thou didst see."

"And how should I know your true love
  From many another one?"
"Oh, by his cockle hat and staff
  And by his sandal shoon."

"O Lady, he is dead and gone;
  Lady, he's dead and gone;
And at his head a green grass turf
  And at his heels a stone."

O FLAME OF LIVING LOVE

SAINT JOHN OF THE CROSS (1549-1591)

O flame of living love,
That dost eternally
Pierce through my soul with so consuming heat,
Since there's no help above,
Make thou an end of me,
And break the bond of this encounter sweet.

O burn that burns to heal!
O more than pleasant wound!
And O soft hand, O touch most delicate,
That dost new life reveal,
That dost in grace abound,
And, slaying, dost from death to life translate!

O lamps of fire that shined
With so intense a light
That those deep caverns where the senses live,
Which were obscure and blind,
Now with strange glories bright,
Both heat and light to His beloved give!

With how benign intent
Rememberest thou my breast,
Where thou alone abidest secretly;
And in thy sweet ascent,
With glory and good possessed,
How delicately thou teachest love to me!
    From the Spanish by Arthur Symons.

THE OBSCURE NIGHT OF THE SOUL

Saint John of the Cross

Upon an obscure night
Fevered with love in love's anxiety,
(O hapless-happy plight!)
I went, none seeing me,
Forth from my house where all things quiet be.

By night, secure from sight,
And by the secret stair, disguisedly,
(O hapless-happy plight!)
By night, and privily,
Forth from my house where all things quiet be.

Blest night of wandering,
In secret, where by none might I be spied,
Nor I see anything;
Without a light or guide,
Save that which in my heart burnt in my side.

That light did lead me on,
More surely than the shining of noontide,
Where well I knew that one
Did for my coming bide;
Where He abode might none but He abide.

O night that didst lead thus,
O night more lovely than the dawn of light,
O night that broughtest us,
Lover to lover's sight,
Lover with loved in marriage of delight!

Upon my flowery breast
Wholly for Him, and save Himself for none,
There did I give sweet rest
To my belovèd one;
The fanning of the cedars breathed thereon.

When the first moving air
Blew from the tower and waved His locks aside.
His hand, with gentle care,
Did wound me in the side,
And in my body all my senses died.

All things I then forgot,
My cheek on Him who for my coming came;
All ceased, and I was not,—
Leaving my cares and shame
Among the lilies, and forgetting them.
From the Spanish by Arthur Symons.

THE IMAGE OF GOD

Francisco de Aldana (1550-1578)

O Lord! who seest from yon starry height,
    Centred in one, the future and the past,
        Fashioned in thine own image, see how fast
The world obscures in me what once was bright
Eternal Sun! the warmth which thou hast given
    To cheer life's flowery April, fast decays;
        Yet, in the hoary winter of my days,
Forever green shall be my trust in heaven.

Celestial King! oh, let thy presence pass
    Before my spirit, and an image fair
        Shall meet that look of mercy from on high,
As the reflected image in a glass
    Doth meet the look of him who seeks it there,
        And owes its being to the gazer's eye.
From the Spanish by W. M. Longfellow.

From JERUSALEM DELIVERED

TORQUATO TASSO (1554-1595)

The sacred armies and the godly Knight
　　That the Great Sepulcher of Christ did free
I sing; much wrought his valour and foresight
　　And in that glorious warre much suffred he;
In vaine gainst him did hell oppose her might,
　　In vaine the Turkes and Morians armèd be;
　　　His soldiers wilde, to braules and mutines prest,
　　　Reducèd he to peace, so heaven him blest.

O heavenly Muse, that not with fading baies
　　Deckest thy brow by th' Heliconian spring,
But sittest crowned with starres immortall raies,
　　In heaven where legions of bright Angels sing;
Inspire life in my wit, my thoughts upraise,
　　My verse ennoble and forgive the thing,
　　　If fictions light I mix with truth divine,
　　　And fill these lines with other praise than thine.
　　　　　　From the Italian by Edward Fairfax.

THE CRUSADERS BEHOLD JERUSALEM

TORQUATO TASSO

The odorous air, morn's messenger, now spread
Its wings to herald, in serenest skies,
Aurora issuing forth, her radiant head
　　Adorned with roses plucked in Paradise;
When in full panoply the hosts arise,
　　And loud and spreading murmurs upward fly,
Ere yet the trumpet sings; its melodies
　　They miss not long, the trumpet's tuneful cry
Gives the command to march, shrill sounding to the sky.

Winged is each heart, and wingéd every heel;
  They fly, yet notice not how fast they fly;
But by the time the dewless meads reveal
  The fervent sun's ascension in the sky,
Lo, toward Jerusalem salutes the eye!
  A thousand pointing fingers tell the tale!
"Jerusalem!" a thousand voices cry,
  "All hail, Jerusalem!" hill, down and dale
Catch the glad sounds, and shout, "Jerusalem, all hail!"
                    From the Italian by Wiffen.

HYMN

Venerable Philip Howard (1557-1595)

O Christ, the glorious Crown
Of virgins that are pure;
Who dost a love and thirst for Thee
Within their minds procure;
Thou art the spouse of those
That chaste and humble be,
The hope, the life, the only help
Of such as trust in Thee.

All charity of those
Whose souls Thy love doth warm;
All simple pleasures of such minds
As think no kind of harm;
All sweet delights wherewith
The patient hearts abound,
Do blaze Thy name, and with Thy praise
They make the world resound.

The sky, the land, the sea,
And all on earth below,
The glory of Thy worthy Name
Do with their praises show.
The winter yields Thee praise,
And summer doth the same,
The sun, the moon, the stars and all
Do magnify Thy name.

The roses that appear
So fair to outward sight;
The violets with their scent
Do yield so great delight;
The pearls, the precious stones,
The birds, Thy praise do sing,
The woods, the wells, and all delights,
Which from this earth do spring.

What creatures, O sweet Lord,
From praising Thee can stay?
What earthly thing but, filled with joy,
Thine honour doth bewray?
Let us, therefore, with praise
Thy mighty works express,
With heart and hand, with mind, and all
Which we from Thee possess.

TO OUR LORD

Francisco Galvam (1560-1635)

O Thou pure fountain of pure love, my Lord!
  O bounty of a Father more than man!
  O God, eternal light and sovereign!
My God—high beauty's new and ancient ward!—
None else but Thee can surety afford;
  None safe where Thou art not custodian.
  How far we stray with madness for our plan
When from Thy side we seek an alien hoard.

Without Thee, how the road and guidance fade;
  Without Thy Tryst, how glory falls away;
    Without Thee, what confusion is the night!
  Yea, in Thee fixed my memory shall stay;
In Thee my soul its dwelling place hath made;
  In Thee my spirit learns its utmost might.
      From the Portuguese by Thomas Walsh.

SEGUIDILLA

José de Valdivielso (1560-1638)

I who once was free,
Sold unto death you see;
Trust not, Mother dear,
Hearts ungrateful here!
With a honeyed smile,
Mother, a false friend
At the banquet's end,
His hand within my dish the while,
Like a lamb betrayed me vile.
Trust not, Mother dear,
Hearts ungrateful here!
I placed him at my side
And passed the dish to him;
I shared and did provide
The best unto the brim.
His bargain rare and grim,—
He sold Thy Son away,
Trust not, Mother dear,
Hearts ungrateful here!
The garden flowers were wet
With the tears I shed thereon;
'Twas Holy Thursday, yet
With me had Judas gone;
He gave unto Thy Son
The kiss I'll not forget—
Trust not, Mother dear,
Hearts ungrateful here!
From the Spanish by Thomas Walsh.

THE NATIVITY OF CHRIST

Luis de Argote y Gongora (1561-1627)

Today from the Aurora's bosom
A pink has fallen—a crimson blossom—
And oh, how glorious rests the hay
On which the fallen blossom lay!

When silence gently had unfurled
Her mantle over all below.
And crowned with winter's frost and snow,
Night swayed the sceptre of the world,
Amid the gloom descending slow,
Upon the monarch's frozen bosom
A pink has fallen,—a crimson blossom.

The only flower the Virgin bore
(Aurora fair) within her breast,
She gave to earth, yet still possessed
Her virgin blossom as before;
That hay that colored drop caressed,—
Received upon its faithful bosom
That single flower,—a crimson blossom.
The manger, unto which 'twas given,
Even amid wintry snows and cold,
Within its fostering arms to fold
The blushing flower that fell from heaven,
Was as a canopy of gold,—
A downy couch,—where on its bosom
That flower had fallen,—that crimson blossom.
                From the Spanish by W. M. Longfellow.

NOT ALL SWEET NIGHTINGALES

LUIS DE ARGOTE Y GONGORA

They are not all sweet nightingales
That fill with songs the flowery vales;
But they are little silver bells,
Touched by the winds in the smiling dells;
Magic bells of gold in the grove,
Forming a chorus for her I love.

Think not the voices in the air
Are from the wingèd Sirens fair,
Playing among the dewy trees,
Chanting their morning mysteries;
Oh! if you listen, delighted there,
To their music scattered o'er the dales,

They are not all sweet nightingales
That fill with songs the flowery vales;
But they are little silver bells,
Touched by the winds in the smiling dells;
Magic bells of gold in the grove,
Forming a chorus for her I love.

Oh, 'twas a lovely song—of art
To charm—of nature to touch the heart;
Sure 'twas some shepherd's pipe, which played
By passion fills the forest shade;
No! 'tis music's diviner part
Which o'er the yielding spirit prevails.

They are not all sweet nightingales
That fill with songs the flowery vales;
But they are little silver bells,
Touched by the winds in the smiling dells;
Magic bells of gold in the grove,
Forming a chorus for her I love.

In the eye of love, which all things sees,
The fragrance-breathing jasmine trees—
And the golden flowers—and the sloping hill—
And the ever melancholy rill—
Are full of holiest sympathies,
And tell of love a thousand tales.

They are not all sweet nightingales
That fill with songs the flowery vales;
But they are little silver bells,
Touched by the winds in the smiling dells;
Bells of gold in the secret grove,
Making music for her I love.
　　　　　From the Spanish by John Bowring.

THE BURNING BABE

ROBERT SOUTHWELL, S.J. (1562-1595)

As I in hoary winter night stood shivering in the snow,
Surprised was I with sudden heat which made my heart to glow;

And lifting up a fearful eye to view what fire was near
A pretty babe all burning bright did in the air appear;
Who scorchèd with excessive heat, such floods of tears did shed
As though His floods should quench His flames with which His
    tears were fed:
"Alas!" quoth He, "but newly born in fiery heats I fry,
Yet none approach to warm their hearts or feel my fire but I!"

"My faultless breast the furnace is; the fuel, wounding thorns;
Love is the fire, and sighs the smoke; the ashes, shames and
    scorns;
The fuel Justice layeth on, and Mercy blows the coals,
The metal in this furnace wrought are men's defiled souls:
For which, as now on fire I am to work them to their good,
So will I melt into a bath, to wash them in my blood."
With this He vanished out of sight and swiftly shrank away,
And straight I callèd unto mind that it was Christmas Day.

A CHILD MY CHOICE

Robert Southwell, S.J.

Let folly praise that fancy loves, I praise and love that Child
Whose heart no thought, whose tongue no word, whose hand no
    deed defiled.
I praise Him most, I love Him best, all praise and love are His;
While Him I love, in Him I live, and cannot live amiss.
Love's sweetest mark, laud's highest theme, man's most desired
    light,
To love Him life, to leave Him death, to live in Him delight.
He mine by gift, I His by debt, thus each to other due,
First friend He was, best friend He is, all times will try Him
    true.
Though young yet wise, though small yet strong; though man yet
    God He is;
As wise He knows, as strong He can, as God He loves to bless.
His knowledge rules, His strength defends, His love doth cherish
    all;
His birth our joy, His life our light, His death our end of thrall.

Alas! He weeps, He sighs, He pants, yet do His angels sing;
Out of His tears, His sighs and throbs, doth bud a joyful spring.
Almighty Babe, whose tender arms can force all foes to fly,
Correct my faults, protect my life, direct me when I die!

STANZAS FROM ST. PETER'S COMPLAINT

Robert Southwell, S.J.

Weep balm and myrrh, you sweet Arabian trees,
With purest gems perfume and pearl your rine;
Shed on your honey drops, you busy bees.
I, barren plant, must weep unpleasant brine.
Hornets I hive, salt drops their labour plies
Sucked out of sin and shed by show'ring eyes.

With easy loss sharp wrecks did he eschew
That sindonless aside did naked slip:
Once naked Grace no outward garments knew;
Rich are his robes, whom sin did never strip,
I that in vaunts displayed Pride's fairest flags,
Disrobed of Grace, am wrapped in Adam's rags.

Sleep, death's ally, oblivion of tears,
Silence of Passions, balm of angry sore,
Suspense of lives, security of fears,
Wrath's lenitive, heart's ease, storms' calmest shore,
Sense's and soul's reprieval from all cumbers,
Benumbing sense of ill with quiet slumbers.

Lazar at Pity's gate I ulcered lie
Craving the refuse crumbs of children's plate;
My sores I lay in view to Mercy's eye,
My rags bear witness of my poor estate:
The worms of Conscience that within me swarm,
Prove that my plaints are less than is my harm.

TO CHRIST CRUCIFIED

ANONYMOUS (Sixteenth or Seventeenth Century)

I am not moved to love Thee, O my Lord,
    By any longing for Thy Promised Land;
    Nor by the fear of hell am I unmanned
To cease from my transgressing deed or word.
'Tis Thou Thyself dost move me,—Thy blood poured
    Upon the cross from nailed foot and hand;
    And all the wounds that did Thy body brand;
And all Thy shame and bitter death's award.

Yea, to Thy heart am I so deeply stirred
    That I would love Thee were no heaven on high,—
That I would fear, were hell a tale absurd!
Such my desire, all questioning grows vain;
    Though hope deny me hope I still should sigh,
And as my love is now, it should remain.

From the Spanish by Thomas Walsh.

TO THE BLESSED SACRAMENT

HENRY CONSTABLE (1562-1613)

When Thee (O holy sacrificed Lamb)
In severed signs I white and liquid see,
As in thy body slain I think on Thee,
Which pale by shedding of Thy blood became.
And when again I do behold the same
Veiled in white to be received of me,
Thou seemest in thy sindon wrapt to be
Like to a corse, whose monument I am.
Buried in me, unto my soul appear,
Prison'd in earth, and banished from Thy sight,
Like our forefathers who in Limbo were.
Clear thou my thoughts, as thou didst give them light,
And as thou others freed from purging fire
Quench in my heart the flames of bad desire.

TO OUR BLESSED LADY

Henry Constable

In that (O Queen of Queens) thy birth was free
From guilt, which others do of grace bereave,
When in their mothers' womb they life receive
God as his sole-borne daughter loved thee.
To match thee like thy birth's nobility,
He thee His Spirit for thy spouse did leave
Of whom thou didst His only Son conceive,
And so wast linked to all the Trinity.
Cease then, O Queens who earthly crowns do wear,
To glory in the pomp of worldly things;
If men such high respect unto you bear
Which daughters, wives, and mothers are of Kings,
What honour should unto that Queen be done
Who had your God for Father, Spouse and Son?

THE LULLABY

Lope de Vega Carpio (1562-1635)

As through the palms ye wander
O Angels of the Blest,
Bend down the branches yonder
To shield my Darling's rest.

O palm-trees stirred and shaken
By every breath that blows,
Lest Bethlehem awaken,
Sway lightly for repose.

Soft sleep serenely squander
From out your dreamy breast;
Bend down the branches yonder
To shield my Darling's rest.

The heavenly Babe is weary
And droops His forehead there;
His tears for earth so dreary
Have dimmed His eyes with care.

Ah, let His young brows ponder;
Come, ease His heart distressed;
Bend down the branches yonder
To shield my Darling's rest.

Ye bitter frosts, congealing
The dampness of the night,
Let me from chill concealing,
Caress and warm Him tight.

Weave your embraces fonder,
O Angels of the Blest,
Bend down the branches yonder
To shield my Darling's rest.

From the Spanish by Thomas Walsh.

THE GOOD SHEPHERD

Lope de Vega Carpio

Shepherd! who with thine amorous, sylvan song
   Hast broken the slumber that encompassed me,
   Who mad'st thy crook from the accursed tree
On which thy powerful arms were stretched so long!
Lead me to mercy's ever flowing fountains;
   For thou my shepherd, guard, and guide shalt be;
   I will obey thy voice, and wait to see
Thy feet all beautiful upon the mountains.

Hear, Shepherd, thou who for thy flock art dying,
   Oh, wash away these scarlet sins, for thou
   Rejoicest at the contrite sinner's vow.
Oh, wait! to thee my weary soul is crying,
   Wait for me; yet why ask it, when I see,
   With feet nailed to the cross, thou'rt waiting still for
     me!

From the Spanish by H. W. Longfellow.

TOMORROW

Lope de Vega Carpio

Lord, what am I, that with unceasing care
  Thou did'st seek after me, that thou did'st wait,
  Wet with unhealthy dews, before my gate,
And pass the gloomy nights of winter there?
Oh, strange delusion, that I did not greet
  Thy blest approach, and oh, to heaven how lost
  If my ingratitude's unkindly frost
Has chilled the bleeding wounds upon thy feet.

How oft my guardian angel gently cried,
  "Soul, from thy casement look, and thou shalt see
How he persists to knock and wait for thee!"
  And oh, how often to that voice of sorrow,
"Tomorrow we will open," I replied,
  And when the morrow came I answered still
    "Tomorrow."
      From the Spanish by H. W. Longfellow.

TO MARY MAGDALEN

Bartolomé Leonardo de Argensola (1564-1631)

Blessèd, yet sinful one, and broken-hearted!
The crowd are pointing at the thing forlorn,
In wonder and in scorn!
Thou weepest days of innocence departed;
Thou weepest, and thy tears have power to move
The Lord to pity and love.

The greatest of thy follies is forgiven,
Even for the least of all the tears that shine
On that pale cheek of thine.
Thou didst kneel down to Him who came from heaven,
Evil and ignorant, and thou shalt rise
Holy and pure and wise.

It is not much that to the fragrant blossom
The ragged briar should change, the bitter fir
Distil Arabian myrrh;
Nor that, upon the wintry desert's bosom,
The harvest should rise plenteous, and the swain
Bear home the abundant grain.

But come and see the bleak and barren mountains
Thick to their tops with roses; come and see
Leaves on the dry dead tree;
The perished plant, set out by living fountains,
Grow fruitful, and its beauteous branches rise,
Forever, to the skies!

From the Spanish by William Cullen Bryant.

OUR LADY'S LULLABY

RICHARD VERSTEGAN (ROWLANDS) (1565-1620)

Upon my lap my Sovereign sits,
And sucks upon my breast;
Meanwhile, his love sustains my life,
And gives my body rest.
    Sing lullaby, my little Boy.
    Sing lullaby, my life's Joy.

When thou hast taken thy repast,
Repose, my Babe, on me;
So may thy Mother and thy Nurse
Thy cradle also be.
    Sing lullaby.

My Babe, My Bliss, My Child, My Choice,
My Fruit, my Flower, and Bud,
My Jesus, and my only Joy,
The Sum of all my good.
    Sing lullaby.

Thy fruit of death from Paradise
Made thee exilèd mourn;
My Fruit of Life to Paradise
Makes joyful thy return.
    Sing lullaby.

The shepherds left their keeping sheep
For joy to see my Lamb;
How may I more rejoice to see
Myself to be the Dam.
    Sing lullaby.

Three kings their treasure hither brought
Of incense, myrrh and gold,
The heaven's Treasure and the King
That here they might behold.
    Sing lullaby.

One sort an angel did direct;
A star did guide the other;
And all the fairest Son to see
That ever had a mother.
    Sing lullaby, my little Boy;
    Sing lullaby, my life's Joy.

THE DIVINE PASSION

FRAY HORTENSIO FELIS DE PARAVICINO Y ARTEAGA (1580-1633)

Pierced are Thy feet, O Lord, pierced are Thy hands;
  Thy head a shaggy grove of bitter thorn;
  Thou hangest on the shameful tree of scorn;
Thy woe my feeble sense half understands!
Ye who love God and who would light the brands
  Of righteous vengeance 'gainst such outrage lorn,
  Look, these are things of wonder made to warn
The hearts of Jew and Greek and Roman lands!

'Tis ye have caused this anguish, of which ye,
    Dishonest, are a witness, judge and part—
        Your sin against this innocence makes war!
O mortal, in your ceaseless wrongs ye see
    The silent victim—I would charge your heart
        With malice that against its God it bore.

From the Spanish by Thomas Walsh.

DEATH WARNINGS

Francisco de Quevedo y Villegas (1580-1645)

I look upon my native city's wall
    That once was mighty, now a ruined mass
    Worn with the march of years where feebly pass
Away the strength and vigor once o'er all.
I sally to the fields where sunbeams fall
    To lap the iceless streams, and shadows glass
    The mountain pastures where the flocks at grass
Lament the swiftness of the day's recall.

I enter in my house, the trophies there
    Displayed are faded out and growing old;
        My staff is bending weak beneath my weight;
I see my sword worn out beyond repair;
    And not a single thing my eyes behold
        But speaks the word of Death's impending fate.

From the Spanish by Thomas Walsh.

TO A CLOISTRESS

Juan de Tassis (1582-1622)

Thou who hast fled from life's enchanted bowers
    In youth's gay spring, in beauty's glowing morn,
Leaving thy bright array, thy path of flowers,
    For the rude convent-garb and couch of thorn;

Thou that escaping from a world of cares,
  Hast found thy haven in devotion's fane,
As to the port the fearful bark repairs,
  To shun the midnight perils of the main;

Now the glad hymn, the strain of rapture pour
  While on thy soul the beams of glory rise!
For if the pilot hail the welcome shore
  With shouts of triumph swelling to the skies,
Oh, how should'st thou the exulting pæan raise
Now heaven's bright harbor opens to thy gaze!
                From the Spanish by Felicia D. Hemans.

THE ASSUMPTION

SIR JOHN BEAUMONT (1583-1627)

Who is she that ascends so high,
  Next the Heavenly King,
Round about whom Angels fly
  And her praises sing?

Who is she that, adorned with light,
  Makes the sun her robe,
At whose feet the queen of night
  Lays her changing globe?

To that crown direct thine eye,
  Which her head attires;
There thou mayst her name descry
  Writ in starry fires.

This is she in whose pure womb
  Heaven's Prince remained;
Therefore in no earthly tomb
  Can she be contained.

Heaven she was, which held that fire,
  Whence the world took light,
And to Heaven doth now aspire
  Flames with flames t' unite.

She that did so clearly shine
When our day begun,
See how bright her beams decline
Now she sits with the Sun.

THE HYMN OF ADAM

JOOST VAN DEN VONDEL (1587-1679)

O Father, we approach Thy throne,
Who bidst the glorious sun arise,
All-good, almighty and all-wise
Great Source of all things, God alone!

We see Thee, brighter than the rays
Of the bright sun, we see Thee shine!
As in a fountain, light divine,
We see Thee, endless fount of days!

We see Thee who our frame hast wrought
With one swift word from senseless clay;
Waked with one glance of heavenly ray
Our never dying souls from naught.

Those souls Thou lightedst with the spark
At Thy pure fire; and gracious still,
Gav'st immortality, free-will,
And language not involved in dark!
From the Dutch by Sir John Bowring.

DIALOGUE AT THE CROSS

FREDERICK SPEE, S.J. (1591-1635)

Jesus:

O Mother dear, didst thou but hear
My plaint of desolation,
Thy tender heart would burst apart
With grief of separation!

I am not stone, yet all alone
  I hush My soul's outcrying,—
Alone to tread the wine-press red,
  To bear the pain of dying.

My lips are dumb, the night has come;
  Ah! solace I might borrow
Had I but thee to bide with Me
  In this wild waste of sorrow.

Mary:

"Gentle moon and stars of midnight,
  Day's fierce orb, and brooklets fair,
Golden apples born of sunshine,
  Precious pearls and jewels rare,—
All things glorious, all things shining,"
  Thus the sorrowing Mother spake;
"E'en ye bright, transfigured faces,
  Mourn with me for Jesus' sake.

"Sparkle, gleam, and glow no longer:
  Only moan and mourn for Him.
Shine not, shine not, weep forever,
  Till your thousand eyes are dim;
For the mighty One has fallen,
  And my Beautiful is slain;
In the dense wood pierced, my Shepherd,—
  Weep ye, weep ye for my pain!
O most oppressed of all oppressed,
  Heart of my heart, my all, my Son!
Grief's keenest sword doth pierce my breast:
  I die with Thee, my only one!
Alas! the pain is all too great,
Since, living, still I share Thy fate.

"Yes, mine Thou wert to bear and rear
  Through life and light, and pain and loss;
And now, ten thousand times more dear,
  I yield Thee to the cruel cross!"
        From the German by Mary E. Mannix.

ON THE VICTORY OF POLAND AND HER ALLIES OVER THE SULTAN OSMAN, 1621

CASIMIR SARBIEWSKI, S.J. (1596-1640)

The air was calm, the sun was low,
Calm was the mighty river's flow,
And silently with footsteps slow
    Labored the yoke;
When fervently with patriot glow,
    The veteran spoke:

"Halt ye, my oxen! Pause we here
Where valor's vestiges appear,
And Islam's relics far and near
    Lurk in the soil;
While Poland on victorious spear
    Rests from her toil.

"Aye! well she may triumphant rest,
Adorn with glory's plume her crest,
And wear of victory the vest,
    Elate and flushed;
Oft was the Paynim's pride repressed—
    Here it was crushed.

"Here the tremendous deed was done,
Here the transcendent trophy won,
Where fragments lie of sword and gun,
    And lance and shield,
And Turkey's giant skeleton
    Cumbers the field!

"Pale and aghast the Crescent fled,
Joyful we clove each turbanned head,
Heaping with holocausts of dead
    The foeman's camp;
Loud echoed o'er their gory bed
    Our horsemen's tramp.

"Sorrow, derision, scorn and hate,
Upon the proud one's footsteps wait;
Both in the field and in the gate
          Accursed, abhorred;
And be his halls made desolate
          With fire and sword!"

But now upon the glorious stream
The sun flung out his parting beam,
The soldier-swain unyoked his team,
          Yet still he chanted
The livelong eve:—and glory's dream
          His pillow haunted—.

From the Latin Ode IV, translated by Francis S. Mahony
(Father Prout).

A SONG OF NUNS

JAMES SHIRLEY (1596-1666)

O Fly, my soul! What hangs upon
     Thy drooping wings
And weighs them down
     With love of gaudy mortal things?

The sun is now the East; each shade
     As he doth rise
Is shorter made
     That earth may lessen to our eyes.

Oh, be but careless then, and play
     Until the Star of Peace
Hide all his beams in dark recess.
Poor pilgrims needs must lose their way
     When all the shadows do increase.

THE HOLY EUCHARIST

PEDRO CALDERON DE LA BARCA (1600-1681)

Honey in the lion's mouth,
Emblem mystical, divine,
How the sweet and strong combine;
Cloven rock for Israel's drouth;
Treasure-house of golden grain
By our Joseph laid in store,
In his brethren's famine sore
Freely to dispense again;
Dew on Gideon's snowy fleece;
Well from bitter turned to sweet;
Shew-bread laid in order sweet,
Bread whose cost doth ne'er increase,
Though no rain in April fall;
Horeb's manna freely given
Showered in white dew from heaven,
Marvellous, angelical;
Weightiest bunch of Canaan's vine;
Cake to strengthen and sustain
Through long days of desert pain;
Salem's monarch's bread and wine;—
Thou the antidote shall be
Of my sickness and my sin,
Consolation, medicine,
Life and Sacrament to me.

From the Spanish by R. C. Trench.

THE CROSS

PEDRO CALDERON DE LA BARCA

Tree which heaven has willed to dower
With that true fruit whence we live,
As that other death did give;
Of new Eden loveliest flower;
Bow of light, that in worst hour

Of the worst flood signal true
O'er the world, of mercy threw;
Fair plant, yielding sweetest wine;
Of our David harp divine;
Of our Moses tables new;
Sinner am I, therefore I
Claim upon thy mercies make;
Since alone for sinners' sake
God on thee endured to die.

From the Spanish by R. C. Trench.

THE DREAM CALLED LIFE

Pedro Calderon de la Barca

A dream it was in which I found myself.
And you that hail me now, then hailed me king,
In a brave palace that was all my own,
Within, and all without it, mine; until,
Drunk with excess of majesty and pride,
Methought I towered so big and swelled so wide
That of myself I burst the glittering bubble
Which my ambition had about me blown
And all again was darkness. Such a dream
As this, in which I may be walking now;
Dispensing solemn justice to you shadows,
Who make believe to listen; but anon
Kings, princes, captains, warriors, plume and steel,
Ay, even with all your airy theatre,
May flit into the air you seem to rend
With acclamations, leaving me to wake
In the dark tower; or dreaming that I wake
From this that waking is; or this and that,
Both waking and both dreaming; *such* a doubt
Confounds and clouds our mortal life about.
But whether wake or dreaming, this I know,
How dreamwise human glories come and go;
Whose momentary tenure not to break,
Walking as one who knows he soon may wake,

So fairly carry the full cup, so well
Disordered insolence and passion quell.
That there be nothing after to upbraid
Dreamer or doer in the part he played;
Whether tomorrow's dawn shall break the spell,
Or the last trumpet of the eternal Day,
When dreaming, with the night, shall pass away.
                    From the Spanish by Edward Fitzgerald.

THE DEMON SPEAKS

Pedro Calderon de la Barca

From the *Magico Prodigioso*

Since thou desirest, I will then unveil
Myself to thee—for in myself I am
A world of happiness and misery;
This I have lost, and that I must lament
Forever. In my attributes I stood
So high and so heroically great,
In lineage so supreme, and with a genius
Which penetrated with a glance the world
Beneath my feet, that won by my high merit
A king—whom I may call the King of Kings,
Because all others tremble in their pride
Before the terrors of His countenance,
In His high palace roofed with brightest gems
Of living light—call them the stars of heaven—
Named me His counsellor. But the high praise
Stung me with pride and envy, and I rose
In mighty competition, to ascend
His seat, and place my foot triumphantly
Upon His subject thrones. Chastised I know
The depth to which ambition falls; too mad
Was the attempt, and yet more mad were now
Repentance of the irrevocable deed:—
Therefore I chose this ruin with the glory
Of not to be subdued, before the shame
Of reconciling me with Him who reigns

By coward cession. Nor was I alone,
Nor am I now, nor shall I be alone;
And there was hope, and there may still be hope.
For many suffrages among His vassals
Hailed me their lord, and many still
Are mine, and many more perchance shall be.
Thus vanquished, though in fact victorious,
I left His seat of empire, from mine eye
Shooting forth poisonous lightning, while my words
With inauspicious thunderings shook heaven,
Proclaiming vengeance, public as my wrong,
And imprecating on His prostrate slaves
Rapine, and death, and outrage. Then I sailed
Over the mighty fabric of the world,
A pirate ambushed in its pathless sands,
A lynx crouched watchfully among its caves
And craggy shores; and I have wandered over
The expanse of these wide wildernesses
In this great ship——

From the Spanish by Percy Bysshe Shelley.

A HEAVENLIE VISITOR

ANONYMOUS (Early Seventeenth Century)

Yet if His Majesty our sovereign lord
  Should of his own accord
Friendly himself invite,
And say, "I'll be your guest tomorrow night,"
How we should stir ourselves, call and command
All hands to work! "Let no man idle stand.
Set me fine Spanish tables in the hall.
See they be fitted all;
Let there be room to eat,
And order taken that there want no meat.
See every sconce and candlestick made bright
That without tapers they may give a light.
Look to the presence; are the carpets spread,
The dazie o'er the head,

The cushions in the chairs,
And all the candles lighted on the stairs?
Perfume the chambers, and in any case
Let each man give attendance in his place."

Thus if the king were coming would we do,
And 'twere good reasons too;
For 'tis a duteous thing
To show all honor to an earthly king.
And after all our travail and our cost,
So he be pleased, to think no labor lost—
But at the coming of the King of Heaven
All's set at six and seven;
We wallow in our sin.
Christ cannot find a chamber in the inn.
We entertain Him always like a stranger
And as at first, still lodge Him in a manger.

WHILE TO BETHLEHEM WE ARE GOING

SISTER VIOLANTE DO CEO (1601-1693)

While to Bethlehem we are going,
Tell me, Blas, to cheer the road,
Tell me why this lovely Infant
Quitted His divine abode?—
"From that world to bring to this
Peace, which, of all earthly blisses,
Is the brightest, purest bliss."

Wherefore from His throne exalted,
Came He on His earth to dwell—
All His pomp an humble manger,
All His court a narrow cell?—
"From that world to bring to this
Peace, which, of all earthly blisses,
Is the brightest, purest bliss."

Why did He, the Lord eternal,
Mortal pilgrim deign to be,
He who fashioned for His glory
Boundless immortality?—
"From that world to bring to this
Peace, which, of all earthly blisses,
Is the brightest, purest bliss."

Well then! let us haste to Bethlehem,
Thither let us haste and rest,
For of all heaven's gifts the sweetest
Sure is peace,—the sweetest, best.
From the Portuguese by John Bowring.

THE NIGHT OF MARVELS

SISTER VIOLANTE DO CEO

In such a marvellous night, so fair
    And full of wonder strange and new,
Ye shepherds of the vale, declare
    Who saw the greatest wonder? Who?

First.   I saw the trembling fire look wan.
Second.   I saw the sun shed tears of blood.
Third.   I saw a God become a man.
Fourth.   I saw a man become a God.

O wondrous marvels! at the thought,
    The bosom's awe and reverence move,
But who such prodigies has wrought?
    What gave such wonders birth? 'Twas love!

What called from heaven that flame divine,
    Which streams in glory from above;
And bade it o'er earth's bosom shine,
    And bless us with its brightness? Love!

Who bade the glorious sun arrest
    His course, and o'er heaven's concave move
In tears,—the saddest, loneliest
    Of the celestial orbs? 'Twas love!

Who raised the human race so high,
  Even to the starry seats above,
That for our mortal progeny,
  A man became a God? 'Twas love!

Who humbled from the seats of light
  Their Lord, all human woes to prove;
Led the great source of day—to night;
  And made of God a man? 'Twas love!

Yes, love has wrought, and love alone,
  The victories all,—beneath,—above,—
And earth and heaven shall shout as one,
  The all-triumphant song of love.

The song through all heaven's arches ran,
  And told the wondrous tales aloud,—
The trembling fire that looked so wan,
  The weeping sun behind the cloud.
A God—a God! becomes a man!
  A mortal man becomes a God!

From the Portuguese by John Bowring.

AMOR MYSTICUS

SISTER MARCELA DE CARPIO (1605-1688)

Let them say to my Lover
That here I lie!
The thing of His pleasure,
His slave am I.

Say that I seek Him
Only for love,
And welcome are tortures
My passion to prove.

Love giving gifts
Is suspicious and cold;
I have all, my Belovèd
When Thee I hold.

Hope and devotion
The good may gain;
I am but worthy
Of passion and pain.

So noble a Lord
None serves in vain,
For the pay of my love
Is my love's sweet pain.

I love Thee, to love Thee,—
No more I desire;
By faith is nourished
My love's strong fire.

I kiss Thy hands
When I feel their blows;
In the place of caresses
Thou givest me woes.

But in Thy chastising
Is joy and peace.
O Master and Love,
Let Thy blows not cease.

Thy beauty, Belovèd,
With scorn is rife,
But I know that Thou lovest me
Better than life.

And because Thou invest me
Lover of mine,
Death can but make me
Utterly Thine.

I die with longing
Thy face to see;
Oh! sweet is the anguish
Of death to me!

From the Spanish by John Hay.

NOX NOCTI INDICAT SCIENTIAM

WILLIAM HABINGTON (1605-1654)

When I survey the bright
　　Celestial sphere;
So rich with jewels hung, that night
　　Doth like an Ethiop bride appear:

My soul her wings doth spread
　　And heavenward flies,
The Almighty's mysteries to read
　　In the large volume of the skies.

For the bright firmament
　　Shoots forth no flame
So silent, but is eloquent
　　In speaking the Creator's name.

No unregarded star
　　Contracts its light
Into so small a character
　　Removed far from our human sight,

But if we steadfast look
　　We shall discern
In it, as in some holy book,
　　How man may heavenly knowledge learn.

It tells the conqueror
　　That far-stretched power,
Which his proud dangers traffic for,
　　Is but the triumph of an hour:

That from the farthest North,
　　Some nation may,
Yet undiscovered, issue forth,
　　And o'er his new-got conquest sway,

Some nation yet shut in
  With hills of ice
May be let out to scourge his sin,
  Till they shall equal him in vice.

And then they likewise shall
  Their ruin have;
For as yourselves your empires fall,
  And every kingdom hath a grave.

Thus those celestial fires,
  Though seeming mute,
The fallacy of our desires
  And all the pride of life confute:

For they have watched since first
  The world had birth;
And found sin in itself accursed,
  And nothing permanent on earth.

EPITAPH FOR ELIZABETH RANQUET

Pierre Corneille (1606-1684)

Shed not a tear upon this burial place,
  O stranger; here is lain the precious bed,
Where limbs most pure unto their ashes trace,
  But warmth of heart with constant flame is fed.
Ere Nature claimed its own, her soul to grace
  Had raised her far beyond what vision shed;
In her Creator joined, in full embrace,
  She walked on earth but heaven knew her tread.

The needy more than she her riches knew;
In help and humbleness her joy was true;
  A sigh of love was latest of her sighs.
O stranger, take her lovely warmth for thine;
  Weep not that exiled from today she lies,
But learn that death is not, if such a fate be thine.
                    From the French by Roderick Gill.

ON ASCENDING A HILL LEADING TO A CONVENT

FRANCISCO MANUEL DE MELLO (1608-1666)

Pause not with lingering foot, O pilgrim, here,
   Pierce the deep shadows of the mountain-side;
Firm be thy step, thy heart unknown to fear,
   To brighter worlds this thorny path will guide.
Soon shall thy foot approach the calm abode
   So near the mansions of supreme delight;
Pause not, but tread this consecrated road
   'Tis the dark basis of the heavenly height.

Behold, to cheer thee on the toilsome way,
   How many a fountain glitters down the hill!
Pure gales inviting softly round thee play,
   Bright sunshine guides—and wilt thou linger still?
Oh, enter there, where, freed from human strife,
Hope is reality and time is life.
                    From the Spanish by Felicia D. Hemans.

DEATH'S APOLOGY

FRANCISCO MANUEL DE MELLO

Once I saw Death go sporting through a plain
   Of living men and some perceived him there;
   The old, of what they did all unaware,
Each moment ran against him to their bane.
The young, trusting their youth, that of the pain
   Of death knows nothing, gave him not a care,

   Purblind were all, none sought to flee the snare,
The while his finger counted out the train.

Then he prepared to shoot, closing each eye;
  He fired and missed. I that.his aim did see
    Thus reckless shouted: "Butcher, hold thy hand!"
He turned and "Such is war," was his reply;
  "If you pass life without a glance at me,
    How greater care of me can you demand?"
                    From the Spanish by Edgar Prestage.

TWO WENT UP TO THE TEMPLE TO PRAY

RICHARD CRASHAW (1613-1649)

Two went to pray? Oh, rather say
One went to brag, the other to pray;

One stands up close and treads on high
Where the other dares not lend his eye;

One nearer to God's altar trod,
The other to the altar's God.

THE FLAMING HEART

RICHARD CRASHAW

Upon the Book and Pictures of the Seraphical Saint Teresa,
as She is Usually Expressed with a Seraphim beside Her.

Well-meaning readers! you that come as friends,
And catch the precious name this piece pretends,
Make not too much haste to admire
That fair-cheek'd fallacy of fire.
That is a seraphim, they say,
And this the great Teresia.
Readers, be ruled by me: and make
Here a well-placed and wise mistake;
You must transpose the picture quite,
And spell it wrong to make it right;
Read him for her, and her for him,
And call the Saint the seraphim.

Painter, what didst thou understand
To put her dart into his hand?
See, even the years and size of him
Shows this the mother-seraphim.
This is the mistress-flame; and duteous he
Her happy fire-works, here, comes down to see.
O most poor-spirited of men!
Had thy cold pencil kissed her pen
Thou couldst not so unkindly err
To show us this faint shade for her.
Why, man, this speaks pure mortal frame;
And mocks with female frost Love's manly flame.
One would suspect thou meanst to paint
Some weak, inferior woman-saint.
But had thy pale-faced purple took
Fire from the burning cheeks of that bright book,
Thou wouldst on her have heaped up all
That could be formed seraphical;
Whate'er this youth of fire wears fair,
Rosy fingers, radiant hair,
Glowing cheeks and glist'ring wings,
All those fair and fragrant things,
But before all, that fiery dart
Had filled the hand of this great heart.
Do then, as equal right requires:
Since his the blushes be, and hers the fires,
Resume and rectify thy rude design;
Undress thy seraphim into mine;
Redeem this injury of thy art;
Give him the veil, give her the dart,
Give him the veil that he may cover
The red cheeks of the rivall'd lover;
Ashamed that our world now can show
Nests of new seraphims here below.
Give her the dart, for it is she
(Fair youth) shoots both thy shaft and thee;
Say, all ye wise and well-pierced hearts
That live and die amidst her darts,
What is't your tasteful spirits do prove
In that rare life of her and Love?

Say, and bear witness. Sends she not
A seraphim at every shot?
What magazines of immortal arms there shine!
Heaven's great artillery in each love-spun line.
Give then the dart to her who gives the flame;
Give him the veil, who gives the shame.
But if it be the frequent fate
Of worse faults to be fortunate:
If all's prescription, and proud wrong
Harken not to an humble song;
For all the gallantry of him,
Give me the suffering seraphim.
His be the bravery of all those bright things,
The glowing cheeks, the glistering wings;
The rosy hand, the radiant dart;
Leave her alone the flaming heart.
Leave her that; and thou shalt leave her
Not one loose shaft, but Love's whole quiver;
For in Love's field was never found
A nobler weapon than a wound.
Love's passives are his activ'st part,
The wounded is the wounding heart
O heart! equal poise of Love's both parts,
Big alike with wound and darts.
Live in these conquering leaves: live all the same;
And walk through all tongues one triumphant flame.
Live here, great heart; and love, and die, and kill;
And bleed, and wound; and yield and conquer still.
Let this immortal life where'er it comes
Walk in a crowd of loves and martyrdoms.
Let mystic deaths wait on't; and wise souls be
The love-slain witnesses of this life of thee.
O sweet incendiary! show here thy art,
Upon this carcass of a hard cold heart;
Let all thy scattered shafts of light that play
Among the leaves of thy large books of day,
Combined against this breast at once break in
And take away from me myself and sin;
This gracious robbery shall thy bounty be,
And my best fortunes such fair spoils of me.

O thou undaunted daughter of desires!
By all thy dower of lights and fires;
By all the eagle in thee, all the dove;
By all thy lives and deaths of love;
By thy large draughts of intellectual day
And by thy thirsts of love, more large than they;
By all thy brim-filled bowls of fierce desire,
By thy last morning's draught of liquid fire;
By the full kingdom of that final kiss
That seized thy parting soul, and sealed thee His;
By all the heavens thou hast in Him
(Fair sister of the seraphim!)
By all of Him we have in thee;
Leave nothing of thyself in me.
Let me so read thy life, that I
Unto all life of mine may die.

QUAERIT JESUM SUUM MARIA

RICHARD CRASHAW

And is he gone, whom these arms held but now
    Their hope, their vow?
Did ever grief and joy in one poor heart
    So soon change part?
He's gone; the fair'st flower that e'er bosom dress'd,
    My soul's sweet rest.
My womb's chaste pride is gone, my heaven-born boy:
    And where is joy?
He's gone; and his lov'd steps to wait upon
    My joy is gone.
My joys and he are gone, my grief and I
    Alone must lie.
He's gone; not leaving with me, till he come,
    One smile at home.
Oh, come then, bring Thy mother her lost joy:
    Oh come, sweet boy.
Make haste and come, or e'er my grief and I
    Make haste and die.

Peace, heart! the heavens are angry, all their spheres
   Rival thy tears.
I was mistaken, some fair sphere or other
   Was thy blest mother.
What but the fairest heaven could own the birth
   Of so fair earth?
Yet sure thou didst lodge here; this womb of mine
   Was once call'd thine.
Oft have these arms thy cradle envied,
   Beguil'd thy bed.
Oft to thy easy ears hath this shrill tongue
   Trembled and sung.
Oft have I wrapped thy slumbers in soft airs,
   And strok'd thy cares.
Oft hath this hand those silken casements kept,
   While their suns slept.
Oft have my hungry kisses made thine eyes
   Too early rise.
Oft have I spoil'd my kisses' daintiest diet,
   To spare thy quiet.
Oft from this breast to thine my love-toss'd heart
   Hath leapt, to part.
Oft my lost soul have I been glad to seek
   On thy soft cheek.
Oft have these arms, alas, show'd to these eyes
   Their now lost joys.
Dawn then to me, thou morn of mine own day,
   And let heaven stay.
Oh, would'st thou here still fix thy fair abode,
   My bosom God:
What hinders but my bosom still might be
   Thy heaven to Thee?

THE HOLY NAME OF JESUS

Richard Crashaw

"Fair, flowery Name! in none but Thee
And Thy nectareal fragrancy
   Hourly there meets
A universal synod of all sweets;

By whom it is defined thus,
    That no perfume
    For ever shall presume
To pass for odoriferous
But such alone whose sacred pedigree
Can prove itself some kin, sweet Name, to Thee.
    Sweet Name! in Thy each syllable
    A thousand blest Arabias dwell.
Oh! that it were as it was wont to be,
When Thy old friends, of fire all full of Thee,
Fought against frowns with smiles! gave glorious chase
To persecutions, and against the face
Of death and fiercest dangers durst, with brave
And sober pace, march on to meet a grave!
On their bold breasts above the world they bore Thee,
And to the teeth of hell stood up to teach Thee,
In centre of their inmost souls they wore Thee,
Where rack and torments strove in vain to reach Thee.
    Each wound of theirs was Thy new morning,
    And reinthroned Thee in Thy rosy nest,
With blush of thine own blood Thy day adorning;
    It was the wit of love o'erflowed the bounds
    Of wrath, and made the way through all these wounds.

    "Welcome, dear, all-adored Name!
      For sure there is no knee
        That knows not Thee;
    Or, if there be such sons of shame,
      Alas! what will they do
    When stubborn rocks shall bow,
And hills hang down their heaven-saluting heads,
    To seek for humble beds
Of dust, where, in the bashful shades of night,
Next to their own low nothing they may lie,
And couch before the dazzling light of Thy dread Majesty?
    They that by love's mild dictate now
      Will not adore Thee
    Shall then with just confusion bow
      And break before Thee."

THE SHEPHERDS' HYMN

RICHARD CRASHAW

We saw Thee in Thy balmy nest,
  Young dawn of our eternal Day;
We saw Thine eyes break from their East,
  And chase the trembling shades away:
We saw Thee: and we blessed the sight,
We saw Thee by Thine own sweet light.

Poor world, said I, what wilt thou do
  To entertain this starry Stranger?
Is this the best thou canst bestow—
  A cold and not too cleanly manger?
Contend, the powers of Heaven and Earth,
To fit a bed for this huge birth.

Proud world, said I, cease your contest,
  And let the mighty babe alone;
The phoenix builds the phoenix' nest,
  Love's architecture is his own.
The babe whose birth embraves this morn,
Made His own bed ere He was born.

I saw the curl'd drops, soft and slow,
  Come hovering o'er the place's head;
Offering their whitest sheets of snow,
  To furnish the fair infant's bed.
Forbear, said I, be not too bold;
Your fleece is white, but 'tis cold.

I saw th' obsequious Seraphim
  Their rosy fleece of fire bestow,
For well they now can spare their wing.
  Since Heaven itself lies here below.
Well done, said I; but are you sure
Your down, so warm, will pass for pure?

No, no! your King's not yet to seek
  Where to repose His royal head;
See, see, how soon His new-bloom'd cheek
  'Twixt mother's breasts is gone to bed!
Sweet choice, said we! no way but so,
Not to lie cold, yet sleep in snow.

She sings thy tears asleep, and dips
  Her kisses in Thy weeping eye;
She spreads the red leaves of Thy lips,
  That in their buds yet blushing lie.
She 'gainst those mother diamonds tries
The points of her young eagle's eyes.

Welcome, all wonders in one sight!
  Eternity shut in a span!
Summer in Winter, Day in Night!
  Heaven in Earth, and God in Man!
Great little One! whose all-embracing birth
Lifts Earth to Heaven, stoops Heaven to Earth.

Welcome, tho' not to gold nor silk,
  To more than Caesar's birthright is;
Two sister-seas of Virgin-milk,
  With many a rarely temper'd kiss,
That breathes at once both maid and mother,
Warms in the one, cools in the other.

Welcome, tho' not to those gay flies,
  Gilded i' the beams of earthly kings;
Slippery souls in shining eyes,
  But to poor shepherds, homespun things,
Whose wealth's their flocks, whose wit's to be
Well-read in their simplicity.

Yet, when young April's husband-showers
  Shall bless the fruitful Maia's bed,
We'll bring the first-born of her flowers
  To kiss Thy feet, and crown Thy head;
To Thee, dread Lamb! whose love must keep
The shepherds more than they keep sheep.

To Thee, meek Majesty! soft King
 Of simple graces and sweet Loves:
Each of us his lamb will bring,
 Each his pair of silver doves:
Till burnt at last in fire of Thy fair eyes,
Ourselves become our own best sacrifice!

THE SHEPHERD FOLK GO TO BETHLEHEM

Nicolas Saboly (1614-1675)

To while the long, long road away
 There is no better thing, O!
Than flute and tambourine to play,
 (Mind the little bagpipe bring, O!)
 And "Noël, Noël, Noël!" pipe and sing, O!

So short, so short the road has been,
 Our journey's end is near, O!
Men, bare your heads ere you go in,
 With reverence draw near, O!
 Pipe "Noël, Noël, Noël!" loud and clear, O!

Ah me, dear God! the pretty one!
 Look how He takes the breast, O!
As if He never would have done,
 So tight His lips are pressed, O!
 Pipe "Noël, Noël, Noël!" Pipe your best, O!

I've brought good eggs and milk and flour
 And a little pipkin with me, O!
If I had fire, in half an hour,
 A fine good soup there'd be, O!
 Pipe "Noël, Noël, Noël," cheerily, O!

Half dead of cold is the sweet thing,
 See Joseph shiver and shake, O!
Quick, the straw and the faggots bring;
 Then what a blaze I'll make, O!
 Pipe "Noël, Noël, Noël!" the world to wake, O!

The little she-ass must crouch down there,
 Else the poor crib will fall, O!
Give me the ribbon from your hair
 To tie the ox in his stall, O!
And "Noël, Noël, Noël" pipe and call, O!

O Mary maiden, Mother of God!
 (Young, brown and sweet is she, O!)
It's time for us to take the road;
 We leave your good company, O!
Pipe "Noël, Noël, Noël!" lustily, O!

From the Provençal by Anne Macdonell.

THE SOUL WHEREIN GOD DWELLS

ANGELUS SILESIUS (JOHANN SCHEFFLER) (1624-1677)

The soul wherein God dwells,
What church could holier be?
Becomes a walking-tent
Of heavenly majesty.
How far from here to heaven?
Not very far, my friend,
A single, hearty step
Will all the journey end.
Though Christ a thousand times
In Bethlehem be born,
If He's not born in thee,
Thy soul is still forlorn.
The cross on Golgotha
Will never save thy soul:
The cross in thine own heart
Alone can make thee whole.
Hold thou—where runnest thou?
Know heaven is in thee—
Seek'st thou for God elsewhere,
His face thou'lt never see.
Oh, would thy heart but be
A manger for His birth;
God would once more become

A child upon the earth.
Go out, God will go in;
Die thou—and let Him live;
Be not—and He will be;
Wait, and He'll all things give.
O shame, a silk-worm works
And spins till it can fly;
And thou, my soul, wilt still
On thine old earth-clod lie!
Anonymous Translation from the German.

SONG OF PRAISE TO MARY

ANGELUS SILESIUS (JOHANN SCHEFFLER)

Thee, O Mary, will I praise,
Love and serve thee all my days.
O thou clearest Morning Star,
I will sing thee near and far;
For through thee to us was given
Jesus, Lord of earth and heaven!

Like the dazzling sun at morn,
Light and splendor thee adorn;
Or as moon and stars endure,
Gentle, holy, chaste and pure.
Yet art thou a host, we know,
To protect us from the foe.

Radiant chariot of gold,
Bearing us into the fold;
Of true Solomon the throne,
Fleece of Gideon, peerless one;
Chosen vessel of the Lord,
Dwelling of the Almighty Word.
O thou brightest Morning Star,
I will sing thee near and far;
Thee, O Mary, will I praise,
Love and serve thee all my days!
From the German by Mary E. Mannix.

THE ROSE

Angelus Silesius (Johann Scheffler)

The rose that here our mortal eyes behold,
Through all eternity in God was old;
It flowers without a reason but to flower,
Nor seeks the idle eye to tell its power.
From the German by Thomas Walsh.

THE TREE OF THE CROSS

Angelus Silesius (Johann Scheffler)

Blest is he that seeketh rest
   In God's pastures green and quiet,
In the shadow of the Cross,
   Far from worldly toil and riot;
He is safe, on holy ground,
Though the tempest rage around.
Sun by day and moon by night
   Shall not there have power to harm him,
Hellish foes with subtle wiles
   Can not there succeed to charm him;
No true ill can him betide
Who beneath the Cross doth bide.
With the fruit that Tree doth bear
   He his hunger keen relieveth,
Closest union with his God
   Through that wondrous food receiveth.
Sweetest fruit, how blest is he
Who doth taste it worthily!
With the dew Christ's Wounds distil
   There his fainting soul he easeth,
Even as the panting hart
   At the brook its thirst appeaseth;
Christ's sweet Blood may well make whole
Every weak and parchèd soul.

Come, then, to the Cross all ye
　　Who do faint beneath your burden;
Rest beneath that Tree, and seek
　　There your labor's ample guerdon—
Peace, which nowhere can be found
Save upon that hallow'd ground.
Let me dwell beneath Thy Cross,
　　Lord, in life and death, I pray Thee;
Let no hostile powers thence
　　Drive me, Lord; do not gainsay me,
Who on earth no comfort own
Save Thy death and Cross alone!

　　　　　Anonymous Translation from the German.

ASCENSION HYMN

Jean-Baptiste de Santeuil (1630-1697)

O Christ, who mountest up the sky
To deck fair thrones for us on high,
Thine exiled sons in love restore
Unto their native land once more.

There gifts to all Thou dost afford,
Thyself shall be our great reward;
How brief below our time of pain!
How long our pleasure shall remain!

With eye unveiled and sated heart
We there shall see Thee as Thou art,
And tell in hymns of sweet accord
Our love and praise of Thee, O Lord.

Lest we be orphaned of Thy love,
Send down from Thy high halls above
The Spirit of adoption sweet,
Salvation's pledge, the Paraclete.

Jesu, to Thee our anthems tend
We shall be judged at time's last end;
To God the Father equal praise
And Holy Ghost through endless days.
From the Parisian Breviary by Allan G. McDougall.

THE CHURCH'S TESTIMONY

JOHN DRYDEN (1631-1700)

But, gracious God, how well dost Thou provide
For erring judgments an unerring guide!
Thy throne is darkness in the abyss of light,
A blaze of glory that forbids the sight.
O teach me to believe Thee thus concealed,
And search no further than Thyself revealed;
But her alone for my director take
Whom Thou hast promised never to forsake!
My thoughtless youth was winged with vain desires,
My manhood, long misled by wandering fires,
Followed false lights; and when their glimpse was gone,
My pride struck out new sparkles of her own.
Such was I, such by nature still I am;
Be Thine the glory, and be mine the shame!

CONVERSION

JOHN DRYDEN

Be vengeance wholly left to powers divine,
And let Heaven judge betwixt your sons and mine:
If joys hereafter must be purchased here
With loss of all that mortals hold so dear,
Then welcome infamy and public shame,
And, last, a long farewell to worldly fame.
'Tis said with ease, but oh, how hardly tried
By haughty souls to human honour tied!
O sharp convulsive pangs of agonizing pride!
Down then, thou rebel, never more to rise;
And what thou didst and dost so dearly prize,
That fame. that darling fame, make that thy sacrifice.

'Tis nothing thou hast given; then add thy tears
For a long race of unrepenting years:
'Tis nothing yet; yet all thou hast to give:
Then add those may-be years thou hast to live.
Yet nothing still: then poor and naked come,
Thy Father will receive his unthrift home,
And thy blest Saviour's book discharge the mighty sum.

CHORUS FROM ATHALIE

Jean Baptiste Racine (1639-1699)

The God whose goodness filleth every clime,
  Let all His creatures worship and adore;
Whose throne was reared before the birth of Time,
  To Him be glory now and evermore!

A Voice:

The sons of violence in vain
Would check His people's grateful strain
  And blot His sacred name.
Yet day to day His power declares,
His bounty every creature shares,
  His greatness all proclaim.

Another Voice:

Dispensing Light and Life at His behest,
Bursts forth the sun by Him in splendor drest;
But of almighty love a brighter sign,
Shines forth His law, pure, perfect and divine.
                    From the French by Charles Randolph.

PROVIDENCE

Vincenzo da Filicaja (1642-1707)

Just as a mother, with sweet, pious face,
  Yearns towards her little children from her seat,
Gives one a kiss, another an embrace,
  Takes this upon her knees, that on her feet;

And while from actions, looks, complaints, pretenses,
    She learns their feelings and their various will,
To this a look, to that a word, dispenses
And, whether stern or smiling, loves them still;

So Providence for us, high, infinite,
    Makes our necessities its watchful task,
        Hearkens to all our prayers, helps all our wants,
And even if it denies what seems our right,
    Either denies because 'twould have us ask,
        Or seems to deny, or in denying grants.

From the Italian by Leigh Hunt.

THE DIVINE NARCISSUS

Sister Juana Inéz de la Cruz (1651-1695)

From *The Auto Sacramental*

Seeking Narcissus in my weariness,
With never a rest to ease my vagrant feet,—
In longing and distress
From many days of journeying I greet
Alone the hedges green,
The only sign of where His step hath been.

Unto this bosky circle come, I yearn
Some tidings of my Well-Beloved to find,—
Though of the paths I learn
That this hath been His meadow twined
With flowery loveliness so rare
Naught but His kisses could have nursed them there.

How many, many days have I explored
The grove; and flower on flower, herb on herb,
Scented and tasted! Yea, without reward—
My heart a burden that my pains perturb,
My step a draggled vagabond,—to rove
Through Time turned centuries, and worlds a grove!

From the Spanish by Roderick Gill.

IN THE FACE OF GRIEF

Sister Juana Inéz de la Cruz

That twilight, dearest, as I spoke with thee,
  I saw in every act and lineament
  That not my words were meeting thine intent,
That 'twas my heart that thou desired'st of me.
And love upbearing me so faithfully
  O'er bonds impossible grew prevalent,
  Since in that flood of grievous tears was spent
My melting heart to seek thy clemency.

Enough of rigors, dearest, and of cares;
  Let not thy tyrant envies rack thee more,
Nor rancor still thy peace of spirit wear
  With senseless shadows and suspicions sore;
Since in those welling tears thou wert aware
  My broken heart thy piteous fingers bore.
                    From the Spanish by Thomas Walsh.

REDONDILLAS

Sister Juana Inéz de la Cruz

Stupid men, forever prone
  To fix the blame on woman's reason,
  When 'tis merely your own treason
That creates her fault alone!

With an unrestrained desire
  For her downfall you are scheming;
  You are of her virtues dreaming
While to ill alone you fire.

Her resistance you oppose,
  Then, all serious, attaint her;
  Fickle, light and faithless paint her,
Though 'twas you the rôle that chose.

Stupidly you would procure
  Baser for a nobler treasure;
  Making Thaïs of your pleasure
A Lucretia chaste and pure.

Nothing could be funnier
  Than the tale of him befouling
  His own mirror, and then scowling
When the image was a blur.

'Twixt your favor and disdain
  You should keep position civil,
  Blaming her if she shows evil,
Mocking not her goodness vain.

Nothing suits your peevish mood;
  You keep changing your opinion,
  Blaming her for harsh dominion,
And blaming her for being kind.

Who commits the greater fault
  In matters of a lawless passion,
  She, destroyed as you would fashion,
Or you who make the rash assault?

The greater evil who is in—
  When both in wayward paths are straying—
  The poor sinner for the paying,
Or he that pays her for the sin?

Come, from your flirting cease, and turn,
  (If maybe) to a cool reflection;
  Then blame the ardor of affection
In her you started first to burn!
      From the Spanish by Garrett Strange.

ENVYING A LITTLE BIRD

Sister Gregoria Francisca (1653-1736)

Envying a little bird
His flight to heaven my heart is stirred,

So hardy is the wing he finds
To breast the bluster of the winds,
So lightly pulsing doth he fare,
Enamored of the sunset there—
And swaying ever higher, higher,
He mounts unto the realms of fire!
Fair plaything of the breeze tonight,
And from thy heart such impulse know
As speeds thy steadfast pinions so!
Would I were with thee in thy flight,
I follow with a lover's sighs
Impatient, where thou cleav'st the skies,
Feeling my body's prison bars
Withhold my spirit from the stars.
For of the Sun supreme am I
A love-delirious butterfly;
By tender dawns I sip,—but claim
The blossom of His noontide flame.
O little bird, my dismal cell
Reflects His sunlit splendors well—
His glorious beauties are for me
But shadowed in my misery!
In envy of thy boundless flight
But one desire can now requite
My heart,—a salamander's soul
To brave His flames without control!—
Thy flight is joyous, little bird,
While I in prison am interred;
But seeing thee my soul is raised
Unto the skies thou seek'st amazed;
A lover and a captive bound
Am I amid my darkness found;
Would that some mighty power would rend
My chains and my harsh durance end!
O what a flight would then be mine,
Could I this shackle-weight resign!
With what warm impulse of the skies
My wing against thine own would rise!
Unto thy heart yon crimson tryst
Of sunset glory hath sufficed;

Thy spirit glad and free of care
Doth to its golden lattice fare;
But I who, knowing, love and pine
For Him that is the Sphere Divine,
Of griefs my only wings can make,
And flights alone on sighings take!
In His immensity of light
I fall into annulling blight;
In the vast clearness of His sphere
My feeble senses disappear.
His brilliance bids my wings expand
To rapid flight unto His hand,—
But oh, my nature's heavy bond
Denies me freedom for beyond!
Do thou, fair bird, on tireless wing
Beyond the heavenly archway spring,
And breasting higher, higher, bear
This message of my fond despair;
Unto that Light and Sun to show
How love doth wound me here below;
Within the inaccessible sky
To say how of my love I die,
Since through my light of faith alone
His radiant beauteousness is known;
To say, the more His splendor shows
The more my dismal blindness grows;
And yet I glory in the dark
His steps in passing by me mark;
To say I wait the joyous hour
When He shall break the mortal power
That holds me prisoned here so long,
And loose me for the wingèd throng,
To say His rays through chink and bar
But only added torments are;—
That all the more His lights display
The more my wounds and burns by day;
That all the noons are full of Him,
Filling joy's goblets to the brim,—
That all my soul is in decline,
Beholding thus His glory shine!

Little bird, if thou of love
Ever the sweet pain didst prove,
Pity take upon my woes
And mourn o'er what my breasts disclose.
Speak to my sweet Lord on high,
That He may grant me liberty,
And lending thy fair wings the while
That I may seek His distant isle,
And from this prison dire be gone,
From this captivity whereon
So many a tear and groan I shed
Unto my dark and exiled bed,—
Where gazing on thy happy flight
I realise my bitter plight,—
And love the more impatient glows
As brighter its far object shows!

From the Spanish by Thomas Walsh.

THE RANN OF THE THREE

(Eighteenth Century)

Three folds in my garment, yet only one garment I bear;
Three joints in a finger, yet only one finger is there;
Three leaves in a shamrock, yet only one shamrock I wear.
Frost, ice and snow, these three are nothing but water;
Three Persons in God, yet only one God is there.

From the Irish.

CHANSON MYSTIQUE

Anonymous

Out for a walk the other day
I met sweet Jesus by the way.
My heart flies, flies, flies,
My heart toward heaven flies!

He said to me: "Daughter, what seekest thou?"
"I was seeking Thee, Jesus sweet, and now
My heart toward heaven flies;
Humility and Charity,
And also holy Chastity,
My heart flies, flies, flies,
My heart toward heaven flies."

"The gifts of perfect love are they,
Daughter, thine shall they be one day."
My heart flies, flies, flies,
My heart toward heaven flies.

From the French by Percy Allen.

CHRISTMAS CAROL

SISTER FRANCISCA JOSEFA DEL CASTILLO (1671-1743)

The land grew bright in a single flower—
    One great Carnation rare—
Against whose bloom no frost had power
    To dim its glowing lair.

Oh, was there ever such another
    So lovely for our lips to kiss,—
To shine where earthly shadows smother,—
    A bud of Heaven, like This?

The sun behind the mists is clouded;
    Haste, shepherds, there to gaze!
See Fire itself in ice beshrouded,
    And Ice in joy ablaze!

From the Spanish by Thomas Walsh.

THE HOLY ECLOGUE

Sister Francisca Josefa del Castillo

Unto Salvation's spring
Amid its thorny reeds
There comes in pilgriming
A weary heart that pleads
Unto the Cross, on which it turns its eyes,
The while it moans and lifts its ceaseless sighs :—

"Thy servant, I, O Lord,
Come thirsting for Thy streams;
With sins so many scored
That penance scarce redeems;
Oh, from Thy presence hold me not away
Unpardoned and unpitied, Lord, I pray!

"Upon the Cross nailed fast—
That sign of peace displayed
Thy full perfection! Cast
Thy glance so long delayed,
Let all my nature and my poor desire
Embrace Thy light and flame and holy fire!

"Thou wert a God of wrath
Unto the Prophets old;
Today my spirit hath
In Thee, made Man, grown bold;
Since, God of love, we now behold Thee bound
Without the arrows of Thy vengeance found.

"To keep me Thou hast shed,
And sealed Thy love, in blood;
And in the Holy Bread
Prepared my sacred food;
Let not my wandering senses lose
The fruits of love and anguish so profuse.

"My sin has led me far
As some wild thirsting bee
Beneath Thy meadow star,
Idly forgetting Thee;
But Thou dost call me home; I hear
Thy voice whose sweetness charms mine ear.

"O Shepherd of the fold,—
That seeks me through the beat
Of tempests and of cold,
As through the burning heat,—
Let me not stray again, but keep
Me folded fast amid Thy little sheep."

From the Spanish by Thomas Walsh.

THE DYING CHRISTIAN TO HIS SOUL

ALEXANDER POPE (1688-1744)

Vital spark of heavenly flame!
Quit, O quit this mortal frame!
Trembling, hoping, lingering, flying,
O the pain, the bliss of dying!
Cease, fond nature, cease thy strife,
And let me languish into life!

Hark! they whisper; angels say,
Sister spirit, come away!
What is this absorbs me quite?
Steals my senses, shuts my sight,
Drowns my spirits, draws my breath?
Tell me, my soul, can this be death?

The world recedes; it disappears!
Heaven opens my eyes! my ears
   With sounds seraphic ring;
Lend, lend your wings! I mount! I fly
O Grave! where is thy victory?
   O Death! where is thy sting?

THE VESTAL

ALEXANDER POPE

How happy is the blameless vestal's lot!
The world forgetting, by the world forgot:
Eternal sunshine of the spotless mind!
Each prayer accepted, and each wish resign'd,
Labour and rest that equal periods keep:
"Obedient slumbers that can wake and weep,"
Desires composed, affections ever even;
Tears that delight, and sighs that waft to Heaven
Grace shines around her with serenest beams,
And whisp'ring angels prompt her golden dreams;
For her th' unfading rose of Eden blooms,
And wings of seraphs shed divine perfumes;
For her the spouse prepares the bridal ring,
For her white virgins hymeneals sing;
To sounds of heavenly harps she dies away,
And melts in visions of eternal day.

VERT-VERT, THE PARROT

LOUIS GRESSET (1709-1777)

In old Nevers, so famous for its
Dark narrow streets and Gothic turrets,
Close on the brink of Loire's young flood,
Flourished a convent sisterhood
Of Ursulines. Now in this order
A parrot lived as parlour-boarder;
Green were his feathers, green his pinions,
And greener still were his opinions;
For vice had not yet sought to pervert
This bird, who had been christened Vert-Vert;
The convent's kindness, need I mention,
Need I detail each fond attention,
Or count the tit-bits which in Lent he
Swallowed remorseless and in plenty?

Dear to each novice and each nun—
He was the life and soul of fun;
Though to be sure some hags censorious
Would sometimes find him too uproarious.
What did the parrot care for these old
Dames while he had for him the household?
Therefore unblamed, he ogled, flirted,
And acted like any unconverted;
Nay, sometimes, too, by the Lord Harry!
He'd pull their caps and scapulary.

.   .   .   .   .   .

Placed when at table near some vestal,
His fare, be sure, was of the best all,—
For every sister would endeavour
To keep for him some sweet hors d'œuvre.

.   .   .   .   .   .

Quick at all arts, our bird was rich at
That best accomplishment, called chit-chat;
For, though brought up within the cloister,
His beak was not closed like an oyster.
Pious withal, and moralising,
His conversation was surprising;
But his tongue ran most smooth and nice on
"Deo sit laus" and "Kyrie eleison";
The maxims he gave with best emphasis
Were Suarez's or Thomas à Kempis's;
In Christmas carols he was famous,
"Orate, fratres" and "Oremus";
Or by particular desire, he
Would chant the hymn of "Dies irae."
Then in the choir he would amaze all
By copying the tone so nasal
In which the sainted sisters chanted—
(At least that pious nun my aunt did.)

.   .   .   .   .   .

Fame, O Vert-Vert! in evil humour
One day to Nantz had brought the rumour
Of thy accomplishments,—"acumen,"
"Nous" and "esprit" quite superhuman;

All these reports but served to enhance
Thy merits with the nuns of Nantz.
How did a matter so unsuited
For convent ears get hither bruited!
Forthwith they taxed their wits to elicit
From the famed bird a friendly visit.
To get this bird they'd pawn the missal;
Quick they indite a long epistle,
Careful with softest things to fill it,
And then with musk perfume the billet.
It was no easy thing to coax
This parrot from the Nevers folks.
What, take their toy from convent belles?
Make Russia yield the Dardanelles!
Filch his good rifle from a "Suliot,"
Or drag her Romeo from a Juliet!
Make an attempt to take Gibraltar
Or try the old corn laws to alter!
Long did the chapter sit in state,
And on this point deliberate;
The junior members of the senate
Set their fair faces quite "again" it;
The elder nuns feel no great scruple
In parting with the charming pupil;
Nor in my surmise am I far out—
For, by their vote, off goes the parrot.

    .   .   .   .

En ce tems là, a small canal-boat
Called by most chroniclers the "Talbot"
(Talbot, a name well known in France)
Travelled between Nevers and Nantz.
Vert-Vert took shipping in this craft,
'Tis not said whether fore or aft;
But in a book as old as Massinger's
We find a statement of the passengers.
For a poor bird brought up in purity
'Twas a sad augur for futurity
To meet, just free from his indentures,
And in the first of his adventures,
Such a strange aggregate of scandals
As to be met but among Vandals;

Rude was their talk, bereft of polish,
And calculated to demolish
All the fine notions and good-breeding
Taught by the nuns in their sweet Eden.
Ear hath not heard such vulgar gab in
The nautic cell of any cabin.
Silent and sad the pensive bird
Shocked at their guilt, said not a word.
Posed, not abashed, the bird refused to
Indulge a scene he was not used to;
And pondering on his strange reception,
"There must," he thought, "be some deception
In the nuns' views of things rhetorical,
And Sister Rose is not an oracle."
Thus in this villainous receptacle
The simple bird at once grew sceptical.
Doubts lead to hell. The arch-deceiver
Soon made of Poll an unbeliever;
And mixing thus in bad society,
He took French leave of all his piety.
His austere maxims soon he mollified,
And all his old opinions qualified
For he had learned to substitute
For pious lore things more astute;
Nor was his conduct unimpeachable,
For youth, alas! is but too teachable;
Such were his curses, such his evil
Practices, that no ancient devil
Plunged to his chin when burning hot
Into a holy water-pot,
Could so blaspheme, or fire a volley
Of oaths so drear and melancholy!
Fondly within the convent bowers
The sisters calculate the hours,
Chiding the breezes for their tardiness,
And in the height of their foolhardiness.
Picturing the bird as fancy painted—
Lovely, reserved, polite, and sainted—
Fit "Ursuline"—and this, I trow, meant
Enriched with every endowment!

Sadly, alas! these nuns anointed,
Will find their fancy disappointed;
When, to meet all those hopes they drew on,
They'll find a regular Don Juan!

.   .   .   .   .   .

Scarce in the port was this small craft
On its arrival telegraphed,
When, from the boat, home to transfer him,
Came the nuns' portress Sister Jerome.
Well did the parrot recognise
The walk demure and downcast eyes,
Nor aught such saintly guidance relished
A bird by worldly arts embellished;
Such was his taste for profane gaiety,
He'd rather much go with the laity.
Thus was Vert-Vert, heart-sick and weary,
Brought to the heavenly monastery;
The bells and tidings both were tolled,
And the nuns crowded, young and old,
To feast their eyes with joy uncommon on
This wondrous talkative phenomenon.
Meantime the Abbess, "to draw out"
A bird so modest and devout,
Broached the most edifying topics,
To start this native of the Tropics;
When to their scandal and amaze, he
Broke forth:—"Morbleu! these nuns are crazy!"
(Showing how well he learnt his task on
The packet-boat from that vile Gascon.)
"Fie! brother Poll!" with zeal outbursting
Exclaimed the Abbess Dame Augustin;
But all the lady's sage rebukes
Brief answer got from Poll—"Gadzooks!"
Scared at the sound,—"Sure as a gun,
The bird's a demon!" cried the nun.
"O the vile wretch! the naughty dog!
He's surely Lucifer *incog*.
What! is the reprobate before us
That bird so pious and decorous—

So celebrated?—Here the pilgrim
Hearing sufficient to bewilder him,
Wound up the sermon of the beldame
By a conclusion heard but seldom—
"Ventre Saint Gris!" "Parbleu!" and "Sacre!"
Three oaths! and every one a whacker.
Still did the nuns, whose conscience tender
Was much shocked at the young offender,
Hoping he'd change his tone and alter
Hang breathless round the sad defaulter;
When, wrathful at their importunity,
And grown audacious from immunity,
He fired a broadside (Holy Mary!)
Drawn from Hell's own vocabulary!
Stunned at these sounds of import Stygian
The pious daughters of religion
Fled from a scene so dread, so horrid,
But with the cross first signed their forehead.
The younger sisters, mild and meek,
Thought that the culprit spoke in Greek;
But the old matrons on the bench
Knew every word was genuine French;
And ran in all directions, pell-mell,
From a flood fit to overwhelm hell;
'Twas by a fall that Mother Ruth
Then lost her last remaining tooth.

·   ·   ·   ·   ·   ·

"Fine conduct this, and pretty guidance!"
Cried one of the most mortified ones;
"Pray, is such language and such ritual
Among the Nevers nuns habitual?
'Twas in our sisters most improper
To teach such curses—such a whopper!
He shan't by me, for one, be hindered
From being sent back to his kindred!"
This prompt decree of Poll's proscription
Was signed by general subscription.
Straight in a cage the nuns insert
The guilty person of Vert-Vert;
Some young ones wanted to detain him;

But the grim portress took the paynim
Back to the boat, close in his litter;
'Tis not said, this time, that he bit her.
Must I tell how, on his return
He scandalised his old sojourn?
And how the guardians of his infancy
Wept o'er their quondam child's delinquency?
One mother counselled "to denounce
And let the Inquisition pounce
On the vile heretic"; another
Thought "it was best the bird to smother!"
Or "send the convict for his felonies
Back to his native land, the colonies."
But milder views prevailed. His sentence
Was, that until he showed repentance,
"A solemn fast and frugal diet,
Silence exact, and pensive quiet,
Should be his lot"; and, for his blister,
He got as gaoler, a lay-sister,
Ugly as sin, bad-tempered, jealous,
And in her scruples over-zealous.
A jug of water and a carrot
Was all the prog she'd give the parrot.
But every eve when vesper-bell
Called Sister Rosalie from her cell,
She to Vert-Vert would gain admittance,
And bring of comfits a sweet pittance.
Taught by his gaoler and adversity,
Poll saw the folly of perversity,
And by degrees his heart relented;
Duly, in fine, "the lad repented."
His Lent passed on, and Sister Brigit
Coaxed the old Abbess to abridge it.

．　　．　　．　　．　　．　　．

The prodigal, reclaimed and free,
Became again a prodigy,
And gave more joy, by works and words,
Than ninety-nine canary-birds—
Until his death, which last disaster
(Nothing on earth endures!) came faster

Than they imagined. The transition
From a starved to a stuffed condition,
From penitence to jollification,
Brought on a fit of constipation,
Some think he would be living still,
If given a Vegetable Pill;
But from a short life and a merry,
Poll sailed one day per Charon's ferry.
By tears from nuns' sweet eyelids wept,
Happy in death this parrot slept;
For him Elysium oped its portals,
And there he talks among immortals.
But I have read, that since that day
(So writes Cornelius a Lapide,
Proving with commentary droll
The transmigration of the soul)
That still Vert-Vert this earth doth haunt,
Of convent bowers a visitant;
And that, gay novices among,
He dwells, transformed into a tongue.

From the French by Francis Mahony (Father Prout).

FOR A BLIND BEGGAR'S SIGN

CLEMENTE BIONDI (1742-)

Take pity, signors, ye who pass me by,
     Where I am but an outcast on the street,
Lest it be said ye are more blind than I,
     That can refuse a brother bread to eat.

For on my brow God's hand hath laid a sign;
     Come, ye with sight—is not His meaning clear?—
"These eyes must virgin wait the Light Divine;
     Who sins, ye rich, if He stands starving here?"

From the Italian by Roderick Gill.

ON A NUN

JACOPO VITORELLI (1749-1835)

Sonnet Addressed by a Father Mourning His Recently Deceased
Married Daughter to the Father Whose Daughter
Had Entered a Convent

Of two fair virgins, modest, though admired,
  Heaven made us happy; and now, wretched sires,
  Heaven for a nobler doom their worth desires,
And gazing upon either, both required.
Mine, while the torch of Hymen newly fired,
  Becomes extinguished, soon, too soon, expires;
  But thine, within the closing grate retired,
Eternal captive, to her God aspires.

But thou at least from out the jealous door
  Which shuts between your never-meeting eyes,
Mayst hear her sweet and pious voice once more;
  I, to the marble where my daughter lies,
Rush—the swoln flood of bitterness I pour,
  And knock, and knock, and knock—but none replies.
From the Italian by Lord Byron.

ODE—IMITATED FROM THE PSALMS

NICOLAS-JOSEPH-FLORENT GILBERT (1750-1780)

My heart is bare to God who knows no wrong;
  And He hath gazed upon my suppliant tears;
Heals my remorse and arms me full and strong;
  The helpless are the children He endears.

My hostile rivals mockingly declare:
  "So let him die and with him go his fame!"
But o'er my calm the Father whispers there:
  "Their hatred shall but add to thy acclaim."

"Those thou hast cherished join them in their rage,
 Deceived in all is thy simplicity;
He whom thy breast hath nourished would engage
 To sell thee, blackened with their infamy."

"But God hath heard thy groan and bounteous brings
 The contrite spirit born of thy chagrins,—
God who doth pardon nature's weakenings
 And man's poor follies in the face of sin.

"My piteousness for thee I shall arouse,
 With justice that the years corrode in vain;
Themselves shall crystallize about thy brows
 Thine honor they would meditate to stain."

Blessèd be Thou, my God, restoring now
 My dole of innocence and noble pride;
Thou who, in peace my ashes to endow,
 Wilt stand as guard my funeral couch beside.

Unto life's banquet, an unhappy guest,
 One day I came and now one day I die;
I pass unto the tomb to gladsome rest
 Where none shall pause to droop a tearful eye.

Hail, ye belovèd fields, ye verdures sweet,
 And you bright exile from the woods outcast—
Sky, roof of man and glorious retreat—
 Hail now forever, hail ye at the last!

Long on your sacred beauties, long may rest
 My friends their gaze, nor hear my last good-bys;
Filled be their days of life, their dying blest
 With tears—a friend at hand to close their eyes!

From the French by Thomas Walsh.

TO JESUS ON THE CROSS

Juan Manuel García Tejada (1774-1845)

To you I hurrying come, O sacred arms
   That stretch so wide upon the lifted Cross
   As though to cherish me for all my loss,
Nailed all too fast to cause my guilt alarms!
To you, O eyes divine eclipsed in night,
   So filled with tears and blood you can but gaze
   Confused in pardon on my sinful ways
And yet to shame me have so little sight!

To you, poor feet so nailed you cannot spurn;
   To you, bowed head that whispers low my name;
To you, O blood outpoured my grace to earn;
To you, O piercèd breast where mine would turn;
   To you, O priceless nails, whose bonds I claim
In rigid union with Him sweet and stern!
             From the Spanish by Thomas Walsh.

COME, YE DISCONSOLATE

Thomas Moore (1779-1852)

Come, ye disconsolate, where'er you languish,
   Come, at God's altar fervently kneel;
Here bring your wounded hearts, here tell your anguish,—
   Earth has no sorrow that heaven cannot heal.

Joy of the desolate, light of the straying,
   Hope when all others die, fadeless and pure,
Here speaks the comforter, in God's name saying,
   "Earth has no sorrow that heaven cannot cure."

Go, ask the infidel, what boon he brings us,
   What charm for aching hearts he can reveal,
Sweet as that heavenly promise hope sings,
   "Earth has no sorrow that God cannot heal."

THE FIFTH OF MAY—NAPOLEON

From the *Ode* of ALESSANDRO MANZONI (1785-1873)

Him on his throne and glorious
Silent I saw, that never—
When with awful vicissitude
He sank, rose, fell forever—
Mixed my voice with the numberless
Voices that pealed on high:
Guiltless of servile flattery
And of the scorn of the coward.
Come I when darkness suddenly
On so great light hath lowered,
And offer a song at his sepulchre
That haply shall not die.

From the Alps unto the Pyramids,
From Rhine to Manzanares,
Unfailingly the thunder-stroke
His lightning purpose carries;
Bursts from Scylla to Tanais,—
From one to the other sea.
Was it true glory? Posterity,
Thine be the hard decision;
Bow we before the Mightiest
Who willed in him the vision
Of His creative majesty
Most grandly traced should be.

Beautiful, deathless, beneficent
Faith! used to triumphs, even
This also write exultantly:
No loftier pride 'neath Heaven
Unto the shame of Calvary
Stooped ever yet its crest.
Thou from his weary mortality
Disperse all bitter passion—
The God that humbleth and hearteneth,

That comforts and that chastens,—
Upon the pillow else desolate
To his pale lips lay pressed!
From the Italian by William Dean Howells.

RETURNING SPRING

COUNT JOSEPH VON EICHENDORFF (1786-1857)

Green were the willows
And heaven—how blue!
The meadow gleamed brightest
About us two.

Are the nightingales
Calling? Rises again
In the mellow air
A lark's swift strain?

From afar, without you,
I hear the singing:
Oh, not for me
Comes spring a-winging.
From the German by George N. Shuster.

POET-HEARTS

COUNT JOSEPH VON EICHENDORFF

Nothing's wholly mine on earth
Other than my lyre's song;
Tell me, has the prosperous throng
More of beauty or of mirth?
All of living's deepest treasure
Mystically is the measure
Which the radiant singer sheaves.
None knows with what radiant weaves
Wonderfully God endows
Poet-hearts that give Him pleasure.
From the German by George N. Shuster.

THE VISION

LOUNKIANOS THE ARMENIAN (About 1790-1860)

When unto heaven the souls elect take flight
    The Master keeps the promise He hath made;
He binds their brows with diadems of light;
    He decks their hands with ruby rings and jade.

Angels and virgins greet them with their songs;
    The strings eternal glad them with sweet sound;
Like stars they see agleam the saints in throngs
    And float with them in ecstasy profound.

Upon this dream are anchored all my joys;
    Come, Mother Mary, take me by the hand
And lead me out where heaven its bloom deploys,—
    So I may breathe the perfumes of that land.
                    From the Armenian by Thomas Walsh.

KOLENDY FOR CHRISTMAS

Lullaby, little Jesus, my little pearl,
Lullaby, belovèd, my little treasure,
Lullaby, little Jesus, lullaby, lullaby,
And thou, His Mother, His weeping calm.
Close Thy little lids, a-blinking with tears,
Close Thy little lips, quivering with sobbing,
Lullaby, little Jesus, lullaby, lullaby,
And thou, His Mother, His weeping calm.

I will give to Jesus sweet berries,
I will go with Him into the garden of His Mother's heart;
Lullaby, little Jesus, etc.

I will give to Jesus butter with bread,
I will place a loaf in His crib;
Lullaby, little Jesus, etc.

Lullaby, Beautiful, my little angel,
Lullaby, gracious flower of the world;
Lullaby, little Jesus, etc.

Lullaby, little rose, most adorning,
Lullaby, lily, most fragrant;
Lullaby, little Jesus, etc.

I will give Thee, Jesus, candies sweet,
Raisins and almonds from my store;
Lullaby, little Jesus, lullaby, lullaby,
And thou, His Mother, His weeping calm.

Lullaby, pleasing to eye, little Star,
Lullaby, most lovely little sun of the world,
Lullaby, little Jesus, etc.

I will give to the little One a beautiful apple,
I will give Him the heart of His beloved Mother;
Lullaby, little Jesus, etc.

Hush, hush, hush! may the little Child slumber,
Look, how He sleeps, the Infant;
Lullaby, little Jesus, etc.

Hush, hush, hush! slumber ye all,
Do not waken my little Child;
Lullaby, little Jesus, etc.

From the Polish by Irena Dalgiewicz.

THE CRUCIFIX

ALPHONSE DE LAMARTINE (1790-1869)

Thou whom I lifted from her pallid lips,
With her last breath and with her last goodbye,
Symbol twice sainted, Death made death's bequest,
    God whom men crucify!

The hour supreme when, from a martyr's breast,
My trembling fingers took you, long has waned,
And on those feet adored what sighs have breathed,
 What bitter tears have rained!

Feebly the hallowed tapers shed their gleam,
On the priest's lips the verses for the dead
Droned, like the plaintive songs a mother croons,
 Bent o'er the cradle's head.

The light of faith still lingered on her brow,
Smit with strange beauty, and upon her face
Death, as he came, had stamped his majesty;
 Pain, as it passed, its grace.

Across her waxen cheek a random tress
Stirred in the breeze that wandered through the room;
So I have seen a cypress shadow sway
 Across a marble tomb.

One of her arms hung limply from the bed:
The other, folded meekly on her breast,
Seemed seeking still, to press upon her mouth,
 The cross my fingers pressed.

Still pursed to kiss—those lips, through which her soul
In one last kiss supreme had sought the skies:
A perfume, which the flame devoured before
 Its fragrant smoke might rise.

Now, on the frozen lips no zephyr moved,
No lightest pulse the stagnant bosom stirred,
And on the glazing eyes the eyelids drooped,
 Wings of a tired bird.

Numbed, as with nameless fear, I stood apart,
Nor ventured to approach the worshipped dead:
It seemed the silent majesty of death
 Turned even love to dread.

I dared not! . . . but the priest my silence heard;
His icy fingers on the relic lay:
"This is your memory, this must be your hope:
    Bear both, my son, away!"

O spectral gift! Have I not treasured thee?
Seven winters since of withered leaves have reft
The tree I planted by her nameless grave:
    My heart thou hast not left.

Borne as an amulet on this fickle breast,
Thou hast defended memory 'gainst the years,
And, drop by drop, thy yellowing ivory shows
    The traces of my tears.

Last confidant of a soul that spread its wings,
Rest on my heart! speak softly, tell me true,
What things her failing whisper spoke, in words
    Heard but by you.

At that last hour when the absorbèd soul,
Behind a pall that thickens on the eyes,
From the numb senses step by step withdraws,
    Heedless of tears and cries:

When, for a moment, poised twixt life and death,
Like some ripe fruit the branches may not keep,
The soul hangs trembling o'er the tomb's abyss,
    For a last breath to reap:

When sobs and prayers, in harmony confused,
No more may pierce the stupor that descends,
Pressed to the dying lips in death's last throe,
    Dearest and last of friends:

To rob that perilous passage of its fears,
To lift t'ward Heaven the pallor of that brow,
Divine Consoler, whose five wounds I kiss,
    Tell me, what answer'dst Thou?

None ever died like Thee! and yet Thy tears,
On that dread night when God His face withdrew,
Watered the grass beneath the olive trees
    From eve till morning dew.

When from the Cross Thine eye the mystery plumbed,
Thou saw'st Thy mother's tears and nature's gloom:
Like us, Thou left'st Thy friends upon the earth,
    Thy body to the tomb.

Cheered by that death, one boon my weakness craves—
To render its last sigh upon Thy breast.
In my last hour remember Thee of Thine,
    Thou who mad'st death Thy guest.

My lips shall seek the spot whereon her lips
Sighed at Thy feet the irreparable farewell:
No hand save hers my errant soul shall guide
    Where souls predestined dwell.

Ah! grant that then, beside my couch of pain,
Sad as some pitiful seraph, yet benign,
A black-robed angel stands, and from my lips
    Gathers the sacred sign.

Solace her loneliness! Make death less hard!
And, like some promise hope and love discern,
From him who goes to her who waits the call,
    Pass, Comforter, in turn.

Until the day when, death and doom upheaving,
A shout from Heaven, seven times multiplied,
Summons the dead who sleep beneath thy shadow
    Around the Crucified!
      From the French by Henry Longan Stuart.

HEILIGE NACHT

JOSEF MOHR (1792-1848)

Silent Night! Holy Night!
Slumber all; in delight
Watch the two saintly guardians there
Over the Child in His ringletted hair:
"Sleep in heavenly Peace!
Sleep in heavenly Peace!"

Silent Night! Holy Night!
Shepherds first learnt its might
From the Angels with Glorias clear
Singing round them from far and near:
"Christ the Saviour is here!
Christ the Saviour is here!"

Silent Night! Holy Night!
God's own Son,—oh, how bright
Shines the love from Thine infinite Face;
While the hour strikes forth for Thy grace—
Christ who is born unto us!
Christ who is born unto us!

From the German by Thomas Walsh.

ERIN

KENELM H. DIGBY (1797-1880)

Island of Saints, still constant, still allied
To the great truths opposed to human pride;
Island of ruins, towers, cloisters grey,
Whence palmer kings with pontiffs once did stray
To Rome and Sion, or to kindle fire
Which amid later darkness can inspire
Lands that in fondest memory and song
Thy pristine glory fearlessly prolong;
Thy peaceful image floating in the West
Denotes a Cause to yield all spirits rest:

Ancient, yet never past, as years gone by
But rising gloriously in eastern sky,
As oft as finding in the setting light
A symbol of thy grandeur in that night
Of ages, when thy fame from sea to sea
Extended as a blissful mystery.
For grandeur, nations, kingdoms have their day,
But Faith like thine will never pass away.

THE CATHOLIC FAITH

KENELM H. DIGBY

Its unobtrusive force leaves you so free
That none besides seems blessed with liberty.
Dear Heart! it is not a Procrustean bed
Whate'er by foes or silly friends is said;
The very name denotes it is for all,
And not more for the great than for the small,
With adaptations infinite for each,
And more, perhaps, than 'twill expressly teach.
Although so varied in their tastes and views
Men find that it will serve them like the Muse,
Receiving with the mildest condescension
The homage e'en of thoughts they dare not mention;
So like a wise and tender mother, still
Regarding less the action than the will,
Which, when it is in harmony with truth,
For all Faith cares may have its freaks in sooth.
Of utterances it makes no parade,
It seeks to work its purpose in the shade;
And one result of its great Presence there,
Of which, or soon or late, men are aware,
Is that it tends to happiness on earth,
And to serene and constant thoughts gives birth.

GETHSEMANE

ANNETTE VON DROSTE-HÜLSHOFF (1797-1848)

Prone in Gethsemane upon His face,—
His eyelids closed,—lay Christ of all our world,—
The winds with endless sorrows seemed enswirled;
A little fountain murmured of its pain
Reflecting the pale sickle of the moon;—
Then was the hour when the Angel brought
From God's high throne the Cup of bitter boon,
While on His hands tears trembling fell like rain.

Before the Christ a cross arose on high;
He saw His own young body hanging there
Mangled, distorted; knotted ropes half-tear
The sinews from their sockets; saw He nigh
The jagged nails' hot rage, the direful Crown
Upon His head, and every dripping thorn
Red-laden, as in fury of its scorn
The thunder battered all kind voices down.
He heard the pattering drops, as from the cross
A piteous sobbing whispered and grew still.
Then Jesus sighed, and every pore did spill
A bloody sweat—

Blackness of night came on, and in a sea
Of ashes swam a lifeless sun and dim;
The agony He read upon the face turned grim
Unto the tossing struggle death must win.
There near the cross the three knelt silently;
He saw them gray as clouds of darkling mist;
He heard the stirring of their heavy breath,
The tremor cloaked within their doleful tryst.
Oh, where is love that knows the flame of His?
His mother, oh!—His piercing glance knew well;
The blood of man, checked in His veins a spell,
Was then in copious sweat poured faster forth.

The spectral sun waned out; an ebon smoke
Enwrapped the cross and grieving in its cloak;

A silence fiercer than the thunder's blare
Moved through the starless highways of the air.
No breath of life was stirred on all the earth—
An endless crater lay in cindrous drouth;
Cried one amid the high vacuity:—
"My God! My God!—Hast Thou forsaken Me!"
And Jesus moaned with a tear-quivering mouth:
"Lord, if it may be, do Thou let this hour
Pass quickly from Me!"
A flash across the night and radiant stood
The cross resplendent with its signs of woe;
He saw a million hands outstretch and go
Clinging in anguish to the bloody wood,
Yes, hands and tiny fingers from afar,
And myriad souls unborn that thronging came
Around the crown in vivid sparks of flame.
Then mists in gentle breath revealed the ground
Where in their tombs the just were buried laid.
And Christ arose, love-blossomed, undismayed:
"Father," He cried to heaven, "let not My will
But Thine be done!"

The sun still sailed the blue; a lily stalk
Greeted the Saviour on the dewy grass,
From out its chaliced pearl the Angel came
To strengthen Him.

From the German by George N. Shuster.

LAST WORDS

ANNETTE VON DROSTE-HÜLSHOFF

When I am gone, brook no complaining,
  Belovèd, shed no tears, I pray!
Where I shall dwell, there peace is reigning,
  There shines an everlasting day.

Where earth's great misery is vanished,
  Your images shall never fade;
I'll pray that all your pain be banished,
  That balm upon your wounds be laid.

At night, when heavenly peace is flying
   Above the world that sorrow mars,
Ah, think not of my grave with sighing!
   For then I greet you from the stars.
       From the German by Margarete Münsterberg.

THE SAGES

ADAM MICKIEWICZ (1798-1855)

In thought that brought no rest nor peace of heart
   The sages fell into uneasy doze—
When far below them in the crowded mart,
   "God comes among us!" loud the cry arose.
"He should be slain," they said, "who breaks our rest;
The crowd protects Him now; by night 'twere best."

So when the night came and their lamps were lit,
   Even as whetstones, books of weighty words
Used they to sharpen their hair-splitting wit
   Till it was keen and cold and swift as swords.
Blind pupils led they forth to capture God,
But to destruction led the path they trod.

"Is't Thou?" they cry unto mild Mary's Son.
   " 'Tis I," He answers, and the pupils fly
In dread; the sages fall before that One.
   "Is't Thou?" They tremble. "Yea," He saith, " 'tis I."
But, seeing that God awes but doth not strike,
They then become more cruel, demonlike.
They stripped Him of His robes of mystery,
   And with cold reasoning they pierced His side;
They flogged His body with their mockery
   And cast Him in a grave digged by their pride;
Yet from their souls, dark as that grave, He came
And offers them salvation in His name!

Thus did the sages fill their cup of pride,
   And terror for her Lord the world o'erwhelm;
Yet 'twas but in their souls that He had died—
   He lives, and peace is in His heavenly realm!
       From the Polish by Dorothy Todd and
           George Rapall Noyes.

TO A POLISH MOTHER

Adam Mickiewicz

O Polish mother, if the radiant eyes
    Of genius kindle in thy darling's face,
If even in his childish aspect rise
    The pride and honor of his ancient race;

If, turning from his playmates' joyous throng,
    He runs to find the bard and hear his lays,
If with bowed head he listens to the song
    Of ancient glory and departed days;

O Polish mother, ill must be his part!
    Before the Mother of Our Sorrows kneel,
Gaze on the sword that cleaves her living heart—
    Such is the craven blow thy breast shall feel!

Though peoples, powers and schisms a truce declare,
    And though the whole wide world in peace may bloom,
In battle—without glory—must he share,
    In martyrdom—with an eternal tomb.

Soon bid him seek a solitary cave
    And ponder there—on rushes lay his head,
Breathe the foul vapors of a hidden grave,
    And with the envenomed serpent share his bed.

There will he learn to hide his wrath from reach,
    To sink his thought as in the abyss profound,
Slyly to poison with miasmic speech,
    And humbly, like the serpent, kiss the ground.

A child in Nazareth, Our Saviour mild
    Fondled the cross whereon He saved mankind;
O Polish mother, I would have thy child
    Thus early learn what playthings he will find.

His young arms load with chains, his body frail
    Full soon have harnessed to a barrow, so
Before the headsman's ax he shall not pale,
    Nor at the swinging halter crimson glow.

Not his to venture like a plumèd knight
    And plant the holy cross on pagan soil,
Nor like a soldier of new faith to fight
    In Freedom's cause, and for her sake to toil.

One day an unknown spy will challenge him,
    A perjured court his adversary be,
The jousting-field, a secret dungeon grim;
    A powerful foe the verdict will decree.

And for the vanquished man as monument
    The gallows-tree will rear its sullen height;
For glory—but a woman's tears, soon spent,—
    And fellow patriots' whispered words by night.

From the Polish by Jewell Parish and
George Rapall Noyes.

EASTER SONG

. Leo Alishan (Nineteenth Century)

Forth welling from the breast of sapphire lakes,
    Oh, tell, my jocund heart, why from their shore
Of emeralds do those pairs of wandering pearls
    Like rain upon the rosy plains downpour?

Less pure, less tender, are the twilight dews
    At eve descending on the crimson rose
And on the lily's petals fine and frail,
    Than those twin drops in which thy sorrow flows.

Speak, why do founts of shining tears descend,
    Mary, from thy love-dropping virgin eyes
To thy cheek's edge and there hang tremulous,
    As the stars twinkle in the evening skies?

As the heart-piercing pupil of the eye
  So sensitive each tear-drop seems to be;
Like the unwinking pupil of the eye,
  Charming my soul, the bright drops look at me.

The heart throbs hard, the gazer holds his breath—
  Ah, now I know the truth! Oh, woe is me!
For me those tears have risen to thine eyes,
  To heal my spirit's wounds eternally.

But still of my unconsecrated heart
  Distrustful, they half-fallen linger there,
And do not dare to drop and moisten me.
  No, Mary! No, O Virgin Mother fair!

I am a land uncultured, rough and wild;
  But, underneath those tender tears of thine,
Let rose and saffron bloom there! With thy love
  Water and cheer this sorrowing heart of mine!
  Translated from the Armenian by Alice Stone Blackwell.

THE AMERICAN FLAG

Charles Constantine Pise (1801-1866)

They say I do not love thee,
  Flag of my native land;
Whose meteor folds above me,
  To the free breeze expand;
Thy broad stripes proudly streaming,
And thy stars so brightly gleaming.

They say I would forsake thee,
  Should some dark crisis lower;
That, recreant, I should make thee
  Crouch to some foreign power;
Seduced by license ample,
On thee, blest flag, to trample!

They say that bolts of thunder,
  Cast in the forge of Rome,
May rise and bring thee under,
  Flag of my native home;
And with one blow dissever
My heart from thee forever.

False are the words they utter,
  Ungenerous their brand;
And rash the oaths they mutter,
  Flag of my native land;
Whilst, still, in hope above me,
Thou wavest—and I love thee!

God is my love's first duty,
  To whose eternal Name
Be praise for all thy beauty,
  Thy grandeur and thy fame;
But ever have I reckoned
Thine, native flag, my second.

Woe to the foe or stranger
  Whose sacrilegious hand
Would touch thee or endanger;
  Flag of my native land!
Though some would fain discard thee,
Mine should be raised to guard thee.

Then wave, thou first of banners,
  And in thy gentle shade,
Beliefs, opinions, manners,
  Promiscuously be laid;
And there, all discord ended,
Our hearts and souls be blended.

Stream on, stream on before us,
  Thou Labarum of light,
While in our generous chorus
  Our vows to thee we plight;
Unfaithful to thee—never!
My native land forever!

THE PILLAR OF THE CLOUD

John Henry Newman (1801-1890)

Lead, kindly Light, through the encircling gloom;
    Lead Thou me on!
The night is dark, and I am far from home;
    Lead Thou me on!
Keep Thou my feet: I do not ask to see
The distant scene; one step enough for me.

I was not ever thus, nor prayed that Thou
    Shouldst lead me on.
I loved to choose and see my path; but now
    Lead Thou me on!
I loved the garish day, and, spite of fears,
Pride ruled my will; remember not past years.

So long Thy power hath blessed me, sure it still
    Shall lead me on
O'er moor and fen, o'er crag and torrent, till
    The night is gone,
And in the morn those angel faces smile
Whom I have loved long since, and lost awhile.

ENGLAND

John Henry Newman

Tyre of the West, and glorying in the name
More than in Faith's pure name!
O trust not crafty fort nor rock renowned
Earned upon hostile ground;
Wielding Trade's master-keys, at thy proud will
To lock or loose its waters, England! trust not still.

Dread thine own powers! Since haughty Babel's prime,
High towers have been man's crime.
Since her hoar age, when the huge moat lay bare,
Strongholds have been man's snare.
Thy nest is in the crags; ah! refuge frail!
Mad counsel in its hour, or traitors will prevail.

He who scanned Sodom for His righteous men
Still spares thee for thy ten;
But, should vain tongues the Bride of Heaven defy,
He will not pass thee by;
For, as earth's kings welcome their spotless guest,
So gives He them by turn, to suffer or be blest.

THE BANDIT PETER MANCINO'S DEATH

(Early Nineteenth Century)

Peter meanwhile perceived the time draw nigh
When he must make his soul prepare to die;
And night and day he called on Heaven's Queen,
His advocate to whom he'd faithful been,
And still had kept her day from sin most clear,
And Saturday alone throughout the year
He wrought no ill. On Mary then, he cried,
And weeping with his priest, in penance died.
              From an Italian Broadsheet by Maria Graham.

THE NIGHTINGALE

GERALD GRIFFIN (1803-1840)

As the mute nightingale in closest groves
    Lies hid at noon, but when day's piercing eye
    Is locked in night, with full heart beating high
Poureth her plain-song o'er the light she loves;
    So, Virgin Ever-pure and Ever-blest,
    Moon of religion, from whose radiant face
    Reflected streams the light of heavenly grace
On broken hearts, by contrite thoughts oppressed:

So, Mary, they who justly feel the weight
  Of Heaven's offended Majesty, implore
Thy reconciling aid with suppliant knee:
Of sinful man, O sinless Advocate,
  To thee they turn, nor Him they less adore;
  'Tis still His light they love, less dreadful seen in thee.

HYMN FOR PENTECOST

James Clarence Mangan (1803-1849).

Pure Spirit of the always-faithful God,
Kindler of Heaven's true light within the soul!
From the lorn land our sainted fathers trod,
Ascends to Thee our cry of hope and dole.
Thee, Thee we praise;
To Thee we raise
Our choral hymn in these awakening days:
O send us down anew that fire
Which of old lived in David's and Isaiah's lyre.

Centuries had rolled, and earth lay tombed in sleep,
The nightmare-sleep of nations beneath kings;
And far abroad o'er liberty's great deep
Death's angel waved his black and stilling wings.
Then struck Thine hour!
Thou, in Thy power,
But breathedst, and the free stood up, a tower;
And tyranny's thrones and strongholds fell,
And men made jubilee for an abolished hell.

And she, our mother-home, the famed, the fair,
The golden house of light and intellect,
Must she still groan in her intense despair?
Shall she lie prone while Europe stands erect?
Forfend this, Thou
To whom we vow
Souls even our giant wrongs shall never bow:
Thou wilt not leave our green flag furled,
Nor bear that we abide the byword of the world.

Like the last lamp that burned in Tullia's tomb
Through ages, vainly, with unwaning ray;
Our star of hope lights but a path of gloom
Whose false track leads us round and round alway.
But Thou canst open
A gate from hope
To victory! Thou canst nerve our arms to cope
With looming storm and danger still,
And lend a thunder-voice to the land's lightning will.

Descend, then, Spirit of the Eternal King!
To Thee, to Him, to His avenging Son,
The Triune of God, in boundless trust we cling:
His help once ours, our nationhood is won.
We watch the time
Till that sublime
Event shall thrill the free of every clime.
Speed, mighty Spirit! speed its march,
And thus complete for earth mankind's triumphal arch.

GONE IN THE WIND

James Clarence Mangan

Solomon! where is thy throne? It is gone in the wind.
Babylon! where is thy might? It is gone in the wind.
Like the swift shadows of Noon, like the dreams of the Blind,
Vanish the glories and pomps of the earth in the wind.

Man! canst thou build upon aught in the pride of thy mind?
Wisdom will teach thee that nothing can tarry behind;
Though there be thousand bright actions embalmed and enshrined,
Myriads and millions of brighter are snow in the wind.

Solomon! where is thy throne? It is gone in the wind.
Babylon! where is thy might? It is gone in the wind.
All that the genius of Man hath achieved and designed
Waits but its hour to be dealt with as dust by the wind.

Pity thou, reader! the madness of poor Humankind,
Raving of Knowledge,—and Satan so busy to blind!
Raving of Glory,—like me,—for the garlands I bind
(Garlands of song) are but gathered, and—strewn in the wind!

PATER VESTER PASCIT ILLA

ROBERT STEPHEN HAWKER (1803-1875)

Our bark is on the waters; wide around
The wandering wave; above, the lonely sky.
Hush! a young seabird floats, and that quick cry
Shrieks to the levelled weapon's echoing sound,
Grasps its lank wing, and on, with reckless bound!
Yet, creature of the surf, a sheltering breast
Tonight shall haunt in vain thy far-off nest,
A call unanswered search the rocky ground.
Lord of leviathan! when Ocean heard
Thy gathering voice, and sought his native breeze;
When whales first plunged with life, and the proud deep
Felt unborn tempests heave in troubled sleep;
Thou didst provide, e'en for this nameless bird,
Home, and a natural love, amid the surging seas.

A CHRIST-CROSS RHYME

ROBERT STEPHEN HAWKER

Christ, His Cross shall be my speed!
Teach me, Father John, to read:
That in Church on Holy Day
I may chant the Psalm and pray.

Let me learn that I may know
What the shining windows show:
Where the lovely Lady stands,
With that bright Child in her hands.

Teach me the letters ABC
Till that I shall able be
Signs to know and words to frame
And to spell sweet Jesus' Name.

Then, dear Master, will I look
Day and night in that fair book
Where the tales of Saints are told
With their pictures all in gold.

Teach me, Father John, to say
Vesper-verse and Matin-lay:
So when I to God shall plead,
Christ His Cross shall be my speed!

THE BELLS OF SHANDON

FRANCIS MAHONY (1804-1866)

With deep affection and recollection,
  I often think of the Shandon bells,
Whose sounds so wild would, in days of childhood,
  Fling round my cradle their magic spells—
On this I ponder, where'er I wander,
  And thus grow fonder, sweet Cork, of thee;
    With the bells of Shandon,
    That sound so grand on
The pleasant waters of the river Lee.

I have heard bells chiming full many a clime in,
  Tolling sublime in cathedral shrine;
While at a glib rate brass tongues would vibrate,
  But all their music spoke nought to thine;
For memory dwelling on each proud swelling
  Of thy belfry knelling its bold notes free,
    Made the bells of Shandon
    Sound far more grand on
The pleasant waters of the river Lee.

I have heard bells tolling "old Adrian's mole" in,
 Their thunder rolling from the Vatican,
With cymbals glorious, swinging uproarious
 In the gorgeous turrets of Notre Dame;
But thy sounds were sweeter than the dome of Peter
 Flings o'er the Tiber, pealing solemnly.
   Oh! the bells of Shandon
   Sound far more grand on
The pleasant waters of the river Lee.

There's a bell in Moscow, while on tower and Kiosko,
 In St. Sophia the Turkman gets,
And loud in air, calls men to prayer,
 From the tapering summit of tall minarets.
Such empty phantom, I freely grant them,
 But there's an anthem more dear to me,
   It's the bells of Shandon,
   That sound so grand on
The pleasant waters of the river Lee.

PRAYER TO GOD

Gabriel de la Concepción Valdéz (1809-1844)

O God of love unbounded! Lord supreme!
In overwhelming grief to thee I fly.
Rending this veil of hateful calumny,
Oh, let thine arms of might my fame redeem!

Thou King of Kings, my fathers' God and mine,
Thou only art my sure and strong defence.
The polar snows, the tropic fires intense,
The shaded sea, the air, the light are thine;
The life of leaves, the water's changeful tide,
All things are thine, and by thy will abide.

Thou art all power; all life from thee goes forth,
And fails or flows obedient to thy breath;
Without thee all is nought; in endless death
All nature sinks forlorn and nothing worth.
Yet even the Void obeys thee; and from nought
By the dread word the living man was wrought.

Merciful God! How should I thee deceive?
Let thy eternal wisdom search my soul!
Bowed down to earth by falsehood's base control,
Her stainless wings not now the air may cleave.
Send forth thine hosts of truth and set her free!
Stay thou, O Lord, the oppressor's victory!

Forbid it, Lord, by that most free outpouring
Of thine own precious blood for every brother
Of our lost race, and by thy Holy Mother,
So full of grief, so loving, so adoring,
Who clothed in sorrow followed thee afar,
Weeping thy death like a declining star.

But if this lot thy love ordains to me,
To yield to foes most cruel and unjust,
To die and leave my poor and senseless dust
The scoff and sport of their weak enmity;
Speak thou, and then thy purposes fulfill;
Lord of my life, work thou thy perfect will.
              Anonymous Translation from the Spanish.

THE RETURN FROM EGYPT

POPE LEO XIII (1810-1903)

A thousand lights their glory shed
On shrines and altars garlanded;
While swinging censers dusk the air
With perfumed prayer.

And shall we sing the ancestry
Of Jesus, Son of God most high?
Or the heroic names retrace
Of David's race?

Sweeter is lowly Nazareth
Where Jesus drew His childish breath—
Sweeter the singing that endears
His hidden years.

An angel leads the pilgrim band
From Egypt to their native land,
While Jesus clings to Joseph's arm
Secure from harm.

"And the Child grew in wisdom's ken
And years and grace with God and men";
And in His father's humble art
Took share and part.

"With toil," saith He, "my limbs are wet,
Prefiguring the Bloody Sweat";
Ah, how He bears the chastisement
With sweet content!

At Joseph's bench, at Jesus' side,
The Mother sits, the Virgin-Bride,
Happy if she may cheer their hearts
With loving arts.

O Blessèd Three, who felt the sting
Of want and toil and suffering,
Pity the needy and obscure
Lot of the poor;

Banish the pride of life from all
Whom ampler wealth and joys befall;
Be every heart with love repaid
That seeks your aid!

From the Latin by H. T. Henry.

MAY CAROL

AUBREY DE VERE (1814-1902)

In vain thy altars do they heap
  With blooms of violated May
Who fail the words of Christ to keep;
  Thy Son who love not, nor obey.

Their songs are as a serpent's hiss;
  Their praise a poniard's poisoned edge;
Their offering taints, like Judas' kiss,
  Thy shrine; their vows are sacrilege.

Sadly from such thy countenance turns;
  Thou canst not stretch thy Babe to such
(Albeit for all thy pity yearns)
  As greet Him with a leper's touch.

Who loveth thee must love thy Son.
  Weak love grows strong thy smile beneath;
But nothing comes from nothing; none
  Can reap Love's harvest out of Death.

THE SACRAMENTS OF NATURE

AUBREY DE VERE

For we the mighty mountain plains have trod
Both in the glow of sunset and sunrise,
And lighted by the moon of southern skies.
The snow-white torrent of the thundering flood
We two have watched together. In the wood
We two have felt the warm tears dim our eyes,
While zephyrs softer than an infant's sighs
Ruffled the light air of our solitude.
O Earth, maternal Earth, and thou, O Heaven,
And Night, first born, who now, e'en now, dost waken
The host of stars, thy constellated train,
Tell me if those can ever be forgiven,
Those abject, who together have partaken
These Sacraments of Nature—and in vain.

THE CHERWELL WATER LILY

FREDERICK WILLIAM FABER (1814-1863)

There is a well, a willow-shaded spot,
  Cool in the noon-tide gleam,
With rushes nodding in the little stream,
  And blue forget-me-not

Set in thick tufts along the bushy marge
With big bright eyes of gold;
And glorious water plants like fans unfold,
Their blossoms strange and large.

That wondering boy, young Hylas, did not find
Beauties so rich and rare,
Where swallow-wort and pale bright maiden's hair
And dog-grass richly twined.

A sloping bank ran round it like a crown,
Whereon a purple cloud
Of dark wild hyacinths, a fairy crowd
Had settled softly down.

And dreaming sounds of never-ending bells,
From Oxford's holy towers
Came down the stream, and went among the flowers,
And died in little swells.

OUR LADY IN THE MIDDLE AGES

FREDERICK WILLIAM FABER

I looked upon the earth: it was a floor
For noisy pageant and rude bravery—
Wassail, and arms, and chase, among the high,
And burning hearts uncheered among the poor:
And gentleness from every land withdrew.
Methought that beds of whitest lilies grew
All suddenly upon the earth, in bowers;
And gentleness, that wandered like a wind,
And nowhere could meet sanctuary find,
Passed like a dewy breath into the flowers.
Earth heeded not; she still was tributary
To Kings and knights, and man's heart well-nigh-failed;
Then were the natural charities exhaled
Afresh, from out the blessed love of Mary.

MUNDUS MOROSUS

Frederick William Faber

I heard the wild beasts in the wood complain;
Some slept, while others wakened to sustain
Through night and day the sad monotonous round,
Half savage and half pitiful the sound.

The outcry rose to God through all the air,
The worship of distress, and animal prayer,
Loud vehement pleadings, not unlike to those
Job uttered in his agony of woes.

The very pauses, when they came, were rife
With sickening sounds of too successful strife;
As when the clash of battle dies away,
The groans of night succeed the shrieks of day.

Man's scent the untamed creatures scarce can bear,
As if his tainted blood defiled the air;
In the vast woods they fret as in a cage,
Or fly in fear, or gnash their teeth with rage.

The beasts of burden linger on their way,
Like slaves who will not speak when they obey;
Their faces, when their looks to us they raise,
With something of reproachful patience gaze.

All creatures round us seem to disapprove;
Their eyes discomfort us with lack of love;
Our very rights, with sighs like these alloyed,
Not without sad misgivings are enjoyed.

Mostly men's many-featured faces wear
Looks of fixed gloom, or else of restless care;
The very babes, that in their cradle lie,
Out of the depths of unknown trouble cry.

Labour itself is but a sorrowful song,
The protest of the weak against the strong;
Over rough waters, and in obstinate fields,
And from dank mines, the same sad sound it yields.

Doth Earth send nothing up to Thee but moans,
Father? Canst Thou find melody in groans?
Oh, can it be that Thou, the God of bliss,
Canst feed Thy glory on a world like this?

Yet it is well with u   From these alarms
Like children scared   fly into Thine arms;
And pressing sorrows   our pride to rout
With a swift faith wh.   has not time to doubt.

We cannot herd in peace with wild beasts rude;
We dare not live in Nature's solitude;
In how few eyes of men can we behold
Enough of love to make us calm and bold?

Oh, it is well with us! With angry glance
Life glares at us, or looks at us askance:
Seek where we will—Father, we see it now!—
None love us, trust us, welcome us, but Thou.

THE HOLY VIATICUM COMES TO ME

GIOVANNI PRATI (1815-1884)

Thou Lord of Life and glorious King of Heaven,
    Thou by the world, the universe, adored,
In Thy mysterious veil Thou now hast given
    To me Thy presence, as my prayer implored.
I thank Thee, God, the aspiring soul is even
    One instant languishing and now restored.
As grass in earth, to be from its root riven,
    Thou canst my death decree, for Thou art Lord.

So be it as Thou wilt; to Thy kind care,
  If I must die, my dear ones I consign,
    Whom now I cannot name with tearless eyes.
Let not my daughter's steps the foe ensnare,
  But guide her lovingly in ways divine.
    I pardon all and thus Thy pardon prize.

From the Italian by Florence Trail.

TOLEDO

JOSÉ ZORILLA (1817-1893)

No more the jousts and tourneys,
No more the Moorish songs,
No more dark battlements with throngs
Of hidden Moslem blades;
Today without their lattices,
Their terraces and glades,
No dance, no fair sultana
Glads with the old *pavana*
Her Sultan's garden shades.

No more the golden chambers
In the palaces of kings;
Nor hidden halls of pleasurings
Of Orient devise;
Nor are there dark-eyed women
On the velvet couches lain,
Where the Faithful may obtain
Their hint of Paradise.

No more the eastern songbirds
In their cages made of gold
Fill the air as once of old
With the color of their songs;
While within his bath reclining,
Half-asleep, with odors shining,
Dreams of love their lord enfold.

No more an age of pleasure
Like the Moorish days gone by;
Age no rival can supply,
Two alike could hardly be;
But beneath the Gothic spire
Of the Christian temple hangs
A great bell whose mighty clangs
Speak of God in verity.

There's today a temple standing
On its hundred Gothic piles;
Crosses, altars in its aisles,
And a creed of holiness;
There's a people bending low,
Lifting unto God its prayer
In the light that's burning there
For the faith their hearts confess!

There's a God the winds have heard
   Mid the foldings of the blast;
The earth trembles at His word,
   And the future mocks the past.
The mere cipher of His name
   On the sinful hearts of men,
Was adored of old the same
   Through the Arab darkness then.

From the Spanish by Thomas Walsh.

IF I WERE DEAD

COVENTRY PATMORE (1823-1896)

"If I were dead, you'd sometimes say, 'Poor Child!'"
The dear lips quiver'd as they spake,
And the tears brake
From eyes which, not to grieve me, brightly smiled.
Poor Child, poor Child!
I seem to hear your laugh, your talk, your song.
It is not true that Love will do no wrong.

How weakly understood,
Thy great commanded good,
Then, fatherly not less
Than I whom Thou hast moulded from the clay,
Thou'lt leave Thy wrath, and say,
"I will be sorry for their childishness."

MAGNA EST VERITAS

COVENTRY PATMORE

Here, in this little Bay,
Full of tumultuous life and great repose,
Where twice a day
The purposeless, glad ocean comes and goes,
Under high cliffs, and far from the huge town
I sit me down.
For want of me the world's course will not fail;
When all its work is done, the lie shall rot;
The truth is great, and shall prevail
When none cares whether it prevail or not.

NIGHTFALL

ANTONIO DE TRUEBA (1823-1889)

The moon is soft arising
    Behind its lattice far,
Serene the air surprising
    As where holy spirits are.
Calm is the sea untroubled,
    And calm the azure skies.
Lord,—when at peace of evening
    Our soul to seek Thee flies
To tell to Thee our sorrows,—
Oh, what despairing morrows,
    If nought to us replies!—
                From the Spanish by Thomas Walsh.

RAPHAEL'S SAN SISTO MADONNA

GEORGE HENRY MILES (1824-1872)

Three hundred years the world has looked at it
Unwearied—it at Heaven—and here it hangs
In Dresden, making it a Holy City!
But let the picture tell its story—take
Your stand in this far corner. Falls the light
As you would have it? That Saint Barbara,
Observe her inclination and the finger
Of Sixtus; both are pointing—where? Now look
Below, those grand boy-angels! Watch their eyes
Fastened on whom? What! not yet catch my meaning?
Step close, half a step—no, nearer. Mark
The Babe's fixed glance of calm equality.
Observe that wondering, rapt, dilated gaze,
The Mother's superhuman joy and fear,
That hushed, that startled adoration! Watch
Those circled cherubs swarming into light,
Wreathing their splendid arch, their golden ring
Around the unveiled vision. Look above
At the drawn curtain! Ah, we do not see
God's self, but they do; they are face to face
With the Eternal Father!

THE EMPTY CRADLE

JOSÉ SELGAS Y CARRASCO (1824-1882)

The angels bending
  To kiss her brow,
Sang unending—
  "Come with us now."

The child replying,
  The angels drew
To her cradle lying:—
  "I'll go with you."

The angel faces
    'Mid wings of gold,
Took her embraces
    Within their hold.

And with the breaking
    Of pallid day,
The crib forsaking,
    They flew away.
        From the Spanish by Thomas Walsh.

GIVE ME THY HEART

ADELAIDE ANNE PROCTOR (1825-1864)

With echoing step the worshippers
Departed one by one;
The organ's pealing voice was stilled,
The vesper hymn was done;
The shadows fell from roof and arch,
Dim was the incensed air,
One lamp alone with trembling ray,
Told of the Presence there!

In the dark church she knelt alone;
Her tears were falling fast;
"Help, Lord," she cried, "the shades of death
Upon my soul are cast!
Have I not shunned the path of sin
And chosen the better part?"
What voice came through the sacred air?
"My child, give me thy heart!

"For I have loved thee with a love
No mortal heart can show;
A love so deep, My Saints in Heaven
Its depths can never know:
When pierced and wounded on the Cross,
Man's sin and doom were Mine,
I loved thee with undying love;
Immortal and divine."

In awe she listened and the shade
Passed from her soul away;
In low and trembling voice she cried,
"Lord, help me to obey!
Break Thou the chains of earth, O Lord,
That bind and hold my heart;
Let it be Thine and Thine alone,
Let none with Thee have part!"

THE LOST CHORD

Adelaide Anne Proctor

Seated one day at the organ
  I was weary and ill at ease,
And my fingers wandered idly
  Over the noisy keys.

I know not what I was playing
  Or what I was dreaming then;
But I struck one chord of music,
  Like the sound of a great Amen.

It flooded the crimson twilight,
  Like the close of an angel's psalm,
And it lay on my fevered spirit
  With a touch of infinite calm.

It quieted pain and sorrow,
  Like love overcoming strife;
It seemed the harmonious echo
  From our discordant life.

It linked all perplexed meanings
  Into one perfect peace,
And trembled away into silence
  As if it were loath to cease.

I have sought but I seek it vainly,
  That one lost chord divine,
Which came from the soul of the organ
  And entered into mine.

It may be that Death's bright angel
  Will speak in that chord again—
It may be that only in Heaven
  I shall hear that great Amen.

THE LAST HOUR

Henry Augustus Rawes, O. S. C. (1826-1885)

Say, would'st thou be
Alone with Him Who calleth thee:
Or dost thou crave
Within the shadow of the grave
Kind faces of the loved to see?

Nay—do not care
When death shall come to thee, nor where,
If then God's arm
Be round thee as a shield from harm
Beneath the Hand that does not spare.

A pitying eye
Shall watch thee when thy death is nigh.
A Heart divine
Will feel for every pang of thine
With man's most perfect sympathy.

He will be near
Who trod for thee the pathway drear.
His kingly power
Will strengthen thee in that dread hour
By Love that casteth out all fear.

Jesus, to Thee,
Rejoicing in Thy kind decree,
We leave the end.
Thou—Thou wilt help us, dearest Friend,
In nature's last infirmity.

O SPRING, COME PRETTILY IN

ADOLF STRODTMANN (1829-1879)

See on what mighty draughts of life
    Spring's first-born night has fed!
Blithely, with wonder in its voice,
    The world comes from its bed.

The swallows drift adown the sky
    Over the blue sea winging;
And to the veiling of the waves
    Is Southland fragrance clinging.

How far the buds have pushed their sides!
    They perfume every breeze,
As if, with song and true welcome,
    They wished us all, heart's ease.

My soul shall wear no mourning now,
    When Nature's eyes are merry:—
Come, let the showers of soothing May
    All sorrow with them carry.

On earth, a truce with bitter pain
    Shall be declared to-day;
Come in, O Spring, come prettily in
    All human hearts, I pray!
                From the German by George N. Shuster.

THE ALISCAMP

FREDERICK MISTRAL (1830-1914)

Far below Arles in those old days
Spread that miraculous burial-place,

The Aliscamp of history,
With legend fraught and mystery,
All full of tombs and chapels thrust,
And hilly with heaps of human dust.
This is the legend ever told:—
When good Saint Trophimus of old
The ground would consecrate, not one
Of all the congregation
Of fathers met, so meek they were,
Dared sprinkle the holy water there.
Then, ringed about with cloud and flame
Of angels, out of heaven came
Our Lord Himself to bless the spot
And left—if the tale erreth not—
The impress of His bended knee
Rock-graven. How so this may be,
Full oft a swarm of angels white
Bends hither on a tranquil night,
Singing celestial harmonies.
Wherefore the spot so holy is,
No man would slumber otherwhere;
But hither kings and priests repair,
And here earth's poor; and everyone
Hath here his deep-wrought funeral stone
Or pinch of dust from Palestine;
The powers of Hell in vain combine
'Gainst happy folk in slumber found
Under the Cross in that old ground.
And all along the river clear
With silver laid upon the bier
For burial fees, men launched and sped
Upon the wave, their kinsfolk dead
Who longed in Aliscamp to lie;
Then, as the coffin floated by,
Balancing on the waters bright,
All sailors turned them at the sight
And helped the little skiffs ashore,
And signed the cross the sleepers o'er,
And, kneeling under the willow-trees,
Piously prayed for their souls' peace.
From the Povençal by Harriet Waters Prescott.

A THOUGHT FROM CARDINAL NEWMAN

MATTHEW RUSSELL, S.J. (1831-1912)

The world shines bright for inexperienced eyes,
   And death seems distant to the gay and strong,
   And in the youthful heart proud fancies throng,
And only present good can nature prize.
How then shall youth o'er these low vapors rise,
   And climb the upward path so steep and long?
   And how, amid earth's sights and sounds of wrong,
Walk with pure heart and face raised to the skies?

By gazing on the Infinitely Good,
   Whose love must quell, or hallow every other—
By living in the shadow of the Rood,
   For He that hangs there is our Elder Brother,
Who dying gave to us Himself as food,
   And His own Mother as our nursing Mother.

OUR MADONNA AT HOME

RAFAEL POMBO (1833-1912)

Couldst thou portray that face whose holy spell
   Still sheds its peace o'er all the loved at home?
   'Tis mine so long in other lands to roam
That her smile only I remember well.
Hers at whose shrine, when sickness on me fell
   In childhood, suppliant thou didst kneel, my mother,
   And I saw both, smile, weep, embrace each other
And which the sweeter was I could not tell.

When memory now in manhood would recall
   Her features who with thee doth share my heart,
   Her half-forgotten face seems like to thine;
And both are still to me the source of all
   That's best in me of poesy and art,
   Nor either mother could my soul resign.

MISERERE

Gaspar Nuñez de Arce (1834-1903)

It is midnight; the great dwelling
Reared at Philip Second's will
The world's wonderment to fill—
All his mighty story telling,—
Lies in haughty shadows spelling
Out the history painfully
Of his vanished majesty,
Giving like some giant writhing
'Neath the mountain, the last tithing
That his ruined glories see.
From the Guadarramas waking
The chill winds have left their caves,
Breasting on the architraves
Of the shrine and ceaseless breaking.
All the stars above are shaking
With a red and sullen flame,
And at times in sorrow's name
Speaks the echo-starting bell
That lugubrious would tell
That the convent prays the same.
While the church morose and sombre
Slumbers in its vast repose,
In its icy silence close
As a tomb the ages cumber;
And the cresset lamps in umber
With uncertain gleam afar
Show the figures now that are
Half advancing, half retreating,
Mingling like the ghost-forms meeting
In a child's or old man's slumber.
Sudden from the royal fosses
Stirs a rumor strange and clear,
And an awesome form of fear
Lifts above the dust and crosses.
Charles the Fifth, the Caesar, tosses

Back the clamping funeral stone,
And with face all fleshless grown,
Rises horrid from the mosses.
Striking hard his bony forehead,
As from lethargy so deep
He would shake his mind from sleep
And disperse his nightmare horrid.
And he stared upon the florid
Burial place so still and lone
Where there towered his funeral stone.
Forth he from the tomb advanced
And took his stand and never glanced
Where his ragged shroud was shown.
"Hark ye!—" cried his warlike voice
In the tone the whole world knew
When the ancient ages threw
At his feet its trembling choice;—
"Throw back your sepulchre's dark walls,
Ye glories of Imperial days,
Ye heroes of immortal rays,
Ye flames of oldtime glory,
And from your places mortuary,
Come forth—'tis Caesar's voice that calls!"—
And answering the haughty word
The very depths with rumor stirred,
And from their marbles surged
Spectres half unpurged;
And the graves opened wide;
And in a line dead kings began
To file before him, each one wan,
And soiled with years, though every man
Still wore his crown of pride.
Grave, solemn, and remote
Came Philip Second, from his wars
Scourged yet unbeaten in his scars;
His son beside him grim would float;
And then the King, the all devout,—
His humbleness beyond a doubt,—
Who saw great Spain, the victim, torn
Like some vast granite mountain, scorn

Of earthquakes, blotted out.
Then came the monarch of the blight,
Whose reign did shame employ
All our grandeur to destroy,
And shaking still with fever's might—
Oh, the dread conspiracy
That the eye might still remark
'Twixt that monarch of the dark
And his wasted monarchy!—
In a terrible confusion
Silently they herd along,
Kings now dead who once were strong!—
Teeming with the grave's profusion.
And the vanished embers start
Gleaming in those brows' dead part,
Throwing shifting lights upon
Eyepits where the eyes are gone,
And empty skulls that grieve the heart.
And following their monarch after,
In answer to the mighty call
As though their very footsteps fall
On Judgment Day, from floor to rafter,
Thronging come Spain's ancient glories,
Through the cloistered corridors,
Princes, Lords and Grand Señores,
Prelates, friars, warriors,
Favorites and counsellors,
Theologues, Inquisitors.
Then with Charles's mandate shaking
From the sceptre that he bore,
To the organ tottered o'er
A poor skeleton all quaking;
Bony hands the keyboard waking
Stirred a torrent of accord
Till the giant music poured,
Litanies and requiems making.
And the voices all in one,
In discordant deadly chant
At the shrine hierophant
To their God and Maker ran.
And the broken echoes, wan

From the victims of the tomb,
Swelled and stirred the startled gloom,
And to such a fervor rose
That it seemed the very close
Of a world beyond its span.
"We were as the mighty stream
Of a river that is dry;
None the source can now espy;
Dry and parched the channels gleam!
Yea, O God, our little power
Was extinguished in an hour—
Miserere!
Cursèd, cursèd the device,
Portent over land and sea,
That spreads the word of life so free
And gives ideas wings of price,
The printed words that all suffice
And wound to death our Sovereignty—
Miserere!
Cursèd be the wire that starts
All lands and peoples into one,
By which to prayers and hopes are run
All the world's pulsating hearts.
Nought in silence can be done;
No injustice lurks or darts—
Miserere!
Now no more each people thrives
In solitary state alone;
To chains of iron have been grown
The bonds where human nature strives;
No more are isolation's gyves
On liberty's strong muscles thrown—
Miserere!
A bitter and a brutal blow
Delivered with unsparing hand
Upon the shoulders with a brand
For priest and king, they did bestow.
And nought there is our sages know
To heal the wound their rage has fanned—
Miserere!

And see, alas, how human pride
Upon the heavens is placing hands!
In arrogance the haughty lands
Would even Thee, the Lord, deride!
Let not their voice blaspheming guide
To peace nor to contentment's strands—
Miserere!
Yet not in hostile turmoil caught,
Nor in their dismal pit of woe
Let Thy world perish, ere it know
That in itself its wrong was fraught.
Unpitying they ceaseless brought
Our death to us—they die also!—
Miserere!
O Life, thou great and mighty river
That hurries onward to the main,
Behold, our channels dust-heaps vain,
Where once did rushing streams deliver!
Let not the impious rule forever—
Nor evil have an endless reign—
Miserere!"
Then suddenly the organ ceased
Its mighty rumble, and the light
Fell swiftly off the throng of blight,
And all to darkness was released.
While in a vast and solemn feast
Of dread and tears the silence grew
And from the eyeless skulls poured through
A flood of weeping never ceased.
Meanwhile the light was fading out
Mysterious and vague, and all
The echoes died along the wall,
And the great vision shrank to doubt.
With daylight breaking from without,
The white procession paled away
As through the scattering mists of day
Came a far locomotive's shout.

From the Spanish by Thomas Walsh.

THE WAITING HARP

GUSTAVO ADOLFO BECQUER (1836-1870)

There in the dusty alcove of the room,
Perchance forgotten by its owner now,
Silent beneath its covering of dust,
The harp was seen.
How many a song was slumbering in its strings,
As in some bird-breast sleeping on the boughs,—
Waiting the snowy hand whose master touch
Should waken it!
Alas, methought—how often genius halts
And drowses thus within the bosom's deeps,
Hoping to hear a voice, like Lazarus,
To say its message,—"Soul, arise and walk."

From the Spanish by Thomas Walsh.

RIMAS

GUSTAVO ADOLFO BECQUER

I am ardorous, I am dark,—
  Passion's symbol do I show;
All desires my spirit mark.—
  Do you seek me?—Thee,—Ah, no!

Pale my brows, my tresses gold;
  I can promise for thy fee
Tender treasuries untold.
  Do you call me?—Nay, not thee!

I am spirit, phantom vain,
  Woof of mist and daylight, now
Bodied, now a ghost again,
  I cannot love thee.—Come, come thou!—

From the Spanish by Thomas Walsh.

THE CARILLON

ROSALÍA DE CASTRO (1837-1883)

I love them—and I hearken
  As the winds their notes prolong,
Like the murmur of a fountain,
  Like a lambkin's distant song,

Like the birds serenely winging
  On their way across the skies,
At the break of daylight soaring
  To salute it with their cries.

In their voices saying ever,
  O'er the plain and mountain peak,
Something that is frank and candid,
  That a soothing charm would speak.

Should their voices cease forever,
  What a sorrow for the air!
What a silence in the belfries!
  And the dead—how strangely bare!
            From the Spanish by Garrett Strange.

INSCRIPTION ON A SHRINE NEAR ISCHL

EMPRESS ELIZABETH OF AUSTRIA-HUNGARY (1837-1898)

Thine arms, O Mother, be outspread
  Here where thy children meet,
And from thy hands be comforted
  The valley at thy feet!

Oh, guard our little dwelling there
  When storms around it play;
Safe let it stand within thy care,
  O Full of Grace, we pray!
            From the German by Thomas Walsh.

A CHILD'S WISH

Abram J. Ryan (1839-1886)

I wish I were the little key
  That locks Love's Captive in,
And lets Him out to go and free
  A sinful heart from sin.

I wish I were the little bell
  That tinkles for the Host
When God comes down each day to dwell
  With hearts He loves the most.

I wish I were the chalice fair
  That holds the Blood of Love,
When every flash lights holy prayer
  Upon its way above.

I wish I were the little flower
  So near the Host's sweet face,
Or like the light that half an hour
  Burned on the shrine of grace.

I wish I were the altar where
  As on His mother's breast
Christ nestles, like a child, fore'er
  In Eucharistic rest.

But oh, my God, I wish the most
  That my poor heart may be
A home all holy for each Host
  That comes in love to me.

TWILIGHT

Joaquín A. Pagaza (1839-   )

Slowly the sun descends at fall of night,
And rests on clouds of amber, rose and red;
The mist upon the distant mountains shed
Turns to a rain of gold and silver light.

The evening star shines tremulous and bright
Through wreaths of vapor, and the clouds o'erhead
Are mirrored in the lake, where soft they spread,
And break the blue of heaven's azure height.

Bright grows the whole horizon in the west
Like a devouring fire; a golden hue
Spreads o'er the sky, the trees, the plains that shine.
The bird is singing near its hidden nest
Its latest song, amid the falling dew,
Enraptured by the sunset's charm divine.

From the Spanish by Alice Stone Blackwell.

AFTER A LITTLE WHILE

JAMES RYDER RANDALL (1839-1908)

After a little while,
   When all the glories of the night and day
   Have fled for aye;
From Friendship's glance and Beauty's winsome smile,
   I pass away,
After a little while.

After a little while,
   The snow will fall, from time and trial shocks,
   Down these dark locks;
Then gliding onward to the Golden Isle,
   I pass the rocks,
After a little while.

After a little while,
   Perchance, when Youth is blazoned on my brow,
   As Hope is now,
I fade and quiver in this dim defile,
   A fruitless bough,
After a little while.

After a little while,
  And clouds that shimmer on the robes of June
  And vestal moon
No more my vagrant fancies can beguile—
  I slumber soon,
After a little while.

After a little while,
  The birds will serenade in bush and tree,
  But not for me;
On billows duskier than the gloomy Nile
  My barque must be—
After a little while.

After a little while
  The cross will glisten and the thistles wave
  Above my grave,
And planets smile;
  Sweet Lord, then pillowed on Thy gentle breast
  I fain would rest,
After a little while.

WHY THE ROBIN'S BREAST WAS RED

James Ryder Randall

The Saviour, bowed beneath His Cross, climbed up the dreary
    hill,
And from the agonizing wreath ran many a crimson rill;
The cruel Roman thrust Him on with unrelenting hand,
Till, staggering slowly 'mid the crowd, He fell upon the sand.

A little bird that warbled near, that memorable day,
Flitted around and strove to wrench one single thorn away;
The cruel spike impaled his breast,—and thus 'tis sweetly said,
The robin has his silver vest incarnadined with red.

Ah, Jesu! Jesu! Son of man! my dolor and my sighs
Reveal the lesson taught by this winged Ishmael of the skies.
I, in the palace of delight or cavern of despair,
Have plucked no thorns from Thy dear brow, but planted
    thousands there!

THE SINNER-SAINT

WILFRED SCAWEN BLUNT (1840-1922)

If I have since done evil in my life,
I was not born for evil. This I know—
My soul was a thing pure from sensual strife.
No vice of the blood foredoomed me to this woe.
I did not love corruption. Beauty, truth,
Justice, compassion, peace with God and man,
These were my laws, the instincts of my youth,
And hold me still, conceal it as I can.
I did not love corruption, nor do love.
I find it ill to hate and ill to grieve.
Nature designed me for a life above
The mere discordant dreams in which I live.
If I now go a beggar on the Earth,
I was saint of Heaven by right of birth.

PRISON SONNET

WILFRID SCAWEN BLUNT

"Honored I lived erewhile with honored men
    In opulent state. My table nightly spread
Found guests of worth—peer, priest, and citizen,
    And poet crowned, and beauty garlanded.
    Nor these alone, for hunger too I fed,
And many a lean tramp and sad Magdalen
    Passed from my doors less hard for sake of bread.
Whom grudged I ever purse or hand or pen?

"To-night, unwelcomed at these gates of woe
    I stand with churls, and there is none to greet
My weariness with smile or courtly show,
    Nor, though I hunger long, to bring me meat.
God! what a little accident of gold
Fences our weakness from the wolves of old!"

HOW SHALL I BUILD

Wilfrid Scawen Blunt

How shall I build my temple to the Lord,
Unworthy I, who am thus foul of heart?
How shall I worship who no traitor word
Know but of love to play a suppliant's part?
How shall I pray, whose soul is as a mart,
For thoughts unclean, whose tongue is as a sword
Even for those it loves, to wound and smart?
Behold how little I can help Thee, Lord.

The Temple I would build should be all white,
Each stone the record of a blameless day;
The souls that entered there should walk in light,
Clothed in high chastity and wisely gay.
Lord, here is darkness. Yet this heart unwise,
Bruised in Thy service, take in sacrifice.

THE BELLS

Antonio Fogazzaro (1842-1911)

The Bells of Oria:
Westward the sky o'ergloometh,
The hour of darkness cometh.
From spirits of Evil,
From Death and the Devil
Keep us, O Lord, night and day!
Let us pray.

The Bells of Osteno:
O'er waters waste we too must sound,
From lonely shores where echoes bound,
Our voice profound.
From spirits of Evil,
From Death and the Devil,
Keep us, O Lord, night and day!
Let us pray.

The Bells of Furia:
We, too, remote and high,
From the dark mountains cry:
Hear us, O Lord!
From Spirits of Evil,
From Death and the Devil,
Keep us, O Lord, night and day!
Let us pray.

The Valley Echoes:
Let us pray!

All the Bells:
The light is born and dies,
  Enduring never!
Sunset follows sunrise
  Forever;
All things, O Lord all-wise!
  Save Thine Eternity
  Are vanity.

The Valley Echoes:
  Vanity!

All the Bells:
  Let us pray and weep,
From the heights and from the deep,
For the living, for them that sleep,
  For so much sin unknown, and so much pain.
    Have mercy, Lord!
  All suffering and pain,
That does not pray to Thee;
  All error that is vain
Does not give way to Thee;
  All love that must complain
  Yet yields no sway to Thee;—
    Pardon, O Holy One!

The Valley Echoes:
  O Holy One!

All the Bells:
Rest for them sleeping
    In blessèd ground:
    Folding profound,
Guilt or innocence keeping,
    Secrets most lonely
    Known to Thee only.

The Valley Echoes:
    Known to Thee only.

All the Bells:
Remember the sorrow
    That covers the world;
The living, the mourning,
    The loving, the yearning.
Pray God of all power
His peace for a dower
    On mountain and shore,
    Then silence once more
    For His Peace.

The Valley Echoes:
Peace.
        Anonymous Translation from the Italian.

From PROMENADES AND INTERIORS

Francois Coppée (1842-1908)

I am writing near the lamp. It's fine weather. Pleasant stillness.
In her black dress, tiny in the great armchair,
Tranquil at the fireside, my mother is there.
She's thinking, no doubt, of the dreadful illness
That sent me away last winter—but without much worry,
For I'm sensible, and stay indoors when there's a flurry.
And then, remembering that an October night
Can grow cold without any warning, suddenly,
She puts a log where the hearth is flaming bright—
Mother, blessed among all women may you be!
        From the French by Joseph T. Shipley.

THE COCOA TREE

Charles Warren Stoddard (1843-1909)

Cast on the water by a careless hand,
  Day after day the winds persuaded me;
  Onward I drifted till a coral tree
Stayed me among its branches, where the sand
  Gathered about me, and I slowly grew,
  Fed by the constant sun and the inconstant dew.

The sea-birds build their nests against my root,
  And eye my slender body's horny case.
  Widowed within this solitary place,
Into the thankless sea I cast my fruit;
  Joyless I thrive, for no man may partake
  Of all the store I bear and harvest for his sake.

No more I heed the kisses of the morn;
  The harsh winds rob me of the life they gave;
  I watch my tattered shadow in the wave,
And hourly droop and nod my crest forlorn,
  While all my fibres stiffen and grow numb
  Beckoning the tardy ships, the ships that never come.

THE TOAST

Charles Warren Stoddard

"Fill me this glass—it is antique Venetian,
  Fair as a bubble from the Adrian Sea;
Pour me a draft of nectar—Cyprian, Grecian—
  None of the *ordinaire* this night for me.

"I drink, my boys, to that entrancing vision,
  A dream o' the summer night, I'll ne'er forget;
I drink to her—Queen of the Land Elysian—
  The dear, delicious girl I never met!

Here's to the heart she gave me as I slumbered,
　The arms that drew me to a haven of bliss;
The melting moments, rapturous, unnumbered,
　World without end—the chrism of her kiss!

Here's to the dreamland home, our Eden dwelling,
　Unchanged forever and forevermore;
And to our mutal love, immortal welling
　Melodiously upon the shadowy shore!

Here's to that perfect one, mine own, mine only—
　And to that dreamful life she shapes for me;
And to those other joys—O Earth, how lonely!—
　The babes I've never dandled on my knee!"

THE BELLS OF SAN GABRIEL

CHARLES WARREN STODDARD

The Mission of San Gabriel Archangel, near Los Angeles,
　founded in 1771, was, for a time, the most flourishing
　　Mission in California

Thine was the corn and the wine,
　The blood of the grape that nourished;
The blossom and fruit of the vine
　That was heralded far away.
　When the wine and fig-tree flourished,
The promise of peace and of glad increase
　Forever and ever and aye.
What then wert thou, and what art now?
　Answer me, oh, I pray!

　　And every note of every bell
　　　Sang Gabriel! rang Gabriel!
　　In the tower that is left the tale to tell
　　　Of Gabriel, the Archangel.

Oil of the olive was thine;
  Flood of the wine-press flowing,
Blood of the Christ was the wine—
  Blood of the Lamb that was slain.
Thy gifts were fat of the kine
  Forever coming and going
Far over the hills, the thousand hills—
  Their lowing a soft refrain.
What then wert thou, and what art now?
  Answer me once again!

      And every note of every bell
        Sang Gabriel! rang Gabriel!
      In the tower that is left the tale to tell
        Of Gabriel, the Archangel.

Seed of the corn was thine—
  Body of Him thus broken
And mingled with blood of the vine—
  The bread and the wine of life.
Out of the good sunshine
  They were given to thee as a token—
The body of Him, and the blood of Him,
  When the gifts of God were rife.
What then wert thou, and what art now?
  After the weary strife?

      And every note of every bell
        Sang Gabriel! rang Gabriel!
      In the tower that is left the tale to tell
        Of Gabriel, the Archangel.

Where are they now, O bells?
  Where are the fruits of the Mission?
Garnered, where no one dwells,
  Shepherd and flock are fled.
O'er the Lord's vineyard swells
  The tide that with fell perdition
Sounded their doom and fashioned their tomb
  And buried them with the dead.
What then wert thou, and what art now?
  The answer is still unsaid.

And every note of every bell
    Sang Gabriel! rang Gabriel!
In the tower that is left the tale to tell
    Of Gabriel, the Archangel.

Where are they now, O tower!
    The locusts and wild honey?
Where is the sacred dower
    That the bride of Christ was given?
Gone to the wielders of power,
    The misers and minters of money;
Gone for the greed that is their creed—
    And these in the land have thriven.
What then wert thou, and what art now,
    And wherefore hast thou striven?

And every note of every bell
    Sang Gabriel! rang Gabriel!
In the tower that is left the tale to tell
    Of Gabriel, the Archangel.

JUSTUS QUIDEM TU ES, DOMINE

GERARD MANLEY HOPKINS, S. J. (1844-1889)

Thou art indeed just, Lord, if I contend
    With Thee; but, sir, so what I plead is just.
    Why do sinners' ways prosper? and why must
Disappointment all I endeavor end?
Wert Thou my enemy, O Thou my friend,
    How wouldst Thou worse, I wonder, than Thou dost
    Defeat and thwart me? Oh, the sots and thralls of lust
Do in spare hours more thrive than I that spend,

Sir, life upon Thy cause. See banks and brakes
    Now, leavèd how thick! lacèd they are again
    With fretty chervil look, and fresh wind shakes
Them; birds build—but not I build; no, but strain,
Time's eunuch, and not breed one work that wakes.
    Mine, O Thou Lord of Life, send my roots rain!

BARNFLOOR AND WINEPRESS

Gerard Manley Hopkins, S. J.

Thou who on Sin's wages starvest,
Behold we have the Joy of Harvest:
For us was gathered the First-fruits,
For us was lifted from the roots,
Sheaved in cruel bands, bruisèd sore,
Scourged upon the threshing floor,
Where the upper millstone roofed His Head,
At morn we found the Heavenly Bread;
And on a thousand altars laid,
Christ our Sacrifice is made.

Thou, whose dry plot for moisture gapes,
We shout with them that tread the grapes;
For us the Vine was fenced with thorn,
Five ways the precious branches torn.
Terrible fruit was on the tree
In the acre of Gethsemane:
For us by Calvary's distress
The wine was rackèd from the press;
Now, in our altar-vessels stored,
Lo, the sweet vintage of the Lord!

In Joseph's garden they threw by
The riven Vine, leafless, lifeless, dry:
On Easter morn the Tree was forth,
In forty days reached Heaven from earth,-
Soon the whole world is overspread:
Ye weary, come into the shade.
The field where He hath planted us
Shall shake her fruit as Libanus,
When He has sheaved us in His sheaf,
When He has made us bear His leaf,
We scarcely call that banquet food,
But even our Saviour's and our blood,
We are so grafted on His wood.

HEAVEN-HAVEN

GERARD MANLEY HOPKINS, S. J.

A Nun Takes the Veil

I have desired to go
　　Where springs not fail,
To fields where flies no sharp and sided hail,
　　And a few lilies blow.

And I have asked to be
　　Where no storms come,
Where the green swell is in the havens dumb,
　　And out of the swing of the sea.

THE WINDHOVER

To Christ Our Lord

GERARD MANLEY HOPKINS, S. J.

I caught this morning morning's minion, king-
　　dom of daylight's dauphin, dapple-dawn-drawn Fal-
　　con, in his riding
　　Of the rolling level underneath him steady air, and
　　striding
High there, how he rung upon the rein of a wimpling wing
In his ecstasy! then off, off forth on swing,
　　As a skate's heel sweeps smooth on a bow-bend: the hurl
　　and gliding
　　Rebuffed the big wind.　My heart in hiding
Stirred for a bird,—the achieve of, the mastery of the
　　thing!

Brute beauty and valour and act, oh, air, pride, plume, here
　　Buckle! and the fire that breaks from thee then, a
　　billion
Times told lovelier, more dangerous, O my chevalier!

No wonder of it: shéer plód makes plough down
   sillion
Shine, and blue-bleak embers, ah, my dear,
   Fall, gall themselves, and gash gold-vermilion.

THE STARLIGHT NIGHT

Gerard Manley Hopkins, S. J.

Look at the stars! Look, look up at the skies!
   O look at all the fire-folk sitting in the air!
The bright boroughs, the quivering citadels there!
The dim woods quick with diamond wells; the elf eyes!
The grey lawns cold where the quaking gold-dew lies!
   Wind-beat white-beams; airy abeles all on flare!
   Flake-doves sent floating out at a farmyard scare!—
Ah well! it is a purchase and a prize.

Buy then! Bid then!—What?—Prayer, patience, alms, vows.—
   Look, look! a May-mess, like on orchard boughs;
   Look! March-bloom, like on mealed-with-yellow sallows.—
These are indeed the barn: within-doors house
The shocks. This piece-bright paling hides the Spouse
   Christ, and the mother of Christ and all his hallows.

THE HABIT OF PERFECTION

Gerard Manley Hopkins, S. J.

Elected Silence, sing to me
And beat upon my whorled ear,
Pipe me to pastures still and be
The music that I care to hear.

Shape nothing, lips; be lovely-dumb:
It is the shut, the curfew sent
From there where all surrenders come
Which only makes you eloquent.

Be shelled, eyes, with doubled dark
And find the uncreated light:
This ruck and reel which you remark
Coils, keeps and teases simple sight.

Palate, the hutch of tasty lust,
Desire not to be rinsed with wine:
The can must be so sweet, the crust
So fresh that come in fasts divine!

Nostrils, your careless breath that spend
Upon the stir and keep of pride,
What relish shall the censers send
Along the sanctuary side!

O feel-of-primrose hands, O feet
That want the yield of plushy sward,
But you shall walk the golden street,
And you unhouse and house the Lord.

And, Poverty, be thou the bride
And now the marriage feast begun,
And lily-coloured clothes provide
Your spouse not laboured-at, nor spun.

A CONFESSION

PAUL VERLAINE (1844-1896)

O my God, Thou hast wounded me with love,
Behold the wound that is still vibrating.
O my God, Thou hast wounded me with love.

O my God, Thy fear hath fallen upon me,
Behold the burn is there and it throbs aloud.
O my God, Thy fear hath fallen upon me.

O my God, I have known all that is vile,
And Thy glory hath stationed itself in me.
O my God, I have known all that is vile.

Drown my soul in floods, floods of Thy wine,
Mingle my life with the body of Thy bread.
Drown my soul in floods, floods of Thy wine.

Take my blood that I have not poured out,
Take my flesh unworthy of Thy suffering,
Take my blood that I have not poured out.

Take my brow that has only learned to blush,
To be the footstool of Thine adorable feet,
Take my brow that has only learned to blush.

Take my hands because they have labored not,
For coals of fire and for rare frankincense,
Take my hands because they have labored not.

Take my heart that has beaten for vain things,
To throb under the thorns of Calvary,
Take my heart that has beaten for vain things.

Take my feet, frivolous travellers,
That they may run to the crying of Thy grace,
Take my feet, frivolous travellers.

Take my voice, a harsh and lying noise,
For the reproaches of Thy penitence,
Take my voice, a harsh and lying noise.

Take mine eyes, luminaries of deceit,
That they may be extinguished in the tears of prayer,
Take mine eyes, luminaries of deceit.

Ah, Thou God of pardon and promises,
What is the pit of mine ingratitude!
Ah, Thou God of pardon and promises.

God of terror and God of holiness,
Alas, my sinfulness is a black abyss!
God of terror, God of holiness.

Thou God of peace, of joy and delight,
All my tears, all my ignorances,
Thou God of peace, of joy and delight.

Thou, O God, knowest all this, all this,
How poor I am, poorer than any man,
Thou, O God, knowest this, all this.
And what I have, my God, I give to Thee.

From the French by Arthur Symons.

MY GOD HAS SPOKEN

PAUL VERLAINE

God has spoken: Love me, son, thou must; oh, see
    My broken side; my heart, its rays refulgent shine;
    My feet, insulted, stabbed, that Mary bathes with brine
Of bitter tears; my sad arms helpless, son, for thee;
With thy sins heavy; and my hands; thou seest the rod;
    Thou seest the nails, the sponge, the gall; and all my pain
    Must teach thee love, amidst a world where flesh doth reign,
My flesh alone, my blood, my voice, the voice of God.
Say, have I not loved thee, loved thee to the death,
    O brother in my Father, in the spirit Son?
    Say, as the word is written, is my work not done?
Thy deepest woe have I not sobbed with struggling breath?
Has not thy sweat of anguished nights from all my pores in pain
Of blood dripped, piteous friend, who seekest me in vain?

From the French by John Gray.

FOREVER

JOHN BOYLE O'REILLY (1844-1890)

Those we love truly never die
Though year by year the sad memorial wreath,
A ring and flowers, types of life and death,
    Are laid upon their graves.

For death the pure life saves,
And life all pure is love; and love can reach
From heaven to earth, and nobler lessons teach
Than those by mortals read.

Well blest is he who has a dear one dead;
A friend he has whose face will never change—
A dear communion that will not grow strange;
The anchor of a love is death.

THE LIGHT OF BETHLEHEM

JOHN BANISTER TABB (1845-1909)

'Tis Christmas Night! the snow
A flock unnumbered lies;
The old Judean stars aglow
Keep watch within the skies.

An icy stillness holds
The pulses of the night;
A deeper mystery enfolds
The wondering Hosts of Light.

Till lo, with reverence pale
That dims each diadem,
The lordliest, earthward bending, hail
The Light of Bethlehem!

OVERFLOW

JOHN BANISTER TABB

Hush!
With sudden gush
As from a fountain, sings in yonder bush
The Hermit Thrush.

Hark!
Did ever Lark
With swifter scintillations fling tne spark
That fires the dark?

Again,
Like April rain
Of mist and sunshine mingled, moves the strain
O'er hill and plain.

Strong
As love, O Song,
In flame or torrent sweep through Life along,
O'er grief and wrong.

CHRIST AND THE PAGAN

JOHN BANISTER TABB

I had no God but these,
The sacerdotal Trees,
And they uplifted me.
"I hung upon a tree."

The sun and moon I saw,
And reverential awe
Subdued me day and night.
"I am the perfect light."

Within a lifeless Stone—
All other gods unknown—
I sought Divinity.
"The Corner-Stone am I."

For sacrificial feast
I slaughtered man and beast
Red recompense to gain.
"So I, a Lamb, was slain.

Yea; such My hungering Grace
That wherever My face
Is hidden, none may grope
Beyond eternal Hope."

TO A ROSE

John Banister Tabb

Thou hast not toiled, sweet Rose,
  Yet needest rest;
Softly thy petals close
  Upon thy breast,
  Like folded hands, of labor long oppressed.

Naught knowest thou of sin,
  Yet tears are thine;
Baptismal drops within
  Thy chalice shine,
  At morning's birth, at evening's calm decline.

Alas! one day hath told
  Thy tale to thee!
Thy tender leaves enfold
  Life's mystery;
  Its shadow falls alike on thee and me!

FIVE ROSES

Jacinto Verdaguer (1845-1902)

Between the roses
Adown the grove,
I saw the Adored One
As fair as love;
He is white and ruddy,
With eyes of a dove;
Like the rim of the lily
His smiles above
With the grace of an angel;

His breast is afire;
He plucked me a rosebloom;
I took it.—Desire
Besought another,
Another rose sweet;
Then five altogether
From hands and from feet.
Still more did I sigh for;—
"Come hither to Me
And pluck from my lips
Where the love-blossoms be,
Yea, drink from the cup
That my lips offer thee!"—
I faint in my rapture
In touching His breast;
From His lips and embraces
I falter distressed.
Alas! Ye embraces,
Bonds rarer than gold!
Through heaven I stagger
Except for their hold.
I know not—I know not
If I live or am dead—
I know that I hold Thee!
Oh, what shall be said
By the Angels who see Thee
And me visited?—

From the Catalan by Thomas Walsh.

A CHRISTMAS CAROL

May Probyn

Lacking samite and sable,
Lacking silver and gold,
The Prince Jesus in the poor stable
Slept, and was three hours old.

As doves by the fair water,
Mary, not touched of sin,
Sat by Him,—the King's daughter,
All glorious within.

A lily without one stain, a
Star where no spot hath room—
Ave, gratia plena,
Virgo Virginum.

Clad not in pearl-sewn vesture,
Clad not in cramoisie,
She hath hushed, she hath cradled to rest, her
God the first time on her knee.

Where is one to adore Him?
The ox hath dumbly confessed,
With the ass, meek kneeling before Him,
"Et homo factus est."

Not throned on ivory or cedar,
Not crowned with a Queen's crown,
At her breast it is Mary shall feed her
Maker, from Heaven come down.

The trees in Paradise blossom
Sudden, and its bells chime—
She giveth Him, held to her bosom,
Her immaculate milk the first time.

The night with wings of angels
Was alight, and its snow-packed ways
Sweet made (say the Evangels)
With the noise of their virelays.

Quem vidistis, pastores?
Why go ye feet unshod?
Wot ye within yon door is
Mary, the Mother of God?

No smoke of spice ascending
There—no roses are piled—
But, choicer than all balms blending,
There Mary hath kissed her Child.

AN OLD WOMAN'S ANSWER TO A LETTER FROM HER GIRLHOOD

Susan L. Emory (1846-1914)

I listen and my hand thy letter presses;
I, time-worn woman, touch it with caresses,
I kiss the faded ink of its addresses.

.   .   .   .   .

In the calm stillness of my meditation,
Here at the ending of my long migration,
I smile at thy young hour of desolation.

.   .   .   .   .

What though the young flowers now are near us never?
The great wind of God's spirit bloweth ever.
I win, with this, the goal of our endeavor.

.   .   .   .   .

Only one youth, but life was still God-given!
Only one youth, but life sped on to Heaven!
For us the gates of glory shall be riven.

.   .   .   .   .

Hush thee! oh hush! no tears mine eyes are dimming;
No grief for mine old age my heart is brimming;
God's mercies, all my days, that heart was hymning.

.   .   .   .   .

I scorn thy foolish fears with sweet derision;
Each year but brought us nearer to the Vision
Of God Himself in His own fields elysian.

.   .   .   .   .

So, while I lay aside thy mournful letter,
The one who wrote, I never can forget her.
God, with unfailing joys at last beset her!

.   .   .   .   .

And then, where youth and age are ever vernal,
We two together shall climb heights supernal,
And see God's face, Ancient of Days, Eternal!

EBBTIDE AT SUNDOWN

Michael Field { Katherine Harris Bradley (1846-1914)
Edith Emma Cooper (1862-1913)

How larger is remembrance than desire!
　How deeper than all longing is regret!
　The tide is gone, the sands are rippled yet;
The sun is gone; the hills are lifted higher,
Crested with rose. Ah, why should we require
　Sight of the sea, the sun? The sands are wet,
　And in their glassy flaws huge record set
Of the ebbed stream, the little ball of fire.

Gone, they are gone! But, oh, so freshly gone,
　So rich in vanishing we ask not where—
So close upon us is the bliss that shone,
And, oh, so thickly it impregns the air!
　Closed in beating heart we could not be
　To the sunk sun, the far, surrendered sea.

BURY HER AT EVEN

Michael Field

Bury her at even
That the stars may shine
Soon above her,
And the dews of twilight cover;
Bury her at even,
Ye that love her.

Bury her at even
In the wind's decline;
Night receive her
Where no voice can ever grieve her!
Bury her at even,
And then leave her!

THE WAY OF THE WORLD

JAMES JEFFREY ROCHE (1847-1908)

The hands of the king are soft and fair—
  They never knew labor's strain.
The hands of the robber redly wear
  The bloody brand of Cain.
But the hands of the Man are hard and scarred
  With the scars of toil and pain.

The slaves of Pilate have washed his hands
  As white as a king's might be.
Barrabas with wrists unfettered stands,
  For the world has made him free.
But Thy palms toil-worn by nails are torn,
  O Christ, on Calvary.

HE WOULD HAVE HIS LADY SING

DIGBY MACKWORTH DOLBEN (1848-1867)

Sing me the men ere this
Who, to the gate that is
A cloven pearl unrapt,
The big white bars between
With dying eyes have seen
The sea of jasper, lapt
About with crystal sheen;

And all the far pleasance
Where linkèd Angels dance,
With scarlet wings that fall
Magnificial, or spread
Most sweetly overhead,
In fashion musical
Of cadenced lutes instead.

Sing me that town they saw
Withouten fleck or flaw,
Aflame, more fine than glass
Of fair Abbayes the boast,
More glad than wax of cost
Doth make at Candlemas
The Lifting of the Host:

Where many Knights and Dames,
With new and wondrous names,
One great Laudate psalm
Go singing down the street;—
'Tis peace upon their feet,
In hand 'tis pilgrim palm
Of Goddess Land so sweet:—

Where Mother Mary walks
In silver lily stalks,
Star-tired, moon-bedight;
Where Cicely is seen,
With Dorothy in green,
And Magdalen all white,
The Maidens of the Queen.

Sing on—the Steps untrod,
The Temple that is God,
Where incense doth ascend,
Where mount the cries and tears
Of all the dolorous years,
With moan that ladies send
Of durance and sore fears:

And Him who sitteth there,
The Christ of purple hair,
And great eyes deep with ruth,
Who is of all things fair
That shall be or that were,
The sum, and very truth.
Then add a little prayer,

That since all these be so,
Our Liege, who doth us know,
Would fend from Sathanas,
And bring us, of His grace,
To that His joyous place;
So we the Doom may pass,
And see Him in the Face.

IN PROVENCE

JEAN AICARD (1848-

'Tis always love in Arles the old—
  An earthly love, or God's dear Word;
Within the church the chants are told,
  But by the door is laughter heard.

And lads awaiting after Mass
  The promise made by ardent eyes,
Or lashes drooping as they pass,
  Come there as to a Paradise.
          From the French by Thomas Walsh

MARY IMMACULATE

ELEANOR C. DONNELLY (1848-1917)

"Pure as the snow," we say. Ah! never flake
  Fell through the air
  One-tenth as fair
As Mary's soul was made for Christ's dear sake.
  Virgin Immaculate,
The whitest whiteness of the Alpine snows,
Beside thy stainless spirit, dusky grows.

"Pure as the stars." Ah! never lovely night
  Wore in its diadem
  So pure a gem
As that which fills the ages with its light.
  Virgin Immaculate,
The peerless splendors of thy soul by far
Outshine the glow of heaven's serenest star.

CHARITY

George Parsons Lathrop (1851-1898)

Unarmed she goeth, yet her hands
Strike deeper awe than steel-caparisoned bands,
No fatal hurt of foe she fears,—
Veiled, as with mail, in midst of gentle tears.

'Gainst her thou canst not bar the door;
Like air she enters; where none dared before,
Even to the rich she can forgive
Their regal selfishness,—and let them live!

A SONG BEFORE GRIEF

Mother M. Alphonsa (Rose Hawthorne Lathrop) (1851-1926)

Sorrow, my friend,
When shall you come again?
The wind is slow, and the bent willows send
Their silvery motions wearily down the plain.
The bird is dead
That sang this morning through the summer rain.

Sorrow, my friend,
I owe my soul to you.
And if my life with any glory end,
Of tenderness for others, and the words are true,
Said, honoring, when I'm dead,—
Sorrow, to you, the mellow praise, the funeral wreath, are due.

And yet, my friend,
When love and joy are strong,
Your terrible visage from my sight I rend
With glances to blue heaven. Hovering along,
By mine your shadow led,
"Away !" I shriek, "nor dare to work my new-sprung mercies
    wrong !"

Still, you are near:
Who can your care withstand?
When deep eternity shall look most clear,
Sending bright waves to kiss the trembling land,
My joy shall disappear,—
A flaming torch thrown to the golden sea by your pale hand.

OUR POETS' BREED

Luis Montoto y Rautenstrauch (1851-   )

"Now whither go ye?"—Would that we did know—
    But who can trace the leaves at midnight torn
From off the storm-swept branches as they go
    Upon the mighty tempest's path of scorn?

"And where abide ye?"—In the refuse heap,
    Our walls and rafters rotting in the dust,—
Dust watered only by the tears we weep—
    Tears bitter with our need and broken trust.

"Had ye no father?"—Yea, he dreamt of fame
    And scorned the thrifty hoardings of the heart,—
He whom the midnight fever overcame,
    To sit, his brows with laurel crowned, apart.

"What seek ye now?"—His legacy decreed,
    The dreamer's treasure buried in the sod;
We are the children of the poet's breed—
    Refuse us not an alms, for love of God !

From the Spanish by Thomas Walsh.

VIGIL OF THE IMMACULATE CONCEPTION

MAURICE FRANCIS EGAN (1852-1924)

A sword of silver cuts the fields asunder—
  A silver sword tonight, a lake in June—
And plains of snow reflect the maples under
  The silver arrows of a wintry moon.

The trees are white with moonlight and with ice-pearls;
  The trees are white, like ghosts we see in dreams;
The air is still; there are no moaning wind-whirls;
  And one sees silence in the quivering beams.

December night, December night, how glowing
  Thy frozen rains upon our warm hearts lie;
Our God upon this vigil is bestowing
  A thousand graces from the silver sky.

O moon, O symbol of our Lady's whiteness;
  O snow, O symbol of our Lady's heart;
O night, chaste night, bejewelled with argent brightness,
  How sweet, how bright, how loving, kind thou art!

O miracle; tomorrow and tomorrow,
  In tender reverence shall no praise abate;
For from all seasons shall we new jewels borrow
  To deck the Mother born Immaculate.

THE FOLDED FLOCK

WILFRED MEYNELL (1852-   )

I saw the shepherd fold the sheep,
With all the little lambs that leap.

O Shepherd Lord, so I would be
Folded with all my family.

Or go they early, come they late,
   Their mother and I must count them eight.

And how, for us, were any heaven
   If we, sore-stricken, saw but seven?

Kind Shepherd, as of old Thou'lt run
   And fold at need a straggling one.

THE WAY OF THE CROSS

Joseph I. C. Clarke (1853-1925)

Onward! Onward!—'neath curse and blow,
   'Neath crushing cross in the darkling day,
With reeling sense, bruised knees that know
   The rocks and flints of Golgotha's way!

Bloody Thy steps?—They must be trod.
   Sweat of Thy brow?—Thirst quenched with gall?—
Thou, being man who wouldst shine as God,
   Must on, though stumbling, rise though fall.

Wouldst Thou rebuild the Temple high?
   Up to Thy Calvary must Thou tread.
Wouldst Thou give life unto men who die?
   Wear Thou the thorns upon Thy head.

They'll nail Thee high, O tottering Christ,
   They'll count Thy torments, pain by pain.
To love—to pity, have not sufficed;
   By those Thou savest Thou shalt be slain.

Who'd tread the god-won heights must fare
   In the piteous steps of the Crucified;
The Cross is his to lift and bear;
   The naked shame, the spear-torn side.

And shall I stoop to count the price?
  Down-borne I'll dare it. Onward till
I drag the cross of sacrifice
  To the top of the cruel hill!

AVE MARIA GRATIA PLENA

Oscar Wilde (1854-1900)

Was this His coming! I had hoped to see
A scene of wondrous glory, as was told
Of some great God who in a rain of gold
Broke open bars and fell on Danaë:
Or a dread vision as when Semele,
Sickening for love and unappeased desire,
Prayed to see God's clear body, and the fire
Caught her brown limbs and slew her utterly.
With such glad dreams I sought this holy place,
And now with wondering eyes and heart I stand
Before this supreme mystery of Love:
Some kneeling girl with passionless pale face,
An angel with a lily in his hand,
And over both the white wings of a Dove.

E TENEBRIS

Oscar Wilde

Come down, O Christ, and help me! reach Thy hand,
  For I am drowning in a stormier sea
  Than Simon on Thy Lake of Galilee:
The wine of life is spilled upon the sand.
My heart is as some famine-murdered land
  Whence all good things have perished utterly,
  And well I know my soul in Hell must lie
If I this night before God's throne should stand.

"He sleeps, perchance, or rideth to the chase,
  Like Baal, when his prophets howled that name
    From morn till noon on Carmel's smitten height."
  Nay, peace I shall behold before the night,
The feet of brass, the robe more white than flame,
The wounded hands, the weary human face.

SHE OF THE GARDEN

Emile Verhaeren (1855-1916)

In such a spot, with radiant flowers for halo,
  I saw the Guardian Angel sit her down;
Vine-branches fashioned a green shrine above her
  And sun-flowers rose behind her like a crown.

Her fingers, their white slenderness encircled
  With humble fragile rings of coral round,
Held, ranged in couples, sprays of faithful roses,
  Sealed with a clasp, with threads of woolen bound.

A shimmering air the golden calm was weaving,
  All filagreed with dawn, that like a braid
Surmounted her pure brow which still was hidden
  Half in the shade.

Woven of linen were her veil and sandals,
  But twined 'mid boughs of foliage in their hem
The Theologic Virtues Three were painted;
  Hearts set about with gold encompassed them.

Her silken hair, slow rippling, from her shoulder
  Down to the mosses of the sward did reach;
The children of her eyes disclosed a silence
  More sweet than speech.

My arms outstretched, and all my soul upstraining,
  Then did I rise,
With haggard yearning, toward the soul suspended
  There in her eyes.

Those eyes, they shone so vivid with remembrance,
    That they confessed days lived alike with me;
Oh, in the grave inviolate can change, then,
    The Long Ago, and live in the To Be?

Sure, she was one, who being dead, yet brought me,
    Miraculous, a strength that comforteth,
And the Viaticum of her survival
    Guiding me from the further side of Death.

        From the French by Alma Strettell.

THE CATHEDRAL OF RHEIMS

EMILE VERHAEREN (1855-1916)

He who walks through the meadows of Champagne
At noon in fall when leaves like gold appear,
Sees it draw near
Like some great mountain set upon the plain.
From radiant dawn until the close of day
Nearer it grows
To him who goes
Across the country. When tall towers lay
Their shadowy pall
Upon his way,
He enters, where
The solid stone is hollowed deep by all
Its centuries of beauty and of prayer.
Ancient French temple! thou whose hundred kings
Watch over thee, emblazoned on thy walls,
Tell me, within thy memory-hallowed halls
What chant of triumph, or what war-song rings?

Thou hast known Clovis and his Frankish train,
Whose mighty hand Saint Remy's hand did keep,
And in thy spacious vault perhaps may sleep
An echo of the voice of Charlemagne.
For God thou hast known fear, when from His side
Men wandered, seeking alien shrines and new,
But still the sky was bountiful and blue
And thou wast crowned with France's love and pride.

Sacred thou art, from pinnacle to base;
And in thy panes of gold and scarlet glass
The setting sun sees thousandfold his face;
Sorrow and joy, in stately silence pass
Across thy walls, the shadow and the light;
Around thy lofty pillars, tapers white
Illuminate, with delicate sharp flames,
The brows of saints with venerable names,
And in the night erect a fiery wall.
A great but silent fervor burns in all
Those simple folk who kneel, pathetic, dumb,
And know that down below, beside the Rhine—
Cannon, horses, soldiers, flags in line—
With blare of trumpets, mighty armies come.

Suddenly each knows fear;
Swift rumors pass, that every one must hear,
The hostile banners blaze against the sky
And by the embassies mobs rage and cry.
Now war has come, and peace is at an end.
On Paris-town the German troops descend.
They are turned back, and driven to Champagne.
And now, as to many weary men,
The glorious temple gives them welcome, when
It meets them at the bottom of the plain.
At once, they set their cannon in its way.
There is no gable now, nor wall
That does not suffer, night and day,
As shot and shell in crushing torrents fall.
The stricken tocsin quivers through the tower;

The triple nave, the apse, the lonely choir
Are circled, hour by hour,
With thundering bands of fire
And Death is scattered broadcast among men.
And then
That which was splendid with baptismal grace;
The stately arches soaring into space,
The transepts, columns, windows gray and gold,
The organ in whose tones the ocean rolled,

The crypts, of mighty shades the dwelling places,
The Virgin's gentle hands, the Saints' pure faces,
All, even the pardoning hands of Christ the Lord,
Were struck and broken by the wanton sword
Of sacrilegious lust.

O beauty slain, O glory in the dust!
Strong walls of faith, most basely overthrown!
The crawling flames, like adders glistening,
Ate the white fabric of this lovely thing.
Now from its soul arose a piteous moan,
The soul that always loved the just and fair.
Granite and marble loud their woe confessed,
The silver monstrances that Popes had blessed,
The chalices and lamps and croziers rare
Were seared and twisted by a flaming breath;
The horror everywhere did range and swell,
The guardian Saints into this furnace fell,
Their bitter tears and screams were stilled in death.

Around the flames armed hosts are skirmishing,
The burning sun reflects the lurid scene;
The German army fighting for its life,
Rallies its torn and terrified left wing;
And, as they near this place
The imperial eagles see
Before them in their flight,
Here, in the solemn night,
The old cathedral, to the years to be
Showing, with wounded arms, their own disgrace.

From the French by Joyce Kilmer.

WOMAN

Thomas O'Hagan (1855-   )

Dipped in the instincts of heaven,
    Robed in the garments of earth,
Maiden and Mother and Queen,
    Wearing each crown at thy birth:

Threefold thy gift to the world,
  Pluck'd from God's ripening sky,
Tending the altar of life,
  Kindred to angels on high.

YOU ARE MY SISTERS

GEORGES RODENBACH (1855-1889)

You are my sisters—souls whose mortal lives
Are passed amid the listless dream that strives
Across my lonely lethargy afar
By the old towns where dreamy rivers are;
Souls in whose silence lives a piety,
Souls whom a sound would mar, whose love alone
Is for what might be, and shall ne'er be known,
Mystics of holy hosts and holy oils,
Hermits whose youth has visioned fabled toils
Toward some illumined land afar, whose gleam
Grows pallid now upon life's paling stream
That winds toward stillness; oh, you are
My sisters, screened beyond the cloister-bar,
Heaven's novices amid Visitandines,
Souls that seem flowers and tones behind the screens
Round which the Angelus is ceaseless wound
As on the loom the gentle fleece is bound!
You, too, my sisters, you whose simple care
Is but to tell the blessed chaplet there
In some sweet hermitage beneath the tower,
O you, my sisters—'tis that name's dear dower
The Church would give you—you are angels wise
Under your snowy coifs with sister eyes,
Chaste in your habits meek and mutely stoled—
Sisters of Silence, in Our Mother's fold!—
                    From the French by Thomas Walsh.

CHRIST IN THE UNIVERSE

ALICE MEYNELL (1855-1925)

With this ambiguous earth
His dealings have been told us.   These abide:
The signal to a maid, the human birth,
The lesson, and the young Man crucified.

But not a star of all
The innumerable host of stars has heard
How He administered this terrestrial ball.
Our race have kept their Lord's entrusted Word.
Of His earth-visiting feet
None knows the secret, cherished, perilous,
The terrible, shamefast, frightened, whispered, sweet,
Heart-shattering secret of His way with us.

No planet knows that this
Our wayside, carrying land and wave,
Love and life multiplied, and pain and bliss,
Bears, as chief treasure, one forsaken grave.

Nor, in our little day,
May His devices with the heavens be guessed,
His pilgrimage to thread the Milky Way,
Or His bestowals there be manifest.

But in the eternities
Doubtless we shall compare together, hear
A million alien Gospels, in what guise
He trod the Pleiades, the Lyre, the Bear.

O, be prepared, my soul,
To read the inconceivable, to scan
The million forms of God those stars unroll
When, in our turn, we show to them a Man.

RENOUNCEMENT

ALICE MEYNELL

I must not think of thee; and, tired yet strong,
　　I shun the thought that lurks in all delight—
　　The thought of thee—and in the blue heaven's height
And in the sweetest passage of a song.
Oh, just beyond the fairest thoughts that throng
　　This breast, the thought of thee waits, hidden yet bright;
　　But I must never, never come in sight;
I must stop short of thee the whole day long.

But when sleep comes to close each difficult day,
　　When night gives pause to the long watch I keep
　　And all my bonds I needs must loose apart,
Must doff my will as raiment laid away,—
　　With the first dream that comes with the first sleep
　　I run, I run, I am gathered to thy heart.

THE YOUNG NEOPHYTE

ALICE MEYNELL

Who knows what days I answer for today?
Giving the bud I give the flower. I bow
This yet unfaded and a faded brow;
Bending these knees and feeble knees, I pray.
Thoughts yet unripe in me I bend one way,
Give one repose to pain I know not now,
One check to joy that comes, I guess not how.
I dedicate my fields when Spring is grey.
O rash! (I smile) to pledge my hidden wheat.
I fold today at altars far apart
Hands trembling with what toils? In their retreat
I seal my love to-be, my folded art.
I light the tapers at my head and feet,
And lay the crucifix on this silent heart.

"I AM THE WAY"

ALICE MEYNELL

Thou art the Way.
Hadst Thou been nothing but the goal,
I cannot say
If Thou hadst ever met my soul.

I cannot see—
I, child of process—if there lies
An end for me,
Full of repose, full of replies.

I'll not reproach
The road that winds, my feet that err.
Access, Approach
Art Thou, Time, Way, and Wayfarer.

THE CHILD'S PRAYER

COMTE ROBERT DE MONTESQUIOU-FEZENSAC (1855-1921)

Teach the child to pray to the blue waves,
    For they are the heavens beneath, the clouds their foam,
The sun's reflection that the bright sea laves
    More gently brings our feeble eyes to home.

Teach the child to pray to the pure sky,
    It is the ocean above, whose waves are clouds,
The gloom of a tempest where spent sailors die
    Is not so sad to follow in those shrouds.

Teach the child to pray to all things;
    The bee of the spirit will form a honey above
On the living AVE, where a rosebud sings
    Chaplet of perfumes on the Rosary of Love.
                    From the French by Joseph T. Shipley.

ROME

MARCELINO MENÉNDEZ Y PELAYO (1856-1912)

Age with devouring fingers spareth naught,—
  Nor populous realm, nor consecrated laws;
  See, now an alien flock to pasture draws
Within the shade where once the Tribunes taught;
No more, behind triumphant chariots caught,
  Go kings in chains to swell the victor's cause;
  Nor do Clitumnian oxen mid the pause
Move toward the altar pompously enwrought.

Like cloud or shadow or swift-fleeting bark,
  Laws, armies, glories, all, are swept away;
    Alone a cross above the ruins, see!
Tell me, O cross, what destiny you mark?—
  Of old Rome's greatness shall the future say,
    'Twas human glory, or God's majesty?
                    From the Spanish by Roderick Gill.

WILD MARJORIE

JEAN LORRAIN (1856-1906)

As on the hedge they danced one night
A breeze blew up and bore in flight
  Wild Marjorie across the sky.

Her homespun socks and petticoat
Within the dizzy air afloat
  Brushed on the clouds as she went by.

Borne far beyond the town's last street,
The strong wind drove her on and beat
  Her body with unsparing might.

Whereon she cries as there she spins:
"Mother of God, forgive my sins
  Since death for me is sure this night.

"And grant me from this dreadful cast
To rise a shriven soul at last
   Into your heaven of starry light!"

Her prayer is answered through the mist
That freezes round her there. Now, hist!
   She's fast upon the steeplecock,

For Marjorie as she goes by
Is caught and held against the sky
   By one poor tatter of her frock.

In the long night a silent spout
With sudden lips of stone speaks out
   And babbles through the rainy swirl:

"There's little strength in that poor stuff
That holds you there. Death's sure enough.
   The Devil's laughing at you, girl."

And hanging there by one poor clout
A thing for all the winds to flout,
   The wench's heart grew very faint.

The gloating Devil, too, had laughed
When suddenly he caught a waft
   Of censers swinging in the night,

And up beyond the steeplecock
With palm in hand there went a flock
   Of venerable men in white;

Old men in white, with giant shapes,
Whose shaven polls upon their capes
   Are ever nodding as they go,

And maids proceeding after them
In robes aflower from sleeve to hem
   With sheen of stars or lily-glow.

Round their pure brows are aureoles.
Great angels with their gleaming stoles
   Leading their flight, look forth and cleave

With their pure glance a burning wake
That shows the way their white souls take
   Over the mistly moonlit eve.

Up soars the throng of glorified
Maidens and men, a phantom tide
   With carolling and chant of psalms,

And there with pomp amid the throng
Wild Marjorie they bear along
   To Paradise and Jesu's arms.
           From the French by Wilfrid Thorley.

THE POET'S HARVESTING

Charles J. O'Malley (1857-1910)

"I gather my poems out of the heart of the clover,
  Out of the wayside weeds, out of the meadows about me—
In gleams from the dewdrop's soul, from wings of birds
    shaken downward,
Poems the night-rain brings, shot through the beeches inces-
    sant;
Poems the grasshopper sings, beating his noonday labor;
The gossamer web is a rhythm, blown from the valley of
    Quiet—
A rondeau that turns on itself, folded in shimmering garments;
And, when the whirling flakes are tangled, at dusk, in the
    thickets,
The voice of Song outcries in the bleat of lambs on the
    hillside.

"All things sing to me—cry: laughter, or tears, or music.
The storm hath its rhythmical beat; the day its musical
    cadence:
Ever an ebb or a flow—a flame, or a mournful nightfall,
A rivulet, bearded with moss, to me is Theocritus singing;
A violet, bursting in spring, thrills me with exquisite music;
A child's voice, heard in the dusk, shakes me with infinite
    pathos,

The flash of the daybreak's sword, the march of the midnight
    planets,
The sweep of the mighty winds, the shout of the prophet-
    voiced thunder,
Restlessly throb in my soul, and shape themselves into
    measure."

CHRISTUS TRIUMPHANS

Condé B. Pallen (1858-   )

i

Mors Victor

Before thy grisly front no man may stand;
    No heart but quakes at sounding of thy feet;
    Thy coming none may flee, though ne'er so fleet,
And trembling earth confesses thy command.
From kings their crowns thou pluck'st and from the hand
    Of Power its scepter; thou mock'st the vacant seat
    Of Pride or Love; or high nor low degree may cheat
Thee of thy tribute, Lord of sea and land.

Dreadful thou art, and terrible thy power
    Against our piteous frailty doomed to die!
    Weakly we lift our fending hands in vain,
And crouching wait the inexorable hour,
    The thunderbolt of thy dark sovereignty
    To smite and blast us with its mighty pain!

ii

Mors Victor

Babes now may smile into thy sunless eye
    And fear thee not, prone in thy kindred dust;
    No longer reck we thine insatiate lust
Of this our crumbling brief mortality.
Time is our bound no more; this narrow sky
    Metes not our vision; vaster is our trust
    Than all the regions of thy moth and rust,
Since passing now we know we do not die.

For risen is our Christ, and with Him we;
And prostrate thou beside His open grave,
O Ancient Victor, in thy first defeat
And everlasting! Smiling now we see
Thou art but shadow with a broken glaive,
Within thy futile hands His winding-sheet.

LE REPOS IN EGYPTE

AGNES REPPLIER (1858-   )

All day I watch the stretch of burning sand;
    All night I brood beneath the golden stars;
Amid the silence of a desolate land,
    No touch of bitterness my reverie mars.

Built by the proudest of a kingly line,
    Over my head the centuries fly fast;
The secrets of the mighty dead are mine;
    I hold the key of a forgotten past.
Yet, ever hushed into a rapturous dream,
    I see again that night. A halo mild
Shone from the liquid moon. Beneath her beam
    Traveled a tired young Mother and the Child.
Within mine arms she slumbered, and alone
    I watched the Infant. At my feet her guide
Lay stretched o'er-wearied. On my breast of stone
    Rested the Crucified.

IN THE DEPTHS OF NIGHT

MANUEL GUTIÉRREZ NÁJERA (1859-1895)

O Lord! O Lord!—how are the seas of thought
    Tonight with waves of direst tempest torn!—
My spirit is in darkness terror-caught
    Like Peter's, on Tiberiades borne!

The waves are cleaving so my little bark
  That to its last destruction it seems nigh;
Thou who didst shed Thy light on blindness dark,
  Oh, let it now unto my faith reply!

Rise, rise, O Star of Jesus, on the world
  That deftly mocks the weakness of my arms!
My soul is chilled; our earthly hopes are furled;
  Our eyes are closing 'mid the dread alarms!

Appear across the blackness of the night!—
  Our spirits call Thee!—here alone we wait!—
And, coming swiftly, let Thy garment white
  Appease the waves where there was tumult late!
                From the Spanish by Thomas Walsh.

THE HOUND OF HEAVEN

Francis Thompson (1860-1907)

I fled Him, down the nights and down the days;
  I fled Him, down the arches of the years;
I fled Him, down the labyrinthine ways
  Of my own mind; and in the mist of tears
I hid from Him, and under running laughter.
          Up vistaed hopes I sped;
          And shot, precipitated,
  Adown Titanic glooms of chasmed fears,
From those strong Feet that followed, followed after.
          But with unhurrying chase,
          And unperturbed pace,
  Deliberate speed, majestic instancy,
          They beat—and a Voice beat
          More instant than the Feet—
"All things betray thee, who betrayest Me."
          I pleaded, outlaw-wise,
By many a hearted casement, curtained red,
Trellised, with intertwining charities
(For, though I knew His love Who followed,
          Yet was I sore adread

Lest, having Him, I must have naught beside);
But, if one little casement parted wide,
    The gust of His approach would clash it to.
    Fear wist not to evade as Love wist to pursue.
Across the margent of the world I fled,
And troubled the gold gateways of the stars,
Smiting for shelter on their clanged bars;
            Fretted to dulcet jars
And silvern chatter the pale ports o' the moon.
I said to dawn: Be sudden; to eve: Be soon;
    With thy young skiey blossoms heap me over
            From this tremendous Lover!
Float thy vague veil about me, lest He see!
    I tempted all His servitors, but to find
My own betrayal in the constancy,
In faith to Him their fickleness to me,
    Their traitorous trueness, and their loyal deceit.
To all swift things for swiftness did I sue;
    Clung to the whistling mane of every wind.
    But whether they swept, smoothly fleet,
    The long savannahs of the blue;
        Or whether, Thunder-driven,
        They clanged His chariot 'thwart a heaven,
Plashy with flying lightnings round the spurn o' their feet.—
    Fear wist not to evade as Love wist to pursue.
            Still with unhurrying chase,
            And unperturbed pace,
    Deliberate speed, majestic instancy,
            Came on the following Feet,
            And a Voice above their beat—
"Naught shelters thee, who wilt not shelter Me."
I sought no more that after which I strayed
            In face of man or maid;
But He still within the little children's eyes
            Seems something, something that replies,
They at least are for me, surely for me!
I turned me to them very wistfully;
But, just as their young eyes grew sudden fair
            With dawning answers there,
Their angel plucked them from me by the hair.
"Come then, ye other children, Nature's-share

With me" (said I). "Your delicate fellowship;
　　Let me greet you lip to lip,
　　Let me twine with you caresses,
　　　　Wantoning
　　With our Lady-Mother's vagrant tresses,
　　　　Banqueting
　　With her in her wind-walled palace,
　　Underneath her azured daïs,
　　Quaffing, as your taintless way is,
　　　　From a chalice
Lucent-weeping out of the dayspring."
　　　　So it was done:
I in their delicate fellowship was one—
Drew the bolt of Nature's secrecies.
　　I knew all the swift importings
　　On the wilful face of skies;
　　I knew how the clouds arise,
　　Spumed of the wild sea-snortings;
　　　　All that's born or dies
　　Rose and drooped with; made them shapers
Of mine own moods, or wailful or divine—
　　With them joyed and was bereaven.
　　I was heavy with the even,
　　When she lit her glimmering tapers
　　Round the day's dead sanctities.
　　I laughed in the morning's eyes
I triumphed and I saddened with all weather,
　　Heaven and I wept together,
And its sweet tears were salt with mortal mine;
Against the red throb of its sunset-heart
　　I laid my own to beat,
　　And share commingling heat;
But not by that, by that, was eased my human smart.
In vain my tears were wet on Heaven's grey cheek.
For ah! we know not what each other says,
　　These things and I; in sound I speak—
Their sound it but their stir, they speak by silences.
Nature, poor stepdame, cannot slake my drouth;
　　Let her, if she would owe me,
Drop yon blue bosom-veil of sky, and show me
　　The breasts o' her tenderness:

Never did any milk of hers once bless
          My thirsting mouth.
          Nigh and nigh draws the chase,
          With unperturbed pace,
Deliberate speed, majestic instancy,
          And past those noised Feet
          A Voice comes yet more fleet—
"Lo! naught contents thee, who contents not Me."
Naked I wait Thy love's uplifted stroke!
My harness piece by piece Thou hast hewn from me,
          And smitten me to my knee;
          I am defenceless utterly.
          I slept, methinks, and woke,
And, slowly gazing, find me stripped in sleep.
In the rash lustihead of my young powers
          I shook the pillaring hours
And pulled my life upon me; grimed with smears,
I stand amid the dust o' the mounded years—
My mangled youth lies dead beneath the heap.
My days have crackled and gone up in smoke,
Have puffed and burst as sun-starts on a stream.
          Yea, faileth now even dream
The dreamer, and the lute the lutanist;
Even the linked fantasies, in whose blossomy twist
I swung the earth a trinket at my wrist,
Are yielding; cords of all too weak account
For earth, with heavy griefs so overplussed.
          Ah! is Thy love indeed
A weed, albeit and amaranthine weed,
Suffering no flowers except its own to mount?
          Ah! must—
          Designer infinite!—
Ah! must Thou char the wood ere Thou canst limn with it?
My freshness spent its wavering shower i' the dust;
And now my heart is as a broken fount,
Wherein tear-drippings stagnate, spilt down ever
          From the dank thoughts that shiver
Upon the sighful branches of my mind.
          Such is; what is to be?
The pulp so bitter, how shall taste the rind?
I dimly guess what Time in mists confounds;

Yet ever and anon a trumpet sounds
From the hid battlements of Eternity;
Those shaken mists a space unsettle, then
Round the half-glimpsed turrets slowly wash again.
　　But not ere him who summoneth
　　I first have seen, enwound
With glooming robes purpureal, cypress-encrowned;
His name I know, and what his trumpet saith.
Whether man's heart or life it be which yields
　　Thee harvest, must Thy harvest fields
　　Be dunged with rotten death?
　　Now of that long pursuit
　　Comes on at hand the bruit;
That Voice is round me like a bursting sea:
　　"And is thy earth so marred,
　　Shattered in shard on shard?
Lo, all things fly thee, for thou fliest Me!
　　Strange, piteous, futile thing,
Wherefore should any set thee love apart?
Seeing none but I makes much of naught" (He said),
"And human love needs human meriting:
　　How hast thou merited—
Of all man's clotted clay the dingiest clot?
　　Alack, thou knowest not
How little worthy of any love thou art!
Whom wilt thou find to love ignoble thee,
　　Save Me, save only Me?
All which I took from thee I did but take,
Not for thy harms,
But just that thou might'st seek it in My arms.
　　All which thy child's mistake
Fancies as lost, I have stored for thee at home:
　　Rise, clasp My hand, and come."
　　　　Halts by me that footfall:
　　　　Is my gloom, after all,
Shade of His hand, outstretched caressingly?
　　　　"Ah, fondest, blindest, weakest,
　　　　I am He Whom thou seekest!
Thou dravest love from thee, who dravest Me."

NIGHT OF THE IMMACULATE CONCEPTION

JUAN MARAGALL (1860-1911)

What sky more lovely than this azure night!
'Twould seem as though it showed the Infinite
In all its grandeur,
In all its candor,
Without a cloud or mist to mar the glow
About the moon and stars that shine arow.

They glow and glow so brilliantly
Amid the endless blue this holy hour
The soul is charméd by their power
On high—

O nightly skies divine, divine,—
The Virgin from God's realms above
Looks down amid the lights that shine
The brighter from her glance of love—

December night she passes by;
The earth is still, the soft winds die—
She passes by so silently—
O night so clear, so fair to see!—

From the Catalan by Thomas Walsh.

CANTO ESPIRITUAL

JUAN MARAGALL

This world we see, O Lord, is made so fair
For those of us who look with eyes of peace,—
What canst Thou give within that other life?—
Hence am I avidous with face and eyes,
With all my body, Lord, and all my soul
That binds me in the oneness of Thy gift—
Therefore this fear, this fear of mine of death—
For with what other senses may I mark

The blue of heaven above the mountain tops?
The mighty sea, the sun ablaze o'er all?—
Grant me these senses in eternal peace;
No other heaven shall I ask than these!"
                    From the Catalan by Thomas Walsh.

BELOVÉD, IT IS MORN

EMILY H. HICKEY (1860-1924)

Belovéd, it is morn!
    A redder berry on the thorn,
    A deeper yellow on the corn,
For this good day new-born.
    Pray, Sweet, for me
    That I may be
    Faithful to God and thee.

Belovéd, it is day!
    And lovers work, as children play,
    With heart and brain untired alway:
Dear love, look up and pray.
    Pray, Sweet, for me
    That I may be
    Faithful to God and thee.

Belovéd, it is night!
    Thy heart and mine are full of light,
    Thy spirit shineth clear and white,
God keep thee in His sight!
    Pray, Sweet, for me
    That I may be
    Faithful to God and thee.

THE WILD RIDE

LOUISE IMOGEN GUINEY (1861-1920)

I hear in my heart, I hear in its ominous pulses
All day, on the road, the hoofs of invisible horses,

All night, from their stalls, the importunate pawing and neighing.
Let cowards and laggards fall back! but alert to the saddle,
Weatherworn and abreast, go men of our galloping legion,
With a stirrup-cup each to the lily of women that loves him.

The trail is through dolour and dread, over crags and morasses;
There are shapes by the way, there are things that appal or
    entice us:
What odds? We are Knights of the Grail, we are vowed to
    the riding.

Thought's self is a vanishing wing, and joy is a cobweb,
And friendship a flower in the dust, and glory a sunbeam:
Not here is our prize, nor, alas! after these our pursuing.

A dipping of plumes, a tear, a shake of the bridle,
A passing salute to this world and her pitiful beauty:
We hurry with never a word in the track of our fathers.

(I hear in my heart, I hear in its ominous pulses
All day, on the road, the hoofs of invisible horses,
All night, from their stalls, the importunate pawing and neigh-
    ing.)

We spur to a land of no name, outracing the stormwind;
We leap to the infinite dark like sparks from the anvil.
Thou leadest, O God! All's well with Thy troopers that follow.

NAM SEMEN EST VERBUM DEI

Louise Imogen Guiney

Springtide of spirits, at the Altar rail:
A mystic Sowing, in the morning light:
A gentleness of Love that yet can smite
As on the granary floor the threshing-flail.
O happy soil! O terror beyond wail,
If never sheaf the Sowing should requite,
And time between were busied but to blight
Good will, which only can make GOD avail!

Till souls be corn and vintage of His feast,
As He was aye of ours, how grave and slow
Like any weary husbandman, a Priest
Fills the long furrow, treading to and fro!
And there my clod of earth, the last, the least,
Vows that pure Seed some harvest, ere the snow.

A CAROL

Louise Imogen Guiney

Vines branching stilly
  Shade the open door,
In the house of Zion's Lily,
  Cleanly and poor.
Oh, brighter than wild laurel
  The Babe bounds in her hand,
The King, who for apparel
  Hath but a swaddling-band,
And sees her heavenlier smiling than stars in His command!

Soon, mystic changes
  Part Him from her breast,
Yet there awhile He ranges
  Gardens of rest:
Yea, she the first to ponder
  Our ransom and recall,
Awhile may rock Him under
  Her young curls' fall,
Against that only sinless love-loyal heart of all.

What shall inure Him
  Unto the deadly dream,
When the Tetrarch shall abjure Him,
  The thief blaspheme,
And scribe and soldier jostle
  About the shameful tree,
And even an Apostle
  Demand to touch and see?—
But she hath kissed her Flower where the Wounds are to be.

THE MAN OF THE HOUSE

Katherine Tynan Hinkson (1861-   )

Joseph, honored from Sea to Sea,
This is your name that pleases me,
    "Man of the House."

I see you rise at the dawn and light
The fire and blow till the flame is bright.

I see you take the pitcher and carry
The deep well-water for Jesus and Mary.

You knead the corn for the bread so fine,
Gather them grapes from the hanging vine.

There are little feet that are soft and slow,
Follow you whithersoever you go.

There's a little face at your workshop door,
A little one sits down on your floor.

Holds His hands for the shavings curled,
The soft little hands that have made the world.

Mary calls you; the meal is ready;
You swing the Child to your shoulder steady.

I see your quiet smile as you sit
And watch the little Son thrive and eat.

The vine curls by the window space,
The wings of angels cover the face.

Up in the rafters, polished and olden,
There's a dove that broods and his wings are golden.

You who kept them through shine and storm,
A staff, a shelter kindly and warm.

Father of Jesus, husband of Mary,
Hold up your lilies for Sanctuary!

Joseph, honored from Sea to Sea,
Guard me mine and my own rooftree.
"Man of the House!"

THE PRESENCE OF THE SPIRIT

GIULIO SALVADORI (1862-   )

Perchance it was the peace that stirless breasts
　　Of forests breathe upon the cliffs on high—
　　Or from the hidden glens the lonely cry
Of nightingale's melodious requests,—
I know not; but the life apart attests
　　Itself unto the wondering passer-by
　　In light so intimate it strikes his eye
As though a festival were on its crests.

While inwardly he turns his wildered eyes,
　　Sensing the Holy Spirit that controls
　　　　The final government of his very heart,
Where mid the starry flowerings of the skies,
　　Lain prone with head immersed, he rolls,
　　　　And sighs the sighs that loves eternal start.
　　　　　　　From the Italian by Thomas Walsh.

THE FRIAR

JULIAN DEL CASAL (1863-1893)

Barefooted, in his hood and cloak of brown,
　　Mounted upon his burro's chubby back
　　To beg the pious alms that fill his sack
The old Franciscan starts at dawn for town.
Behind him sounds the early belfry down
　　To call to Mass the faithful in his track;
　　The summons floats afar into the wrack
Of pink and golden clouds, the dawning's crown.

His breviary at his elbow tucked away,
His rosary rattling heavily with his sway,
   He reckons that his givers shall not lag;
And hearkens as he paces down the road,
Between the burro's braying for the load,
   The wind that whistles through his empty bag.
                                        From the Spanish by Thomas Walsh.

LOST YOUTH

SIR ROGER CASEMENT (1864-1916)

Weep not that yon no longer feel the tide
   High breasting sun and storm that bore along
   Your youth in currents of perpetual song;
For in these mid-sea waters, still and wide,
A sleepless purpose the great deep doth hide.
   Here spring the mighty fountains, pure and strong,
   That bear sweet change of breath to city throng,
Who, had the sea no breeze, would soon have died.

So, though the sun shines not in such a blue,
   Nor have the stars the meaning youth devised,
The heavens are nigher, and a light shines through—
   The brightness that not sun nor stars sufficed;
And on this lonely waste we find it true
   Lost youth and love not lost, are hid with Christ.

ANNUNCIATION NIGHT

KATHERINE E. CONWAY (1865-1927)

It was night in the village of Nazareth,
But the dark, like the dusk of a blessed death,
Was pierced with splendor and voices tender,
And the breeze died down to a zephyr's breath.

Stars sang as they swung in their ordered courses
And planets circling around the sun;
And all life stirred at its inmost sources,
With sense of the Wonder on earth begun.

But the little fair Virgin of Nazareth slept,
Dreaming the touch of the hand of her Child.
And angels above her their vigil kept,
And oft in her sleep she tenderly smiled.

For God to His own Creation knit
His life and hers not a breath apart;
While Heaven was a-thrill at the thought of it—
The Hope of the Worlds hidden under her heart!

FIRST COMMUNION

José Asunción Silva (1865-1896)

That moment all the world respired
With mystic piety;
The early morning light that shone
Adown the chapel aisles;
The rhythmic chants that soared above,—
It seemed to highest heaven;
The aromatic cloud that rose
In incense spirals up;
The voices from another world
Sonorous and serene;
The little children sweetly grouped
Before the altar rail;
Yea, even the ancient Saints, aligned
In shadows vaguely dim
Beneath the cumbering dust of years,
In silence seemed to smile!

From the Spanish by Thomas Walsh.

ART

José Asunción Silva

Verse is a chalice; place within it only
   A stainless thought;
From out whose deeps the smouldering radiance sparkles
   Like bubbles in a golden vintage caught.

Bind 'round it flowers to tell their long endeavors
    Against the numbing world;
Gentle reminders of the season's unreturning
    As pearly seedlings in the dews' flight whirled.
To consecrate our hapless days with balsam,
    Pour on the mystic draught,
Warmed in the very first-breast of the spirit,
    A simple drop alone.

From the Spanish by Thomas Walsh.

THE IRISH FRANCISCAN

Rosa Mulholland (-1924)

A barefoot friar all in brown,
Weather-beat face and storm-rent gown,
Tattered hood over shaven crown,
Travelled as the sun goes down.

Whither ere morning goeth he
Over the bog he moveth free;
Bog so brown it were hard to see
That brown man travelling patiently.

Hidden under his threadbare best
He holdeth One close to his breast;
"O Lord, in what poor place of rest
This winter's eve thou harbourest!"

Deep in the pools the red lights die;
Darkness veileth the western sky;
Only the plovers cry and cry
Amen to prayers as they flutter by.

Who are these, thou barefoot man,
Weak and weary and under a ban,
Who meet thee in the starlight wan?—
Columb, and Patrick, and Adamnan!

Three with torches faint and white,
Threading the holes to give thee light,
Bowing before the One of might
Thou bearest with thee through the night.

Now the dawn opens in the east,
There's the altar, and here the priest;
Welcome now to the last and least,
Who hunger for the Master's feast.

Table of rock and cloth of moss;
(Gold and silver are Mammon's dross)
Rude is the stone and rude the cross,—
O Christ, our gain, O World, our loss!

Ye banned and outlawed of the faith!
Shrive ye now with bated breath;
Hither the hunter hasteneth,
Fear not the little pain of death.

Shines the moon on the curling sea,
Sighs the wind in the white-thorn tree;
Forth from the bough, as the gale blows free,
Swingeth a figure dolorously—

A barefoot friar all in brown,
Weather-beat face and threadbare gown,
Girdle of rope and shaven crown—
Swingeth he as the moon goes down.

KNOWEST THOU ISAAC JOGUES?

FRANCIS W. GREY (1865-   )

A wayworn pilgrim from a distant shore
  Knocked at the convent gate, at early day,
  Then waited patiently: "Whence com'st thou, pray?"
The Brother asked. "From Canada"; the door

Was opened wide in welcome; faint and sore
  With many a toil, he seemed, and long the way
  That he had journeyed; greatly marvelled they
To see the cruel wounds and scars he bore.

"Com'st thou from Canada?" the Rector said,
  —Vested was he for Mass, yet came to see
The travelled guest,—who answered. "Yes"; they led
To welcome food and rest; then asked, "Maybe
Thou knowest Isaac Jogues?" He bowed his head,
  As one who shunneth honor—"I am he."

THE SECRET

José Joaquin Casas (1866-   )

With solemn benediction at the end,
  The Cura's rites are done. The joyous sound
  Starts all the childish choir's hearts to bound
Like when at school their singsong lessons blend;
And rumors vague a silver music lend,
  As through the town the dwellers drift around.
  The glad old priest feels all his breast enwound
With breaths of balsam pure and reverend.

Now of this placid Eden-spot I hold
  The secret key, which all the world ignores—
  Nor Plutarch nor wise Epictetus knew!—
Child, youth and woman, townsmen young and old,
  All, all in Villasuta know it too,—
The saving Wisdom that mankind adores!—
                    From the Spanish by Thomas Walsh.

MEA CULPA

Ethna Carbery (1866-1902)

Be pitiful, my God!
  No hard-won gifts I bring—
But empty, pleading hands
  To Thee at evening.

Spring came, with-browed and young;
   I, too, was young with spring.
There was a blue, blue heaven
   Above a skylark's wing.

Youth is the time for joy,
   I cried, it is not meet
To mount the heights of toil
   With child-soft feet.

When summer walked the land
   In passion's red arrayed,
Under green sweeping boughs,
   My couch I made.

The noontide heat was sore,
   I slept the summer through;
An angel waked me—"Thou
   Hast work to do."

I rose and saw the sheaves
   Upstanding in a row;
The reapers sang Thy praise
   While passing to and fro.

My hands were soft with ease;
   Long were the autumn hours;
I lift the ripened sheaves
   For poppy-flowers.

But lo! now winter glooms
   And gray is in my hair;
Whither has flown the world
   I found so fair?

My patient God, forgive!
   Praying Thy pardon sweet
I lay a lonely heart
   Before Thy feet.

MARQUETTE ON THE SHORES OF THE MISSISSIPPI

JOHN JEROME ROONEY (1866-   )

Here, in the midnight of the solemn wood,
    He heard a roar as of a mighty wind,
    The onward rush of waters unconfined
Trampling in legions through the solitude.
Then lo! before him swept the conquering flood,
    Free as the freedom of the truth-strong mind
    Which hills of Doubt could neither hide nor bind,
Which, all in vain, the valley mounds withstood!

With glowing eye he saw the prancing tide
    With yellow mane rush onward through the night
        Into the vastness he had never trod;
Nor dreamt of conquest of that kingdom wide
    As down the flood his spirit took its flight
        Seeking the long-lost children of his God.

CROCUSES IN THE GRASS

JOHN GRAY (1866-   )

Purple and white the crocus flowers
    And yellow, spread upon
The sober lawns; the hours
    Are not more idle in the sun.

Perhaps one droops a prettier head,
    And one would say: Sweet Queen,
Your lips are white and red,
    And round you lies the grass most green.

And she, perhaps, for whom is fain
    The other, will not heed;
Or, that he may complain,
    Babbles, for dalliance, with a weed.

And he dissimulates despair,
    And anger, and surprise;
The while white daisies stare—
    And stir not—with their yellow eyes.

LORD, IF THOU ART NOT PRESENT

John Gray

Lord, if Thou art not present, where shall I
    Seek Thee the absent? If Thou art not everywhere,
How is it that I do not see Thee nigh?

Thou dwellest in a light remote and fair.
    How can I reach that light, Lord? I beseech
Thee, teach my seeking, and Thyself declare

Thyself the sought to me. Unless Thou teach
    Me, Lord, I cannot seek; nor can I find
Thee, if Thou wilt not come within my reach.

Lord, let me seek, with sturdy heart and mind,
    In passion of desire and longingly.
Let me desire Thee, seeking Thee; and find—
    Loving Thee, find Thee; love Thee, finding Thee.

BENEDICTIO DOMINI

Ernest Dowson (1867-1900)

Without, the sullen noises of the street!
    The voice of London inarticulate,
Hoarse and blaspheming, surges in to meet
    The silent blessing of the Immaculate.
Dark is the church, and dim the worshippers,
    Hushed with bowed heads as though by some old spell,
While through the incense-laden air there stirs
    The admonition of a silver bell.

Dark is the church, save where the altar stands,
　　Dressed like a bride, illustrious with light
Where one old priest exalts with tremulous hands
　　The one true solace of man's fallen plight.
Strange silence here: without, the sounding street
　　Heralds the world's swift passage to the fire;
O Benediction, perfect and complete!
　　When shall men cease to suffer and desire?

EXTREME UNCTION

ERNEST DOWSON

Upon the eyes, the lips, the feet,
On all the passages of sense,
The atoning oil is spread with sweet
Renewal of lost innocence.

The feet that lately ran so fast
To meet desire, are soothly sealed;
The eyes that were so often cast
On vanity, are touched and healed.

From troublous sights and sounds set free;
In such a twilight hour of breath,
Shall one retrace his life or see,
Through shadows, the true face of death?

Vials of mercy, sacring oils,
I know not where nor when I come,
Nor through what wanderings and toils,
To crave of you Viaticum.

Yet, when the walls of flesh grow weak,
In such an hour it well may be,
Through mist and darkness, light will break,
And each anointed sense will see.

THE MURMUR FROM THE STABLE

RUBEN DARÍO (1867-1916)

'Twas in the lonely stable whence the Holy Babe had gone,
Fleeing the wrath of Herod and had left His cradle lone.
Shepherds and kings had gone before, and none remained behind
But the gentle beasts of burden, more true than humankind;
The patient ox and quiet ass still chewed their fragrant hay;
But spared the corner where so late the Lord of Glory lay.
Sad was their talk together, spite of the breath of love,
Like a warm perfume from the nest of the celestial Dove.
"Surely," the ox said, "do we know that He is Lord of all";
"Yes," said the ass, " 'tis He who yet shall save us from the fall."
"Save whom?"
                    "Why all."
                              "Oh, no!"
                                        "What then?"
                                                  "Alas! the heavenly grace
Is meant but for our masters of the cruel human race."
"But we can read the future. It is our priceless gift
To look behind the veil that they may not hope to lift.
Our tranquil eyes can gaze beyond the breaking of the dawn,
And pierce the cloud of mystery o'er sacred secrets drawn.
We are dumb beneath the lash of the cruel human kind,
But we breathe our knowledge to the sun, the moon, the fields,
    the wind!
And sure, though low our lot may be, He never will forget
How we shared with Him our bed where His presence lingers
    yet.
But, meanwhile, here we must be sad—" "No! happy and con-
    tent!"—
So spoke the Angel of the Lord, whose sudden swift descent
Upon the wild wind's rushing wings, a flash of glory shed
On the patient heads that bowed themselves above the Baby's
    bed.
"The day shall come for all of you to know redeeming love,
And hear the summons of the Lord to taste the joys above.
For the humble service that so long and patiently was given,
The gentle animals shall join the ransomed souls of Heaven.

The more that they have suffered here, the more bliss shall
    they see
And for you both yet greater the recompense shall be.
For you two who have parted with your Lord your lowly bed,
And watched with love above Him in Bethlehem's humble shed;
Who have given all you could, without thought of gain or loss,
Shall be the charge of him who shared the burden of His cross;
And on the golden hills of Heaven, for thus it is decreed,
Saint Simon the Cyrenean shall lead you forth to feed."

From the Spanish by Agnes Blake Poor.

PORTICO

Rubén Darío

I am the singer who, of late, put by
    The verse azulean and the chant profane;
Across whose nights a rossignol would cry
    And prove himself a lark at morn again.

Lord was I of my garden-place of dreams,
    Of heaping roses and swan-haunted brakes,
Lord of the doves; lord of the silver streams,
    Of gondolas and lyres upon the lakes.

And very eighteenth century; both old
    And very modern; bold, cosmopolite;
Like Hugo daring, like Verlaine half-told,
    And thirsting for illusions infinite.

From infancy 'twas sorrow that I knew;
    My youth—was ever youth my own indeed?—
Its roses still their perfume round me strew,
    Their perfume of a melancholy seed—

A reinless colt, my instinct galloped free;
    My youth bestrode a colt without a rein;
Intoxicate I went, a belted blade with me;
    If I fell not—'twas God who did sustain—

Within my garden stood a statue fair;
 Of marble seeming yet of flesh and bone;
A gentle spirit was incarnate there
 Of sensitive and sentimental tone.

So timid of the world, it fain would hide
 And from its walls of silence issue not,
Save when the spring released upon its tide
 The hour of melody it had begot—

The hour of sunset and the hidden kiss;
 The hour of gloaming twilight and retreat;
The hour of madrigal, the hour of bliss,
 Of "I adore thee" and "Alas" too sweet.

And mid the gamut of the flute, perchance,
 Would come a ripple of crystal mysteries
Recalling Pan and his old Grecian dance
 With the intoning of old Latin keys.

With such a sweep and ardor so intense,
 That on the statue suddenly were born
The muscled goat-thighs shaggy and immense
 And on the brows the satyr's curvéd horn.

As Cóngora's Galatea, so in fine
 The fair marquise of Verlaine captured me;
And so unto the passion half divine
 Was joined a human sensuality;

All longing, and all ardor, the mere sense
 And natural vigor; and without a sign
Of stage effect or literature's pretence—
 If there was ever soul sincere—'twas mine.

The ivory tower awakened my desire;
 I longed to enclose myself in selfish bliss,
Yet hungered after space, my thirst on fire
 For heaven, from out the shades of my abyss.

As with the sponge the salt sea saturates
  Below the oozing wave, so was my heart
Tender and soft, bedrenched with bitter fates
  That world and flesh and devil here impart.

But, through the grace of God, my conscience
  Elected unto good its better part;
If there were hardness left in any sense,
  It melted soft beneath the touch of Art.

My intellect was freed from baser thought;
  My soul was bathed in the Castalian flood;
My heart a pilgrim went, and so I caught
  The harmony from out the sacred wood.

O sacred wood! O rumor, that profound
  Stirs from the sacred woodland's heart divine!
O plenteous fountain in whose power is wound
  And overcome our destiny malign!

Grove of ideals, where the real halts,
  Where flesh is flame alive, and Psyche floats—
The while the satyr makes his old assaults,
  Let Philomel loose her azure-drunken throats.

Fantastic pearl and music amorous
  Adown the green and flowering laurel tops;
Hypsipyle stealthily the rose doth buss
  And the faun's mouth the tender stralklings crops.

There, where the god pursues the flying maid,
  Where springs the reed of Pan from out the mire,
The life Eternal hath its furrows laid
  And wakens the All-Father's mystic choir.

The soul that enters there, disrobed should go
  A-tremble with desire and longing pure,
Over the wounding spine and thorn below,—
  So should it dream, be stirred, and sing secure.

Life, Light and Truth, as in a triple flame
  Produce the inner radiance infinite;
Art, pure as Christ, is heartened to exclaim:
  "I am indeed the Life, the Truth, the Light!"

The Life is mystery; the Light is blind;
  The Truth beyond our reach both daunts and fades;
The sheer perfection nowhere do we find;
  The ideal sleeps, a secret in the shades.

Therefore to be sincere is to be strong.
  Bare as it is what glitter hath the star;
The water tells the fountains soul in song
  With voice of crystal flowing out afar.

Such my intent was,—of my spirit pure
  To make a star, a fountain music-drawn,
With horror of the thing called literature—
  And mad with madness of the gloam and dawn.

From the blue twilight such as gives the word
  Which the celestial ecstasy inspires,
The haze and minor chord,—let flutes be heard!
  Aurora, daughter of the Sun,—sound, lyres!

Let pass the stone if any use the sling,
  Let pass, should hands of violence point the dart.
The stone from out the sling is for the waves a thing,
  Hate's arrow of the idle wind is part.

Virtue is with the tranquil and the brave;
  The fire interior burneth well and high;
The triumph is o'er rancor and the grave;
  Toward Bethlehem—the caravan goes by!
           From the Spanish by Thomas Walsh.

SIMPLE THINGS

PAUL-JEAN TOULET (1867-1920)

Infinite! let me not think on you;
    Let me still portray
Springtime with its flowered view,
    The wave that ebbs away,
Her who perfumes fair eves
    With her light breath,
Love—fallen leaves—
    Roses of death—
        From the French by Joseph T. Shipley.

THE DARK ANGEL

LIONEL JOHNSON (1867-1902)

Dark Angel, with thine aching lust
To rid the world of penitence;
Malicious Angel, who still dost
My soul such subtile violence!

Because of thee, no thought, no thing,
Abides for me undesecrate:
Dark Angel, ever on the wing,
Who never reachest me too late!

When music sounds, then changest thou
Its silvery to a sultry fire:
Nor will thine envious heart allow
Delight untortured by desire.

Through thee, the gracious Muses turn
To Furies, O mine Enemy!
And all the things of beauty burn
With flames of evil ecstasy.

Because of thee, the land of dreams
Becomes a gathering place of fears:
Until tormented slumber seems
One vehemence of useless tears.

When sunlight glows upon the flowers,
Or ripples down the dancing sea:
Thou, with thy troop of passionate powers,
Beleaguerest, bewilderest, me.

Within the breath of autumn woods,
Within the winter silences:
Thy venomous spirit stirs and broods,
O Master of impieties!

The ardour of red flame is thine,
And thine the steely soul of ice:
Thou poisonest the fair design
Of nature, with unfair device.

Apples of ashes, golden bright;
Waters of bitterness, how sweet!
O banquet of a foul delight,
Prepared by thee, dark Paraclete.

Thou art the whisper in the gloom,
The hinting tone, the haunting laugh:
Thou art the adorner of my tomb,
The minstrel of mine epitaph.

I fight thee, in the Holy Name!
Yet, what thou dost, is what God saith,
Tempter! should I escape thy flame,
Thou wilt have helped my soul from Death.

The second Death, that never dies,
That cannot die, when time is dead:
Live Death, wherein the lost soul cries,
Eternally uncomforted.

Dark Angel, with thine aching lust
Of two defeats, of two despairs:
Less dread, a change to drifting dust,
Than thine eternity of cares.

Do what thou wilt, thou shalt not so,
Dark Angel! triumph over me:
Lonely, unto the Lone I go;
Divine, to the Divinity.

THE PRECEPT OF SILENCE

LIONEL JOHNSON

I know you: solitary griefs,
Desolate passions, aching hours,
I know you: tremulous beliefs,
Agonized hopes, and ashen flowers!

The winds are sometimes sad to me;
The starry spaces, full of fear:
Mine is the sorrow on the sea,
And mine the sigh of places drear.

Some players upon plaintive strings
Publish their wistfulness abroad:
I have not spoken of these things,
Save to one man, and unto God.

TE MARTYRUM CANDIDATUS

LIONEL JOHNSON

Ah, see the fair chivalry come, the companions of Christ!
  White Horsemen, who ride on white horses, the
Knights of God!
They, for their Lord and their Lover who sacrificed
All, save the sweetness of treading where He first trod!

These through the darkness of death, the dominion of night,
Swept, and they woke in white places at morning tide:
They saw with their eyes, and sang for joy of the sight,
They saw with their eyes the Eyes of the Crucified.

Now, whithersoever He goeth, with Him they go:
White Horsemen, who ride on white horses, oh fair to see!
They ride, where the Rivers of Paradise flash and flow,
White Horsemen, with Christ their Captain: for ever He!

THE CATHEDRAL OF RHEIMS

Edmund Rostand (1868-1918)

They make it only more immortal still.
   Though vandals mar, yet lives the work of Art.
   Let Phidias witness and Rodin impart
How in these fragments speaks the primal thrill.
The fortress crumbles on the gunless hill;
   The shrine though broken lives with nobler heart;
   Our eyes raised wistful where its spires would start
Find heaven grown lovelier through its shattered grille.

Let us be grateful—Fate would long withhold
What Greece could boast of on her hill of gold,
   A Beauty in its outrage sanctified,—
Let us be grateful, now the hands upon
   The blundering German cannon would provide
Their shame forever and our Parthenon.

From the French by Thomas Walsh.

LITTLE GREGORY

Theodore Botrel (1868-1925)

"Gregory," his dam would chide,
"Where could one find smaller?
Why, the kneading-trough outside
Is two inches taller!'

Though apprentices are sought
On the land and sea,
None would give your suit a thought;
You're too weak and wee, my bonny;
You're too weak and wee.
Jesu Domine!"

"Gad," the merry Captain said,
"Pigmy, I'll be sworn,
Once aboard you'd soon be dead.
Harkee, Peppercorn,
Though you have a waggish look,
Who will ever see
You as swab or billy-cook?
You're too weak and wee, my bonny;
You're too weak and wee.
Jesu Domine!"

At the Palace of Versailles
He besought the King:
"Sire, a lad of Cornouailles
Comes a soldiering!"
But King Louis laughed aloud:
"Guardsman would you be?
Though with heart you're well endowed,
You're too weak and wee, my bonny,
You're too weak and wee.
Jesu Domine!"

Springtime broke in Brittany
And the war had come.
Jean Chouan, his friend, and he
Marched behind the drum.
Soon the bullets swept the plain,
Missing Gregory,
Singing in their high disdain;
"He's too weak and wee, this Johnny;
He's too weak and wee.
Jesu Domine!"

But a bullet found at last
Rest between his eyes.
Through the hole his spirit passed
To the azure skies.
There, Saint Peter, golden-keyed,
Said: "Begone from me!
Though for seraphs we have need,
You're too weak and wee, my bonny,
You're too weak and wee.
Jesu Domine!"

But the Lord our God above,
Here and everywhere,
Bared His riven heart of love,
Hiding Gregory there;
And the warden of the keys
Sank down upon his knees
When he heard the voice that spake
In distant Galilee:
"Whoso receiveth one of these
In sooth receiveth Me!"

"Jesu Domine!"
From the French by Richard Cloudesley Savage.

THE HEDGE SCHOOLMASTERS

SEUMAS MACMANUS (1868-   )

When the night shall lift from Erin's hills, 'twere shame if we
    forget
One band of unsung heroes whom Freedom owes a debt.
When we brim high cups to brave ones then, their memory let
    us pledge
Who gathered their ragged classes behind a friendly hedge.

By stealth they met their pupils in the glen's deep-hidden nook
And taught them many a lesson was never in English book;
There was more than wordy logic shown to use in wise debate;
Nor *amo* was the only verb they gave to conjugate.

When hunted on the heathery hill and through the shadowy
    wood,
They climbed the cliff, they dared the marsh, they stemmed the
    tumbling flood;
Their blanket was the clammy mist, their bed the wind-swept
    bent;
In fitful sleep they dreamt the bay of blood-hounds on their
    scent.

Their lore was not the brightest, nor their store, mayhap, the
    best,
But they fostered love undying in each young Irish breast;
And through the dread, dread night and long that steeped our
    island then,
The lamps of hope and fires of faith were fed by these brave
    men.

The grass waves green above them; soft sleep is theirs for aye;
The hunt is over and the cold; the hunger passed away.
Oh, hold them high and holy! and their memory proudly
    pledge,
Who gathered their ragged classes behind a friendly hedge.

SHADOWS

PAUL CLAUDEL (1868-   )

I am here, the other elsewhere, the silence seems to live;
We are wretched ones, and Satan sifts us in his sieve.

I suffer, the other suffers, and there is no travelled land
Between her and me, from the other to me no word and no
    hand.

Naught but the common and incommunicable night,
The night where naught is done, and love's incredible affright.

I feel a subtle wind, and my horror is released.
Flee from the danger of death, from the jaws of the beast!

Here once more the savor of death is between my teeth.
The travail, and the vomit, and the turning beneath.

I was alone in the wine-press, I trod the grape, accursed
That night, as I walked from wall to wall, while maniac laughter
burst.

He who has made the eyes, without eyes shall He behold me?
He who has made the ears, without ears shall He be told me?

I know that where sin abounds, superabounding is your compas-
sion pearled.
I must pray, for it is the hour of the Sovereign of the world.
From the French by Joseph T. Shipley.

SEVENTH STATION

Paul Claudel

'Tis not the stones that conquer now, nor the knotted flails;
It is the soul that falters here, it is the soul that fails.

Oh, midway of our mortal life when the strong soul is spent,
When the compass loses its polar star and faith is firmament,

Because the flinty road is long, the steep climb without end,
We seem to sink, abandoned by every hope and friend.

Oh, lengthening years of weariness, inflexible cold fate!
Borne down by secret self-disgust and the cross's cruel weight

We fall at last, not on our knees in supplicating prayer,
But wretchedly, face downward, in agonized despair.

The jaded body falls, ah yes, but not till the tired will stumbles—
Save us, Lord, from this second fall when the weary spirit
crumbles!
From the French by Henry Marton Robinson.

Lines from the GÉORGIQUES CHRÉTIENNES

Francis Jammes (1868-   )

This day, O Father, give us daily bread
For without Thee, our wit and goods are sped.

Thou, teaching well, dost superintend the care
Of kneading fingers, crossed as if in prayer,—

And drawest from the breathless worker's sigh
The words of love which halting poets try.

Our Father of Heaven, this humble folk is Thine;
Be for them every one an overseer benign.

Father of harvesters, here is Thy sickle lying—
To Thee like fields of wheat are families, dying.

Father of millers, here is Thy strong mill—
This turning world, the which like grains we fill.

From the French by George N. Shuster.

PRAYER THAT AN INFANT MAY NOT DIE

Francis Jammes

Lord, spare to them this very little child
as You preserve a grass-blade in the wind!
What will it cost You, since the mother weeps,
not to have it die there in a brief while
as a matter that cannot be avoided?
If You grant it life, it will go next year
to toss roses in the Lord's Day festival!
But You are too good! 'Twould not be You, good Lord,
Who place blue death upon the rosy cheek
while there are still fine places where You can set
sons beside their mothers at the window.
But why not here? Ah, since the hour calls,
remember, Lord, before the dying child,—
You live forever at Your mother's side!

From the French by Joseph T. Shipley.

PALM SUNDAY

Francis Jammes

At last the beautiful Palm Sunday comes.
When I was a little child, they gave some cakes to me
And I went to vespers, docile and sad.
My mother would say, "In my country there are olives . . .
Jesus was weeping once in an olive garden . . .
They went with great pomp to seek Him again . . .
The people wept, calling His name at Jerusalem . . .
He was gentle like the sky, and the little ass carried Him,
Trotting joyously over the strewn palms. And when
The beggars saw Him, they sobbed with joy along His path,
And followed Him, because they had faith.
All the bad women became good,
Seeing Him pass by with His halo so fair,
So beautiful that they thought it was the sun.
He had a smile, and like honey was His hair.
He raised the dead . . . they crucified Him then . . ."
I remember this childhood and the vespers,
And I weep, my throat convulsed at being no more
That little boy of those old months of March;
At being no more in the village church,
Where I carried incense in the procession,
And where I heard the good priest say the Passion.
From the French by Theodore Yung.

ALONE

Francis Jammes

Alone amid the forest of his soul
The poet wearies of the distant goal,—
Bunalli lianas and balm-trees in vain,
He watches for the Good Samaritan.
He prays. God is silent. He with anger
Is seized, and grief weighs on him like thunder.
Answer me, Lord, what with me would You do?
I am entirely dispossest of you,

And I feel within me a great dryness.
Return! Give me only the happiness
Of this bird chanting in the cherry tree.
What is Your motive in thus breaking me?
—I labour thy heart—that I may be kind
To thee, my child! Thou hast injuries borne.
Guard Me in thy heart, even when the wind
Has the last roses from the bushes torn.
Didst thou forsake Me great would be thy loss . . .
I need thy tears, well-loved son, for My dole;
I need a bird to sing upon the Cross.
Wouldst thou then leave Me, redbreast of the soul?—
Lord, where a hedge of thorns cinctures Your brow,
During Your Passion, singing, I will sit:
But when the blossoms in the hedge shall blow,
You will the bird let build her nest in it.

From the French by J. Ffrench-Mullen.

TOLEDO

Antonio Gómez Restrepo (1869—)

Perched on its yellow peak beneath a sky
    Inclement as of Africa, there lifts
    Toledo, with its brows of wrinkled rifts
Crowned with the belfries of the long gone-by.
The sacred city shuts its midday eye
    To take siesta mid the Orient wifts:
    Only from out the forge the rumor drifts
Where on the sword-blade still the armorers ply.

Deep in the choir's ancient glooms, behind
    The Gothic lattices, there bends in prayer
        A pallid monk upon his ritual.
And on the balcony outside there wind
    The garlanded carnations, burning there
        Fresh as the lips love's earliest sighs enthrall.

From the Spanish by Thomas Walsh.

THE FINAL FAITH

GEORGE STERLING (1869-1926)

Not often, when the carnal dance is mad—
　　Not often, in our youth's audacity,
　　Shall one, aware, have final faith in thee,
O soul, for he that knows thee shall be sad
Betimes, and youth would be forever glad.
　　Then, craving freedom, never are we free;
　　Through many-colored mists we call or flee,
And in illusion's raiment are we clad.

But when the humiliation of the flesh
　　Is ours, like truant children going home
　　We turn to thee, the beautiful and best,
Whose dew-remembered flowers are ever fresh—
　　Whose winds are from the snows and ocean-foam—
　　Who hast the starlight on thy marble breast.

III

CONTEMPORARY POETS FROM 1870

TO DIVES

HILAIRE BELLOC (1870-

Dives, when you and I go down to Hell
Where scribblers end and millionaires as well,
We shall be carrying on our separate backs
Two very large but very different packs;
And as you stagger under yours, my friend,
Down the dull shore where all our journeys end,
And go before me (as your rank demands)
Toward the infinite flat underlands,
And that dear river of forgetfulness—
Charon, a man of exquisite address
(For as your wife's progenitors could tell,
They're very strict on etiquette in Hell),
Will, since you are a lord, observe, "My lord,
We cannot take these weighty things aboard!"
Then down they go, my wretched Dives, down—
The fifteen sorts of boots you kept for town,
The hat to meet the Devil in; the plain
But costly ties; the cases of champagne;
The solid watch, and seal, and chain, and charm;
The working model of a Burning Farm
(To give the little Belials; all the three
Biscuits for Cerberus; the guarantee
From Lambeth that the rich can never burn,
And even promising a safe return;
The admirable overcoat, designed
To cross Cocytus—very warmly lined;
Sweet Dives, you will leave them all behind
And enter Hell as tattered and as bare
As was your father when he took the air
Behind a barrow-load in Leicester Square.
Then turned to me, and noting one that brings
With careless step a mist of shadowy things;
Laughter and memories, and a few regrets,
Some honor, and a quantity of debts,

A doubt or two of sorts, a trust in God,
And (what will seem to you extremely odd)
His father's granfer's father's father's name,
Unspoilt, untitled, even spelt the same;
Charon, who twenty thousand times before
Has ferried Poets to the ulterior shore,
Will estimate the weight I bear, and cry—
"Comrade!" (He has himself been known to try
His hand at Latin and Italian verse
Much in the style of Vergil—only worse.)
"We let such vain imaginaries pass!"
Then tell me, Dives, which will look the ass—
You, or myself? Or Charon? Who can tell?
They order things so damnably in Hell.

DREAMING OF CITIES DEAD

Eleanor Rogers Cox

Dreaming of cities dead,
Of bright Queens vanishéd,
Of Kings whose names were but as seed wind-blown
E'en when white Patrick's voice shook Tara's throne,—
My way along the great world-street I tread
And keep the rites of Beauty lost, alone.

Cairns level with the dust—
Names dim with Time's dull rust—
Afar they sleep on many a wind-swept hill,
The beautiful, the strong of heart and will—
On whose pale dreams no sunrise joy shall burst,
No harper's song shall pierce with battle-thrill.

Long from their purpled heights,
Their reign of high delights,
The Queens have wended down Death's mildewed stair,
Leaving the scent of lilies on the air,
To gladden earth through all her days and nights,
That once she cherished anything so fair.

INDIA THE MAGIC

JULES BOIS (1870-   )

With light of magic India shines afar,
  Calling the weary heart with shadowy dance;
She is the flower of Dream, the Mystic Star
  That through the Orient gardens casts her glance.

Birthland is she of gods and goddesses;
  Pure are her heavens as are an infant's eyes;
Lurking with terrors, fertile of caress;
  The tiger's triumph mid her jungle lies.

Along her balconies the monkey plays;
  The peacock struts on her pagoda eaves;
The elephant majestic plods her ways;
  A glare of stone her serpents' long gaze leaves.

India brings jewelled tribute from the kings;
  From cupolas of pearl and pools of sky;
Eternal, smile her walls' rememberings—
  And he who sees no longer fears to die!

From the French by Thomas Walsh.

THE LORD

JOSÉ MARIA GABRIEL Y GALÁN (1870-1908)

In the name of God—Who shall open—
I close the doors of my ancestral dwelling,—
closing my life out from the horizons,
closing my God as in a temple!—
Oh, there is need of a heart of stone,
blood of hyenas, and a breast of steel,
to speak the farewells that in my throat
are struggling from my brooding breast.
Oh, there is need of a martyr's lips
to meet today

The icy chalice trembling in my hold
beneath my clouded eyes of hope.—
Now is the house deserted,
the elders silently have stolen forth;
Alone, it is for me to seek the loving Christ,—
There with His arms stretched wide—

From the Spanish by Thomas Walsh.

A PRAYER

Lord Alfred Douglas (1870-   )

Often the western wind has sung to me,
  There have been voices in the streams and meres,
And pitiful trees have told me, God, of Thee:
  And I heard not. Oh! open Thou mine ears

The reeds have whispered low as I passed by,
  "Be strong, O friend, be strong, put off vain fears,
Vex not thy soul for doubts, God cannot lie";
  And I heard not. Oh! open Thou mine ears.

There have been many stars to guide my feet,
  Often the delicate moon, hearing my sighs,
Has rent the clouds and shown a silver street;
  And I saw not. Oh! open Thou mine eyes.

Angels have beckoned me unceasingly,
  And walked with me; and from the sombre skies
Dear Christ Himself has stretched out hands to me;
  And I saw not. Oh! open Thou mine eyes.

MYSTICAL POETS

Amado Nervo (1870-1919)

Bards of brow funereal,
With your profiles angula
As in medals old and grand,—

Ye with air seignorial,
Ye whose glances lie afar,
Ye with voices of command,

Theologians grave in pride,
Vessels of love's holy grace,
Vessels filled with griefs profound,

Ye who gaze with vision wide,
Ye whose Christ is in your face,
Ye in tangled locks enwound,—

My Muse—in mood marmoreal
That seeks oblivion as a star,
Can find alone her raptures fanned

Amid your air seignorial,
Amid your glance that lies afar,
Amid your voices of command.

My soul that would your spirits trace
Behind the incense rising tide
Within the nave's calm shadow-ground,

Hath loved the Christ upon your face,
Hath loved your sweep of vision wide,
Hath loved your tangled locks enwound.
                 From the Spanish by Thomas Walsh.

VESPERS

Louis Mercier (1870-   )

'Tis Sunday at home.
  The country around
Stirs in the sad, soft winter sun.
  Vespers sound.

No one's at work in the fields,
  The trees, wind-browned,
Look like sowers walking
  Through the farther ground.

Closed doors of the few houses
  Shut in their folk;
Through the chimney wavers
  A film of smoke.

Nothing disturbs the quiet.
  The wind dreams, the woods hark,
The few leaves that are left them
  Bend to the dark.

The hour is pensive. You might say
  So gravely its smiles well,
That the earth knows a secret
  It's about to tell.

The quiet, under the sleeping sky,
  Is so profound,
It gives foretaste of goodly death.
  Vespers sound.

From the French by Joseph T. Shipley.

AT HIGH MASS

ROBERT HUGH BENSON (1871-1914)

Thou who hast made this world so wondrous fair,—
  The pomp of clouds; the glory of the sea;
  Music of waters; song-birds' melody;
The organ of Thy thunder in the air;
Breath of the rose; and beauty everywhere—
  Lord, take this stately service done to Thee,
  The grave enactment of Thy Calvary
In jewelled pomp and splendor pictured there!

Lord, take the sounds and sights; the silk and gold;
  The white and scarlet; take the reverent grace
    Of ordered step; window and glowing wall—
Prophet and Prelate, holy men of old;
  And teach us, children of the Holy Place
    Who love Thy Courts, to love Thee best of all.

THE TERESIAN CONTEMPLATIVE

Robert Hugh Benson

She moves in tumult; round her lies
  The silence of the world of grace;
The twilight of our mysteries
  Shines like high noonday on her face;
Our piteous guesses, dim with fears,
She touches, handles, sees, and hears.

In her all longings mix and meet;
  Dumb souls through her are eloquent;
She feels the world beneath her feet
  Thrill in a passionate intent;
Through her our tides of feeling roll
And find their God within her soul.

Her faith the awful Face of God
  Brightens and blinds with utter light;
Her footsteps fall where late He trod;
  She sinks in roaring voids of night;
Cries to her Lord in black despair,
And knows, yet knows not, He is there.

A willing sacrifice she takes
  The burden of our fall within;
Holy she stands; while on her breaks
  The lightning of the wrath of sin;
She drinks her Saviour's cup of pain,
And, one with Jesus, thirsts again.

TO A THRUSH

T. A. Daly (1871-   )

Sing clear, O! throstle,
  Thou golden-tongued apostle
And little brown-frocked brother
  Of the loved Assisian!
Sing courage to the mother,

Sing strength into the man,
For they, who in another May
Trod Hope's scant wine from grapes of pain,
Have tasted in thy song today
The bitter-sweet red lees again.
To them in whose sad May-time thou
Sang'st comfort from thy maple bough,
To tinge the presaged dole with sweet,
O! prophet then, be prophet now
And paraclete!

That fateful May! The pregnant vernal night
Was throbbing with the first faint pangs of day,
The while with ordered urge toward life and light,
Earth-atoms countless groped their destined way;
And one full-winged to fret
Its tender oubliette,
The warding mother-heart above it woke,
Darkling she lay in doubt, then, sudden wise,
Whispered her husband's drowsy ear and broke
The estranging seal of slumber from his eyes:
"My hour is nigh: arise!"

Already, when, with arms for comfort linked,
The lovers at an eastward window stood,
The rosy day, in cloudy swaddlings, blinked
Through misty green new-fledged in Wister Wood.
Breathless upon this birth
The still-entranced earth
Seemed brooding, motionless in windless space.
Then rose thy priestly chant, O! holy bird!
And heaven and earth were quickened with its grace;
To tears two wedded souls were moved who heard,
And one, unborn, was stirred!

O! Comforter, enough that from thy green
Hid tabernacle in the wood's recess
To those care-haunted lovers thou, unseen,
Should'st send thy flame-tipped song to cheer and bless.
Enough for them to hear
And feel thy presence near;

And yet when he, regardful of her ease,
  Had led her back by brightening hall and stair
To her own chamber's quietude and peace,
  One maple-bowered window shook with rare,
  Sweet song—and thou wert there!

Hunter of souls! the loving chase so nigh
  Those spirits twain had never come before.
They saw the sacred flame within thine eye;
  To them the maple's depths quick glory wore,
    As though God's hand had lit
    His altar-fire in it,
And made a fane, of virgin verdure pleached,
  Wherefrom thou might'st in numbers musical
Expound the age-sweet words thy Francis preached
  To thee and thine, of God's benignant thrall
  That broodeth over all.
And they, athirst for comfort, sipped thy song,
  But drank not yet thy deeper homily.
Not yet, but when parturient pangs grew strong,
  And from its cell the young soul struggled free—
    A new joy, trailing grief,
    A little crumpled leaf,
Blighted before it burgeoned from the stem—
  Thou, as the fabled robin to the rood,
Wert minister of charity to them;
  And from the shadows of said parenthood
  They heard and understood.

Makes God one soul a lure for snaring three?
  Ah! surely; so this nursling of the nest,
This teen-touched joy, ere birth anoint of thee,
  Yet bears thy chrismal music in her breast.
    Five Mays have come and sped
    Above her sunny head,
And still the happy song abides in her.
  For though on maimed limbs the body creeps,
It doth a spirit house whose pinions stir
  Familiarly the far cerulean steeps
  Where God His mansion keeps.

So come, O! throstle,
   Thou golden-tongued apostle
And little brown-frocked brother
   Of the loved Assisian!
Sing courage to the mother,
   Sing strength into the man,
That she who in another May
   Came out of heaven, trailing care,
May never know that sometimes gray
   Earth's roof is and its cupboards bare.
To them in whose sad May-time thou
Sang'st comfort and thy maple bough,
   To tinge the presaged dole with sweet,
O! prophet then, be prophet now
   And paraclete!

HELEN, THE SAD QUEEN

PAUL AMBROISE VALÉRY (1871-   )

Azure, 'tis I; from the caves of death withdrawn
   To hear the waves break rhythmic on the shores,
To see swift galleys clear, across the dawn,
   Lifting from darkness on the blades of golden oars.
My lonely hands now summon forth the kings
   Whose salt-grey beards amuse my chaste fingers—
I wept—And each his gloomy triumph sings
   And behind the stern of his bark the furrow lingers.

I hear sonorous conchs and clarion calls
Marking the lift of the oars and their even falls.
   The clear chant of the undulant oarsmen charms
      The tumult; and the gods! heroic at the prow
      With their olden smile and the spray hurled at their brow,
   Stretch toward me their indulgent, graven arms.

From the French by Joseph T. Shipley.

JESUS

Ramón Pimentel Coronel (1872-1909)

Dear Sons of God,—of Him whom Sinai saw
Mid rolling thunders trace the road of Right,
Clear carven on the tables of the Law,—
A road, rough cast or smooth, for day and night.

I come not from my Father to enslave,
But with the lamp of knowledge that ye crave,
To hear the prayers of those who grace implore,
Drying wet eyes and soothing bosoms sore;
Yea, dying on the Cross the world to save.

Behold the King of whom the Prophet told!
The Son of God—Messiah—see in me.
I quench the flame and quiet down the sea,
I guide the child and help the weak and old!

If to a stiffened corpse my cry "arise
And live again" be spoken,
Look where the cere-cloth fallen lies,
And death's cold seal upon the tomb is broken.

No kingly robe I wear; no golden sceptre bear;
No haughty frontlet can my brows endure;
Love and the lowly heart my treasures rare;
My law, the law of all the good and pure.—

Mine is the army of the worn and sad,
Beaten by sun and wind,
No spearsmen have I in brave armor clad,
Yet thus I come to rule mankind!

The works that smile to God as things of worth
Can lend no glow to the satanic fires:
Strike down the things of evil at their birth,
And stifle in your robe-folds base desires.

Let little children gather at my knees;
Their snow-white innocence shall be
The garb of those who mount to Heaven with me.
Verily I say, be ye as one of these!

Drive from your soul the vengeful thought; .
Vengeance is His who rules the realms above;
Give good for evil that your foe has wrought;
I am the Lord of Hope, the Lord of Love!

Do good, do good, but free of vaunt or boast,
Without vainglorious show,
So that of which your right hand knows the cost,
Your left hand shall not know.

No golden key of wealth may ope the door
Of God's great temple in the heavenly mead;
Yea, I who give you precepts, go before,
To give example of the deed;

Behold me humbled and a-hungered, poor;
The fishes have their homes beneath the waves,
The birdling holds his downy nest secure,
The wild things of the forest have their caves,
The insect has its place of lure . . .

Jesus alone
Who comes from sin to bring release
And free man's life from dread,
Preaching the faith of poverty and peace,
Yea, Jesus, Son of God, has not a stone
Whereon to lay His head!

From the Spanish by Joseph I. C. Clarke.

THE LATIN TONGUE

JAMES J. DALY, S. J. (1872-   )

Like a loud-booming bell shaking its tower
    Of granite blocks, the antique Latin tongue
    Shook the whole earth; over all seas it flung
Triremes of war, and bade grim legions scour

The world's far verges. Its imperial dower
  Made Tullius a god ; and Flaccus strung
  Its phrases into garlands ; while among
The high enchanters it gave Maro power.

Then Latin lost its purple pomp of war,
  Its wine-veined laughter and patrician tears ;
  It cast its fleshly grossness, won a soul,
And trafficked far beyond the farthest star
  With angel-cohorts, echoing through the years
  In sacred Embassies from pole to pole.

NOX IGNATIANA

James J. Daly, S. J.

His vigil was the stars ; his eyes were bright
  With radiance of them.   Mystically slow
  Was their processional, while far below
Rome's quick and dead slept—fellows in the night.
These very stars had marched in crytic rite
  For Vergil in clear evenings long ago,
  Gliding, like motes, athwart the overflow
Of splendor from immortal tides of Light.

"What is this ant-life on a sphere of sand
  That it must drive, with ant-like cares, my soul
  Than all the stars together more sublime ?"
So in the spacious night Ignatius planned
  His spacious morrows—centuries his scroll—
  Upon a background of Eternal Time.

IN COVENTRY

James J. Daly, S. J.

My friends the leaves, who used to entertain me
  On summer afternoons with idle chatter,
Are dropping off in ways that shock and pain me.
  I wonder what's the matter.

My friends the birds are quietly withdrawing;
　The meadowlarks are gone from fence and stubble;
Even the crows are gone; I liked their cawing.
　I wonder what's the trouble.

My friend the sun is here, but altered slightly;
　He acts more coolly than than he has been doing;
He seems more distant, and he smiles less brightly.
　I wonder what is brewing.

SONG OF THE LITTLE VILLAGES

James B. Dollard (1872-   )

The pleasant little villages that grace the Irish glynns
Down among the wheatfields—up amid the whins,
The little white-walled villages crowding close together,
Clinging to the Old Sod in spite of wind and weather:
Ballytarsney, Ballymore, Ballyboden, Boyle,
Ballingarry, Ballymagorry by the Banks of Foyle,
Ballylaneen, Ballyporeen, Bansha, Ballysadare,
Ballybrack, Ballinalack, Barna, Ballyclare.

The cozy little villages that shelter from the mist,
Where the great West Walls by ocean spray are kissed;
The happy little villages that cuddle in the sun
When blackberries ripen and the harvest work is done.
Corrymeela, Croaghnakeela, Clogher, Cahirciveen,
Cappaharoe, Carrigaloe, Cashel and Coosheen,
Castlefinn, Carrigtohill, Crumlin, Clara, Clane,
Caringaholt, Carrigaline, Cloghjordan and Coolrain.

The dreamy little villages, where by the fires at night,
Old Sanachies with ghostly tale the boldest hearts affright;
The crooning of the wind-blast is the wailing Banshee's cry,
And when the silver hazels stir they say the fairies sigh,
Kilfenora, Kilfinnane, Kinnity, Killylea,
Kilmoganny, Kiltamagh, Kilronan and Kilrea.
Killashandra, Kilmacow, Killiney, Killashee,
Killenaule, Killmyshall, Killorglin and Killeagh.

Leave the little villages, o'er the black sea go,
Learn the stranger's welcome, learn the exile's woe,
Leave the little villages, but think not to forget,
Afar they'll rise before your eyes to rack your bosoms yet.
Moneymore, Moneygall, Moniva and Moyne,
Mullinahone, Mullinavatt, Mullagh and Mooncoin,
Shanagolden, Shanballymore, Stranorlar and Slane,
Toberaheena, Toomyvara, Tempo and Strabane.

On the Southern Llanos,—north where strange light gleams,
Many a yearning exile sees them in his dreams;
Dying voices murmur (passed all pain and care),
"Lo, the little villages, God has heard our prayer."
Lisdoonvarna, Lissadil, Lisdargan, Lisnaskea,
Portglenone, Portarlington, Portumna, Portmagee,
Clondalkin and Clongowan, Cloondara and Clonae,
God bless the little villages and guard them night and day!

MY SONG OF TODAY

Saint Thérèse of the Child Jesus (1873-1897)

My life is but an instant, a fleeting hour above me,
  My life is but a moment escaping swift away;
Thou knowest, O my God, on earth, in time, to love Thee
  Naught have I but today.

Oh, how I love Thee Jesus,—for Thee my soul aspires,
  For this one day remain, my sweet and gentle stay;
Come, reign within my heart; Thy smile my soul desires,
  If only for today.

What matters it, O Lord, if dark the future hover?
  One prayer for its tomorrow—oh, no, I cannot say;
My heart untouched preserve—and with Thy shadow cover,
  If only for today.

If I dream of the morrow, my changeful thought affrights me,
  My heart, inconstant, mourns and wearies of the way;
I long, my God, that pain and trial to Thee unites me,
  If only for today.

I fain would see Thee soon upon the eternal shores,
   O Pilot of my soul, whose guidance I obey;
Steer Thou in peace my bark, while angry tempest roars,
   If only for today.

O hide me in Thy Face, sweet Lord, my heart imploreth,
   There shall I hear no more earth-follies at their play;
Give me Thy love, and grant Thy grace my bosom storeth,
   If only for today.

Near to Thy heart divine, all passeth me unheeded,
   I dread no more the foe—the arrows of the fray;
Ah! give me in Thy Heart the home my heart hath needed,
   If only for today.

O living Bread of heaven, O Sacrament most tender,
   O mystery of love—love only can repay,
Come, lift within my heart, Jesus, Thy Host's white splendor,
   If only for today.

Unite me unto Thee, O sacred Vine most holy,
   My feeble branch will yield its fruit without delay;
And I my ripened grape will offer to Thee solely,
   If only for today.

Cluster of love, each sphere a soul of my desires,—
   And I must form it now e'er time flees swift away;
Cast in my heart, O Jesus, Thine apostolic fires,
   If only for today.

Virgin Immaculate, O thou sweet star whose shining
   Uniteth me to Jesus, its clear and lucent ray;
O Mother, hide me close beneath thy veil confining,
   If only for today.

O Angel Guardian mine, o'erspread me with thy pinions,
   Enlighten with thy fires, O sweetest friend, my way;
Aid me, come, guide my steps into thy bright dominions,
   If only for today.

I long to see Thee, Jesus, unveiled to me—unclouded,—
  But while I wait, how near Him each moment shall I stay;
His countenance of love shall ne'er from me be shrouded,
  If only for today.

Soon shall I wing my flight afar to heavenly choirs,
  Where His fair day undying shall o'er my soul have sway;
There shall I sing in bliss amid angelic lyres,
  The eternal, glad today!

*From the French by the Prioress Augustine
of the Mother of God.*

THE UNPETALLED ROSE

SAINT THÉRÈSE OF THE CHILD JESUS

Jesus, when from Thy Mother's clasp I see Thee go,   2
  Held by her hand;
To set Thy first wee step on this sad earth below,
  And trembling stand;
Before Thee I would strew most tenderly a rose
  In opening hour;
That Thy dear little feet so softly might repose
  Upon a flower.

This rose unpetalled would a faithful image be,
  O Child Divine,
Of heart unshared and immolate for Thee,
  Each moment Thine.
Oft on Thine altar, Lord, a rose all fresh, all fair,
  Would dazzling gleam,
For Thee—but to bestrew my dropping petals there
  Is my one dream!

O lovely Child, how beautiful the rose full-blown
  For festal day!
But fallen petals are forgot and idly thrown
  Wind-tossed away.
The rose unpetalled, seeking nought, doth offer all,
  No more to be;
I, too, O little Jesus, give without recall
  My life to Thee.

Heedless, we tread the scattered petals of a rose;
    Simply they fell,
Adorning without art as nature might dispose;
    I know full well—
O Jesus, for Thy love, my life, my future lie
    O'erspent for Thee,
To fall as withered rose 'neath glance of mortal eye
    Is death for me.

For Thee to die, O Jesus, loveliness divine!
    What joy for me!
Oh, may I strew my life to prove my love is Thine,
    All, all for Thee!
Lost 'neath Thy first wee infant steps in mystery
    I wish to live,
That solace to Thy last, worn steps on Calvary
    Gently to give.

From the French by the Prioress Augustine
of the Mother of God.

AGNUS DEI

VICTOR KINON (1873-   )

O Lamb of God, O little infant lying
    Between the ox and ass, within the stall,
    Absolve us of the sin that stains us all
With Thy sweet, delicate hand all-purifying.

O Lamb of God, O little infant laden
    With all the shame that man has heaped on earth,
    Now dissipate our night and pulse to birth,
With light of innocence, our soul-sought Aidenn.

O Lamb of God, O little infant, sigh it!
    Thy word that wakes auroral cool and calm.
    Drop from Thy lips the petals of Thy balm!
Drop from Thy lips Thy syllables of quiet!

From the French by Richard Cloudesley Savage.

THE CHERUB-FOLK

Enid Dinnis (1873-   )

In highest Heaven, at Mary's knee,
  The Cherubs sit with folded wings,
And beg her by St. Charity
  To tell them tales of human things.

They throw their harps down on the floor,
  And all their heavenly playthings leave,
And clamor to be told once more
  The faerie tale of faulty Eve.

Up into Mary's lap they climb
  To hear how on a place called Earth
Once, in a wondrous thing called Time,
  The Uncreated One had birth.

And she to whom a Son was given,
  Plays there her Mother's part to them
And tells the Cherub-folk in heaven
  The wonder tale of Bethlehem.

A FRANCISCAN PRAYER

Enid Dinnis

When I am old and tutored by
  The grim experience of days;
  When I have proved men in their ways,
Oh, do not let the dreamer die.

When I have learned aside to toss
  The foolish things that wise men hate,
  Lest Littleness should hold me great,
Be mine the folly of the Cross.

When comes detachment's strength to me,
    Let mine the weakness be that wept
    O'er Lazarus's grave and kept
Three comrades in Gethsemane.

When head bids heart herself forget,
    When Reason's lure would love deceive,
    May my poor foolish heart achieve
A few life-giving blunders yet.

When I have grown too sane, too sad,
    To join the angels' faerie ring
    And serve the play-time of the King,
Then, Sweet Saint Francis, make me mad.

SURSUM

Guillermo Valencia (1873-   )

A pallid taper its long prayer recites
    Before the altar, where the censers spread
    Their lifting clouds, and bells toll out their dread,
In grief's delirious sanctuary rites.
There—like the poor Assisian—invites
    A cloistered form the peace All-Hallowéd;
    Against the dismal portals of the dead
Resting his wearied brows for heavenly flights.

Grant me me honey-taste of the Divine;
Grant me the ancient parchments' ruddy sign
    Of holy psalmody to read and prize!
For I would mount the heights immortal crowned,
Where the dark night is 'mid the glories drowned,
    And gaze on God, into His azure eyes!
                    From the Spanish by Thomas Walsh.

From THE MYSTERY OF THE INNOCENT SAINTS

CHARLES PEGUY (1873-1914)

I have often played with man, saith the Lord. But it is a play, a
  fearsome play whereat I tremble.
I have often played with man,—saith the Lord—it is for his
  salvation, and I am atremble with fear that I may not find
  power to save him,
May not win his salvation. Nay, I am atremble, indeed, fearing
  lest I win not to save him,
Asking whether the goal of his salvation has been won.
I have often played with man, and I know how stealthy is my
  grace, how many and how varied its turning plays. It is
  older in subtlety than woman.
But it plays with man and turns him and turns the outcome of
  his deeds that it may win him salvation, may preserve him
  from sin.
Often do I play against men, saith the Lord, but he in his fool-
  hardiness desires to lose, and I am enanguished that he shall
  gain.
Sometimes I bring it to pass
That he gain
For indeed it must be said, we play that whoso losses, gains.
Of man be that said, for when I lose, verily do I lose.
But he, when he loses, then only does he gain.
Strange play, I his partner and his adversary.
And he would gain at my expense, though thereby he would lose.
And I his adversary desire that he shall gain.

From the French by Joseph T. Shipley.

IN MY OLD VERSES

CHARLES GUÉRIN (1873-1907)

In my old verses you could find
  Poetry that took
Artless airs, that used to wind
  Like a babbling brook.

I released it from my spirit
  As it pleased to turn;
It had but freshness to endear it,
  And its unconcern.

Worry? Then I did not know it,
  Perfection to achieve;
Why couldn't I have stayed a poet
  Thus naive!
        From the French by Joseph T. Shipley.

TWILIGHT

Olive Custance

Spirit of Twilight, through your folded wings
  I catch a glimpse of your averted face,
And rapturous on a sudden, my soul sings
  "Is not this common earth a holy place?"

Spirit of Twilight, you are like a song
  That sleeps, and waits a singer,—like a hymn
That God finds lovely and keeps near Him long,
  Till it is choired by aureoled cherubim.

Spirit of Twilight, in the golden gloom
  Of dreamland dim I sought you, and I found
A woman sitting in a silent room
  Full of white flowers that moved and made no sound.

These white flowers were the thoughts you bring to all,
  And the room's name is Mystery where you sit,
Woman whom we call Twilight, when night's pall
  You lift across our Earth to cover it.

IN MEMORIAM, A. H. 1916

Maurice Baring (1874-   )

God, who had made you valiant, strong and swift,
And maimed you with a bullet long ago,
And cleft your riotous ardor with a rift,
And checked your youth's tumultuous overflow,
Gave back your youth to you,
And packed in moments rare and few
Achievements manifold
And happiness untold,
And bade you spring to Death as to a bride,
In manhood's ripeness, power and pride,
And on your sandals the strong wings of youth.
He let you leave a name
To shine on the entablatures of truth,
Forever:
To sound forever in answering halls of fame.
For you soared onwards to that world which rags
Of clouds, like tattered flags,
Concealed; you reached the walls of chrysolite,
The mansions white;
And losing all, you gained the civic crown
Of that eternal town,
Wherein you passed a rightful citizen
Of the bright commonwealth ablaze beyond our ken.

        .   .   .   .   .

And in the portals of the sacred hall
You heard the trumpet's call,
At dawn upon the silvery battlement,
Re-echo through the deep
And bid the sons of God to rise from sleep,
And with a shout to hail
The sunrise on the city of the Grail:
The music that proud Lucifer in Hell
Missed more than all the joys that he forewent.
You hear the solemn bell
At vespers, when the oriflammes are furled;
And then you know that somewhere in the world.

That shines far off beneath you like a gem,
They think of you, and when you think of them
You know that will wipe away their tears,
And cast aside their fears;
That they will have it so,
And in no otherwise;
That it is well with them because they know,
With faithful eyes,
Fixed forward and turned upwards to the skies,
That it is well with you,
Among the chosen few,
Among the very brave, the very true.

CARE IS HEAVY

CONAL O'RIORDAN (1874-   )

Dear God, though Thy all-powerful hand
Should so direct my earthly fate
That I may seem unfortunate
To them who do not understand
That all things follow Thy decree,
Staunchly I'll bear whate'er's Thy will—
Praying Thee but to grant me still
That none shall come to harm through me;
For, God, although Thou knowest all,
I am too young to comprehend
The windings to my journey's end;
I fear upon the road to fall
In the worst sin of all that be
And thrust my brother in the sea.

LEPANTO

GILBERT K. CHESTERTON (1874-   )

White founts falling in the Courts of the sun,
And the Soldan of Byzantium is smiling as they run;
There is laughter like the fountains in that face of all men
    feared,
It stirs the forest darkness, the darkness of his beard;

It curls the blood-red crescent, the crescent of his lips;
For the inmost sea of all the earth is shaken with his ships.
They have dared the white republics up the capes of Italy,
They have dashed the Adriatic round the Lion of the Sea,
And the Pope has cast his arms abroad for agony and loss,
And called the kings of Christendom for swords about the
     Cross.
The cold queen of England is looking in the glass;
The shadow of the Valois is yawning at the Mass;
From evening isles fantastical rings faint the Spanish gun,
And the Lord upon the Golden Horn is laughing in the sun.

Dim drums throbbing, in the hills half heard,
Where only on a nameless throne a crownless prince has stirred,
Where, risen from a doubtful seat and half attainted stall,
The last knight of Europe takes weapons from the wall,
The last and lingering troubadour to whom the bird has sung,
That once went singing southward when all the world was
     young.
In that enormous silence, tiny and unafraid,
Comes up along a winding road the noise of the Crusade.
Strong gongs groaning as the guns boom far,
Don John of Austria is going to the war,
Stiff flags straining in the night-blasts cold
In the gloom black-purple, in the glint old-gold,
Torchlights crimson on the copper kettle-drums,
Then the tuckets, then the trumpets, then the cannon, and he
     comes.
Don John laughing in the brave beard curled,
Spurning of his stirrups like the thrones of all the world,
Holding his head up for a flag of all the free.
Love-light of Spain—hurrah!
Death-lights of Africa!
Don Juan of Austria
Is riding to the sea.

Mahound is in his paradise above the evening star.
(*Don Juan of Austria is going to the war.*)
He moves a mighty turban on the timeless houri's knees
His turban that is woven of the sunsets and the seas.
He shakes the peacock gardens as he rises from his ease,
And he strides among the tree-tops and is taller than the trees;

And his voice through all the garden is a thunder sent to bring
Black Azrael and Ariel and Ammon on the wing.
Giants and the Genii,
Multiplex of wing and eye,
Whose strong obedience broke the sky
When Solomon was king.

They rush in red and purple from the red clouds of the morn,
From the temples where the yellow gods shut up their eyes in
    scorn;
They rise in green robes roaring from the green hells of the
    sea
Where fallen skies and evil hues and eyeless creatures be,
On them the sea-valves cluster and the grey sea forests curl,
Splashed with a splendid sickness, the sickness of the pearl;
They swell in sapphire smoke out of the blue cracks of the
    ground,—

They gather and they wonder and give worship to Mahound.
And he saith, "Break up the mountains where the hermit-folk
    can hide,
And sift the red and silver sands lest bone of saint abide,
And chase the Giaours flying night and day, not giving rest,
For that which was our trouble comes again out of the west.
We have set the seal of Solomon on all things under sun,
Of knowledge and of sorrow and endurance of things done.
But a noise is in the mountains, in the mountains, and I know
The voice that shook our palaces—four hundred years ago:
It is he that saith not 'Kismet'; it is he that knows not Fate;
It is Richard, it is Raymond, it is Godfrey at the gate!
It is he whose loss is laughter when he counts the wager worth,
Put down your feet upon him, that our peace be on the earth."
For he heard drums groaning and he heard guns jar,
(*Don John of Austria is going to the war.*)
Sudden and still—hurrah!
Bolt from Iberia!
Don John of Austria
Is gone by Alcalar.

St. Michael's on his Mountain in the sea-roads of the north
(*Don John of Austria is girt and going forth.*)

Where the grey seas glitter and the sharp tides shift
And the sea-folk labour and the red sails lift.
He shakes his lance of iron and he claps his wings of stone;
The noise is gone through Normandy; the noise is gone alone;
The North is full of tangled things and texts and aching eyes,
And dead is all the innocence of anger and surprise,
And Christian killeth Christian in a narrow dusty room,
And Christian dreadeth Christ that hath a newer face of doom,
And Christian hateth Mary that God kissed in Galilee,—
But Don John of Austria is riding to the sea.
Don John calling through the blast and the eclipse
Crying with the trumpet, with the trumpet of his lips,
Trumpet that sayeth *ha!*
   Domino gloria!
Don John of Austria
Is shouting to the ships.

King Philip's in his closet with the Fleece about his neck,
(*Don John of Austria is armed upon the deck.*)
The walls are hung with velvet that is black and soft as sin,
And little dwarfs creep out of it and little dwarfs creep in.
He holds a crystal phial that has colours like the moon,
He touches, and it tingles, and he trembles very soon,
And his face is as a fungus of a leprous white and grey
Like plants in the high houses that are shuttered from the day,
And death is in the phial and the end of noble work,
But Don John of Austria has fired upon the Turk.
Don John's hunting, and his hounds have bayed—
Booms away past Italy the rumour of his raid.
Gun upon gun, ha! ha!
Gun upon gun, hurrah!
Don John of Austria
Has loosed the cannonade.

The Pope was in his chapel before day or battle broke,
(*Don John of Austria is hidden in the smoke.*)
The hidden room in man's house where God sits all the year,
The secret window whence the world looks small and very dear.
He sees as in a mirror on the monstrous twilight sea
The crescent of his cruel ships whose name is mystery;

They fling great shadows foe-wards, making Cross and Castle
　　dark,
They veil the plumèd lions on the galleys of St. Mark;
And above the ships are palaces of brown, black-bearded chiefs,
And below the ships are prisons, where with multitudinous griefs,
Christian captives sick and sunless, all a labouring race repines
Like a race in sunken cities, like a nation in the mines.
They are lost like slaves that sweat, and in the skies of morning
　　hung
The stair-ways of the tallest gods when tyranny was young.
They are countless, voiceless, hopeless as those fallen or flee-
　　ing on
Before the high King's horses in the granite of Babylon.
And many a one grows witless in his quiet room in hell
Where a yellow face looks inward through the lattice of his cell,
And he finds his God forgotten, and he seeks no more a sign—
(*But Don John of Austria has burst the battle-line!*)
Don John pounding from the slaughter-painted poop,
Purpling all the ocean like a bloody pirate's sloop,
Scarlet running over on the silvers and the golds,
Breaking of the hatches up and bursting of the holds,
Thronging of the thousands up that labour under sea
White for bliss and blind for sun and stunned for liberty.
Vivat Hispania!
Domino Gloria!
Don John of Austria
Has set his people free!

Cervantes on his galley sets the sword back in the sheath
(*Don John of Austria rides homeward with a wreath.*)
And he sees across a weary land a straggling road in Spain,
Up which a lean and foolish knight for ever rides in vain,
And he smiles, but not as Sultans smile, and settles back the
　　blade. . . .
(*But Don John of Austria rides home from the Crusade.*)

ON THE ANNUNCIATION OF FRA ANGELICO

MANUEL MACHADO (1874-   )

The silver carolling of Matins woke
  The angel artist from his couch to paint,
  While round him throng a rosy chorus quaint
Of cherubs waiting on his brush's stroke.
They guide his hand to set the snowy light
  On Mary's brow and o'er her lovely cheeks,
  To show the eyes wherein her pureness speaks,
To limn her slender fingers amber-white.

Their angel wings unto his eyes they hold
  So he may copy of their childlike snows
The plumes of him who brought her message here;
Who rays, amid his pearly vestment stoled,
  His light upon the Virgin's breast of rose,
Like vivid sunburst on some crystal sphere.
                    From the Spanish by Thomas Walsh.

INTEMPESTIVA

HENRY LONGAN STUART (1875-   )

Once more the lumbering earth heaves its chill flank
  Through tempered sun and blessedness of rain;
  Spring wears to summer; now forget thy pain
With quickened pulse the quickening season thank.
Leave thy close room, that, couched 'mid grasses rank,
  While a wood's warbled woes for thine complain,
  Nature thy wounded heart may salve again,
With simples that of old Antaeus drank.

But stir me not! My soul begins to tire,
  With loveless summer sated, and is grown
    Kin to the winter it was wont to hate.
For I could weep because they quench my fire,
  Flinging the windows open, and have strown
    Forgotten flowers on the empty grate.

RESURREXIT

Henry Longan Stuart

All you that weep, all you that mourn,
   All you that grieving go,
Lift up your eyes, your heads adorn,
   Put off your weeds of woe.
The sorrows of the Passion week
   Like tearful dreams are fled.
For He hath triumphed Whom you seek,
   Is risen—That was dead.

Oh! you who to the Sepulchre
   At break of morning bring
The tribute of your spice and myrrh
   To balm our murdered King,
Each cleft of his forsaken tomb
   With Easter sun is red,
For He you laid amidst its gloom
   Is risen That was dead.

See! all about the prostrate stone
   Its abject sentries stand,
Death, with his diadem downthrown,
   And Fear, with fettered hand.
Lo! captive of the nails and spear
   Captivity is led,
For Love, that conquers Death and Fear,
   Is risen—That was dead.

THE PARISH CHURCH

Julio Herrera Reissig (1875-1911)

In blesséd silence vegetates the place;
   The wax-faced Virgins sleep in their attire
   Of livid velvets and discolored wire,
And Gabriel's trumpet wearies on his face.

A marble yawn the dried-up font would trace;
 There sneezes an old woman in the choir;
 And in the sun-shaft dust the flies aspire
As though 'twere Jacob's ladder for their grace.

The good old soul is starting at her chores;
 She shakes the poor-box, and in reverence pores
   To find how the Saint Vincent alms are going;
 Then here and there her feather-duster hies;
 While through the vestry doorway come the cries
   From out the barnyard and the gallant crowing.
                    From the Spanish by Thomas Walsh.

TEARS AGAINST THE MOON

THOMAS WALSH (1875-   )

Tears on my pillow—who has wept
Here while my worn eyes slept?
Tears—many tears—within what ghost-world shed—
For what persistent dead?
By day my lids have opened, dried
And wise with that old grief that died;
Tears on my pillow—ah, what lovely face
Has visited my sleeping-place!
What lovely voice has said
Ineffable canticles of the dead?
What soft reproaches spoken
For love-troths broken?
What sweet confession made
Of heart-desires delayed?
What long adieux sighed o'er and o'er?—
—My mind recalls no more—
Tears on my pillow—witnesses in vain
Of half-remembered pain!
Her vision draws away unto eternal day,
Leaving the noon for my content
But holding a lament
To slake the moon and stars of our commune,—
Tears on my pillow—tears against the moon.

THE FEAST OF PADRE CHALA

THOMAS WALSH

There are solemn figures walking up the Tocaïma roadway;
There are gestures and loud talking 'neath sombreros and
umbrellas;
For the sun is shining brightly through the palms along the
valley,
And the bells are tinkling lightly for the feast-day of Saint
Thomas.
Padre Chala, with bandanna stands and greets them from the
doorway—
And the belfry rings Hosanna as they mount unto the chapel;
Padre Gomez de Camilla, on his easy-pacing mula,
And the Padre Carrasquilla, reining in his restive stallion.
While on foot come Fray Ansado, rector of the Recoletos,
Padre Roman de Tejado, preacher from the Jesuitas,
And the portly Fray Rosildo, from the house of San Domingo.
And lean Fray Hermenegildo, from Our Lady de la Pena.
Carmelites and Augustinians, Escolapians and Marists,
All are airing their opinions, as they tread the dusty highway;
And their steps become the faster near the belfry of Tocaïma,
Where the Padre Chala, pastor, is awaiting with his dinner.
In the early morn the squawking from the barnyard of the Cura,
Set the neighborhood a-talking of the chickens old Jesusa
Was preparing for the dinner of the feast-day of the parish.
What a spread for saint and sinner!—Cool papayas, aguacates;
Juicy yuccas and melones, with the platanos and pinas,
And the maizes and rinones, from the sopa to the dulces!
As the Cura asked the blessing, and his guests were bowed in
silence,
One could hear the parrot calling from the garden a petition—
"Pray for us!" (it was the loro) "Pray for us, O great Saint
Thomas!"
As it learned it from the coro and had chanted and repeated,
Years without a variation—"Pray for us, O great Saint
Thomas!"
And from this demure oration, it had never deigned to vary,

Though the brightest minds had striven, with most implicating
    questions
To have explanations given for devotion so exclusive;
But the Cura their endeavor answered—"Ask not what Saint
    Thomas—
'Tis our patron-saint, however, our Saint Thomas of Tocaïma!"
Padre Ramon, forward leaning, with his finger made objection;
"Yet the customary meaning of the Church in such connections,
With no other term appended, is to indicate Apostles—
So 'twould seem to us intended, that this sole ejaculation
Of the loro, is the Doubter—Thomas Didymus, Apostle!"
Fray Rosildo, red and stouter, choking down a piece of chicken,
Gave it out as his opinion, where there was a greater figure
In theology's dominion, such as Thomas the Aquinas,
That his claims should be admitted in the naming of the patron.
Padre Carrasquilla twitted Padre Ramon's orthodoxy,
Blinking through his glasses merry: "Should we seek distin-
    guished patrons,
There is Thomas Canterbury, if we won't accept Apostles!"

While an Augustinian friar: "He, of Spanish Villanova,
Our Saint Thomas," he'd inquire—"how about him as a patron?"
While they argued, there came swooping o'er the patio a falcon,
Which dropped down upon the parrot, scooping it amid its talons,
While the priests and servants hurried, as it rose above the
    garden,
Where poor Padre Chala worried, and bemoaned his ravished
    loro.
Sudden in the upper reaches of the noontide's blazing splendor,
Woke the startled loro's screeches: "Pray for us, O great Saint
    Thomas!"
And the frightened falcon, hearing, loosed its prey and soared
    defeated—
While the loro reappearing, took his perch and sat unruffled.
Then the Padre Chala kneeling, with his pious guests around him,
Raised his broken voice, appealing: " 'Tis a miracle of Heaven!
Let us cease our disputations, raise no further points about him—
Praise Saint Thomas, of Tocaïma—none can question now or
    doubt him!"

TO A CARMELITE POSTULANT

MICHAEL EARLS, S. J. (1875-   )

Oh, the banks of May are fair,
  Charm of sound and sight,
Breath of heaven fills the air,
  To the world's delight.

Far more wondrous is a bower,
  Fairer than the May,
Love-of-God it wears in flower,
  Blooming night and day.

Love-of-God within the heart
  Multicolored grows,
Now a lily's counterpart,
  Now the blood-red rose.

Come the sun or chilling rain,
  Come the drought or dew,
Crocus health or violet pain,
  Love-of-God is true.

Hard may be the mountain-side,
  Soft the valley sod,
Yet will fragrance sure abide
  With the Love-of-God.

Where the grace of Heaven leads,
  There it makes a home,
Hills a hundred and the meads
  Will its pathway roam.

Carmel by the western sea
  Holds your blessed bower:
Love-of-God eternally
  Keep your heart a-flower.

THE YOUNG PRIEST TO HIS HANDS

Edward F. Garesché, S. J. (1876-   )

Time was when ye were powerless,
To shrive and sing, anoint and bless.
Clasped, ye worshipped from afar,
That Host, as distant as a star.
Your palms were barren still, and cold,
Ye might not touch, ye might not hold
God, whom the signs of bread enfold.

But now, ah, now, most happy hands,
Ye fold the Saviour's swaddling bands,
Ye lift His tender limbs and keep
The snowy bed where He doth sleep.
His heart, His blood, His being fair,
All God and Man is in your care!
Ye are His guardians everywhere.

Ye pour the wine, ye break the bread
For the great Supper, sweet and dread!
Ye dress the rood of Sacrifice
Whereon the morning Victim lies,
And when my trembling accent calls,
Swift leaping from His Heaven's walls,
On you the Light of Glory falls!

You are the altar where I see
The Lamb that bled on Calvary,
As sacred as the chalice shrine,
Wherein doth glow the Blood divine.
As sacred as the pyx are ye,
O happy hands—an angel's fee!
That clasp the Lord of Majesty!

WHAT NO MAN KNOWETH

HUGH FRANCIS BLUNT (1877-   )

When I am lying cold and dead,
With waxen taper at my head,
The night before my Mass is said;
And friends that never saw my soul
Sit by my catafalque to dole
And all my life's good deeds unroll;
O Jesu, Jesu, will it be
That Thou wilt turn away from me?

WHAT IS WHITE?

THOMAS MACDONOUGH (1878-1916)

What is white?
  The soul of the sage, faith-lit,
The trust of Age,
  The infant's untaught wit.
What more white?
  The face of Truth made known,
The Voice of Youth
  Singing before her throne.

OF A POET PATRIOT

THOMAS MACDONOUGH

His songs were a little phrase
  Of Eternal Song
Drowned in the harping of lays
  More loud and strong.

His deed was a single word
  Called out alone
In a night when no echo stirred
  To laughter or moan.

But his songs new souls shall thrill
    That loud harps dumb,
And his deed the echo fill
    When the dawn is come.

IDEAL

P. H. Pearse (1879-1916)

Naked I saw thee,
    O beauty of beauty!
And blinded my eyes
    For fear I should flinch.

I heard thy music,
    O sweetness of sweetness!
And I shut my ears
    For fear I should fail.

I kissed thy lips,
    O sweetness of sweetness!
And I hardened my heart
    For fear of my ruin.

I blinded my eyes,
    And my ears I shut,
I hardened my heart
    And my love I quenched.

I turned my back
    On the dream I had shaped,
And to this road before me
    My face I turned.

I set my face
    To the road here before me,
To the work that I see,
    To the death that I shall meet.
        From the Irish by Thomas MacDonough.

THE FAIR AGNETE

Agnes Miegel (1879-   )

When Sir Ulrich's widow in church knelt to pray,
From the churchyard toward her floated a lay.
The organ on high did cease to sound,
The priests and the boys all stood spell-bound;
The congregation hearkened, old man, child and bride,
To singing like a nightingale's so fair outside:
"Dear mother, in the church where the sexton's bell rings,
Dear mother, hark outside how your daughter sings!
For I cannot come to you in the church—ah, nay,
Before the shrine of Mary I cannot kneel to pray,
For I have lost salvation in everlasting time,
For I wedded the water-sprite with all his black slime.
My children—they play in the lake with fish-tribes fleet,
They have fins on their hands and fins on their feet,
Their little pearly frocks no sunlight ever dries—
Not death nor yet a dream can close my children's eyes—
Dear mother, oh, I beg of thee,
Lovingly, longingly:
Wilt thou and all thy servants pray
For my green-haired water-sprites alway—
Will ye pray to the Saints and Our Lady kind,
By every church and every Cross that on the fields ye find!
Dearest mother, I beseech thee so—
Every seven years I may hither go;
Unto the good priest tell
The church door to leave open well
That I may see the candle light
And see the golden monstrance bright,
That my little children may be told
How the gleam of the Chalice is sunlight gold!"
The organ pealed when the voice sang no more,
And then they opened wide the door—
And while they all inside High Mass were keeping,
A wave all white—so white—outside was leaping.

From the German by Margarete Münsterberg.

TO MY DAUGHTER BETTY, THE GIFT OF GOD

THOMAS M. KETTLE (1880-1916)

In wiser days, my darling rosebud, blown
    To beauty proud as was your mother's prime,
    In that desired, delayed, incredible time,
You'll ask why I abandoned you, my own,
And the dear heart that was your baby throne,
    To dice with death. And oh, they'll give you rhyme
    And reason; some will call the thing sublime,
And some decry it in a knowing tone.

So here, while the mad guns curse overhead,
    And tired men sigh with mud for couch and floor,
Know that we fools, now with the foolish dead,
    Died not for flag, nor King, nor Emperor,—
But for a dream, born in a herdsman's shed,
    And for the secret Scripture of the poor.

MUSIC

CHARLES PHILLIPS (1880-   )

There is a hunger in my heart to-night,
    A longing in my soul, to hear
The voice of heaven o'er the noise of earth
    That doth assail mine ear:

For we are exiled children of the skies,
    Lone and lost wanderers from home . . .
The stars come out like lamps in windows lit
    Far, far from where we roam;

Like candles lit to show the long late way,
    Dear kindly beacons sure and bright;
But O, the heavy journeying, and O
    The silence of the night!—

The dark and vasty silences that lie
    Between the going and the goal!
Will not God reach a friendly hand to lift
    And land my weary soul?

Will not God speak a friendly word to me
    Above the tumult and the din
Of earthly things—one little word to hush
    The voice of care and sin? . . .

He speaks! He answers my poor faltering prayer!
    He opens heaven's lattice wide;
He bids me bathe my brow in heavenly airs
    Like to a flowing tide!

He calls; He gives unto my famished soul,
    Unto my eager heart, its meed:
He breathes upon me with the breath of song,
    And O, my soul is freed,

And I am lifted up and up, and held
    A little while—a child, to see
The beauties of my Father's house, which shall
    No more be shut from me!

THE CALLING

Luis Felipe Contardo (1880-   )

Lord, Thou dost know with what implacable hand
    Life cut its wound across my inmost breast;
How I was lost amid the worldly band—
    How I have suffered where its blade was pressed!
Lord, Thou dost know how, from all healing banned,
    No cure I found in all the world possest;
How I in gloom would walk, and trembling stand
    Before Thy mystery with doubt confest!

Thy words came then unto mine ear—so sweet,
  Yea, sweeter far than mother's lullaby.
Unto the path, O Lord, Thou drewst my feet;
  My wounded wing against Thy breast did fly,
And there, as in predestined grief's retreat,
  Within Thy heart, as in' its nest, did lie!

From the Spanish by Thomas Walsh.

THE GAELIC

BLANCHE MARY KELLY (1881-   )

What are these words that beat their wings in vain
Against the holden portals of my brain,
Yet with swift flight and sure
Find my heart's inmost citadel
And rest secure?
Whence is their might?
How have they power to rouse me, as a bell
Rouses a sleeping city in the night?
Whence is this Pentecostal miracle?
They fall with alien sound upon mine ear,
And yet I hear,
I hear, I answer. Gael with Gael speaks
Across what seas of time, athwart what peaks
Of silence, from what deeps!
Not with my ears I hearken, but my blood.
Its surges are at flood.
There is a music in the fragrant night,
A flame, a thunder,
A beacon breaks in light,
The chains are reft asunder,
Torrent to torrent leaps
Across the sundering gulf of griefs and years,
Not with my tongue I answer, but my tears.

SILENTIUM ALTUM

Blanche Mary Kelly

I know a wind-swept hill where all day long
Comes never footfall nor the sound of word,
Only by swallow's wing or woodlark's song
Is that immense and brooding stillness stirred.

I sat awhile in that lost, listening place,
And felt the pulse of Time beat slow, beat slow,
Watching, upon the mountain sides of space,
The bright feet of God's heralds come and go.

On pinions of that silence was I raised,
With awe pervaded and pierced utterly,
Like theirs that from an Ostian window gazed
Beyond the bastions of eternity.

AN OLD WOMAN OF THE ROADS

Padraic Colum (1881-   )

Oh, to have a little house!
    To own the hearth and stool and all!
The heaped-up sods upon the fire,
    The pile of turf against the wall!

To have a clock with weights and chains
    And pendulum swinging up and down!
A dresser filled with shining delph,
    Speckled and white and blue and brown!

I could be busy all the day
    Clearing and sweeping hearth and floor,
And fixing on their shelf again
    My white and blue and speckled store!

I could be quiet there at night
    Beside the fire and by myself,
Sure of a bed, and loth to leave
    The ticking clock and the shining delph!

Och! but I'm weary of mist and dark,
    And roads where there's never a house or bush,
And tired I am of bog and road
    And the crying wind and the lonesome hush!

And I am praying to God on high,
    And I am praying Him night and day,
For a little house—a house of my own—
    Out of the wind's and the rain's way.

CHRIST THE COMRADE

Padraic Colum

Christ, by Thine own darkened hour,
Live within me, heart and brain—
Let my hands slip not the rein!

Ah, how long ago it is
Since a comrade went with me!
Now a moment let me see

Thyself, lonely in the dark,
Perfect, without wound or mark!

A CRADLE SONG

Padraic Colum

O men from the fields,
    Come gently within.
Tread softly, softly,
    O men coming in!

Mavourneen is going
From me and from you,
Where Mary will fold him
With mantle of blue!

From reck of the smoke
And cold of the floor
And the peering of things
Across the half-door.

O men of the fields,
Soft, softly come thro'.
Mary puts round him
Her mantle of blue.

DAVID AP GWILLAM'S MASS OF THE BIRDS

Padraic Colum

The thrush, the lark, and, chief, the nightingale,
With one small bird whose name I do not ken,
Offered a Mass; the little bird was clerk,
At intervals he struck his silver bell.
The stars above that were not whitened then
The candles were; the altar was a stone;
Myself was there with meet observances
Hearing the Mass the birds said in the dell.

It was the lark who sang in dark's decrease
Kyrie Eleison; then the nightingale
The Consecration chanted solemnly.
(The silver bell was rung for him in chief.)
And then the thrush, the dweller in the vale,
Orate Fratres sang—how near, how clear!
It was the thrush who, as the sun appeared,
Held up the Monstrance, a dew-circled leaf.

ROSES

J. CORSON MILLER (1883-   )

Last night, against the wall of the moon
I heard a crowd of roses speak—
If you will listen at the lips of June,
Oh, you will hear what the roses seek.
For Spring comes late, but Summer soon,
And a red rose lives for a lover's cheek.

'Twas under the roof of the radiant moon
I heard a white rose softly sing
A strange, wild song with a ghostly tune,
Of a girl's white feet gone wandering.
For never a white rose weaves a rune,
But the ear of a dead girl's listening.

Though Spring come late, and Summer soon,
And June make Summer's gift complete,
The life of a rose is sadly fleet,
And fleet are the dancing feet of June.
If you will listen when the wind is sweet,
You'll hear the roses speak to the moon.

MEDIÆVAL APPRECIATIONS

WILLIAM MILLER THOMAS GAMBLE

Now a knightlier sort you'll never find
Than the university modern mind;
Generous even to serious fault—
When not directly under assault.
To the glories of elder Christian days
It gives no end of its choicest praise.
Of course the loveliest things are said
Provided the past stays decently dead;
It must never be hinted to ears polite
That the ancient Faith is not moribund, quite;

For 'twere shocking bad form, in this urbane day
If a corpse kept kicking its shroud away
And spurning the elegant floral wreath
Meant for its grave, when it lies beneath!
So long as the Past consents to behave
In decorous quiet within its grave;
And public power still seems secure
As a mainly Protestant sinecure;
So long as good circles, as heretofore,
Still find it possible to ignore
Faith's life as "insignificant,"
Faith's indignation as "ignorant"—
The "ages of faith" shall not lack due praise
In such allusion and stately phrase,
As "athletes" are Becket, Aquinas and Scotus,
Whose fame should reëcho from Thule to Azotus!
"Olympians" are Gerbert and Hildebrand,
Who daringly, sublimely planned
Their "vast, too-perfect theocracy
Of variegated unity!
Unwitting dream-precursors they
Of actuality's urgent day!
What though their childish subtleties
Of code or creed must find surcease
As light dawned slow—" (with muffled shock)
Through Wycliffe, Bacon, Hobbes and Locke,
Till Kant (with true Promethean
Audacity, befriending man)
Snatched dogma from the indignant skies
And taught all men to dogmatize?
"Ye, with the foes that faced your ban—
King, Kaiser, Jew, Arabian—
Together by your very strife
Begot our world, with all its life!
Unbroken march of Mind we sing
From Anselm down (or up) to Inge!"

COMMUNION

CAROLINE GILTINAN (1884-   )

Mother Mary, thee I see
Bringing Him, thy Babe, to me,
Thou dost say, with trusting smile:
"Hold Him, dear, a little while."
Mother Mary, pity me,
For He struggles to be free!
My heart, my arms—He finds defiled:
I am unworthy of thy Child.
Mary, Mother, charity!
Bring thy Baby back to me!

THE MOTHER

KATHRYN WHITE RYAN

On a center staff and on two cross bars
  I would hang my heart for him.
On a center staff and on two cross bars
  I would nail my life for him.

Love spread out from me like a shading tree
  Rich it was, that stable floor!
Love spread out from me like a shading tree
  I withheld an endless store.

I who fought through storms, bore a man of peace;
  Hand clasped hand in Lebanon.
I whom shadows dimmed, bore a man of light;
  They are wise, where he has gone.

To him life I gave, on him life I thrust,
  On the cross his lips went blue.
To him life I gave, on him life I thrust—
  Was it—death—too?

AUT CÆSAR AUT NULLUS

LILIAN WHITE SPENCER

"Come; sun and laughter wait us at the end!"
  You whisper as I walk a darkened road
Bowed with my burden. God grows kind to send
  A guide who leads me from this crushing load.

—No further! He is beautiful, the dead,
  Thrust from my heart: so empty now and free—
I must go back. It aches still where his head
  Long pressed against my bosom heavily.

A FADED LETTER

WILLIAM J. FISCHER

Upon a letter old I came to-day,
  'Twas faded much, yet it was worth the prize,
  And, when I read it, tears crept to my eyes;
Like drops of dew on blushing rose, they lay
Upon my cheek and, when they rolled away,
  I saw you, gentle, loving, brave and wise,
  Your lips the color of the crimson skies—
And we were boys, friends of life's tender May,

But now the scene has changed and we are men.
  In lonely walls, a cassocked priest, you pray,
  Giving your life to God through ev'ry day,
Fighting grim vice with fiery voice and pen.
  You left me at the parting of the way
And sacrificed the world and all its ken.

EVENSONG

Ruth Schaumann

Music, murmur me to slumber;
Take the task from out my hands.
Gentle sheep, of sheep the mothers,
Climb my spirit's pasturelands.
Music mingle strong with sweet,
Murmur, lay me at God's feet.

Dusk-time crimson, sickled moon
Arm on arm the spaces view.
In the mountainous sky's valleys
Gleams a star, and glimmer two.
Music, bid your bud-filled loom
Weave all beauty to its bloom.

Willows tremble in the twilight
By a far-off wildling stream.
My heart's fitful beating plunges
In the long breath of a dream.
Music, murmur—'tis His will
Life should listen and be still.

From the German by George N. Shuster.

THE BRIDGE

Willibald Köhler

Streams would wander, bridges stay;
Together shores desire to be.
Bears me this footpath faithfully,
Or go my steps to the sea astray?

Ripples sing and the bridge declares—
Has road or crossroad ever mattered?
On the sea all stones are scattered
And streamward every traveler fares.

From the German by George N. Shuster.

CLOISTER

CHARLES L. O'DONNELL, C.S.C. (1884-   )

"Show me your cloister," asks the Lady Poverty.

Well, that were a cloister; for its bars
Long strips of sunset; and the roofs its stars.

Four walls of sky, with corridors of air
Leading to chapel, and God everywhere.

Earth beauteous and bare to lie upon,
Lit by the little candle of the sun.

The wind gone daily sweeping like a broom—
For these vast hearts it was a narrow room.

THE DEAD MUSICIAN

CHARLES L. O'DONNELL, C.S.C.

In Memory of Brother Basil

He was the player and the played upon,
He was the actor and the acted on,
Artist, and yet himself a substance wrought;
God played on him as he upon the keys,
Moving his soul to mightiest melodies
Of lowly serving, hid austerities,
And holy thought that our high dream out-tops,—
He was an organ where God kept the stops.
          Naught, naught
Of all he gave us came so wondrous clear
As that he sounded to the Master's ear

Wedded he was to the immortal Three,
Poverty, Obedience and Chastity,
And in a fourth he found them all expressed,
For him all gathered were in Music's breast,
          And in God's house
He took her for his spouse,—
High union that the world's eye never scans
          Nor world's way knows.
Not any penny of applauding hands
He caught, nor would have caught,
          Not any thought
          Save to obey
Obedience that bade him play,
          And for his bride
To have none else beside,
That both might keep unflecked their virgin snows.

Yet by our God's great law
Such marriage issue saw,
As they who cast away may keep,
          Who sow not reap.
          In Chastity entombed
          His manhood bloomed.
          And children not of earth
          Had spotless birth.
With might unmortal was he strong
          That he begot
          Of what was not,
Within the barren womb of silence, song.
          Yea, many sons he had
          To make his sole heart glad—
Romping the boundless meadows of the air,
Skipping the cloudy hills, and climbing bold
The heavens' nightly stairs of starry gold.
          Nay, winning heaven's door
          To mingle evermore
With deathless troops of angel harmony.
          He filled the house of God
          With servants at his nod,
A music-host of moving pageantry.
Lo, this priest, and that an acolyte:

Ah, such we name aright
Creative art,
To body forth love slumbering at the heart . . .
Fools, they who pity him,
Imagine dim
Days that the world's glare brightens not.
Until the seraphim
Shake from their flashing hair
Lightnings, and weave serpents there,
His days we reckon fair . . .

Yet more he had than this;
Lord of the liberative kiss,
To own and yet refrain,
To hold his hand in reign.
High continence of his high power,
That turns from virtue's very flower,
In loss of that elected pain
A greater prize to gain.
As one who long had put wine by
Would now himself deny
Water, and thirsting die.
So, sometimes he was idle at the keys,
Pale fingers on the aged ivories;
Then, like a prisoned bird,
Music was seen, not heard,
Then were his quivering hands most strong
With blood of the repressed song,—
A fruitful barrenness. Oh, where
Out of angelic air,
This side the heavens' spheres
Such sight to start and hinder tears.
Who knows, perhaps while silence throbbed
He heard the De Profundis sobbed
By his own organ at his bier today,—
It is the saints' anticipative way,
He knew both hand and ear were clay.
That was one thought
Never is music wrought,
For silence only could that truth convey.

Widowed of him, his organ now is still
His music-children fled, their echoing feet yet fill
The blue, far reaches of the vaulted nave,
The heart that sired them, pulseless in the grave.
Only the song he made is hushed, his soul,
Responsive to God's touch, in His control
Elsewhere shall tune the termless ecstasy
Of one who all his life kept here
          An alien ear,
Homesick for harpings of eternity.

A PRAYER FOR ST. INNOCENT'S DAY

HELEN PARRY EDEN (1885-   )

Wisdom, be Thou
The only garland of my burdened brow,

The nearest stage
And vowed conclusion of my pilgrimage,

Shade whence I shun
The untempered supervision of the sun,

Planet whose beams
Dispel the desperate ambuscade of dreams;

Through the Red Sea
Of mine own passion, Wisdom, usher me.

For this I pray
The four austere custodians of today,

Urge mine intent—
Nazarius, Celsus, Victor, Innocent!

SORROW

Helen Parry Eden

Of Sorrow, 'tis as Saints have said—
That his ill-savoured lamp shall shed
A light to Heaven, when, blown about
By the world's vain and windy rout,
The candles of delight burn out.

Then usher Sorrow to thy board,
Give him such fare as may afford
Thy single habitation-best
To meet him half-way in his quest,
The importunate and sad-eyed guest.

Yet somewhat should he give who took
My hospitality, for look,
His is no random vagrancy;
Beneath his rags what hints there be
Of a celestial livery.

Sweet Sorrow, play a grateful part,
Break me the marble of my heart
And of its fragments pave a street
Where, to my bliss, myself may meet
One hastening with pierced feet.

PRIEST OR POET

Shane Leslie (1886-   )

O Lord, why must thy poets peak and pine
    Why fall thy singers into fate?
When all thy priests do sup on amber wine
    And walk in purples delicate?

Thy Prophets of the desert honey sip,
    And sate their souls with loneliness,
Yet breakest Thou Thy flame upon their lip
    And givest camel's hair for dress.

To Poets, Lord, Thou givest neither drink.
  Nor raiment, fire nor peace nor food;
Enhungered, thirsting as they daily sink
  Beneath the trampling multitude.

DAW'S DINNER

Joyce Kilmer (1886-1918)

Poor little daws, hungry little daws,
  Do you want some wholesome eating?
Here's my heart on my sleeve for your beaks
    and claws,
  All ruddy and warm and beating!

Come, birdies, come, for my heart is young,
  And now is the time for feeding!
. . . And the very best songs that ever are sung
  Are sung while the heart is bleeding.

PENNIES

Joyce Kilmer

A few long-hoarded pennies in his hand
Behold him stand;
A kilted Hedonist, perplexed and sad.
The joy that once he had,
The first delight of ownership is fled.
He bows his little head.
Ah, cruel Time to kill
That splendid thrill,
Then in his tear-dimmed eyes
New lights arise.
He drops his treasured pennies on the ground,
They roll and bound
And scattered, rest
Now with what zest
He runs to find his errant wealth again!

So unto men
Doth God, depriving that He may bestow.
Fame, health and money go,
But that they may, new-found, be newly sweet.
Yea, at His feet
Sit, waiting us, to their concealment bid,
All they, our lovers, whom His Love hath hid.
Lo, comfort blooms on pain, and peace on strife,
And gain on loss!
What is the key to Everlasting Life?
A blood-stained Cross.

PRAYER OF A SOLDIER IN FRANCE

Joyce Kilmer

My shoulders ache beneath my pack
(Lie easier, Cross, upon His back)

I march with feet that burn and smart
(Tread, Holy Feet, upon my heart)

Men shout at me who may not speak
(They scourged Thy back and smote Thy cheek)

I may not lift a hand to clear
My eyes of salty drops that sear.

(Then shall my fickle soul forget
Thy Agony of Bloody Sweat)

My rifle hand is stiff and numb
(From Thy pierced palm red rivers come)

Lord, Thou didst suffer more for me
Than all the hosts of land and sea.

So, let me render back again
This millionth of Thy gift. **Amen.**

THE PEACEMAKER

Joyce Kilmer

Upon his will he binds a radiant chain,
    For Freedom's sake he is no longer free,
    It is his task, the slave of Liberty,
With his own blood to wipe away a stain.
That pain may cease, he yields his flesh to pain.
    To banish war, he must a warrior be,
    He dwells in Night, eternal Dawn to see,
And gladly dies, abundant life to gain.

What matters Death, if Freedom be not dead?
    No flags are furled, if Freedom's flag be furled.
Who fights for Freedom, goes with joyful tread
    To meet the fires of Hell against him hurled,
And has for captain Him whose thorn-wreathed head
    Smiles from the Cross upon a conquered world.

MARY'S BABY

Shaemas O'Sheel (1886-   )

Joseph, mild and noble, bent above the straw:
A pale girl, a frail girl, suffering, he saw;
"O my Love, my Mary, my bride, I pity thee!"
"Nay, Dear," said Mary, "All is well with me!"
    "Baby, my Baby, O my Babe," she sang.
Suddenly the golden night all with music rang.

Angels leading shepherds, shepherds leading sheep:
The silence of worship broke the mother's sleep.
All the meek and lowly of the world were there;
Smiling she showed them that her Child was fair.
    "Baby, my Baby," kissing Him she said.
Suddenly a flaming star through the heavens sped.

Three old men and weary knelt them side by side,
The world's wealth forswearing, majesty and pride;

Worldly might and wisdom before the Babe bent low:
Weeping, maid Mary said, "I love Him so!"
"Baby, my Baby," and the Baby slept.
Suddenly on Calvary all the olives wept.

DIADUMINIUS

Pierre Benoit (1886-   )

The mournful majesty of human greatness,
    The monument of desires, kisses, tears,
What name better than yours, Diaduminius,
    Gathers its pride into a symbol for the years?

For you were the strange and silent Cæsar
    Who leaned at night upon the terraces of flame
When the swift storm over the urns' black waters
    With blue metallic lightnings came.

And who that has known your story now can say;
    "Live, thrust skyward still more proud and bold—
Happiness is with the women of one's desire,
    In a marble palace, beside a sceptre of gold."

It lies, O Cæsar, near an old bell-tower,
    With sapphires strewn in a rippling burn,
In an old garden flowered with young roses,
    In the old house to which one will return.
                    From the French by Joseph T. Shipley.

THE OLD WOMAN

John Bunker (1886-   )

She keeps her nook, sitting with folded hands
And looking abroad with dim unquestioning gaze,
Her heart grown strangely quiet and tolerant.
She has learnt patience—those she loved are gone,
And youth has gone, and all the dreams of youth,
And grief itself hath found its natural ending,
And now she feels there is no more to learn.

Placid she sits in gnarled simplicity,
Not hills nor rocks more tranquil, and even as they
She bears Time's marks upon her patiently.
Hers is the sober wisdom of the years,
And now she waits for what she knows will come,.
Breathing the calmness of all quiet things,
Twilight and silence and a heart at peace.

PETITION OF YOUTH BEFORE BATTLE

John Bunker

Lo, I, a maiden knight,
Keeping lone vigil before this shrine of grace
Silent and still throughout the solemn hours
In lowlihead of my untested powers,
Here in this holy place
To Thee and right
My sword and shield do plight;
Yet ere that moment come when for the fray
I put me on my battailous array,
A boon I'd crave of Thine enduring might.

If in the treacherous ways
Of comfortable days
Too confident I tread life's daily round
Nor know it for precarious ground,—
Lord, I pray Thee well
To show,
My casual feet below,
The ravenous gape of Hell.

If in mine own despite
I take undue delight
In common things the world accounts most dear
(Though ashy with decay),
And all too little mindful of my quest
Subdue my waving crest
Beneath the cold-proud world's tyrannic sway,—
Within her central stronghold make me hear
The stirring discord of Thy trumpet's bray.

If in the midst of life,
The stress of this hot strife,
Thee
I cannot see
For the surrounding foe,
And stricken sore
Unto my spirit's core
Do hide my grievous hurt beneath a prideful pall
And so
Irrevocably fall,—
Even in the thick of fight
Purge Thou my sight
With euphrasy of woe.

And if it so should be
That, wearied utterly,
For one weak moment on this warring field
Base thoughts I'd have to yield,
That so with easy breath
Heedless of what the Captain saith
I might recline me prone in soft desires,—
Oh, rouse me from this life in death,
Quicken my spirit with Thy quenchless fires!

If clouded with despair
I see naught fair
And in midday yet walk in darkest night,
Girt round with hopelessness unriven
By friendly light,—
In any simplest thing
That from the sod may spring,
In bird-notes trilling wild,
In laughter of a child,
Give me faint glimpse of Heaven.

KNIGHTS ERRANT

Sister M. Madeleva (1887-   )

Death is no foeman, we were born together;
He dwells between the places of my breath,

Night vigil at my heart he keeps and whether
I sleep or no, he never slumbereth.
Though I do fear thee, Knight of the Sable Feather,
Thout wilt not slay me, Death!

But one rides forth, accoutered all in wonder:
I know thee, Life, God's errant that thou art,
Who comest to make of me celestial plunder;
To wound me with thy Love's immortal smart!
Life, thou wilt rend this flesh and soul asunder;
Love, thou wilt break my heart!

DIALOGUE

Sister M. Madeleva (1887-   )

A Word, a Word
Thou, Lord, didst utter which Thy willing handmaid heard,
And infinite, small Life within my own life breathed and stirred.

A blessed space
My Lord in me and I in Him found resting place;
In such divine repose I waited, silent and full of grace.

Answer is nigh;
O God, I lift a Child up heart-and-heaven high
And say, "This is my Flesh and Blood"; Thy Word is my reply.

O SOWER OF SORROW

Joseph Mary Plunkett (1887-1916)

O Sower of Sorrow,
  From the seed of your sowing
Tomorrow the mower
  The wheat will be mowing.

O Reaper of ruth,
  'Mid the roots of your reaping
Springs the truth that in sleep
  Bears the fruit of all sleeping.

O Binder of sheaves,
   That are loose for your binding,
Withered leaves you shall find
   And shall lose after finding.

I SEE HIS BLOOD UPON THE ROSE

Joseph Mary Plunkett

I see His blood upon the rose
   And in the stars the glory of His eyes,
His body gleams amid eternal snows,
   His tears fall from the skies.

I see His face in every flower;
   The thunder and the singing of the birds
Are but His voice—and carven by His power
   Rocks are His written words.

All pathways by His feet are worn,
   His strong heart stirs the ever-beating sea,
His crown of thorns is twined with every thorn,
   His Cross is every tree.

THE STIRRUP CUP

Aline Kilmer (1888-   )

Here where each road-worn one
Rests till the night is done
   In the gray dawning I saw my horse stand,
And as I left the inn
With his smooth face of sin
   Smiling, mine host with a cup in his hand.

"Drink now, my merry friend,
Drink to your journey's end.
   Let not the hour of our parting be sad.
Follow what road you will
One thought will cheer you still—
   This warm and fragrant cup you shall have had.

"Traveller, the ride is sweet,
God speed your flying feet,
 Thinking you hasten to lover and friend.
Gather the bridle up,
Drain dry the stirrup cup,
 Only a cup of tears waits at the end."

REMEMBRANCE

Aline Kilmer

I went back to a place I knew
 When I was very, very small;
The same old yellow roses grew
 Against the same old wall.

Each thing I knew was in its place;
 The well, the white stones by the road,
The box-hedge with its cobweb lace,
 And a small spotted toad.

And yet the place seemed changed and still;
 The house itself had shrunk, I know.
And then my eyes began to fill—
 For I had always loved it so!

THE MAID

Katherine Brégy

The whiteness of the lily once was thine,
O little maid, who watched Domremy's sheep—
Thy converse with the saints, whose words occult
Thou, like Another, in thy heart didst keep.

And thine the whiteness of the cleaving sword,
So blinding pure from out earth's blood-shedding,
When, in the gloom of Rheims' imperial shrine,
Thy lord of France was hallowed unto King.

But now, more ardent whiteness wraps thee round,
O martyr-saint, rejected and betrayed . . .
The sacrificial whiteness of the flame
Is thine—swift-soaring, unafraid!

The smoke is ours; its shame, its blindness, too,
And tears of the way thou valiantly hast trod;
But thou, white warrior maid, on high art raised,
A votive taper between us and God!

"I THIRST . . ."

KATHERINE BRÉGY

Yea, Lord, I too—
Only in this insatiate torment like to You:
For *love,* that still must give, and ask, the whole,
That may not rest short of the flame-wrapped goal,
Nor find surcease in any timorous part:
I am the human heart!

THE LAST COMMUNION

LEO WARD (1890-   )

There is a time wherein eternity
Takes rest upon the world; King Charity
Bowed to our fallen state, the God of Grace
Made visible upon a human face;—
When the deep Harmony, the eternal Word,
The unfallen Wisdom, only love has heard,
Touches the troubled body, bruised and hard
With the long fight, yet now set heavenward,—
When the deep argument of souls must cease,
Dying, to meet the victory of peace.

THE LAST ABBOT OF GLOUCESTER

WILFRED ROWLAND CHILDE (1890-   )

The Middle Ages sleep in alabaster
    A delicate fine sleep. They never knew
The irreparable hell of that disaster
    That broke with hammers Heaven's fragile blue.

Yea, crowned and robed and silent he abides,
    Last of the Romans, and that ivory calm,
Beneath whose wings august the minster-sides,
    Trembled like virgins to the perfect Psalm.

Yea, it is gone with him, yea, it returns not;
    The gilt proud sanctuaries are dust, the high
Steam of the violet fragrant frankincense burns not:
    All gone; it was too beautiful to die.

It was too beautiful to live; the world
    Ne'er rotted it with her slow-creeping hells:
Men shall not see the Vision crowned and pearled,
    When Jerusalem blossomed in the noon-tide bells!

BROTHER DOG

LUIS ANIBAL SÁNCHEZ

In the enormous tragic silence of the night, Francis, the monk
    of Assisi, with sunken eyes of immense tenderness, caressed
    the white body, the snow-white body, of a poor dog that
    died in the war.

To that body which had no soul, but which felt much, loved
    much, suffered much, Francis has given a tear and infinite
    pity.

Francis has wept, while afar nations made war.

It is the apocalyptic hour. Humanity is condensed into one long
  shriek. Hate asserts its supremacy. The great red cataclysm
  sows earth with tears and blood; tears of the child and of
  the beloved, and ancient crystallized tears of the venerable
  mothers who weep in dark alcoves where the cat whines
  sybaritically without knowing why.

Before the white body of the poor dog slain by chance bullets,
  the divine Francis wept.

  From the Spanish by Muna Lee.

SAN SABAS

Luis Palés Matos

There is here an ancient anchorite
  Who so spring-like shows
That on a cliff inaccessible
  He tended his mystic rose,
Intoxicate with April and hair-cloth
  And censers; and over all—
Since no earthly dew fell there—
  The dew celestial.

He lived remote in a cave
  Viscous as an evil mind;
Amid thistles and brambles
  He was animal and divine.
The thorn spoke to his feet
  With an especial blessing
By his blood sanctified.
  No flower its perfumes shed
On that gentle old body,
  An azure calm possessing.
Little poisonous creatures
  Were his only friends, and gray
Mists were dispelled from his eyelids
  When he began to pray.

Below him the pale hamlet
   A flock at dawn seemed to be;
And the sonorous sound of the anvil,
   The bell of eternity:

     Men going to the mountain,
     And women to their praying,
     Children to their playing,
     Dogs to their barking,
     Oxen to the plow,
     Cows to the milking;
     All birds to flight
     And all the flights to sea,
     All seas to the wind,
     All the winds to blowing,
     All the blowing to life,
     All life to labor.

And above this intranquillity,
   In the refuge he had made,
San Sabas, ample as a tree,
   Giving his paternal shade.
          From the Spanish by Muna Lee.

SORROW'S LADDER

GERTRUDE CALLAGHAN

Only by sorrows' ladder shall we rise,
For joy is an abbreviated stair,
We come upon its threshold unaware—
High sorrow's ladder reaches to the skies!
I, who have made this world my paradise,
Now find earth strangely filled with towering fears—
The sea a multitude of undried tears—
The way of grief lies bared before my eyes.

O Life, that I have jested with so long,
Capered into your pitfalls, wound each snare
About my heedlessness; too debonair
For further reckoning, now make me strong
That I, though bruised, may fearlessly ascend
High sorrow's ladder, singing, to the end!

THE WORLD'S MISER

THEODORE MAYNARD (1890-   )

I

A miser with an eager face
Sees that each roseleaf is in place.

He keeps beneath strong bolts and bars
The piercing beauty of the stars.

The colours of the dying day
He hoards as treasure—well he may!—

And saves with care (lest they be lost)
The dainty diagrams of frost.

He counts the hairs of every head,
And grieves to see a sparrow dead.

II

Among the yellow primroses
He holds His summer palaces,

And sets the grass about them all
To guard them as His spearmen small.

He fixes on each wayside stone
A mark to show it as His own,

And knows when raindrops fall through air
Whether each single one be there

That, gathered into ponds and brooks,
They may become his picture books

To show in every spot and place
The living glory of His face.

ON THE EDGE OF THE PACIFIC

Theodore Maynard

A bright beach glittering in the morning sun,
  Between the lofty promontories that stand
Shaggily capped with cypress and the dun
  Mass of the pines. The long waves on the sand
Fall weary of travelling from their still lagoon
  In Java or the plumed Pacific isles,
Urged on by the winds and the insistent moon
  Across immensity and its aching miles.

No marvel that, seeing this vast, Balboa ran,
  Amazed and shouting waist-deep in the sea,
His fierce eyes turned to China and Japan
  And India fabulous in antiquity,
Beyond those deeps where ships sail on and on,
Eager to reach the land of Prester John.

THE DUEL

Theodore Maynard

Love me, that I may die the gentler way;
Hate me, because thy love's too great for me.
                    Donne's "Prohibition"

May God be praised! I have an equal skill
To that which nerves your thin and supple wrist;
And while our striving bodies lunge and twist
And parry the naked blades flashed out to kill
I worship you with insults. For my will

Is like your own, O dear antagonist,
And in it strive the saint and sensualist,
Exquisite enemies who are never still.

I have no wish to die upon your sword;
Nor any wish to see you die on mine.
I charge you have a care, for I decline
An easy safety! Hated and adored,
This is a duel to the death, and when
We part as friends we meet as foes again.

POEM OF CIRCUMSTANCE

JEAN COCTEAU (1892-   )

Carve your name upon a tree
    That thrusts its roots below.
Better than marble this will be,
    For you can watch it grow.
            From the French by Joseph T. Shipley.

MUTANS NOMEN EVAE

ERIC GILL

Again God plants the tree of doom
On Calvary to branch and bloom
Himself the fruit. He bids us eat
And grow unto God's increase. Sweet
Art Thou, O Vine, whose fibres bleed
For us to know the Good indeed.
We taste the Truth of God seeing
The Shining out of God's Being.
Bind Thou us with straw and clay
To Thy opened side where may
Thy sap revive these branches faded
And all our life with Thine invaded
Grow fragrant for the Judgment day.

QUATRAINS

CHARLES J. QUIRK, S. J.

On the Parapet of Notre Dame

Paris lay hushed beneath the midday sun,
Her evil hid in smile's oblivion.
Then, suddenly I heard the gargoyles' jeering cry,
Answered beneath by carven angels' sigh.

The Countersign

An erstwhile sinner knocked at Heaven's gate,
Without the password dread.
"I know no countersign, save sorrow, Lord."—
"Pass in," our Saviour said.

MUSIC

ANNE RYAN (1892-   )

Hold how you may what masks to hide your dreaming,
I will delight in beauty as you go,
Solaced awhile for what was lately seeming
Waiting and woe—

Bent is my head, in little nods caressing
The warmth of these old, spangled melodies,
Or swept with wind that sobs this night confessing
But wintry trees!

Wound me anew, let fly the lightest arrows
Winged and adrip with sound, old cares among—
Be still the speech that silence narrows
Into fresh song!

THE EEL

EVAN MORGAN (1893-   )

I have floated far too long on the surface of the wave,
Far too long upon the surface of the wave.

Better had I died and been buried in my grave
Than have floated on the surface of the wave.
Let me sink then as a stone, as a rock into the sea,
Let me hide from myself, let me hide myself from Thee,
I have floated far too long, far too long and wantonly.

I have lain among the seaweeds, the dim flowers of the deep,
Half asleep amongst the flowers of the deep,
What sort of count I wonder of those hours did I keep
While I drowsed among the flowers of the deep?
Let me drop then as a stone, as a rock into the sea,
Let me tumble to destruction in a stricken misery,
Be frozen as my heart is; my heart to His heart's plea.

From the deeps there let me cry and when smothered by the
        wave,
Entirely hid and smothered by the wave.
Let me cry, and hear my cry, my cry to Thee to save,
When my bones are knocked together by the wave.
Let me rise then as an eel, as an eel up through the sea,
Let me creep unto His feet to lie there patiently
Until His eyes of mercy are turned with love on me.

THE ABBEY

José M. Eguren

Through the deep monastic halls
Ancient chime of Matins calls
Solemnly and mournfully,
Where the cloistered knights of prayer
Put away their love-dreams fair,
Thoughts of tourney, and of feast,
In profound obscurity—
Courtiers, poets, who have ceased
From their plays and learned to feel
Sorrows sharper than the steel.
In oblivion's shrine, despite
Smothered groanings, they recite,
Sheathing in their anguished breasts
Farewells to glories laid to rest

Deep in abbey crypts of night.
And the bell their story says,
In its bitterness contrite,
To the clouds upon their ways;
Says their boast, desire, and all,
To the sainted knights of prayer,
As it sounds the Matins there
O'er the graves conventual.

From the Spanish by Thomas Walsh.

AN ETCHING

Sister Imelda, O.S.D.

The Harper draws his golden string,
And over-head, like birds awing—
That soar and flutter as they sing—
    The music floats
    In liquid notes,
    And all is still.

The dreamer lives in the far away,
Where fancy's children ever play—
His vision fair as fields in May—
    The dreamer dreams,
    When moonlight gleams,
    On the rippling rill.

A Mother reads in baby eyes,
A message writ in Paradise—
Deep in her heart all gladness dies—
    A Mother weeps,
    When darkness sweeps
    O'er Calvary's Hill.

A NEW ORLEANS BALCONY—1880

DOROTHY HAIGHT (1897-   )

In simple muslin delicately dressed,
Fair and receptive for her husband's beckoning,
She stands on the grilled balcony that overlooks
The square and the Cathedral, lovely beyond reckoning,
With palm trees against the scarlet west,
And a great sunset going down in Orleans bay.

The mariners are due at home again,
In those low rolling vessels from the far away,
That raise glad masts like the Cathedral spire,
Over a cargo that is brought by men.

Ashore. Behold. It is a sight to take the voyage-tire
From Captain's heart, and to his head like wine,
To see her standing on the balcony,
Wrought pillars, valences of iron tracery,
Framing her like the borders of a valentine!

FINDING YOU

MARY DIXON THAYER (1897-   )

Dear God, I wish I could have been
Among those girls and boys
You called to come and talk with You,
And who left all their toys,
And ran and climbed up on Your knee,
And held Your hand, and sat
Around You, learning lovely things—
I wish I had done that!
But God, I know that even now
I can get close to You.
I know You still love children—yes
Indeed! I know You do.
And so I often slip away

Into the Church and kneel
Down at the altar where You are,
And tell You all I feel.
I cannot see Your face, and yet
I know that You are there.
I know I'm just as close to You
As all those children were!

BIRD-SONG

MARY DIXON THAYER

Do you see that bird in the sky?
It is my love for you!
My love is like a bird—
A bird with shining wings;
Like a bird in the dusk, it flies,
Like a bird in the dusk, it sings . . .
And under the moon it drifts,
And over the curving sea,
And my love blows with the wind
Through gates of mystery.

Ah, catch the shadow that falls
Along the meadow-grasses!
My love is a bird that calls—
My love a shadow that passes . . .

THE MAD LOVER

SPEER STRAHAN (1898-   )

He was lovelier than the white birch
The wind holds
Against the sky . . .
But now,
Since His death,
His body is warm
And fragrant as the body of a cherry tree.

They say, my love,
The bark of pomegranates has grazed your cheek—
But tell me
Why have your hands and feet a deeper dye?

The wine presses are running
While the song lifts of those who tread out the vintage . . .
And your feet
Are as red as wine . . . or blood.

Wearing a casque of silver
And helmet of beaten gold,
The moon walked last night between
　　two slim young pine trees . . .
Like Pharaoh's daughter.

All night long
She wandered among the reeds,
Searching, searching something
That had been lost . . .

THE POOR

Speer Strahan

The poor I saw at the cloister gate
　　Mutely beg with their patient eyes
An alms, for the love of Him who sate
　　And supped with the poor in human guise.

And there were monks saw the nails' deep scars
　　In the shrunken hands that reached for bread,
Who heard a Voice from beyond the stars
　　In the broken thanks of them they fed.

I, too, at the gates of God each day
　　Seek for an alms of strength and grace,
Beggar am I that wait and pray
　　To feast my soul on His beauteous Face.

IN THE AZURE NIGHT

Bartolomé Galindez (1899-   )

The pilgrim of the night
  Passed down the azure road,
The chrism of the moonlight shone
  Upon his pallid brow.

He bore a staff with flowers
And white with dust were his sandals,
A smile was on his lips—
  Like a star turned human!—

Softly—softly in the azure night
  The silvery form
Of the pilgrim of Thebais
  Faded from sight!
           From the Spanish by Thomas Walsh.

THE LAST SONG

Eileen Duggan

"God has so many singing birds
To lilt from sunny throats,
Proud birds with slow strong notes,
Like stately Dons of Spain:
God has full many singing birds
To mock on hill and plain
The tabor of the wind,
The viol of the rain.
God has so many troubadours
With songs of March and May
On pipe and flageolet
To flute of flower and seed,
God has so many troubadours
To sing in court and train,
He will not miss my bitter reed,
I shall not sing again."

JUNIPER

Eileen Duggan

I am Juniper and I am wicked.
    That's as sure as steel is blue,
Juniper, the fool, is wicked,
    Little Father, it is true.

Sin is like a little field-clock flying,
    Like a dandelion fruit.
Lo! I let it rest a minute on me,
    And the seed sent down a root.

I was good that night when you were dying,
    And your cold hands touched my head.
Oh, I beat my breast then with the others,
    But it came when you were dead.

For if I went first you know I'd blunder,
    Setting angels by the ears,
And who'd say "Poor Juniper is sorry,
    Do not mind him! See his tears."

While the rest are sobbing I am singing
    Out of tune upon my stool;
You have gone before me into heaven,
    You will answer for your fool.

PHANTOMS

Harry McGuire (1904-   )

At the end I will bellow my challenge;
Holding my gun on the stoop;
They will come with the hordes of evening
In a silver sloop.

Their faces fantastic and painted,
Revealed to the look of the moon,
Silently they will disembark—
Weird platoon.

Then I will raise my musket
For its last shot;
There will be a sound in the stillness . . .
A barrel hot,

The despairing glance of a watered eye
As the smoke clears, and I see
The phantom marchers moving still . . .
Moving upon me.

Cold as the kiss of hell their steel—
Cold as the dread of cost
To a man who has waited to battle his sins
To the last—and lost.

Then he will die at the sword-point
Who knew not how to live,
Who thought his sins were phantoms . . .
God, forgive!

IV

CATHOLIC POEMS BY NON-CATHOLIC POETS

THE PILGRIMAGE

SIR WALTER RALEIGH (1552-1618)

Give me my scallop-shell of quiet,
　My staff of faith to walk upon;
My scrip of joy, immortal diet,
My bottle of salvation;
My gown of glory, hope's true gauge,
And thus I'll make my pilgrimage!
Blood must be my body's 'balmer,
　No other balm will there be given;
Whilst my soul, like quiet palmer
　Travelleth towards the land of Heaven;
Over the silver mountains
Where spring the nectar fountains.
There will I kiss the bowl of bliss,
　And drink mine everlasting fill
　Upon every milken hill.
My soul will be a-dry before,
But after, it will thirst no more.
Then by that happy, blissful day,
　More peaceful pilgrims I shall see
That have cast off their rags of clay
　And walk apparelled fresh like me.
I'll take them first to quench their thirst
　And taste of nature's suckets
At those clear wells where sweetness dwells
　Drawn up by saints in crystal buckets.
And when our bottles and all we
Are filled with immortality,
Then the blest paths we'll travel
Strewed with rubies thick as gravel,—
Ceilings of diamonds, sapphire floors,
High wall of coral, and pearly bowers.
From thence to Heaven's bribeless hall,
Where no corrupted voices brawl;

449

No conscience molten into gold,
No forged accuser bought or sold,
No cause deferred, no vain-spent journey,
For there Christ is the King's Attorney;
Who pleads for all without degrees,
And He hath angels, but no fees;
And when the grand twelve-million jury
Of our sins, with direful fury,
'Gainst our souls black verdicts give,
Christ pleads His death and then we live.
Be Thou my speaker, taintless pleader,
Unblotted lawyer, true proceeder!
Thou giv'st salvation even for alms,—
Not with a bribéd lawyer's palms.
And this is mine eternal plea
To Him that made heaven, earth, and sea,
That since my flesh must die so soon,
And want a head to dine next noon,
Just at the stroke when my veins start and spread,
Set on my soul an everlasting head;
Then am I, like a palmer, fit
To tread those blest paths which before I writ
Of death and judgment, heaven, and hell
Who oft doth think, must needs die well.

EASTER

Edmund Spenser (1553-1598)

Most glorious Lord of life that on this day
　Didst make Thy triumph over death and sin,
And having harrowed hell didst bring away
　Captivity thence captive us to win;
　This joyous day, dear Lord, with joy begin
And grant that we, for whom Thou didest die
　Being with Thy dear blood clean washed from sin,
May live forever in felicity.

And that Thy love we weighing worthily,
   May likewise love Thee for the same again;
And for Thy sake that all like dear didst buy,
   With love may one another entertain.
So let us love, dear love, like as we ought,
Love is the lesson which the Lord us taught.

SONNET

WILLIAM SHAKESPEARE (1564-1616)

Poor soul, the centre of my sinful earth,
   !—these rebel powers that thee array,
Why dost thou pine within and suffer dearth,
   Painting thy outward wall so costly gay?
Why so large cost, having so short a lease,
   Dost thou upon thy fading mansion spend?
Shall worms, inheritors of this excess,
   Eat up thy charge? is this thy body's end?
Then, soul, live thou upon thy servant's loss,
   And let that pine to aggravate thy store;
Buy terms divine in selling hours of dross;
   Within be fed, without be rich no more;
So shalt thou feed on Death, that feeds on men,
And Death once dead, there's no more dying then.

Dirge from CYMBELINE

WILLIAM SHAKESPEARE

Fear no more the heat of the sun,
   Nor the furious winter's rages;
Thou thy worldly task hast done,
   Home art gone, and ta'en thy wages.
Golden lads and girls all must,
As chimney-sweepers, come to dust.

Fear no more the frown o' the great;
    Thou art past the tyrant's stroke.
Care no more to clothe and eat;
    To thee the reed is as the oak.
The sceptre, learning, physic, must
All follow this, and come to dust.

Fear no more the lightning flash,
    Nor the all-dreaded thunder-stone;
Fear not slander, censure rash;
    Thou hast finished joy and moan.
All lovers young, all lovers must
Consign to thee and come to dust.

THE DAWNING

Henry Vaughan (1621-1693)

Ah! what time wilt thou come? when shall that crie
The Bridegroome's comming! fil the sky?
Shall it in the evening run,
When our words and works are run,
Or wil thy all-surprising light
                Break at midnight?
When either sleep, or some dark pleasure,
Possesseth mad man without measure;
Or shall these early, fragrant hours
                Unlock thy bowres?
And with their blush of light descry
Thy locks crown'd with eternitie.

THE RETREAT

Henry Vaughan

Happy those early dayes! when I
Shin'd in my angell-infancy.
Before I understood this place
Appointed for my second race,

Or taught my soul to fancy aught
But a white, celestiall thought.
When yet I had not walk'd above
A mile or two from my first love,
And, looking back (at that short space),
Could see a glimpse of his bright face;
When on some gilded cloud or flow're
My gazing soul would dwell an houre,
And in those weaker glories spy
Some shadows of eternity.

CORRUPTION

Henry Vaughn

Man, in those early days,
Was not all stone and earth.
He shin'd a little, and of those weak rays,
Had some glimpse of his birth.
He sigh'd for Eden, and would often say,
Ah! what bright days were those?

Nor was Heav'n cold unto him; for each day
The valley or the mountain
Afforded visits, and still Paradise lay
In some green shade or fountain.
Angels lay leiger there: each bush and cel,
Each oke and high-way knew them.
Walk but the fields, or sit down at some wel,
And he was sure to view them.

THE LAMB

William Blake (1757-1827)

Little Lamb, who made thee?
Dost thou know who made thee?
Gave the life and bade thee feed,
By the stream and o'er the mead;

Gave thee clothing of delight,
Softest clothing, wooly, bright,
Gave thee such a tender voice,
Making all the vales rejoice?
Little Lamb, who made thee?
Dost thou know who made thee?

Little Lamb, I'll tell thee;
Little Lamb, I'll tell thee;
He is callèd by thy name,
For He calls Himself a Lamb.
He is meek and He is mild;
He became a little child.
I a child, and thou a Lamb,
We are callèd by His name.
Little Lamb, God bless thee!
Little Lamb, God bless thee!

THE VIRGIN

WILLIAM WORDSWORTH (1770-1850)

Mother! Whose virgin bosom was uncrost
    With the least shade of thought to sin allied;
    Woman! Above all women glorified,
Our tainted nature's solitary boast;
Purer than foam on central ocean tost;
    Brighter than eastern skies at daybreak strewn
    With fancied roses, than the unblemished moon
Before her wane begins on heaven's blue coast;

Thy image falls to earth. Yet some, I ween,
    Not unforgiven, the suppliant knee might bend
    As to a visible power, in which did blend
        All that was mixed and reconciled in thee
        Of mother's love with maiden purity,
Of high with low, celestial with terrene.

THE MONKS OF BANGOR'S MARCH

SIR WALTER SCOTT (1771-1832)

When the heathen trumpet's clang
Round beleaguered Chester rang
Veiléd nun and friar gray
Marched from Bangor's fair Abbaye;
High their holy anthem sounds
Cestria's vale the hymn rebounds,
Floating down the silvan Dee,
    O miserere, Domine!

On the long procession goes,
Glory round their crosses glows,
And the Virgin Mother mild
In their peaceful banner smiled;
Who could think such saintly band
Doomed to feel unhallowed hand?
Such was the divine decree,
    O miserere, Domine!

Bands that masses only sung,
Hands that censers only swung,
Met the northern bow and bill
Heard the war-cry wild and shrill;
Woe to Brockmael's feeble hand,
Woe to Olfrid's bloody brand,
Woe to Saxon cruelty,
    O miserere, Domine!

Weltering amid warriors slain,
Spurned by steeds with bloody mane,
Slaughtered down by heathen blade
Bangor's peaceful monks are laid;
Word of parting rest unspoke,
Mass unsung and bread unbroke,
For their souls for charity,
    Sing O miserere, Domine!

Bangor! o'er the murder wail!—
Long thy ruins told the tale,
Shattered towers and broken arch
Long recalled the woeful march;
On thy shrine no tapers burn,
Never shall thy priests return;
The pilgrim sighs and sings for thee,
  O miserere, Domine!

A VOICE SINGS

SAMUEL TAYLOR COLERIDGE (1772-1834)

Hear, sweet spirit, hear the spell,
Lest a blacker charm compel!
So shall the midnight breezes swell
With thy deep long-lingering knell.

And at evening evermore,
In a chapel by the shore,
Shall the chaunters, sad and saintly,
Yellow tapers burning faintly,
Doleful masses chaunt for thee,
  Miserere, Domine!

Hark, the cadence dies away
  On the quiet moonlight sea;
The boatmen rest their oars; and say,
  Miserere, Domine!

ASPIRATION

CHARLES LAMB (1775-1834)

Maternal Lady with the virgin grace,
  Heaven-born thy Jesus seemeth sure,
  And thou a Virgin pure.
Lady most perfect, when thy sinless face
  Men look upon, they wish to be
  A Catholic, Madonna fair, to worship thee.

SIT DOWN, SAD SOUL

BRYAN WALLER PROCTOR (1787-1874)

Sit down, sad soul, and count
  The moments flying;
Come—tell the sweet amount
  That's lost by sighing!
How many smiles?—a score?
Then laugh and count no more;
  For day is dying.

Lie down, sad soul, and sleep,
  And no more measure
The flight of Time, nor weep
  The loss of leisure;
But here, by this lone stream
Lie down with us, and dream
  Of starry treasure.

We dream: do thou the same:
  We love—forever;
We laugh; yet few we shame,
  The gentle never.
Stay, then, till Sorrow dies;
Then—hope and happy skies
  Are thine forever!

NOCTURNE

VICTOR HUGO (1802-1885)

I walked beside the deep, one night of stars;
  No cloud above, no sail upon the sea.
All nature semed to question waves and sky
  Of their dread majesty and mystery.

And the great breakers bowed their haughty crests,
  And thundered forth, with voice of full accor'
The diapason of their ceaseless hymn
  Of "Holy, holy, holy to the Lord!"

The starry legions cast their crowns of fire
  Before the feet of God, and made reply,
In swelling anthems jubilant and strong,
  "It is the Lord! It is the Lord Most High!"
          From the French by Sister Mary Angelita.

HYMN OF THE ANGELUS

EDGAR ALLAN POE (1809-1849)

At morn, at noon, at twilight dim,
Maria, thou hast heard my hymn!
In joy and woe, in good and ill,
Mother of God, be with me still!
When the hours flew brightly by,
And not a cloud obscured the sky,
My soul, lest it should truant be,
Thy grace did guide to thine and thee;
Now, when the storms of fate o'ercast
Darkly my present and my past,
Let my future radiant shine
With sweet hopes of thee and thine.

ST. AGNES

ALFRED TENNYSON (1809-1892)

Deep on the convent-roof the snows
  Are sparkling to the moon:
My breath to heaven like vapor goes:
  May my soul follow soon!
The shadows of the convent-towers
  Slant down the snowy sward,
Still creeping with the creeping hours
  That lead me to my Lord:
Make Thou my spirit pure and clear
  As are the frosty skies,
Or this first snowdrop of the year
  That in my bosom lies.

As these white robes are soiled and dark,
To yonder shining ground;
As this pale taper's earthly spark,
To yonder argent round;
So shows my soul before the Lamb,
My spirit before Thee;
So in mine earthly house I am,
To that I hope to be.
Break up the heavens, O Lord! and far,
Thro' all yon starlight keen,
Draw me, thy bride, a glittering star,
In raiment white and clean.

He lifts me to the golden doors;
The flashes come and go;
All heaven bursts her starry floors,
And strews her lights below,
And deepens on and up! the gates
Roll back, and far within
For me the Heavenly Bridegroom waits,
To make me pure of sin.
The sabbaths of Eternity,
One sabbath deep and wide—
A light upon the shining sea—
The Bridegroom with his bride!

ST. MICHAEL THE WEIGHER

JAMES RUSSEL LOWELL (1819-1891)

Stood the tall Archangel weighing
All man's dreaming, doing, saying,
All the failure and the pain,
All the triumph and the gain,
In the unimagined years,
Full of hopes, more full of tears,
Since old Adam's hopeless eyes
Backward searched for Paradise,
And, instead, the flame-blade saw
Of inexorable Law.

Waking, I beheld him there,
With his fire-gold flickering hair,
In his blinding armor stand,
And the scales were in his hand:
Mighty were they, and full well
They could poise both heaven and hell.
"Angel," asked I humbly then,
"Weighest thou the souls of men?
That thine office is, I know."
"Nay," he answered me, "not so:
But I weigh the hope of Man
Since the power of choice began,
In the world, of good or ill."
Then I waited and was still.

In one scale I saw him place
All the glories of our race,
Cups that lit Belshazzar's feast,
Gems, the lightning of the East,
Kublai's sceptre, Cæsar's sword,
Many a poet's golden word,
Many a skill of science, vain
To make men as gods again.

In the other scale he threw
Things regardless, outcast, few,
Martyr-ash, arena sand,
Of St. Francis' cord a strand,
Beechen cups of men whose need
Fasted that the poor might feed,
Disillusions and despairs
Of young saints with grief-grayed hairs,
Broken hearts that brake for Man.

Marvel through my pulses ran
Seeing then the beam divine
Swiftly on this hand decline,
While Earth's splendor and renown
Mounted light as thistledown.

JACOPONE DA TODI

MATTHEW ARNOLD (1822-1888)

That son of Italy who tried to blow,
  Ere Dante came, the trump of sacred song,
  In his bright youth amid a festal throng
Sate with his bride, to see a public show.
Fair was the bride and on her front did glow
  Youth like a star; and what to youth belong—
  Gay raiment, sparkling gauds, elation strong.
A prop gave 'way! Crash fell a platform! lo,

Mid struggling sufferers, hurt to death, she lay!
  Shuddering they drew her garments off—and found
    A robe of sackcloth next her smooth white skin.
Such, poets, is your bride, the Muse! young, gay,
  Radiant, adorned outside, a hidden ground
    Of thought and of austerity within.

MARY'S GIRLHOOD

DANTE GABRIEL ROSSETTI (1828-1882)

This is the blessèd Mary, pre-elect
  God's virgin. Gone is a great while, and she
  Dwelt young in Nazareth of Galilee.
Unto God's will she brought devout respect
Profound simplicity of intellect.
  And supreme patience. From her mother's knee
  Faithful and hopeful; wise in charity;
Strong in grave peace; in pity circumspect.

So held she through her girlhood; as it were
  An angel-watered lily, that near God
    Grows and is quiet. Till, one day at home
She woke in her white bed, and had no fear
  At all—yet wept till sunshine, and felt awed:
    Because the fulness of the time was come.

A SONG OF FLIGHT

CHRISTINA ROSSETTI (1830-1894)

While we slumber and sleep
The sun leaps up from the deep
—Daylight born at a leap!—
Rapid, dominant, free,
Athirst to bathe in the uttermost sea.

While we linger at play
—If the year would stand at May!—
Winds are up and away
Over land, over sea,
To their goal wherever their goal may be.

It is time to arise,
To race for the promised prize,
—The Sun flies, the Wind flies—
We are strong, we are free,
And home lies beyond the stars and the sea.

THE LAUD OF SAINT CATHERINE

From *Siena*

ALGERNON CHARLES SWINBURNE (1837-1909)

O gracious city well-beloved,
Italian, and a maiden crowned,
Siena, my feet are no more bound
Toward thy strange-shapen mountain bound;
But my heart in me turns and moves,
O lady loveliest of my loves,
Toward thee, to lie before thy feet
And gaze from thy fair fountain-seat
Up the sheer street;

And the house midway hanging see
That saw Saint Catherine bodily,
Felt on its floors her sweet feet move,
And the live light of fiery love
Burn from her beautiful strange face
As in the sanguine sacred place
Where in pure hands she took the head
Severed, and with pure lips still red
Kissed the lips dead.

For years through, sweetest of the saints,
In quiet without cease she wrought,
Till cries of men and fierce complaints
From outward moved her maiden thought;
And prayers she heard and sighs toward France,
"God, send us back deliverance,
Send back thy servant, lest we die!"
With an exceeding bitter cry
They smote the sky.

Then in her sacred saving hands
She took the sorrows of the lands,
With maiden palms she lifted up
The sick time's blood-embittered cup,
And in her virgin garment furled
The faint limbs of a wounded world.
Clothed with calm love and clear desire,
She went forth in her soul's attire,
A missive fire.

Across the might of men that strove
It shone, and over heads of kings;
And molten in red flames of love
Were swords and many monstrous things;
And shields were lowered, and snapt were spears,
And sweeter-tuned the clamorous years;
And faith came back, and peace, that were
Fled; for she bade, saying "Thou, God's heir,
Hast thou no care?"

"Lo!—men lay waste thine heritage
Still, and much heathen people rage
Against thee, and devise vain things.
What comfort in the face of kings,
What counsel is there? Turn thine eyes
And thine heart from them in like wise;
Turn thee unto thine holy place
To help us that of God for grace
Require thy face.

"For who shall hear us if not thou
In a strange land? What doest thou there?
Thy sheep are spoiled, and the ploughers plough
Upon us; why hast thou no care
For all this, and beyond strange hills
Liest unregardful what snow chills
Thy foldless flock, or what rains beat?
Lo, in thine ear, before thy feet,
Thy lost sheep bleat!

"And strange men feed on faultless lives,
And there is blood, and men put knives,
Shepherd, unto the young lambs' throat;
And one hath eaten, and one smote,
And one hath hunger and is fed
Full of the flesh of these, and red
With blood of these as who drinks wine,
And God knoweth, who that sent thee a sign,
If these were thine."

But the Pope's heart within him burned,
So that he rose up, seeing the sign
And came among them; but she turned
Back to her daily way divine,
And fed her faith with silent things,
And lived her life with curbed white wings,
And mixed herself with heaven and died;
And now on the sheer city-side
Smiles like a bride.

You see her in the fresh clear gloom
Where walls shut out the flame and bloom
Of full-breathed Summer, and the roof
Keeps the keen ardent air aloof
And sweet weight of the violent sky;
There bodily beheld on high,
She seems as one hearing in tune
Heaven within heaven, at heaven's full noon,
In sacred swoon.

A solemn swoon of sense that aches
With imminent blind heat of heaven,
While all the wide-eyed spirit wakes,
Vigilant of the supreme Seven,
Whose choral flames in God's sight move,
Made unendurable with love,
That without wind or blast of breath
Compels all things through life and death
Whither God saith.

There on the dim side-chapel wall
Thy mighty touch memorial,—
Razzi,—raised up for aged dead,
And fixed for us her heavenly head;
And, rent with plaited thorn and rod,
Bared the live likeness of her God
To men's eyes turning from strange lands,
Where, pale from thine immortal hands,
Christ wounded stands;

And the blood blots His holy hair
And white brows over hungering eyes
That plead against us, and the fair
Mute lips forlorn of words or sighs
In the great torment that bends down
His bruised head with the bloomless crown,
White as the unfruitful thorn-flower,—
A God beheld in dreams that were
Beheld of her!

PRAYER TO THE VIRGIN OF CHARTRES

HENRY ADAMS (1838-1918)

Gracious Lady:—
Simple as when I asked your aid before;
   Humble as when I prayed for grace in vain
Seven hundred years ago; weak, weary, sore
   In heart and hope, I ask your help again.

You, who remember all, remember me;
   An English scholar of a Norman name,
I was a thousand who then crossed the sea
   To wrangle in the Paris schools for fame.

When your Byzantine portal was still young
   I prayed there with my master Abailard;
When Ave Maris Stella first was sung
   I helped to sing it here with Saint Bernard.

When Blanche set up your gorgeous Rose of France
   I stood among the servants of the Queen;
And when Saint Louis made his penitence
   I followed barefoot, where the King had been.

For centuries I brought you all my cares
   And vexed you with the murmurs of a child;
You heard the tedious burden of my prayers;
   You could not grant them, but at least you smiled.

If then I left you, it was not my crime,
   Or if a crime, it was not mine alone.
All children wander with the truant Time.
   Pardon me too; you pardoned once your Son!

For He said to you:—"Wist ye not that I
   Must be about my Father's business?" So,
Seeking His Father He pursued His way
   Straight to the Cross toward which we all must go.

So I too wandered off among the host
    That racked the earth to find the Father's clue.
I did not find the Father, but I lost
    What now I value more, the Mother, You!

I thought the fault was yours that foiled my search;
    I turned and broke your image on its throne,
Cast down my idol, and resumed my march
    To claim the Father's empire for my own.

Crossing the hostile sea, our greedy band
    Saw rising hills and forests in the blue;
Our Father's kingdom in the Promised Land!
    —We seized it and dethroned the Father too.

And now we are the Father, with our brood,
    Ruling the Infinite, not Three but One;
We made our world and saw that it was good;
    Ourselves we worship, and we have no Son.

Yet we have gods, for even our strong nerve
    Falters before the energy we own.
Which shall be master? Which of us shall serve?
    Which wears the fetters? Which shall have the crown?

Brave though we be, we dread to face the Sphynx,
    Or answer the old riddle she still asks;
Strong as we are, our reckless courage shrinks
    To look beyond the piece-work of our tasks.

But when we must, we pray, as in the past
    Before the Cross on which your Son was nailed.
Listen, dear Lady! You shall hear the last
    Of the strange prayers Humanity has wailed.

.   .   .   .   .   .

But years, or ages, or eternity
    Will find me still in thought before your throne,
Pondering the mystery of Maternity,
    Soul within Soul—Mother and Child in One!

Help me to see! not with my mimic sight—
　With yours! which carried radiance, like the sun,
Giving the rays you saw with light in light—
　Tying all suns and stars and worlds in one.

Help me to know! not with my mocking art—
　With you, who knew yourself unbound by laws;
Gave God your strength, your life, your sight, your heart,
　And took from Him the Thought that Is—the Cause.

Help me to feel! not with my insect sense,—
　With yours that felt all life alive in you;
Infinite heart beating at your expense;
　Infinite passion breathing the breath you drew!

Help me to bear! not my own baby load,
　But yours; who bore the failure of the light,
The strength, the knowledge and the thought of God,—
　The futile folly of the Infinite.

A BALLAD OF TREES AND THE MASTER

SIDNEY LANIER (1842-1881)

Into the woods my Master went,
Clean forspent, forspent.
Into the woods my Master came,
Forspent with love and shame.
But the olives they were not blind to Him,
The little gray leaves were kind to Him;
The thorn-tree had a mind to Him
When into the woods He came.

Out of the woods my Master went,
And he was well content.
Out of the woods my Master came,
Content with death and shame.
When Death and Shame would woo Him last
From under the trees they drew Him last;
'Twas on a tree they slew Him—last
When out of the woods He came.

NOEL: CHRISTMAS EVE, 1913

ROBERT BRIDGES (1844-   )

Pax hominibus bonæ voluntatis

A frosty Christmas Eve
    when the stars were shining
Forth I fared alone
    where westward falls the hill,
And from many a village
    in the water'd valley
Distant music reach'd me
    peals of bells aringing.
The constellated sounds
    ran sprinkling on earth's floor
As the dark vault above
    with stars was spangled o'er.

Then sped my thought to keep
    that first Christmas of all
When the shepherds watching
    by their folds ere the dawn
Heard music in the fields
    and marveling could not tell
Whether it were angels
    or the bright stars singing.

Now blessed be the tow'rs
    that crown England so fair,
That stand up strong in prayer
    unto God for our souls:
Blessed be their founders
    (said I) an' our country folk
Who are ringing for Christ
    in the belfries to-night
With arms lifted to clutch
    the rattling ropes that race
Into the dark above
    and the mad romping din.

But to me heard afar
        it was starry music,
Angels' song comforting
        as the comfort of Christ
When he spake tenderly
        to his sorrowful flock:
The old words came to me
        by the riches of time
Mellow'd and transfigur'd
        as I stood on the hill
Heark'ning in the aspect
        of th' eternal silence.

THE LORD OF ALL

EDWIN MARKHAM (1852-   )

Milton, you did them wrong the hour you sang
    The Lord's Nativity: the fair young gods,
    Scorched by your scorn and stricken by your rods,
Were loved of Him who took the mortal pang.
He knew their cliffs that shone, their wells that sprang
    And all the wonder of their purple clime;
    And as his feet descended into Time,
Their voices on the hills and sea-reefs rang.

So the young gods of Hellas knew the hour
When life's bough was to break in sudden flower;
And in the hush they knelt without a word
Beside the Stall; for in the little one
    They saw Apollo come again, and heard
His name cried in the porches of the sun!

OUR LADY

Mary Coleridge (1861-1907)

Mother of God! no lady thou:
  Common woman of common earth!
Our Lady ladies call thee now,
  But Christ was never of gentle birth;
  A common man of the common earth.

For God's ways are not as our ways.
  The noblest lady in the land
Would have given up half her days,
  Would have cut off her right hand
  To bear the Child that was God of the land.

Never a lady did He choose,
  Only a maid of low degree,
So humble she might not refuse
  The carpenter of Galilee.
  A daughter of the people, she.

Out she sang the song of her heart.
  Never a lady so had sung.
She knew no letters, had no art;
  To all mankind, in woman's tongue
  Hath Isrealitish Mary sung.

And still for men to come she sings,
  Nor shall her singing pass away.
"He hath filled the hungry with good things"—
  Oh, listen, lords and ladies gay!—
  "And the rich He hath sent empty away."

THE MYSTERY

Ralph Hodgson (1871-   )

He came and took me by the hand
  Up to a red rose tree,
He kept His meaning to Himself
  But gave a rose to me.

I did not pray Him to lay bare
    The mystery to me,
Enough the rose was Heaven to smell,
    And His own face to see.

From THE SONG OF HONOUR

Ralph Hodgson

I climbed a hill as light fell short,
And rooks came home in scramble sort,
And filled the trees and flapped and fought
And sang themselves to sleep;
An owl from nowhere with no sound
Swung by and soon was nowhere found,
I heard him calling half-way round,
Holloing loud and deep;

A pair of stars, faint pins of light,
Than many a star, sailed into sight,
And all the stars, the flower of night,
Were round me at a leap;
To tell how still the valleys lay
I heard a watchdog miles away,
And bells of distant sheep.

.   .   .   .   .

I heard it all, each, every note
Of every lung and tongue and throat,
Ay, every rhythm and rhyme
Of every thing that lives and loves
And upward, ever upward moves
From lowly to sublime!
Earth's multitudinous Sons of Light,
I heard them lift their lyric might
With each and every chanting sprite
That lit the sky that wondrous night
As far as eye could climb!

I heard it all, I heard the whole
Harmonious hymn of being roll
Up through the chapel of my soul
And at the altar die,
And in the awful quiet then
Myself I heard, Amen, Amen,
Amen I heard me cry!
I heard it all, and then although
I caught my flying senses, Oh,
A dizzy man was I!
I stood and stared; the sky was lit,
The sky was stars all over it,
I stood, I knew not why,
Without a wish, without a will,
I stood upon that silent hill
And stared into the sky until
My eyes were blind with stars and still
I stared into the sky.

SING THOU, MY SOUL

THEODOSIA GARRISON (1874-   )

The black night came down in rain and wrath and storm,
Men lifted from a cross a broken Form;
Dawn came with song and sun—Sing thou, my Soul!—
Rose, radiant, from the tomb the Christ made whole.

Mine eyes and yours have seen joy bound and slain,
Your eyes and mine shall see joy rise again;
To each his Easter day when Love shall rise
With the same outstretched hands and the same eyes.

Some while they live shall see, even as those
Who wept beneath a cross at the day's close;
Some eyes Lord Death must seal ere yet they see—
Sing thou, my Soul—Love's face—yet this shall be!

From THE BOOK OF HOURS

RAINER MARIA RILKE (1875-   )

Many have painted her. But there was one
Who drew his radiant colors from the sun.
Mysteriously glowing through a background dim
When he was suffering she came to him,
And all the heavy pain within his heart
Rose in his hands and stole into his art.
His canvas is the beautiful bright veil
Through which her sorrow shines. There where the frail
Texture o'er her sad lips is closely drawn
A trembling smile softly begins to dawn—
Though angels with seven candles light the place
You cannot read the secret of her face.

.   .   .   .   .   .

By day Thou art the Legend and the Dream
    That like a whisper floats about all men,
The deep and brooding stillnesses which seem
    After the hour has struck, to close again.

And when the day with drowsy gesture bends
    And sinks to sleep beneath the evening skies,
As from each roof a tower of smoke ascends—
    So does Thy Realm, my God, around me rise.
                    From the German by Jessie Lemont.

THE LADY POVERTY

EVELYN UNDERHILL (1875-   )

I met her on the Umbrian hills
    Her hair unbound, her feet unshod;
As one whom secret glory fills
    She walked, alone with God.

I met her in the city street;
  Oh, changed was all her aspect then!
With heavy eyes and weary feet
  She walked, alone with men.

MESSENGERS

CHARLES HANSON TOWNE (1877-   )

The apple-trees, with burdens of white bloom,
And lavish with mysterious perfume,
Opened their great clean arms as I went by.
They whispered softly under the blue spring sky—
"We are the ghosts of all earth's beauty you lost
In vanished summers, in days of piercing frost;
We are the dreams of youth you would not dream.
And now, by many a roadway, many a stream,
We come in pale battalions, leaning out,
Bidding you, wounded soul, no longer doubt;
Daring you take us, after the jubilant rain,
Back to your perishing goodness, back to your heart again."

FRANCISCAN ASPIRATION

VACHEL LINDSAY (1879-   )

Would I might wake Saint Francis in you all,
Brother of birds and trees, God's Troubadour,
Blinded with weeping for the sad and poor;
Our wealth undone, all strict Franciscan men,
Come, let us chant the canticle again
Of mother earth and the enduring sun.
God make each soul the lowly leper's slave;
God make us saints, and brave.

DRAKE

The Coming of the Armada

ALFRED NOYES (1880-   )

Bring on the pomp and pride of old Castile,
  Blazon the skies with royal Aragon,
Beneath Oquendo let old ocean reel,
  The purple pomp of priestly Rome bring on;
And let her censers dusk the dying sun,
  The thunder of her banners on the breeze
Following Sidonia's glorious galleon
  Deride the sleeping thunder of the seas,
  While twenty thousand warriors chant her litanies.

Lo, all their decks are kneeling! Sky to sky
  Responds! It is their solemn evening hour.
Salve Regine, though the daylight die,
  Salve Regina, though the darkness lour;
Have they not still the kingdom and the power?
  Salve Regina, hark, their thousands cry,
From where like clouds to where the mountains tower
  Their crowded galleons looming far or nigh,
  Salve Regina, hark, what distant seas reply!

What distant seas, what distant ages hear?
  Bring on the pomp! the sun of Spain goes down;
The moon but swells the tide of praise and prayer;
  Bring on the world-wide pomp of her renown;
Let darkness crown her with a starrier crown,
  And let her watch the fierce waves crouch and fawn
Round those huge hulks from which her cannon frown,
  While close inshore the wet sea-mists are drawn
  Round England's Drake; then wait, in triumph, for the dawn.

The sun of Rome goes down; the night is dark!
  Still are her thousands praying, still their cry
Ascends from the wide waste of waters, hark!
  Ave Maria, darker grows the sky!

Ave Maria, those about to die
  Salute thee! Nay, what wandering winds blaspheme
With random gusts of chilling prophecy
  Against the solemn sounds that heavenward stream!
The night is come at last. Break not the splendid dream.

SAINT THOMAS AQUINAS

Thomas S. Jones, Jr. (1882-   )

The lord of all the lore that man had found,
  He placed the dream the longing heart had won
  Above the webs of logic subtly spun,
And reason with white revelation crowned;
In skies too vast for wondering thought to sound
  His soul was lifted like a lonely sun
  About whose fire mysterious planets run
And by whose law the scattered stars are bound.

Beyond the garnered wisdom of the earth
  He sought the starlight deep with spirit led
    Through adoration to Love's dwelling-place;
Till in the Host where life has mystic birth
  He saw the God who gave the Wine and Bread
    Unveil the hidden beauty of His Face.

TO THE LIGHTED LADY WINDOW

Marguerite Wilkinson (1883-   )

I kiss my hand to you,
  Mary, Holy Mother!
I kiss my hand to you,
  Jesus, little brother!

    Lady, I love your robe
      Like a wave in a deep sea;
    Your aureole of stars
      Is very dear to me;

And the beauty of the soul
　　That met the Holy Ghost,
And the wonder of the life
　　Wherein the guest was Host.
But lady, even more,—
　　And you would have it said,—
I love the little child
　　That shines above your head.

I kiss my hand again,
　　Mary, Holy Mother;
I kiss my hand again,
　　Jesus, little brother.

THE MADONNA'S LAMP

Prince Wilhelm of Sweden (1884-   )

When we two, friends from childhood, wanderers are,
　　And fate like dice would cast me 'gainst the wall,—
With paths before me steep and many a scar,
　　And only echoings attend my call,—
　　Then will your face across my memory fall
Like some Madonna dimly shrined afar
Where I shall be the lamp's unquenching star
　　To shed a tender radiance over all.

Long as the oil shall last the flame shall light
The soft reflection of two eyes as bright
　　As those of happy days we used to know;
Then should it shrink and flicker out of sight,
　　Still, still the mild Madonna face will glow,
　　Although the lamp has darkened long ago.

From the Swedish by Thomas Walsh.

BALLAD OF THE GOODLY FREE

(Simon Zelotes speaketh it somewhile after the Crucifixion)

EZRA POUND (1885-   )

Ha' we lost the goodliets fere o' all
    For the priests and the gallows tree?
Aye lover he was of brawny men,
    O' ships and the open sea.

When they came wi' a host to take our Man
    His smile was good to see,
"First let these go!" quo' our Goodly Frere,
    "Or I'll see ye damned," says he.

Aye he sent us out through the crossed high spears
    And the scorn of his laugh rang free,
"Why took ye not me when I walked about
    Alone in the town?" says he.

Oh we drunk his "Hale" in the good red wine
    When we last made company,
No capon priest was the Goodly Fere
    But a man o' men was he.

I ha' seen him drive a hundred men
    Wi' a bundle o' cords swung free,
That they took the high and holy house
    For their pawn and treasury.

They'll no' get him a' in a book I think
    Though they write it cunningly;
No mouse of the scrolls was the Goodly Fere
    But aye loved the open sea.

If they think they ha' snared our Goodly Fere
    They are fools to the last degree.
"I'll go to the feast," quo' our Goodly Fere,
    "Though I go to the gallows tree."

"Ye ha' seen me heal the lame and blind,
    And wake the dead," says he,
"Ye shall see one thing to master all:
    'Tis how a brave man dies on the tree."

A son of God was the Goodly Fere
    That bade us brothers be.
I ha' seen him cow a thousand men.
    I have seen him upon the tree.

He cried no cry when they drave the nails
    And the blood gushed hot and free,
The hounds of the crimson sky gave tongue
    But never a cry cried he,

I ha' seen him cow a thousand men
    On the hills o' Galilee,
They whined as he walked out calm between,
    Wi' his eyes like the grey o' the sea,

Like the sea that brooks no voyaging
    With the winds unleashed and free,
Like the sea that he cowed at Geneseret
    Wi' twey words spoke suddenly.

A master of men was the Goodly Fere,
    A mate of the wind and sea,
If they think they ha' slain our Goodly Fere
    They are fools eternally.

I ha' seen him eat o' the honey-comb
    Sin' they nailed him to the tree.

IN THE MONASTERY

NORREYS JEPHSON O'CONOR (1885-   )

Cold is the wind tonight, and rough the sea,
    Too rough for even the daring Dane to find
A landing-place upon the frozen lea.
    Cold is the wind.

The blast sweeps round the chapel from behind,
  Making the altar-fire flare fitfully,
While I must kneel and pray with troubled mind.

Patrick and Bridget, I have prayed to thee!
  The night is over and my task resigned
To Colum. Though God's own dwelling shelter me,
  Cold is the wind.

THE FALCONER OF GOD

WILLIAM ROSE BENÉT (1886-   )

I flung my soul to the air like a falcon flying.
I said, "Wait on, wait on, while I ride below!
I shall start a heron soon
In the marsh beneath the moon—
A strange white heron rising with silver on its wings,
Rising and crying
Wordless, wondrous things;
The secret of the stars, of the world's heart-strings
The answer to their woe.
Then stoop thou upon him and grip and hold him so!"

My wild soul waited on as falcons hover.
I beat the reedy fens as I trampled past.
I heard the mournful loon
In the marsh beneath the moon.
And then—with feathery thunder—the bird of my desire
Broke form the cover
Flashing silver fire.
High up among the stars I saw his pinions spire.
The pale clouds gazed aghast
As my falcon stoopt upon him, and gript and held him fast.

My soul dropt through the air—with heavenly plunder?—
Gripping the dazzling bird my dreaming knew?
Nay! but a piteous freight,
A dark and heavy weight

Despoiled of silver plumage, its voice forever stilled,—
All of the wonder
Gone that ever filled
Its guise with glory. Oh, bird that I have killed,
How brilliantly you flew
Across my rapturous vision when first I dreamed of you!

Yet I fling my soul on high with new endeavor,
And I ride the world below with a joyful mind.
I shall start a heron soon
In the marsh beneath the moon—
A wondrous silver heron its inner darkness fledges!
I beat forever
The fens and the sedges.
The pledge is still the same—for all disastrous pledges,
All hopes resigned!
My soul still flies above me for the quarry it shall find.

HE IS THE LONELY GREATNESS

Madeleine Caron Rock

He is the lonely greatness of the world—
    (His eyes are dim),
His power it is holds up the Cross
    That holds up Him.

He takes the sorrow of the threefold hour—
    (His eyelids close)
Round Him and round the wind—His Spirit—where
    It listeth blows.

And so the wounded greatness of the world
    In silence lies—
And death is shattered by the light from out
    Those darkened eyes.

ST. BRIDGET'S LULLABY

Doroth Una Ratcliffe

Hushoo! hushoo! tiny King,
God never made a dearer thing;
Thy poor father's very worn
And would sleep, now Thou art born.
Thy wee Mother needeth rest,
Suckle now at Bridget's breast.

Hushoo! hushoo! little dear,
Hushoo! or the ass will hear
And the cattle cannot sleep
If they hear their Saviour weep.
All the village Thou wilt wake
Hushoo! for Thy parents' sake.

Hushoo! hushoo! or Thy cry
Will make the blesséd angels sigh;
And those Kings who travelled far,
Following a guiding star,
Will think Thou art not pleased with them.
Hush! they rest in Bethlehem.

THE END OF THE DUEL

Rachel Annand

There's an end to the duel long fought in the Dark
  In the dangerous moonlighted Past.
Monseigneur my God, a chivalrous lady
  Surrenders at last.

Idly magnanimous, tolerant, intolerant
  Of cowards, frank, fierce, Florentine,—
Monseigneur my God, a chivalrous lady
  Thou alone canst divine.

If I be defeated, 'tis by inviolate
   Stroke of Thy mystical Lance.
Monseigneur my God, a chivalrous lady
   Still dares risk the chance.

If I be unvizored, I gaze at my victor
   With smiling and reconciled eyes.
Monseigneur my God, play fair by the lady—
   Unhelm ere she dies.

AFTER READING SAINT TERESA, LUIS DE LEON AND RAMON LULL

Muna Lee

There is a joy I have not known, a splendor
   That never flashed across my darkened heart.
   There is a bliss in which I have no part
Of passionate welcome and of rapt surrender.
It is the Vision, terrible and tender,
   Whose ecstasies Teresa's songs impart;
   The spring from which Luis's praises start;
The Fire and Dew that Ramon's altars render.

Yet even I, the cold and blind, have been
   Led by an echo toward the Holy Wood,
      Hearing the Voice that thrilled its sentient air,
   And, as an alien at its edge I stood,
Afar within its depths I too have seen
      The star that glitters on the lilies there.

BIOGRAPHICAL DATA

ABELARD, PETER (1079-1142), was born near Nantes, France. He studied under Roscelin and William of Campaigne and taught at Melun and Paris. He built the Oratory of the Paraclete after being compelled to burn his Introduction to Theology. He was controverted by Saint Bernard. His love affair with Héloise is famous.

ADAM DE ST. VICTOR (1130-1180), was one of the greatest poets of his time. There are 106 of his Hymns and Sequences still extant.

ADAMS, HENRY (1838-1918), was born and educated in New England. He was author of Essays in Anglo-Saxon Law (1876), the Life of Gallatin (1879), the Life of John Randolph (1882), a History of the United States, The Degradation of the Democratic Dogma, The Education of Henry Adams, Mont-Saint-Michel and Chartres, and Letters to a Niece.

AGOSTINHO DA CRUZ, FREI (1540-1619), was a younger brother of the poet Diogo Bernardez. He joined the Franciscans in 1561. There is an edition of his poems by Mendes dos Remedios (Vol. XXI, Subsidios).

AICARD, JEAN (1848-....), was born at Toulon, France, and is a well-known poet and dramatist.

ALDANA, FRANCISCO (1550-1578), was born at Tortosa, Spain, and perished in the African War of the Portuguese King Sebastian in 1578. Menendez y Pelayo ranks him high among the Spanish mystical poets.

ALISHAN, LEO, was born at Erzeroum early in the nineteenth century. He became a monk in the Mechitarist community in Venice and won distinction as a linguist, antiquarian, scientist and historian. He translated into Armenian many poems from European languages. He died revered and beloved.

ALPHONSA, MOTHER M. (Lathrop, Rose Hawthorne) (1851-1926), was the daughter of Nathaniel Hawthorne. She was married to George Parsons Lathrop the poet in 1871 and entered the Catholic Church with him in 1891. She became the superior of the Dominican Community of the Third Order and founded the Charitable Home for Cancer Patients in New York City.

AMBROSE, SAINT (340-397), was born of a Christian family, his

485

father being pretorian prefect at Treves, and when he settled at Milan the future bishop was entrusted with the government of Liguria and Aemilia. His election to the bishopric of Milan was on the unanimous vote of the Christian assembly. He was certainly the author of the hymns, Aeterne Rerum Conditor, Deus Creator Omnium, Jam Surgit Hora Tertia, and Veni Redemptor Gentium. Many others are attributed to him. He is one of the Doctors of the Church.

ANATOLIUS, SAINT (died 458), was Patriarch of Constantinople in the reign of Theodosius the Younger. He was born at Alexandria and distinguished himself against Nestorius. The Bollandists commend him as a Catholic, a saint, and a prophet.

ANGELUS SILESIUS (Johannes Scheffler) (1624-1677), was born in Breslau, the son of a Lutheran Polish nobleman. He graduated from the University of Padua and became a Catholic in 1653. In 1661 he was ordained priest and retired to the monastery of the Knights of the Cross in Breslau where he died. His famous religious songs, Heilige Seelenlust, were published in 1657. His long poem, The Cherubic Pilgrim (Cherubinische Wandersmann), is his most famous work. He also left a number of controversial tracts collected under the title of Ecclesiologia.

ANNAND, RACHEL, is an authority on the Italian Renaissance. She resides at Edinburgh.

ANSELM, SAINT (1033-1109), was born near Aosta, Italy. He studied under Lanfranc and is considered one of the founders of scholastic theology. He became archbishop of Canterbury in 1093 and died there with the repute of great sanctity. His writings comprise The Soliloquy on the Essence of God, The Proslogion, and Apologies Against Gaunilo. His hymns are of a high order, especially the long tribute to Mary known as the Mariale. He is sometimes called the Saint of Le Bec, from the French abbey of which he was prior and abbot (1063-1093).

ANTHONY OF PADUA, SAINT (1195-1231), was born in Lisbon; he spent ten years with the Augustinians of Coimbra and then, with their consent, took the habit of Saint Francis. There are many stories of his thaumaturgic powers. He was very famous as a preacher and by chance came to his end near Padua, where he is enshrined. His vision of the Christ-Child is a favorite subject with the old painters and sculptors. He was a companion of Saint Francis of Assisi in his last years.

ARGENSOLA, BARTOLOMÉ LEONARDO DE (1564-1631), was a native of Aragon who, with his brother, attempted to resist the influence of Gongorism in Spain. His Rimas were published in 1634.

ARIOSTO, LUDOVICO (1474-1533), was born at Reggio. He studied law but early devoted himself to poetry. He enjoyed the patronage of Cardinal d'Este and his brother the Duke. Retiring to Ferrara he wrote comedies and satires and his famous Orlando Furioso (1532). His work is considered classic in Italian literature.

ARNOLD, MATTHEW (1822-1888), was born at Laleham, Middlesex, England, the son of Thomas Arnold (1795-1842). He was educated at Winchester, Rugby, and Oxford. He became professor of poetry at Oxford in 1857. He made two visits to the United States. His works include Poems (1854 and 1867), Empedocles on Aetna (1853), Essays in Criticism (1865), of Celtic Literature (1867), Literature and Dogma (1873) and Last Essays on Church and Religion.

ATHENOGENES, SAINT (2nd century), was a martyr whose works are quoted by Saint Basil.

AUGUSTINE OF HIPPO, SAINT (354-450), was born at Thegaste in Numidia, his mother Monica a Christian, his father Patricius a pagan. He was sent to study in Carthage and turned from a life of pleasure to an interest in religion, first allying himself with the Manicheans. He taught for some time in Rome and then passed on to Milan. Here he encountered Saint Ambrose and was baptized in 387, his mother Saint Monica dying in the same year. He returned to Carthage and Thegaste, received the priesthood and in 395 was consecrated bishop of Hippo. His writings are numerous, comprising his Confessions, the City of God, and Christian Doctrine.

AUGUSTINE OF THE MOTHER OF GOD, SISTER, is the Prioress of the Carmelites of Santa Clara, California.

BARCLAY, ALEXANDER (1475-1552), was probably of Scottish birth and joined the monks of Ely and Canterbury and later was the rector of All Hallows in London. His works include The Ship of Fools and Eclogues.

BARING, MAURICE, THE HONORABLE MAJOR (1874-....), was educated at Eton and Trinity College, Oxford. He served in the British diplomatic service and later became correspondent for The Morning Post in Manchuria, Russia, Constantinople and the Balkans. His works include Hildesheim, Quatre Pastiches (1899), The Black Prince (1902), Gaston de Foix (1903), Desiderio (1906), Sonnets (1906), and Collected Poems (1911-1914-1918).

BEAUMONT, SIR JOHN (1583-1627), was born at Grace-Dieu, Leicestershire, a brother of the English poet and dramatist Francis Beaumont. His works include Bosworth Field and sacred poems.

BECQUER, GUSTAVO ADOLFO (1836-1870), was a native of Seville whence he passed to Madrid for a poverty-stricken career. His Obras (Madrid, 1871) show marked German influences.

BEDE, SAINT, THE VENERABLE (672-735), was born in Northumberland, England, and educated by Saint Benedict Bishop and Ceolfrid in the Monastery of St. Peter and St. Paul at Wearmouth and Jarrow where his whole life was passed. He was ordained priest in his thirtieth year. The title of Venerabilis dates from thirty or forty years after his death. Leo XIII in 1899 declared him Doctor Ecclesiæ. His works are numerous and there has been no adequate edition of them in full. His great work is the Historia Ecclestiastica Gentis Anglorum. He mentions his book of hymns, but only a few may be identified as his own.

BELLOC, HILAIRE (1870-....), was born and educated at Edgbaston and Oxford. He entered the House of Commons in 1906, and is author of The South Country and The Path to Rome.

BENÉT, WILLIAM ROSE (1880-....), was born at Fort Hamilton, New York, and educated at the Albany Academy, Sheffield Scientific School and Yale University. He is literary editor of the Literary Review. His works are: Merchants from Cathay (1913), The Falconer of God (1914), The Great White Wall (1916), The Burglar of the Zodiac (1918) and Moons of Grandeur (1920).

BENIVIENI, GIROLAMO (1453-1542), was born at Florence, Italy, and became famous among the religious poets of his country. He was an intimate friend of Pico della Mirandola, who wrote a commentary on his Canzone dell amor celeste e divino.

BENOIT, PIERRE (1886-....), has won the Grand Prize of the French Academy for his novel Atlantis (1919). His poems are collected under the title of Diaduminius.

BENSON, ROBERT HUGH (1871-1914), was born in England, the son of the Archbishop of Canterbury. He was educated at Clivedon and Eton and completed his classical course at Cambridge in 1893. In 1894 he took orders in the Anglican Church. In 1903 he became a Catholic and went to Rome where he was ordained priest in 1904. He lectured in the United States in 1910 and 1912. His works include Light Invisible (1903), By What Authority (1904), Come Rack, Come Rope (1912), Lord of the World, and Confessions of a Convert (1913).

BERCEO, GONZALO DE (1180-1246), was born at Berceo, Spain. He became a priest in the Benedictine Monastery of San Millán in Calahorra. An edition of his Vida de Santo Domingo was published by J. D. Fitzgerald (Paris, 1904).

BERNARD OF CLAIRVAUX, SAINT (1090-1153), was born at Fontaines, near Dijon, France. He joined the Cistercian Order and became abbot of Clairvaux in 1115. He championed the claims of Innocent III to the papacy and procured the condemnation of the writings of Abelard. See his works by Mabillon (Paris, 1667).

BERNARD OF MORLAS (about 1140), was a monk at Cluny whose long poem De Contemptu Mundi was rendered into English by Dr. Neale.

BIONDI, CLEMENTE, was an Italian poet who flourished after 1742.

BLAKE, WILLIAM (1757-1827), was born in London. He became noted as a poet, engraver and painter. His principal writings are The

Book of Thel (1780), Songs of Innocence (1789), Marriage of Heaven and Hell (1790) and Gates of Paradise (1793).

BLOUZ, HOVHANNES (1250-1326), was born at Erzenga, studied at the Monastery of Saint Minas and Cain on the border of Georgia and Eastern Armenia. He composed the hymn in honor of St. Nerses. He studied Latin and translated parts of St. Thomas into Armenian. His works are to be found in MS. 234 of the Mekhitaristes of Venice.

BLUNT, HUGH FRANCIS (1877-....), was born at Medway, Massachusetts, and educated at Boston College and St. John's Seminary where he received Holy Orders. His collected works are to be found in Poems, Songs for Sinners, The Book of the Mother of God, and Spiritual Songs (1925).

BLUNT, WILFRID SCAWEN (1840-1922), was born near Crawley, England, and educated at Stonyhurst and St. Mary's Oscott. He spent some time in the British diplomatic service and eventually espoused the cause of Arabi Pasha and the Irish nationalist party. He published Love Sonnets of Proteus (1880), Esther (1892), Griselda (1893), Quatrains of Youth (1898), Satan Absolved 1899) and Seven Golden Odes of Arabia (1903).

BOCCACCIO, GIOVANNI (1313-1375), was born in Paris of Florentine family; there he began his studies and later prosecuted them in the Naples law schools. He turned early to literature, but went back to Florence where he held public offices and was entrusted with diplomatic missions to Padua and Avignon. His friendship with Petrarch began in 1350. In 1373 he began his lectures in Florence on the works of Dante. His principal work is the Decameron, finished in 1353, the indecencies of which are no more than reflections of the free speech prevailing at his time. His personal character is, generally speaking, estimable.

BOIS, JULES (1870-....), was born at Marseilles, France, and educated there at the College of St. Sebastian. His works include Le Monde Invisible, Les Petites Religions de Paris, Le Satanisme et la Magie, and Humanité Divine.

BONADVENTURE, SAINT GIOVANNI DI FIDENZA (1221-1274), was born at Bagnores, Italy. He was surnamed Doctor Seraphicus for his achievements in scholastic philosophy. His works are Breviloquium and Centiloquium and Biblia Pauperum.

BOTREL, THEODORE (1868-1925), was born at Dinon, France, and gained great popularity with his Chansons de Chez-Nous, Chansons en Sabots, Chansons en Dentelle, Chansons de Bivouac, etc.

BRÉGY, KATHERINE, is a native of Philadelphia, Pennsylvania, whose poetry and criticism reveal high culture and refinement. Her essays are collected in two volumes: The Poet's Chantry and Poets and Pilgrims.

BRIDGES, ROBERT (1844-....), Poet Laureate of England, was educated at Eton and Corpus Christi College, Oxford. He studied and practiced medicine but gave himself wholly to letters after 1882. His poetical product has resulted in many volumes, his later works being The Spirit of Man, An Anthology (1916), Yatterdon Hymnal, and Ibant Obscuri.

BRIGID OF KILDARE, SAINT (453-523), was the daughter of a slave-woman and Dubhthach who sent her to a druid for keeping. She was baptized and, returning to her father's house, refused all offers of marriage. She at length took the convent vows, and with seven companions founded the Convent of Kildare. This became one of the greatest monasteries in Ireland, noted for the learning of its monks and nuns. She is known in Irish literature as "The Mary of the Gael," and there are many miracles and legends gathered around her name.

BUNKER, JOHN (1886-....), was born in Cincinnati, Ohio, of German-Irish parents. He was educated by the Jesuits of St. Xavier's College, Cincinnati, and has published his poems under the title Shining Fields and Dark Towers (1919).

CAEDMON, SAINT (died in 680), was a laborer in the monastery founded by St. Hilda at Whitby. Following her request he took the monastic vows and pursued a life of great holiness. His writings in Anglo Saxon survive in a tenth-century MS. in the Bodleian Library. Bede declares that his work knew no rival.

CALDERON DE LA BARCA, PEDRO (1600-1681), was a native of Madrid, Spain, and a favorite dramatist of Philip IV. He has been frequently translated into English, French and German. See Calderon, His Life and Genius, by R. C. Trench (New York, 1856).

CALLAGHAN, GERTRUDE, is a native of New York City. Her poems are published under the titles of Inheritance (1924) and Witch Girl (1926).

CAMOENS, LUIS VAZ DE (1524-1579), was born in Lisbon and died there after a life of many wanderings. He lost an eye at the battle of Ceuta and suffered imprisonment at Goa. His master-piece, Os Lusiados, was published in 1572.

CARBERY, ETHNA (1866-1902), was born at Ballymena, Ireland. Her name was Anna Johnston before she became the wife of Seumas MacManus, who after her death collected her poems under the title of The Four Winds of Eirinn (1902). She is a poet of unusual charm.

CASAL, JULIAN DEL (1863-1893), was a native of Habana, Cuba, who followed French forms in his poetry. His works are Hojas al Viento (1890) and Bustas y Rimas (1893).

CASAS, JOSÉ JOAQUIN (1866-....), is a native of Bogotá, Colombia, where he is a leading statesman and poet. His metrical works may be found in Recuerdos de Fiestas (1912) and Crónicas de Aldea (1919).

CASEMENT, SIR ROGER (1864-1916), was born at Kingstown, Ireland. He served as British consul in the Congo Free State and Brazil (1895-1913). In 1916 he joined in the activities of the Irish Sinn Fein Party and was arrested on landing from a German submarine and executed for treason. He joined the Catholic Church shortly before his execution.

CASTRO DE MURGUIA, ROSALÍA (1837-1885), was born at Santiago de Compostela. She stands at the head of modern Galician poetry. Her chief work may be found in Cantares Gallegos (1863) and Follas Novas (1880).

CHAUCER, GEOFFREY (1340-1400), was born in London, the son of the royal vintner whom he followed into France. In 1372 he was sent on a diplomatic mission into Italy and became a friend of Petrarch. His whole life was passed in official positions, some of them of importance (see Louise Imogen Guiney's Chaucer in The Catholic Encyclopedia). The standard editions of his poems and tales are Saunder's edition (London, 1894), Complete works by Skeat (Oxford, 1894), The Student's Chaucer by Skeat (Oxford, 1895) and Canterbury Tales, in the King's Classics Series (1904). Catholics, who are the best judges of such questions, hold that Chaucer's religion was at base true and orthodox and his life, on the whole, correct and regular.

CHESTERTON, GILBERT (1874-....), was born at Campden Hill, Kensington, England. He studied at St. Paul's School and at Slade Institute. His works include The Wild Knight, The Napoleon of Notting Hill (1904), Heretics (1905), The Man Who Was Thursday (1908), Orthodoxy (1908), All Things Considered (1908), The Ball and the Cross (1910), The Innocence of Father Brown (1911), Manalive (1912), Poems (1915) and The Everlasting Man (1926)

CHILDE, WILFRID ROWLAND (1890-....), was born at Wakefield, Yorkshire, England, and educated at Harrow and Magdalen College, Oxford. He became a Catholic in 1914 and is at present on the faculty of English in the University of Leeds. He has published seven collections of poems, the first of which is The Little City (1911).

CLARKE, JOSEPH I. C. (1853-1925), was born at Dunleary, Kingstown, Ireland, and educated at Mountrath and the Christian Brothers' School in Kingstown. He passed ten years in London, but becoming involved in some of the Fenian activities of 1868, he made his escape to America where he spent the rest of his life as a journalist and editor on the New York Herald (1870-1883), the Morning Journal and The World (1883-1898), The Criterion (1898-1900), New York Herald (1900-1901), and as publicity agent for the Standard Oil Company (1901-....). His works for the stage include The Prince of India and Heartsease; his poems appeared under the titles Malmorda and The Fighting Race (1911).

CLAUDEL, PAUL (1868-....), was born in the Vosges of Picardy, France, and early came under the literary influences of Renan, Mallarmé and Verlaine. In his consular service he came to the United States and was sent in 1875 to Tientsin, China, and still later to Prague, Frankfort-on-the-Main and Hamburg. He eventually became ambassador to Tokio and Washington. His dramatic works were gathered together in 1901 under the title of L'Arbre. His other books are Muses, Tête d'Or, L'Echange, La Ville, L'Otage, L'Annonce Faite à Marie, Corona Benignitatis, and Connaissance de l'Est.

CLEMENT OF ALEXANDRIA (160-215), was one of the leaders of the Christian Academy at Alexandria. He advocated Greek culture which was then suspect among the Christians. His works include Exhortation to the Greeks, The Instructor, and Miscellanies.

COCTEAU, JEAN (1892-....), is a contemporary French poet, recently converted to the Church.

COLERIDGE, MARY ELIZABETH (1861-1907), was a cousin of Samuel Taylor Coleridge. Her first novel was The Seven Sleepers of Ephesus (1893). Her other works are Fancy's Following (1896), The King with Two Faces (1897), A Romance of Gustav III of Sweden, Non Sequitur (1900), and Poems, New and Old (1907).

COLERIDGE, SAMUEL TAYLOR (1771-1834), was born at Ottery, Devonshire, England. He was educated at Cambridge and published his first poems at Bristol. He was an associate of Southey and Wordsworth. He later studied at Göttingen. His works include Remorse, a Tragedy (1813), Christabel (1816) and Biographia Literaria (1817). The Ancient Mariner appeared in Lyrical Ballads, published in collaboration with Wordsworth in 1798.

COLUM, PADRAIC (1881-....), was born in Longford, Ireland, and early won recognition as a poet of unusual delicacy. He has resided for some years in the United States. His works in poetry are Wild Earth (Dublin, 1910, and New York, 1916) and Dramatic Legends and Other Poems (New York, 1922). His prose volumes of tales are numerous, including The Children Who Followed the Piper and The Road Round Ireland (1926).

COLUMCILLE, SAINT (521-597), was born at Gartan in Donegal, the son of Fergus, a descendant of Niall of the Nine Hostages. His first teacher was Saint Finnian and later he studied at Clonard. His first religious foundation was at Derry; then he founded the monastic schools of Durrow and Kells. Becoming involved in the disputes of rival chieftains, Columcille appealed to his kinsfolk, with the result that in a battle at Benbulbin he was defeated with the loss of some three thousand slain. He thereupon decided that the interests of peace demanded his retirement from Ireland and he went into exile on the Island of Iona, from which he carried on his work of converting the Picts. Three of his Latin hymns are extant: the Altus, the Trinity and Noli Pater. There are some hymns in Gælic also attributed to him.

CONSTABLE, HENRY (1562-1613), was born at Newark, England, and graduated at Cambridge. Becoming a Catholic, he settled in Paris. In 1603 on his return to London he was imprisoned in the Tower. His sonnet-sequence Diana was published in 1592.

CONTARDO, LUIS FELIPE (1880-....), a poet of Chile, South America, was educated for the priesthood in Rome. He has published Cantos del Camino (1918).

CONWAY, KATHERINE ELEANOR (1865-1927), was born at Rochester, New York, and studied at the Sacred Heart Convents in Rochester and New York City. She was for a long time a member of the editorial staff of The Pilot, Boston. Her poetical works are: On the Sunrise Slope (1881) and A Dream of Lilies (1893).

COPPÉE, FRANCOIS (1842-1908) was born in Paris. He was a member of the French Academy, and author of Passant, Jacobites, and Pour la Couronne. He was a poet deeply moved by scenes of humble life.

CORMAC OF CASHEL (837-903) was born Mac Culinan, and became king of Munster and archbishop of Cashel. He was betrothed to the Princess Gormly, but renounced her to enter the Church. He was the great literary and political figure of his time. His works include Cormac's Glossary, the oldest vernacular dictionary of modern Europe, and the Saltair of Cashel. He was killed in battle between the clans of Munster and Leinster.

CORNEILLE, PIERRE (1606-1684), was a native of Rouen, France, and became a protégé of Cardinal Richelieu. He is considered the father of French tragedy and left numerous plays including the Cid, Horace, Cinna, and Polyeucte.

COSMAS, SAINT (died in 760), was a confrere of Saint John Damascene. His Golden Canon is considered "the grandest piece in Greek sacred poetry."

COX, ELEANOR ROGERS (1865-....), was born at Enniskillen, Ireland, and coming in her youth to the United States was educated at St. Gabriel's High School, New York. Her works are A Hosting of Heroes (1911), Singing Fires of Erin (1916) and Finovar of the Fair Eyelids (1918).

CRASHAW, RICHARD (1613-1649), was born in London, the son of a Puritan divine. He entered the Charterhouse School and later Pembroke Hall, Cambridge, where in 1632 he obtained a pensionership. As a result of his studies and affiliations he became one of the most cultivated men in an age of high culture. Shortly before 1646 he had entered the Catholic Church. He became a member of the household of Cardinal Palotta, but his criticism of the private lives of his Italian companions induced His Eminence to obtain for him a benefice at the shrine of Loretto. After four weeks in this post he died of his exertions during a pilgrimage. He is one of the greatest of modern Catholic poets, the inspiration of all who have succeeded him in religious lyrical fields. His work may be found in Epigrammatum Sacrorum Liber (1634), Carmen Deo Nostro (1652) and The Delights of the Muses (1648).

CUSTANCE, OLIVE (1874-....), was born at Weston Park, Norwich, England. She was married to Lord Alfred Douglas and has published some very choice poetry. She is the daughter of Colonel Custance.

DALY, JAMES J. (1872-....), was born at Chicago, Illinois, and educated by the Jesuits, making his profession in their Society in 1890. He is at present stationed in St. Louis, Missouri, but has served as editor of America and as professor at Campion College. He is the literary editor of the Jesuit quarterly, Thought.

DALY, THOMAS AUGUSTINE (1871-....), was born at Philadelphia, Pennsylvania, and educated at Villanova and Fordham Colleges. He is author of Canzoni (1906), Carmina (1909), Madrigali (1912), Songs of Wedlock (1916) and McAroni Ballads (1919).

DANTE ALIGHIERI (1265-1321) was born at Florence, the son of a notary belonging to an old Guelph family. He was matriculated in the Guild of Physicians and Apothecaries' and in 1694 had completed his poem Vita Nuova, celebrating his spiritual love for Beatrice Portinari. He became involved in the rivalries of the Whites and Blacks of the Guelph party and was sent into exile on account of his anti-papal activities. He married Gemma di Manetto Donati and had four children. His exile was passed in various cities of North Italy, and he gradually withdrew from political intrigues. Settled in Ravenna, he completed the Divine Comedy in 1317. Here he died on the Feast of the Exaltation of the Cross, 1321. Dante holds a place in Catholic poetry of supreme honor. His criticism of popes and prelates never leads him astray from the norms of Church philosophy, and his works in general, from the Vita Nuova and the Convivio to the Divina Comedia, are a glorious exemplification of eternal beauty and truth.

DARIO, RUBÉN (1867-1916), a native of Leon, Nicaragua, engaged in journalism in several countries of South America. He later took up residence in Madrid and Paris and exerted marked influence on modern Spanish literature. His works include: Azul (1888), Prosas Profanas (1896) and El Canto Errante (1907).

DESCHAMPS, EUSTACHE (1340-1410), was born at Vertus, Marne,

France. He was both knight and cleric and spent many years at the courts of Charles V and Charles VI. He is the earliest realist in French literature and left many ballads and other poems in elaborate forms; also the Miroir de Marriage and the Art de Dicter. His works were published by the Societé des Anciens Textes Francais (1878-1894).

DE VERE, AUBREY (1814-1902), was born at Curragh Chase, Limerick, Ireland. In 1832 he entered Trinity College, Dublin, and later studied at Oxford and in Rome. He was received into the Catholic Church in 1857. He was interested in bettering Irish conditions, but he is best known as a poet. His chief works are The Legend of St. Patrick (1872), The Search After Proserpine (1843), May Carols (1857), Mediæval Records and Sonnets (1898). He was much esteemed as a literary critic. His Recollections were published in London (1897).

DIGBY, KENELM HENRY (1797-1877), was born at Geashill, King's County, Ireland. He left his country as a boy and was educated at Petersham and Trinity College, Cambridge, where he graduated in 1819, but remained for ten years in residence. He spent the greater part of his life in Southern Europe. In 1825 he was received into the Catholic Church. His Broadside of Honor was first published in 1822 and, after his conversion, was issued in an enlarged edition in 1826. His Mores Catholici (1831-1842) had an American edition (Cincinnati, 1905). His other works are Compitum (1849-1854), Short Poems (1865), Ouranogia (1872).

DINIS, KING (1261-1325), was the grandson of Alfonso X of Castile, and one of the most famous monarchs of Portugal. There are extant 138 of his poems edited in Cancioneiro d'el Rei D. Denis by H. R. Lang (Halle, 1894)

DINNIS, ENID MAUD (1873-....), is an English poet, converted to the Church in 1897. Her books include God's Fairy Tales; Mystics All; Mr. Coleman, Gent; The Anchorhold; Meadowsweet and Thyme; More Mystics; and The Three Roses.

DOLBEN, DIGBY MACKWORTH (1848-1867), was born at Finedon Hall, Northampton, England, and educated at Eton and Oxford. He joined the High Church Anglicans and in 1866 asked Newman to receive him in the Catholic Church. The Cardinal desired him to wait till he came of age. See studies of his work by B. Cornish in The Dublin Review; Louise J. Guiney in The Catholic World; Robert Bridges' Oxford edition of his Poems (1911). He was drowned in the Thames on June 28, 1867.

DOLLARD, JAMES B. (1872-....), was born in Kilkenny, Ireland, and emigrating to Canada in 1890 he studied for the priesthood and was ordained in 1896. He is now a pastor in the diocese of Toronto. He has published several collections of his poems.

DOMINICI, GIOVANNI (1356-1419), was born at Florence, Italy, of humble parents. Pope Gregory XII created him archbishop of Ragusa in 1407 and cardinal in 1408. He was active as a preacher against the Hussites. Only one of his books has been printed, A Treatise on Charity (Latin, 1555; Italian, 1736).

DONNELLY, ELEANOR C. (1848-1917), was the daughter of Ignatius Donnelly of Shakespeare cryptogram fame. She did yeoman service in the cause of Catholic letters in the United States and left several volumes of poetry full of delicate charm.

DOUGLAS, LORD ALFRED (1870-....), is the son of the Marquis of Queensbury and was educated at Winchester and Oxford. He became the editor of The Academy (1807-1910) and was converted to the Church in 1911. His works include Opals (1897), Rainbows (1902), The Blue Bird (1905), The Inn of Dreams (1910), City of the Soul (1899), Sonnets (1900) and Collected Poems (1919).

DOWSON, ERNEST (1867-1900), was born in Kent, England, and grew up in Italy and the south of France. He spent a few years at Queen's College, Oxford, and lived the rest of his life between London and France. Between 1887 and 1890 he had entered the Catholic Church. His scanty production of poems was scattered through the periodicals of the nineties, and his dainty comedy The Pierrot of the Minute was published in 1897.

DRACONTIUS, BLOSSIUS AEMILIUS (5th century), was a native of Carthage, author of De laudibus Dei. He was imprisoned by the Vandal King Gunthamund (484-496), but was released after his poem in elegiacs, entitled Satisfactio.

DROSTE HÜLSHOFF, ANNETTE VON (1797-1848), was born at Hülshoff near Münster. She is counted among the greatest of the nineteenth-century German poets.

DRYDEN, JOHN (1631-1700), was born at Oldwinkle All Saints, Northamptonshire, England, of a Parliamentary family. He was educated at Westminster and Trinity College, Cambridge. After celebrating Cromwell in Heroic Stanzas (1658), he welcomed the return of King Charles II in Astraea Redux (1660). His Annus Mirabilis appeared in 1667. Following a series of dramatic poems, he was made poet laureate in 1670. His masterpiece for the stage is the story of Anthony and Cleopatra in All for Love (1678). In 1681 he began his satires of Absalom and Achitophel and became involved in a polemical warfare which called forth MacFlechnoe (1682). He was converted to the Catholic Church in 1686. His allegorical poem The Hind and the Panther appeared in 1687. He returned to this writing for the stage and began a series of translations from the Latin and Greek classics, including a valuable version of Vergil's Georgics and the Aeneid. His Alexander's Feast was written for St. Cecilia's Day in 1697.

Du Bellay, Joachim (1524-1560), was nephew of General Guillaume and Cardinal Jean Du Bellay. His Defense et Illustration de la Langue Francaise places him at the head of the poetical school of the Pleiade.

Duggan, Eileen, is a contemporary poet of Wellington, New Zealand.

Dunbar, William (1460?-1520?), "The Chaucer of Scotland," was educated at St. Andrew's University. He celebrated his first Mass in 1504 but never obtained the benefice he petitioned for. His poem The Thrissil and the Rois was published in 1503. His other well-known poems are the Goldyn Targe and Dance. In 1834 his complete works were published by Dr. David Laing.

Earls, Michael (1875-....), was born at Southbridge, Massachusetts, and educated at Holy Cross College (Worcester), Georgetown (Washington) and in Paris. He joined the Jesuits in 1899 and is professor of English at Holy Cross College. He has published his poems in four volumes.

Eden, Helen Parry (1885-....), was born in England and educated at Manchester University. In 1906 she was married to the artist Denis Eden and continued her study of painting. She and her husband became Catholics in 1909. Her books include Bread and Circuses, Coal and Candlelight, and a children's life of Christ in rhymes entitled a String of Sapphires.

Egan, Maurice Francis (1852-1924), was born at Philadelphia, Pennsylvania, of Irish parents. He was educated at La Salle College, Philadelphia, and Georgetown, Washington. He became assistant to the editor, James McMaster, of the Freeman's Journal and at his death took up his lectures in English literature at Notre Dame and St. Mary's College, South Bend, Indiana. Later he became a professor of English literature at the Catholic University, Washington. From this post he was sent as American minister to Copenhagen and remained in Denmark until 1918. His works include Preludes (1879), Songs and Sonnets (1885), Sexton Maginnis Stories (1902) and Sonnets de Heredia (World's Best Literature).

Egurén, José M., is a native of Lima, Peru, and author of collections of poems including Simbólicas (1911) and La Canción de las Figuras (1916).

Eichendorff, Count Joseph von (1786-1857), was born near Ratibor, Silesia, served in the War of Liberation (1813-1815) and became a counselor at Dantzic and Konigsberg. He retired to Berlin and wrote Ahnung und Gegenwart. His complete poetical works appeared in 1842.

Elizabeth, Empress of Austria-Hungary (1837-1898), was the daughter of Duke Maximilian of Bavaria and was married to the Emperor Franz Josef in 1854. She was assassinated on the Italian Lakes in 1898.

EMERY, SUSAN (1846-1914), was born at Dorchester, Massachusetts, of an old New England family. She was editor of The Young Christian Soldier (1871-1874), and entered the Catholic Church in 1875. Her writings include Messages for the Ecclesiastical Year and Inner Life of the Soul.

EPHREM, SAINT, THE SYRIAN (306-373), was born at Nisibis, Mesopotamia. His works were published in Rome (1732-1743).

FABER, FREDERICK WILLIAM (1814-1863), was born at Calverley, Yorkshire, England, of Huguenot descent. He was educated at Harrow and at Balliol and University Colleges, where he came under the influence of Newman. In 1839 he was admitted to Anglican Orders and undertook High Church activities at his church in Elton. He became a Catholic in 1845 and in 1847 was ordained a Catholic priest and joined Newman at the Oratory of St. Philip Neri. His hymns were composed for use in his Oratory in London. His works include Lives of Modern Saints (1847), All for Jesus (1853), Growth in Holiness (1854), The Foot of the Cross (1858) and The Precious Blood (1860). His holiness and devotion to the Faith are reflected in all his writings.

FIELD, MICHAEL, is the pseudonym of Katherine Harris Bradley and her niece Edith Emma Cooper (1846-1913). Together they entered the Catholic Church in 1907. Their joint works include Callirhoe (1884), Fair Rosamund, Long Ago (1889), Sight and Song (1893), Poems of Adoration (1912), Cedar and Hyssop (1913).

FILICAJA, VINCENZIO DA (1642-1707), was born at Florence, Italy. His poems were highly appreciated by Macaulay. He published Poesie Toscane (1607).

FISCHER, WILLIAM J. (1880-1912), was born at Windsor, Ontario, where he was educated. He practiced medicine for some years before his death at an early age; and among his published works left two collections of poems: Songs By the Wayside (1903) and The Toiler (1907).

FOGAZZARO, ANTONIO (1842-1911), was born at Vicenza, Italy. He began his literary career in 1874. His novel Il Santo was taken as a sort of gospel for the Modernist societies of North Italy and was thereupon prohibited by the Holy Index. Fogazzaro immediately submitted to the condemnation and in another novel, Leila, criticized his former followers. Other novels from his pen are Piccolo Mundo Antico and Piccolo Mundo Moderno.

FORREST, WILLIAM (1510-1565), was a priest and poet during the reign of Henry VIII in England. Very little is known of his life, but he was an excellent musician and collected the writings of the composers of his time. His works, mostly unpublished, are History of Joseph the Chaste, The Pleasant Poesie of Princely

Practice, Catherine of Aragon and her Divorce, a poem, with other poems in the Harleian MS. (1703).

FORTUNATUS, VENANTIUS HONORIUS CLEMENTIANUS (about 530-400), was born near Treviso, Italy and educated at Ravenna. He became a traveler courtier composing eulogies for saints, churches, prelates and kings, and at last took up a residence at Poitiers where Saint Radegunde had established a great monastery. His poems Vexilla Regis and the Pange Lingua were written to thank the Emperor Justin for the piece of the True Cross he had sent to this monastery. His works are the best pictures we have of society in the Merovingian period. The best edition is that of F. Leo and B. Krusch (Berlin 1881-1885).

FRANCIS OF ASSISI, SAINT (1181-1226), was born at Assisi, Umbria, Italy, the son of a wealthy cloth merchant. He received his education from the priests of St. George in Assisi and devoted himself to the pleasures of life in the troubadour period. He took some minor part in the civil warfares between Assisi and Perugia. In spite of the opposition of his father he retired to a hermitage and returned to Assisi only to collect materials to restore some ruined chapels. He was soon joined by a choice body of companions, known by the name of Penitents of Assisi and, later, as Friars Minor, after they had received the approbation of Pope Innocent III. "They wandered from place to place singing in their joy and calling themselves God's minstrels. The whole world their cloister." In 1212 Francis was joined by Clare, a young heiress of Assisi, who was to become the founder of the female branch of the Franciscan Order. In the same year Francis embarked for Syria but was shipwrecked and returned to Ancona, Italy. In 1214 he set out for Morocco but was seized by a serious illness in Spain and forced to return again to Italy. The vast and intricate story of the founding and spread of the Franciscan Order is a study to be highly recommended to all who would understand the spirit of thirteenth-century Europe. The rule of Francis remained the model of communities mendicant, missionary and educational throughout the Christian world. He was the "Troubadour of God" in the constant poetry of his actions and his words. The legends that have gathered about his name only reflect the actual character of his life. He has been called the precursor of Dante. The actual writings accepted as authentic works of Francis may be summed up in the Rule of the Friars Minor, some exhortatory fragments and the Canticle of the Sun. The Life of St. Francis by Paul Sabatier (Paris, 1894) is recognized for its great erudition and absence of sympathy with his spiritual significance. See The Writings of St. Francis of Assisi by Pascal Robinson (Philadelphia, 1906).

FRANCIS XAVIER, SAINT (1506-1552), was born in the Castle of

Xavier, near Sanguesa, Navarre, Spain. He went to Paris in 1525 for study at the Collège de Sainte-Barbe and there met Saint Ignatius Loyola then planning the foundations of the Jesuit Society. He made his vows in 1534 and was ordained with Ignatius in 1537. In 1541 he embarked for India, his missions spreading from Goa to the Island of Ceylon. He continued with marvelous success his evangelization of Malacca and the Moluccas, and is said by some authorities to have reached Mindanao in the Philippines. He and his companions landed in Japan in 1549, but after two years he returned to Goa. He was on his way to establish his missions in China when he was taken off his ship in a dying condition on the Island of Sancian near the coast of China. He was canonized with St. Ignatius by Gregory XV in 1622.

FRANCISCA JOSEFA DEL CASTILLO, SISTER (1691-1743), was born at Tunja, Columbia, and died there in the Convent of Santa Clara. Her works were published in Philadelphia in 1817.

GABRIEL Y GALÁN, JOSÉ MARÍA (1870-1908), was a native of Frades de la Serna, Salamanca, Spain, whose life was given to schoolteaching and farming. His Obras Completas were published in Madrid-Seville, 1909.

GALINDEZ, BARTOLOMÉ (1899-....), is a young poet of Argentina, who has published a collection of poems, Humanidad (1922).

GALVAM, FRANCISCO (1540-1635), was born at Villa Viçosa, Portugal. He was equerry to the Duke of Braganza. His authorship of the sonnet To Our Lord has been questioned.

GAMBLE, WILLIAM MILLER T., is a contemporary American poet and scholar, a convert to the Church.

GARESCHÉ, EDWARD F. (1876-....), was born at St. Louis, Missouri, and educated at St. Louis University and Washington University. He was ordained in the Society of Jesus in 1912; founded The Queen's Work and edited it (1914-1922); and at present edits Hospital Progress. He has published several volumes of poetry.

GARRISON, THEODOSIA (1874-....), was born at Newark, New Jersey, and was educated in the Newark schools. Her works are: Joy of Life (1909), Earth Cry (1910) and The Dreamer (1917).

GILBERT, NICOLAS-JOSEPH-FLORENT (1750-1780), was born at Fontenay-le-Chateau and died in Paris from a fall from his horse. He is author of some satires and his Adieu à la Vie is among the French classics.

GILL, ERIC (1882-....), is an English convert to the Church who has done some unique work in bookmaking and illustrating, and has written some quaint religious poems. His books include Sculpture, and Songs Without Clothes.

GILTINAN, CAROLINE (1884-....), was born at Philadelphia, Pennsylvania, and now resides at Alexandria, Virginia. She published The Divine Image (1917).

GOMEZ RESTREPO, ANTONIO (1869-....), was born in Colombia and has become a leader in literary and national affairs. He is the author of the editions of Rafael Pombo (1917) and Miguel Antonio Caro (1918).

GONGORA, LUIS DE ARGOTE Y (1561-1627), was born at Cordoba, Spain, and educated at Salamanca. In 1613 he became chaplain to the king. His reputation was established in 1600 with the publication of his Romancero General. He established the style known as Gongorism in Spain, equivalent to Marinism in Italy and Euphuism in England.

GRAY, JOHN (1866-....), was born in London and became a Catholic in his early youth. He was associated with the authors generally represented in The Yellow Book and The Savoy and published his Blue Calendar in 1897, a book of child's verse in 1904, and in 1901 he was ordained in Rome and took up his priestly duties in Edinburgh where he built St. Peter's Church, of which he is now the pastor. His verse was published under the title of Spiritual Poems. He wrote the preface to the Letters of Aubrey Beardsley.

GREGORIA FRANCISCA, SISTER (1653-1736), was born of half-Flemish, half-Spanish parentage at San Lucar de Barrameda. She entered the Carmelite Convent in Seville and rose to eminence for her sanctity and the precious mystical quality of her poems. See Discurso sobre Sor Gregoria Francisca by Santiago Montoto (Seville, 1913).

GREGORY OF NAREK (951-1011), is a saint of the Armenian Rite.

GREGORY THE GREAT, SAINT (538-594), was born in Rome and about 574 was appointed pretor urbanus by the Emperor Justin. He joined the priesthood and founded six monasteries in Sicily and one in Rome to which he retired. In 590 he was elected pope. He sent Saint Augustine and forty monks to convert the English. He reformed the chant of the Church and left a Sacramentary, which was the base of the Roman Missal. The chief edition of his works is the Benedictine (1706).

GRESSET, LOUIS (1709-1777), was born at Amiens, France, and became a member of the Society of Jesus. His literary expansions led to his retirement from the order but his private life remained exemplary. His most famous poem is Vert-Vert, translated with much spirit by Father Prout. The present version has been somewhat bowdlerized by the editor.

GREY, FRANCIS W. (1860-....), was born in England and resided for some years in Canada and the United States. He is a convert from Anglicanism and a valued contributor to the leading English and American reviews. His Love Crucified was published at

Bruges, Belgium, 1902. He is also author of The Curé of St. Philippe.

GRIFFIN, GERALD (1803-1840), was born at Limerick, Ireland, and received a good education. His first ambitions turned toward the stage, but he had died before Macready produced his tragedy Gisippus in 1842. He had made some success with stories of Munster when he produced The Collegians (1828) followed by The Invasion (1832). His desire to serve others led to his entrance to the teaching congregation of the Christian Brothers in 1838, and as Brother Joseph he was transferred from Dublin to Cork where he passed to his reward.

GUÉRIN, CHARLES (1873-1907), was born at Lunéville, Meurthe-et-Moselle, France. His works are: Fleurs de Neige (1893), L'Art Perjure (1894), Joies Grises (1894), Le Sang des Crepuscules (1895), Le Coeur Solitaire (1898) and L'Eros Funebre (1900).

GUINEY, LOUISE IMOGEN (1861-1920), was born in Boston, Massachusetts, the daughter of General Patrick R. Guiney, and finished her education at the Elmhurst Convent, Providence, Rhode Island. She immediately engaged in literary work and after 1904 made her home at Oxford, England. Her chief works are: Songs at the Start (1884), The White Sail (1887), A Roadside Harp (1893), Nine Sonnets Written at Oxford (1895), Patrins (1897), The Martyr's Idyl (1900) and Happy Ending (1909). She edited many volumes and devoted years of preparation to a book on Henry Vaughan the Silurist, which was never altogether finished.

GUITTONE D'AREZO (1230-1294) was a native of Arezzo, Italy. He became a leader in the religious Knighthood of the Cavalieri Gaudenti. His sonnets are considered models of perfection and he is counted among the founders of the Italian tongue.

GUTIERREZ NÁJERA, MANUEL (1859-1895), was the Mexican precursor of the Modernista movement in Spanish poetry. He is one of the glories of Mexican letters and founded La Revista Azul.

HABINGTON, WILLIAM (1605-1654), was born at Hindlip, Worcestershire, England. He studied at Saint-Omer and Paris. He married in 1632 and in 1634 published his Castara. In 1640 appeared his Queen of Aragon, his other works being chiefly histories.

HAIGHT, DOROTHY (1897-....), is an American poetess of a very original charm. Her work is as yet uncollected.

HAWKER, ROBERT STEPHEN (1803-1875), was born at Plymouth, England, and was educated at Liskeard, Cheltenham, and at Pembroke College, Oxford. He took his degree in 1828 and orders in the Anglican Church in 1831. In 1834 he was appointed vicar of Morwenstow on the coast of Cornwall. He lived there until his death, before which he was received into the Catholic Church. His Cornish Ballads had an edition (London, 1904), and his finest poems are The Quest of the San Graal and the Ballad of Trelawney.

HENRYSON, ROBERT (1430?-1500?), was a Scottish poet, author of the Schoolmaster of Dunfermline and fables retold from more ancient sources. His Robene and Makyne is said to be the first pastoral poem in English.

HERRERA, FERNANDO DE (1534-1594), was a native of Seville where he became a parish priest. In 1580 he published an annotation of the poems of Garcilasso de la Vega and a Life of Sir Thomas More (1592). See Fernando de Herrera by M. A. Coster (Paris, 1908).

HERRERA Y REISSIG, JULIO (1875-1911), was born in Montevideo, Uruguay, and passed an unhappy life. His works collected after his death include Los Peregrinos de Piedra, Las Lunas de Oro, Las Pascuas del Tiempo, and La Vida (Montevideo, 1914).

HEYWOOD, JOHN (1497-1580) was probably a native of London and a student at Pembroke College, Oxford. He was attached to the royal court as a musician. He was a Catholic and delivered a Latin oration of welcome to Queen Mary Tudor, and at her death retired on account of his faith to Mechlin, Brabant, where it is believed he died in exile. His principal work is The Four P's. His wit and humor are highly appreciated by the best critics.

HICKEY, EMILY (1860-1924), was born in County Wexford, Ireland. Her works include A Sculptor and Other Poems (1881), Verse Tales, Lyrics and Translations (1889), and Michael Villiers, Idealist, and Other Poems (1891). She was one of the founders of the Browning Society.

HINKSON, KATHERINE TYNAN (1861-....), was born in Dublin and published her first book Louise de la Valliere (1885), followed by Shamrocks (1887), Cuckoo Songs (1894), Miracle Plays (1895), The Wind in the Trees (1898), Collected Poems (1901), New Poems (1911), Innocencies (1905), Experiences (1908) and Irish Poems (1913).

HODGSON, RALPH (1871-....), is an English poet whose works include Poems (1917) and The Last Blackbird and Other Lines (1917).

HOPKINS, GERARD MANLEY, S.J. (1844-1889), was born at Stratford, near London, and received his education at Cholmondeley School, Highgate. In 1866 he became a Catholic; in the following year he entered Balliol College, Oxford, and studied under Walter Pater. He left the university to enter the Birmingham Oratory with Father John Henry Newman and in 1868 he joined the Society of Jesus. He served as priest in Liverpool, London and Oxford. In 1884 he was appointed classical examiner at Dublin where he died. His poems are still uncollected.

HOWARD, VENERABLE PHILIP (1557-1595), Earl of Arundel, was born at Arundel House, London. He was educated under John Foxe and sent to Cambridge. He entered the Catholic Church in 1584 and reformed his life. In attempting to fly from the power of Queen Elizabeth he was captured on the seas and brought back to the Tower where he remained from 1585 till his death in 1595. His works are the Epistle of Christ to the Faithful Soul (translated from Lanspergius, Antwerp (1505), Fourfold Meditations of Four Last Things (London, 1895) and Verses on the Passion.

HUGO, VICTOR (1802-1885), was born at Besançon, France. In early youth his poetical talents were widely acknowledged but his real fame began with the performance of Hernani (1830). He took part in political affairs. His principal works are Odes et Ballades, Orientales, Feuilles d'Automne, and romances like Les Miserables and Notre Dame de Paris.

IMELDA, SISTER, is a contemporary American poet, a member of the Order of St. Dominic.

INNOCENT III, P. M. (1161-1216), was born at Anagni, Italy, Lotario de Conti, son of Count Trasimund of Segni and nephew of Clement III. He studied in Rome and Bologna and returning to the papal city was created cardinal in 1190. He was elected pope on the death of Celestine III. During the vacancy on the imperial throne he restored the papal power in Rome and expelled the German rulers from central Italy. He became protector of the young emperor Frederick VI. The elections of the German empire falling into a confused state, Innocent III made his famous declarations regarding the papal rights in imperial affairs, which he put into effect after the disorders of Otto IV, as well as in the royal revolt of Philip Augustus of France, the excommunication of King John of England and the troubles of the entire Christian world. He convoked the Fourth Council of the Lateran in 1215. He was a great politico-ecclesiastical figure in the most powerful period of Church history.

ITA, SAINT (480-570), was the foster mother of Saint Brendan the Navigator (484-577), the Irish monk who set out for the Fortunate Isles in an expedition known to Columbus under the title of Navigatio Sancti Brendani.

JACOPONE DA TODI (1228-1306), was born at Todi, between Perugia and Rome, his baptismal name being Jacomo. After a fantastic youth similar to that of St. Francis of Assisi, he married Vanna di Guidone, a beautiful woman, who one year later was killed by the collapsing of a balcony at a marriage feast; she was found after her death to be wearing a harsh hair shirt under her splendid attire. A sudden conversion was operated in Jacopone; he joined the Franciscans of his native town and began a life of extraordinary piety and fantastical character, half-troubadour, half-preacher, which made him the delight of the enthusiast and the troublemaker of the authorities. Becoming involved in the protests of the Spiritual party, Jacopone fell under the excommunication of Pope Boniface VIII, who refused to absolve him. The new Pope Benedict XI granted him his release after five years of imprisonment. He died at the Convent of Poor Clares at Collazzone, on Christmas Eve, 1306. Some of the greatest poems of his time are attributed to him. His authenticated work is of the supremest beauty and devotion. See Jacopone da Todi (London, 1919) by Evelyn Underhill.

JAMES of the Protevangelium was at the head of the school of Nisibis, which counted among its adherents St. Ephrem, Rabula Bishop of Edessa (412-435) and Bishop Ibas (435-457).

JAMMES, FRANCIS (1868-....). His works are: De L'Angelus de l'Aube (1888-1897), Le Deuil des Primeveres (1898-1900), Le Triomphe de la Vie (1900-1901), Clairières dans le Ciel (1902-1906), Les Georgiques Chretiénnes, La Vierge et les Sonnets, and Le Tombeau de Jean de la Fontaine.

JESUS CHRIST, the Son of God.

JOHN DAMASCENE, SAINT (680-760), was a native of Damascus; he was surnamed Chrysorrhoas, and the Arabs called him Mansur. He was highly esteemed as a theologian of the Eastern Church. His works are The Fountain of Knowledge, Orations on the Images, and the Book of Right Thoughts. He is one of the greatest of the ancient hymnologists.

JOHN OF THE CROSS, SAINT (1549-1591), was born Juan de Yepes y Álvarez, at Ontiveros, Spain. He joined the Carmelites in 1563 and became known as the Ecstatic Doctor. His few poems are considered the greatest productions of mystical literature.

JOHN THE EVANGELIST, SAINT, was the "Disciple whom Jesus loved." He was the son of Zebedee and brother of James, with whom he shared the name of Boanerges "the sons of Thunder." Tradition holds that he died at an advanced age at Ephesus, having returned from a long exile on the island of Patmos. He is the author of a Gospel, three Epistles and the Apocalypse, or Book of Revelations. There has been much discussion of these authorships.

JOHNSON, LIONEL (1867-1902), was born at Broadstairs, Kent. He was of Anglo-Irish Protestant blood with a cross of Hebrew and American forbears, his family for generations having produced military men for England. He was educated at Winchester and New College, Oxford. In 1891 he became a Catholic. His love of Ireland was one of his personal passions. His death was the result of a slight fall. His books are only three: The Art of Thomas Hardy (1894), Poems (1895) and Ireland and Other Poems (1897).

JONES, THOMAS S., JR. (1882-....), was born at Boonville, New York, and educated at Hoolbrook's Military Academy and Cornell University. His works include The Path of Dreams (1904), The

Rose Jar (1906), From Quiet Valleys (1907), Interludes (1908) and Sonnets of the Saints (1926).

JUANA INÉS DE LA CRUZ, SISTER (1651-1695), was born Juana de Asbaje at San Miguel de Napantla, Mexico. She entered the Hieronymite Convent in Mexico in 1667 and died there of the plague. There is no satisfactory edition of her poems.

KELLY, BLANCHE M. (1881-....), was born at Troy, New York, and educated at the Sacred Heart Convent, Albany, New York. She served on the editorial staff of The Catholic Encyclopædia and on the teaching staff of Mount St. Vincent's College, New York. Her works include The Valley of Vision (1917) and Mary the Mother (1919).

KETTLE, THOMAS M. (1880-1816), was born in Ireland and graduated at University College, Dublin. Admitted to the bar in 1905, he was elected on the Nationalist ticket to Parliament in 1906. He enlisted at the outbreak of the war and fell in action in 1916. He had a great reputation as an orator.

KILMER, ALINE (1888-....), was born Aline Murray at Norfolk, Virginia, and educated at Rutgers Preparatory School. She was married to Joyce Kilmer the poet in 1908, and has published Candles That Burn (1908), Vigils (1921), Hunting a Hair Shirt (1923) and The Poor King's Daughter (1925).

KILMER, JOYCE (1886-1918), was born at New Brunswick and educated at Rutgers and Columbia University where he graduated in 1908. He engaged in newspaper and magazine work and held editorial positions on The Standard Dictionary, The Churchman and the New York Times. He enlisted in the 7th Regiment and was transferred to the 69th Regiment, with which contingent he went to France. He entered the Catholic Church in 1913, and was killed in action near the River Ourcq where he lies buried. His works include Summer of Love (1911), Trees (1915), Main Street (1917), Literature in the Making (1917), The Circus and Other Essays (1916) and Dreams and Images, An Anthology (1917).

KINON, VICTOR (1873-....), is a contemporary poet of France.

KÖHLER, WILLIBAD, is a contemporary poet of Germany.

KOUTCHAK, NAHABED (early 16th century), was a wandering singer of poems at Kharagonis, near Van, and also lived at Eghine. He was not a cleric but an Oriental popular poet of the gnomic order.

LAMARTINE, ALPHONSE DE (1790-1869), was born at Macon, France. He was educated abroad, principally in Italy. He shares with Alfred de Musset and Victor Hugo the highest rank in French poetry. His work includes Meditations Poetiques (1823), Jocelyn (1836), Histoire de Girondins (1847) and Histoire de la Restauration (1851).

LAMB, CHARLES (1775-1834), was born in the Temple, London. He was a friend of the poet Coleridge. His most successful book was Tales from Shakespeare (1807), in which he treated the tragedies and his sister Mary the comedies. His Essays of Elia appeared in book form in 1823, and the Last Essays of Elia, in 1833.

LANGLAND, WILLIAM (1330?-1400?), was born, probably, in South Shropshire, England. He was, probably also, in minor orders, although later he married. Most of his life was passed in London. He is the author of The Vision of Piers Plowman. Another poem, Richard the Redeless, is attributed to him.

LANIER, SYDNEY (1842-1881), was born at Macon, Georgia. In 1879 he was appointed lecturer on English literature in Johns Hopkins University. He was an intimate friend of Father John B. Tabb, the poet. His works include: Tiger Lilies, a novel (1867), Centennial Ode (1876), The English Novel and its Development (1883) and Poems (1884).

LATHROP, GEORGE PARSONS (1851-1898), was born at Honolulu, Hawaii, and educated in New York and Dresden, Germany. He married Rose, the daughter of Nathaniel Hawthorne, in 1871. In 1883 he founded the American Copyright League and in 1891 he and his wife entered the Catholic Church. His works are Rose and Rose-tree (1873), Afterglow (1876), Spanish Vistas (1883), Dreams and Days (1892) and A Story of Courage (1894).

LEE, MUNA (Mrs. Luis Muñoz-Marin), is an American poet, distinguished also as a translator from the Spanish. Her collected poems are entitled Sea-Change.

LEO XIII, POPE (1810-1903), was born at Carpineto, Italy, the son of Count Lodovico Pecci. He studied under the Jesuits at Viterbo and gained special distinction for his Latin. He was ordained priest in 1837 after courses in the College of Noble Ecclesiastics and Sapienza University. He succeeded in stamping out brigandage in the regions of Benevento and was then sent to Perugia, a seat of revolutionary outbreaks. In 1843 he was appointed nuncio to Brussels and consecrated archbishop of Damiata; he reunited the Belgian Catholics and established the Belgian College in Rome. He was recalled to the bishopric of Perugia where he remained for thirty-two years. He was made cardinal in 1853, and in 1877 Pius IX appointed him cardinal-camerlengo, which necessitated his residence in Rome. In 1878 he was elected to the papacy. The principal events of his reign are matters of current history. He called upon Catholics to coöperate with the French Republic; came to terms with Bismarck in German affairs; acted as arbitrator between Germany and Spain; established a rapprochement with Russia; appointed the Apostolic Delegation to the United States in 1892. His encyclicals were received with profound reverence by Protestants as well as Catholics and won the highest encomiums for their literary beauty.

His Latin Poems were published in English versions excellently rendered by Monsignor H. T. Henry.

LEON, FRAY LUIS DE (1528-1591), was born at Belmonte de Cuenca, Spain, of Hebrew origins. He joined the Augustinians of Salamanca where he came to great distinction at the university. In 1572 he was tried before the Inquisition and spent five years in prison on unproved charges of heresy.

LESLIE, SHANE (1885-....), was born in Ireland of distinguished ancestry and educated at Eton and King's College, Cambridge. He has passed some years in America and returned to London to edit The Dublin Review (1916-1926). His works include Songs of Oriel, The Isle of Columcille, The End of the Chapter (1916), Verses on Peace and War, The Oppidan (1922), The Life of Cardinal Manning, and an Anthology of Catholic Poets (1925).

LINDSAY, VACHEL (1879-....), was born in Springfield, Illinois, and is the author of General William Booth Enters Heaven, The Chinese Nightingale, and Collected Poems (1923).

LOPEZ DE AYALA, PERO (1332-1407), was a native of the Basque countries and a courtier of Pedro the Cruel and his successors Henry, John I and Henry III. He is author of the Rimado de Palacio.

LORRAIN, JEAN (Paul Duval) (1855-1906), was born at Fecamp, France, and became known as the translator of Tennyson. His books include M. de Phocas and La Maison Philibert.

LOUNKIANOS (1790-1860) was born at Erzeroum and made his early studies in Persia. He prepared for the priesthood with the Congregation of the Antonians of Liban. He went to Cairo, became secretary to Ibrahim Pasha, but left Egypt for the Crimea and Petrograd and Tiflis, living in great poverty in spite of recognition by the Catholic Armenians. He died at Varevan.

LOWELL, JAMES RUSSELL (1819-1891), was born at Cambridge, Massachusetts and graduated from Harvard College in 1838. In 1855 he succeeded Longfellow in the chair of English and spent some years of further study in Europe. He was editor of the Atlantic Monthly (1857-1862) and of the North American Review (1863-1872). His poetical works include A Year's Life (1841), Poems (1844-48-49-54), The Vision of Sir Launfal (1845), A Fable for Critics (1848), The Bigelow Papers (1848 and 1867), Commemoration Ode (1865) and Three Memorial Poems (1876).

LULL, BLESSED RAMÓN (1235-1315), was born at Palma on the Island of Majorca and brought up at the royal court. In 1266 he reformed his life, sold his property and retired to a Cistercian monastery where he undertook the study of Arabic in order to convert the Moslems. He lectured at Miramar, Montpellier, Rome, Paris; traveled through Palestine, Egypt and Morocco;

and endeavored to inaugurate a new crusade. He became known as the Doctor Illuminatus. His passion for the conversion of the Moslems consumed his long life, and while preaching at Bugia he was seized by them and stoned to death outside the city. His writings were very numerous: some four hundred and eighty-six treatises on theology, physics, medicine, mathematics and chemistry, the Libre de Amich e Amat, Horas de Nostra Dona Sancta Maria, Els Cent Noms de Deu, and a fantastical novel, Blanquerna. E. Allison Peers has published in English The Book of the Lover and the Beloved (1923), The Tree of Love (1926) and The Art of Contemplation.

LYDGATE, JOHN (1370?-1471?), was born at Lydgate, Suffolk, England. As a boy he entered the Benedictine Abbey of Bury and is said to have studied also at Oxford and Cambridge. He was ordained in 1397. He left a large body of poetry, much of which is still in manuscript, including the Falls of Princess, Troy Book, Story of Thebes, The Life of Our Lady, The Dance of Death, and The Temple of Glass.

MAC CONGLINNE was a famous Irish bard of the twelfth century. His Vision seems to have been the inspiration of the poets who in a later century produced The Land of Cokaigne.

MACDONOUGH, THOMAS (1878-1916), was born at Cloughjordan, Tipperary, Ireland. Relinquishing his intention to join the priesthood he devoted himself to teaching and the revival of Gaelic literature. He took part in the starting of the Irish Review. He had command of a corpse in the revolt of Easter Week and was condemned to death by the British commanders.

McGUIRE, HARRY (1904-....), was born at Denver, Colorado, and educated at Notre Dame University. He was editor of the poetry magazine Pan.

MACHADO, MANUEL (1874-....), is a poet of the Sevillian Spanish school, noted for his fine qualities as shown in his collections Alma, Museo, and Cantares (1907).

MACMANUS, SEUMAS (1868-....), was born at Inver, Donegal, Ireland, and became known as a story-teller throughout Ireland and America, reproducing the old legends of his country in popular form and becoming famous under the name of "The Country Boy." He was first married to Ethna Carbery (1866-1902) and later to Catalina Paez of Venezuela. His most striking poems are collected under the title of Ballads of a Country Boy (Dublin, 1905) and Shuilers from Heathy Hills (1893).

MADELEVA, SISTER MARY, C.S.C. (1887-....), is a graduate of the University of Notre Dame, Indiana, and the University of California. Her works are Knights Errant (1923), Chaucer's Nuns and other Essays (1925) and Pearl, a Study in Spiritual Dryness (1925).

MAEL-ISU (died 1038), was the grandson of Brolcan, of Derry. His name signifies Client or Tonsured of Jesus.

MAHONY, FRANCIS SYLVESTER (FATHER PROUT) (1804-1866), was born in Cork, Ireland, and educated at St. Clongowes Wood College and St. Acheul, France. He joined the Jesuits but retired and entered the Irish College in Rome and was ordained at Lucca in 1832. After some differences with his bishop he took up a literary career in London, and twelve years later (1858) went to Paris as correspondent for The Globe where he remained till his death. He never wavered in deep loyalty to the Church. His chief work is The Reliques of Father Prout (1859); his contributions to Fraser's Magazine represent the best of his production.

MALON DE CHAIDE, PEDRO (1530-1589), was an Augustinian friar, a native of Navarre and a graduate of Saragossa. His most famous work is the Conversión de la Magdalena, published after his death.

MANGAN, JAMES CLARENCE (1803-1849), was born in Dublin, Ireland, of poor parents. In 1831 he contributed to the Journal of the Comet Club and he became a writer on The Nation, The United Irishman and The Irish Tribune. The chief collections of his poems have been issued by Father C. P. Meehan (1884), Mitchel, New York (1859), Louise Imogen Guiney (1897) and the Centenary Edition (Dublin and London, 1903).

MANRIQUE, JORGE (1440-1479), was the son of Don Rodrigo, grandmaster of Santiago. He was killed in the battle at Muñoz. His famous Coplas were written after the death of his father in 1476. They have had many commentaries and musical settings.

MANZONI, ALESSANDRO (1785-1873), was born at Milan of a feudal family, his grandfather being Beccaria the political economist. After studying at the University of Pavia he went to Paris and became identified with the Voltairian group. He married a Protestant in Milan, 1808, but she became a Catholic and Manzoni returned to the Church and devoted the rest of his life to religion, patriotism and literature. He settled at Milan where he became a friend of Rosmini. His works include The Triumph of Liberty, Sacred Hymns, The Napoleonic Ode, The Fifth of May, and I Promessi Sposi, his masterpiece.

MARAGALL, JUAN (1860-1911), was born in Barcelona. His works, published since his death in eleven volumes, constitute him one of the leaders of the Catalan renascence.

MARCELA DE CARPIO, SISTER (1605-1688), was the daughter of the great Lope de Vega. She became a nun of the Trinitarian Convent in Madrid where she obtained the reputation of unusual sanctity.

MARCH, AUZIAS (1397-1459), Lord of Beniarjo, stands at the head of Catalan lyrical poetry. He was Grand Falconer to Alfonso V.

MARKHAM, EDWIN (1852-....), was born at Oregon City, Oregon, and educated at San José Normal School. He undertook teaching and journalism in California until 1899. He has resided in New York for many years. His works include The Man with the Hoe (1899), Lincoln (1901), The Shoes of Happiness and Gates of Paradise.

MARY, QUEEN OF SCOTS (1542-1587), was born at Linlithgow, Scotland, daughter of James V, and was only six days old when she became queen of Scotland. She was excellently educated in France and married to Francis the dauphin, who soon became king of France. As Queen Elizabeth was of illegitimate birth, Mary was the rightful queen of not only Scotland but England, and her heralds gave her the emblazonments to that effect. The troubles in France made it impossible for her to assert her claims. Francis II died, leaving Mary no alternative but to strive to assert her claims to the Scottish throne. The general histories give an account of her failures in Scotland due to the hostility of the Covenanters and the nobility enriched with the confiscated properties of the Church. Her marriage with Darnley, who in a fit of jealousy murdered her courtier Rizzio, was followed by his own assassination. The Earl of Bothwell, who was charged with the murder, carried Mary off by force to Dunbar where she consented to marry him. The nobles seizing the couple, Bothwell made his escape but Mary was immured in Lochleven Castle. She managed to escape when her army was defeated at Langside (1568) and she took refuge in England, where she was made a prisoner. The story of intrigue and slander took on a most ferocious character. A scheme to have her married to the Duke of Norfolk resulted in his losing his head on the block; Elizabeth was publicly excommunicated by Pius V. Mary's condemnation and execution under the power of Elizabeth were, without doubt, inspired by a fear of the Catholic powers and her fidelity to her faith. She was an unfortunate pawn in the international and religious warfares of her time.

MARY, THE BLESSED MOTHER OF GOD (1st century).

MAYNARD, THEODORE (1890-....), was born at Madras, India, and received his education in England. In recent years he has made his home in the United States. His works include Laughs and Whiffs of Song (1915), Drums of Defeat (1916), Carven from the Laurel Tree (1918), A Tankard of Ale (1919), The Last Knight (1921), The Divine Adventure (1921) and The Book of Modern Catholic Verse (1926).

MELLO, FRANCISCO MANUEL DE (1608-1666), was an historian and poet, born of distinguished family in Lisbon. See his Obras Métricas (Lyons, 1665).

MENDOZA, FRAY INIGO DE (about 1482), was a Franciscan friar, a favorite of Isabel la Catolica. His devotional Cancionero was published in 1480.

MENENDEZ Y PELAYO, MARCELINO (1856-1912), was the leading literary critic of modern Spain. His critical works are valuable and numerous. His original metrical works are in Odas, Epistolas y Tragedias (Madrid, 1883).

MERCIER, LOUIS (1870-....), was born in the South of France where he has remained consistently. He is the editor of the Journal of Roanne. He shows a marked sympathy for natural beauties.

MEYNELL, ALICE (1855-1925), was born Alice Thompson, in London, and lived for a long time in Italy. She married Wilfred Meynell and published Preludes (1875), The Rhythm of Life (1893), The Color of Life (1896), The Children (1896) and The Flower of the Mind, An Anthology (1898).

MEYNELL, WILFRID (1852-....), published his early work under the name of John Oldcastle. He is known as the editor of Merry England and the patron of the poet Francis Thompson. His works are Benjamin Disraeli, Come and See, Aunt Sarah and the War, Verses and Reverses, and Rhymes with Reason.

MICHELANGELO BUONARROTI (1475-1564), was born at Caprese of an old Florentine family; he studied under Ghirlandajo, copied the antiques collected by the Medici rulers and began a career in art that placed him at the head of sculpture, architecture and painting of the entire world. His poetry was written under the inspiration of Vittoria Colonna, widow of the Marquis di Pescara, who became a center for the literary life in Rome where he spent his last years.

MICKIEVICZ, ADAM (1798-1855), was born near Novogrodek, Lithuania. His life was passed principally in Paris. His epic Konrad Wallenrod (1830) and Pan Tadewsz are considered masterpieces of Slavonic literature.

MIEGEL, AGNES (1879-....), was born at Königsberg, Germany, and has taken a high place among the Catholic poets of her time. She has published Gedichte (1901) and Balladen und Lieder (1907).

MILES, GEORGE HENRY (1824-1871), was born at Baltimore, Maryland, and graduated from Mount St. Mary's, Emmitsburg, in 1842. His success with dramatic writing took him away from his practice of law in 1850, when he won the Edwin Forrest prize with his drama Mahommed. His De Soto (1859), Mary's Birthday, and Señor Valiente were successes of the same year. In 1860 Laura Keene produced his Seven Sisters. Other writings were Cromwell, Glimpses of Tuscany, Christine (1866) and Christian Poems. He delivered in 1874 his Discourse in Commemoration of the Landing of Pilgrims of Maryland. From 1859 until his death he was professor of English Literature at Mount St. Mary's, Emmitsburg.

MILLER, J. CORSON (1883-....), was born at Buffalo, N. Y., and graduated from Canisius College. His poems are collected under the title Veils of Samite (1821).

MISTRAL, FREDERICK (1830-1914), was born at Maillane, Bouches-du-Rhone, and became the principal poet of the Provençal brotherhood of the Felibriges. His works are Mireio (Mireille, 1859), Calendau (1867), Provencal-French Dictionary (1884), Nerto (1884) and La Reine Jeanne (1890).

MOHR, JOSEF (1792-1848), was born in Salzburg, Austria, and ordained priest in 1815. He was an assistant priest at the Church of St. Nicolas in Oberndorf, near Salzburg, when he composed the words of the famous hymn Heilige Nacht. The music was written by his friend Franz Gruber (1787-1863), who was born at Hochburg and had become a teacher and church organist at Hallein, also near Salzburg. The hymn was sung for the first time in St. Nicholas Church of Obenndorf, Christmas Eve, 1818.

MONTESQUIOU-FEZENSAC, COMTE ROBERT DE (1855-1921), was born in Paris, France, where he became a leader in letters and fashion. He published Les Chauves-Souris (1892), Felicité (1894), Le Chef des odeurs suaves (1894), Le Parcours du Reve au Souvenir (1895), Les Hortensias bleus (1896) and Autels privilegiés (1899).

MONTOTO Y RAUTENSTRAUCH, LUIS (1851-....), is a native of Sevilla, Spain, whose works include Noches de Luna, La Sevillana, and Toros en Sevilla.

MOORE, THOMAS (1779-1852), was born in Dublin of a Kerry family and educated at Trinity College. He published Odes of Anacreon (1800). In 1803 he traveled in America. In 1806 he published his Odes and Epistles and Irish Melodies, The Twopenny Postbag (1813), Lalla Rookh (1817) and Lives of Lord Edward Fitzgerald, Sheridan and Lord Byron. His Memoirs, Journals and Correspondence were published in 1853.

MORE, BLESSED SIR THOMAS (1478-1535), was born in London and educated at St. Anthony's School and at Canterbury Hall, Oxford. He was recalled to enter as a law student at New Inn about 1494. In 1518 he published, with Lilly, the Progymnasmata of epigrams from the Greek and Latin. He married in 1505. His popular tendencies gradually won for him the royal opposition, but his great abilities secured for him the favor of Wolsey and Henry VIII. In 1529 he succeeded Wolsey as chancellor of England. In 1530 came the demand that the clergy recognize Henry VIII as the head of the Church, but More, who had opposed the King's divorce from Catherine and his renouncement of the papal supremacy, resigned his post in 1532 and went into seclusion. In 1534 he was summoned to take the Oath of Succession and on his refusal was imprisoned in the Tower, charged with treason; on July 6, 1535, he was beheaded at Tower Hill. His beatification was by decree of Leo XIII in 1886. His Latin works were published at Basle (1556) and at Louvain (1565 and 1566). He left a long series of answers and apologies of a polemical order, treatises on the Scripture and devotions. For a complete list see Gillow's Bibliographical Dictionary of English Catholics. More's most famous work, the Utopia, was first published in Louvain (1516) in Latin.

MORGAN, HON. EVAN FREDERICK (1893-....), was born in Wales and educated at Eton and Christ Church, Oxford. After studying painting he entered the Welsh Guards (1915-1916) and served at the Allied Peace Conference. In 1919 he became a Catholic. He is author of Fragments, Gold and Ochre, At Dawn, The Eel, and Trial By Ordeal.

MULHOLLAND, ROSA (Lady Gilbert) (....-1924), was born in Belfast, Ireland, and is well known in English and Irish literature for her stories as well as for her poetry in her volume published in 1886 entitled Spirit and Dust.

NERSES IV (1098-1173), surnamed Klaientsi and "The Gracious," was born in Rome and educated by his grand-uncle the Patriarch Gregory Vkaiaser. He was consecrated bishop by his brother Patriarch Gregory III, attended the Council of Antioch in 1141 and was made patriarch in 1166. He endeavored to effect the union of the Armenian and Greek churches and gives testimony of the primacy of the See of Peter. His poems include Jesu Orti and many hymns.

NERVO, AMADO (1870-1919), was a Mexican poet, much of whose life was passed in France. His best work is to be found in Perlas Negras and in Misticas.

NEWMAN, JOHN HENRY (1801-1890), was born in London, became a leader in the Tractarian Movement at Oxford, took Anglican Orders, entered the Catholic Church in 1845, was ordained in Rome in 1846 and founded the Oratory of St. Philip Neri in 1847. His experiences in the Irish University, his lawsuit with Achilli, his controversy with Charles Kingsley are outstanding. In 1879 he was created cardinal deacon. His bibliography is highly valuable and extensive. The Lead Kindly Light was composed in his Protestant days while he was lying in a calm in the Straits of Bonafacio.

NOTKER BALBULUS, THE BLESSED (840-912), was born at Jonswil, Switzerland, of distinguished family, and educated at St. Gall where he became a monk. He is accepted as the author of Gesta Caroli Magni. He introduced the singing of sequences into Germany. The hymn Media Vita was attributed to him in the Middle Ages. His beatification took place in 1512, and he was called "a vessel of the Holy Spirit without equal in his own time."

NOYES, ALFRED (1880-....), was born in Staffordshire, England, and educated at Exeter College, Oxford. He lectured in the United States, principally at Princeton College (1913-1923), and has published The Loom of the Years (1902), The Flower of Old Japan (1903), Poems (1904), The Forest of Wild Thyme (1905), Drake (1908), Forty Singing Seamen (1907), The Enchanted Island (1909), Collected Poems (1910), The Elphin Artist (1920) and The Torchbearers (1922).

NUÑEZ DE ARCE, GASPAR (1834-1903), was a native of Vallodolid, Spain. His Gritos del Combate appeared in 1875 and his Un Idilio in 1879. There is no complete edition of his poems.

O'CONOR, NORREYS JEPHSON (1885-....), was born in New York City and educated at Harvard College. He is author of The Child's Hansel and Gretel (1909), Celtic Memories (1914), Beside the Blackwater (1915), The Fairy Bride (1916), Songs of the Celtic Past (1918) and Battles and Enchantments (1922).

O'DALY, MUIREADACH, was called Albanach on account of his flight into Scotland. He flourished about the year 1215 and had his bardic home at Lissadil. His poems are important in bardic literature.

O'DONNELL, CHARLES L. C.S.C. (1884-....), was born at Greenfield, Indiana. He received his education at Notre Dame and The Catholic University. He entered the Congregation of the Holy Cross and was ordained in 1910. He was father-provincial from 1922 to 1926 and is now assistant-general. His works are The Dead Musician and Cloister and Other Poems.

O'HAGAN, THOMAS (1855-....), was born at Toronto, Canada, and educated at St. Michael's College, Toronto, Ottawa University, and the Universities of Syracuse, Cornell, Wisconsin, Chicago, Grenoble, Louvain, Bonn and Fribourg. His works are A Gate of Flowers (1887), In Dreamland (1893), Songs of the Settlement (1899), Songs of Heroic Days (1916) and Complete Poetical Works (1922).

O'MALLEY, CHARLES J. (1857-1910), was for a long time the editor of The New World (Chicago).

O'REILLY, JOHN BOYLE (1844-1890), was born at Douth Castle, Drogheda, Ireland, and educated by his father. He enlisted in the Tenth Hussars and later joined the Fenian Brotherhood and was condemned by court-martial to twenty years penal servitude in Australia. In 1869 he made his escape to Massachusetts and became editor of The Pilot in Boston (1870-1890). His books include Songs of the Southern Seas, Songs, Legends and Ballads, The Statues in Block, and In Bohemia; his prose works are

Moondyne, and collaboration in The King's Men and Athletics and Manly Sport.

O'RIORDAN, CONAL H. (1874-....), was born at Dublin, Ireland, and educated by the Jesuits. He early took to the stage and succeeded J. M. Synge as director of the Abbey Theatre, Dublin. His works include In the Green Park (1894), The House of the Strange Woman (1895), The Fool and His Heart (1896), The Nigger Knights (1900), In London (1922) and Rowena (1925).

O'SHEEL, SHAEMAS (1886-....), was born in New York City and graduated from Columbia University. He founded a magazine called Moods in 1908 and published The Blossomy Bough (1911) and The Light Feet of Goats (1915).

PAGAZA, JOAQUIN ARCADIO¹ (1839-....), bishop of Vera Cruz, Mexico, was much admired for his Castilian sonnets, although he is chiefly remembered as the translator into Spanish of the Latin poem Rusticatio Mexicana by the Jesuit author Rafael Landivar (1731-1793), his work sharing with Balbuena's Grandeza Mexicana the merit of fixing the classical style of letters in Hispanic America.

PALÉS MATOS, LUIS, is a contemporary poet of the Island of Porto Rico.

PALLEN, CONDÉ BENOIST (1858-....), was born at St. Louis, Missouri, and educated at Georgetown and St. Louis Universities. He was editor of The Church Progress (1887-1897) and managing editor of The Catholic Encyclopedia (1912-1920). His works include The Philosophy of Literature (1897), Epochs of Literature (1898), The New Rubaiyat (1899), The Feast of Thalarchus (1901), The Death of Sir Launcelot (1902) and Collected Poems (1915).

PARAVICINO Y ARTEAGA, FRAY HORTENSIO—FELIS DE (1580-1633), was born in Madrid, studied with the Jesuits and in 1599 joined the Order of the Trinitarios Calzados. He was court preacher to Philip III and IV and a friend of the painter El Greco.

PATMORE, COVENTRY (1823-1896), was born at Woodford, England, of a literary family. His works include Tamerton Church Tower (1853), The Angel in the House (1854-1862), The Unknown Eros, Principle in Art, and Rod, Root and Flower. He was married three times and is considered one of the profounder influences in modern English poetry.

PATRICK OF TARA, SAINT (387-493), "The Apostle of Ireland," was born at Dumbarton, Scotland, of a Roman father. In his sixteenth year he was carried into captivity by Irish marauders and sold as a slave to Milchu in the present County of Antrim where he remained as a shepherd for six years. He escaped to England and later went to his uncle St. Martin of Tours. St. Germaine took him back to England to combat the Pelagian heresies, and, after the abandonment of the Irish mission by Palladius, he was sent by Pope Celestine to convert the pagan Irish. He landed there in 433. See The Catholic Encyclopedia for details of his foundations. The hymn The Breastplate of St. Patrick is now universally recognized as his composition, also the Confessio and the Epistola ad Coroticum. There are other canonical compositions attributed to him on excellent authority.

PEARSE, PADRAIC H. (1879-1916), was born in Dublin, Ireland. In 1903 he became Irish lecturer in the Catholic University College and in 1908 he founded St. Enda's School, a Gaelic-Catholic institute. He was commander-in-chief of the Army and president of the Provisional Government in the Easter Rising of 1916. He was executed by the British authorities. His gifts of mystical exaltation were extraordinary.

PEGUY, CHARLES (1873-1914), was the founder of the Cahiers de la Quinzaine (1899), in which the principal writers of his day made their first appearance. He died in battle for France. His works include Le Mystere de la Charité de Jeanne d'Arc and Victor Marie Comte Hugo.

PETRARCH, FRANCESCO (1304-1374), was born at Arezzo, Italy. Between 1315 and 1319 he studied at Carpentras, and later at Montpellier and Bologna. In 1323 he abandoned law and took minor Orders at Avignon. It was here he is said to have seen his Laura, whose existence has been doubted by some of his critics. In 1330 he began his wanderings through France and Germany and in 1337 he settled at Vaucluse. His Latin works and correspondence are extant to prove his encyclopedic learning. His Italian poetry, however, is the base of his modern reputation and may be found in his compilations I Trionfi and Canzoniere.

PHILIPA OF AVIS AND LANCASTER, PRINCESS (1437-1497), entered the Convent of Odivellas near Lisbon and became famous for her sanctity.

PHILLIPS, CHARLES (1880-....), was born at New Richmond, Wisconsin, and educated at De la Salle High School and St. Mary's College, Oakland, California. He was engaged in editorial work in The Northwestern Chronicle (St. Paul), The New Century (Washington) and The Monitor (San Francisco). During the war he served with the Knights of Columbus in France and Germany and the American Red Cross in Poland. He has published Back Home (1913), The Divine Friend (1915), Tarcisius (1917), A Buccaneer of Christ (1918) and The New Poland (1923).

PICO DELLA MIRANDOLA, GIOVANNI FRANCESCO (1463-1494), belonged to the higher nobility of Modena. He resigned his property rights to devote himself to study, entered Bologna and traveled through

France and Italy, learning Greek, Latin, Hebrew, Syriac and Arabic. He was deeply interested in cabalism and lost himself in philosophical subtleties. His propositions were condemned by the Church and he destroyed his writings and devoted his old age to the defense of Christianity against the Jews, Mohammedans and astrologers. He is interred at San Marco, Florence, where Savonarola preached his funeral oration. Numerous editions of his studies of Platonic and Oriental philosophies appeared during the sixteenth century.

PIMENTEL CORONEL, RAMON (1872-1909), was a well-known poet of Venezuela, born at Caracas. His work has never been collected.

PISE, CHARLES CONSTANTINE (1801-1866), was born at Annapolis, Maryland, educated at Georgetown College, and for a while was a member of the Society of Jesus. He later taught rhetoric at Mount St. Mary's, Emmitsburg, and served as a priest in Washington where he was made chaplain of the United States Senate, the only Catholic priest who has occupied that office. In 1848 he was pastor of St. Peters, Barclay Street, New York, and in 1849 he was appointed pastor of St. Charles Borromeos, Brooklyn, where he died. He is conspicuous as the first Catholic poet whose works were produced in the United States. His works include a History of the Catholic Church (1829), Pleasures of Religion and Other Poems (1833), Father Rowland, a novel, and Christianity and the Church (1850).

PLUNKETT, JOSEPH MARY (1887-1916), was born in Dublin, the son of Count Plunkett. He was educated at Belvidere College and Stonyhurst. He joined Padraic Colum and Thomas MacDonough in editing the Irish Review. He planned out the campaign for the Easter Rising in 1916 and was condemned to death by the British authorities upon the suppression of the revolt.

POE, EDGAR ALLAN (1809-1849), was born at Boston, Massachusetts. He was adopted by John Allan of Richmond who placed him at the Manor House School at Stoke-Newington, England. In 1826 he entered the University of Virginia. On his failure there he ran away and published his poems Tamerlane and Other Poems by a Bostonian (1827). He later settled in Baltimore. In 1835 he married Virginia Clemm and became assistant editor of the Southern Literary Messenger; in 1844 he took up his post on The Mirror. Falling into deterioration after the death of his wife he died in Washington College Hospital, Baltimore. His criticism and fiction were highly appreciated; his poems were published under the titles Al Aaraaf, Tamerlane and Minor Poems (1829), and Poems (1831).

POMBO, RAFAEL (1833-1912), was born in Bogotá, Colombia, of mingled Irish and Spanish blood. He visited the United States on a diplomatic mission in 1854. His sonnet Our Madonna at Home

was composed originally in English and won the admiration of
William Cullen Bryant.

POPE, ALEXANDER (1688-1744), was born in London, England, the son
of a convert to the Catholic Faith. His excellent education was
received privately on account of the restrictions put upon his
religion in the larger schools. In 1713 he settled at Twickenham
which became a resort of the smart world of letters and fashion.
His works include Essay on Criticism (1711), The Rape of the
Lock (1712), Windsor Forest (1713), his version of the Iliad
(1720), the Odyssey (1725), Miscellanies by Pope and Swift
(1727), The Dunciad (1728) and The Essay on Man (1732).

POTHINUS OF LYONS, SAINT (2nd century), was the Christian bishop
martyred during the persecutions of Marcus Aurelius in the year
177.

POUND, EZRA (1885-....), was born at Haily, Idaho, and educated at
Hamilton College and the University of Pennsylvania. His principal books are Personae, Provenca, Ripostes, Umbra, and Personae Collected Poems (1926).

PRATI, GIOVANNI (1815-1884), was born at Davido, Trentino, Italy,
and is distinguished for some inspired patriotic songs.

PROBYN, MAY, is an English poet of unusual mystical quality. Her
Poems appeared in 1881, and A Ballad of the Road, in 1883. She
also published some fiction, but retiring into the Dominican Order
she ceased her literary work.

PROCTOR, ADELAIDE ANNE (1825-1864), was the eldest daughter of the
poet Bryan Waller Proctor (Barry Cornwall) and was born in
London. In 1851 she became a Catholic. Her first book of poems,
Legends and Lyrics, appeared in two series in 1858-1860. She
devoted herself to the charity of reforming fallen women. In
1862 she published A Chaplet of Verses and some of her verses
have been considered so devotional that they are used as hymns.

PROCTOR, BRYAN WALLER (Barry Cornwall) (1787-1874), was born in
London, England. He was educated at Harrow. His works
include Dramatic Scenes and Other Poems (1819), Mirandola
(1821), Flood of Thessaly (1823), Effigies Poetica (1824) and
English Songs (1832).

PRUDENTIUS, AURELIUS CLEMENS (348-405), was born in the Ter-
raconensis, in Spain, probably of Christian parents. He was at
first a lawyer, served twice as provincial governor and was summoned to Rome by the emperor. It was not until the later years
of his life that he thoroughly renounced the vanities of paganism.
He collected his own poems which he dated 405. His works
include Peristephanon and Cathemerinon. His most personal
poem is that known as Contra Symmachum.

QUEVEDO Y VILLEGÁS, FRANCISCO DE (1580-1645), was a nobleman of
Madrid, educated at Álcala de Henaers. He was imprisoned for

four years for lampooning Olivares. He is one of the greater poets of Spain.

QUIRK, CHARLES J.S.J. (1889-....), was born at New Orleans, Louisiana, and educated at Spring Hill College, Mobile, Alabama. He has published Sails on the Horizon (1926).

RACINE, JEAN BAPTISTE (1639-1699), was born at La Ferte-Milon, France. He studied at the College of Beauvais and the College d'Harcourt and came to Paris in 1663. His first play La Thebáide was performed in 1664. His great successes were gained in Andromaque, Les Plaideurs, Britannicus, Bernice, and Iphigenie. The failure of his Phedre was followed by a silence of twelve years, but in 1689 he reappeared with Esther and Athalie (1691), written for the institution at Saint-Cyr founded for poor girls by Madame de Maintenon.

RALEIGH, SIR WALTER (1552-1618), was born at Hayes, Devonshire, England. He studied at Oriel College, Oxford, and took up a military career in France and Ireland. He became a favorite of Queen Elizabeth and undertook colonization in Virginia. In 1584 he introduced the potato into Ireland. He was imprisoned in the Tower for eloping with Elizabeth Throckmorton and was released to take part in capturing the Spanish fleet off Cadiz. In 1603 he was charged with treason by James I. While in the Tower he wrote his History of the World. On his return from an expedition to Guiana he was executed.

RANDALL, JAMES RYDER (1839-1908), was born at Baltimore, Maryland. He was educated at Georgetown College, traveled in South America and returned to take the chair of English in Poydras College, Louisiana. His Southern sympathies were aroused by the attack on the Federal troops in Baltimore, April 21, 1861, and he wrote his famous Maryland, My Maryland, which was published in the New Orleans Sunday Delta. After the war he became the Washington correspondent of the Augusta Chronicle.

RASCAS, BERNARD, who died in 1353, was a poet of the Limousin school. He became a priest and enjoyed the patronage of Clement VI and Innocent VI. His works are Las Recoysinadas de l'Amor Recalviar and Les Elegias y Les Sereaades. At his death he endowed the Hospital of St. Bernard in Avignon.

RATCLIFFE, DOROTHY UNA, is a contemporary poet of Yorkshire, England, and author of Singing Rivers, Dale Dramas, and Dale Lyrics.

RAWES, HENRY AUGUSTUS, O.S.C. (1826-1885), was born at Easington, England, and after graduating at Trinity College, Cambridge, entered the Anglican ministry. In 1856 he became a Catholic. In 1857 he joined the English Congregation of Oblates of St. Charles at Bayswater. In 1880 he became superior of his Congregation and remained in that office until his death. His hymns are preserved in Foregleams of the Desired and are deserving of a wider circle of readers.

REPPLIER, AGNES (1858-....), was born at Philadelphia, Pennsylvania, and educated at the Sacred Heart Convent in Torresdale. Her works are Books and Men (1888), Points of View (1891), Essays in Idleness (1893), Varia (1897), In Our Convent Days 1905) and Points of Friction (1920).

RHABANUS MAURUS (784-856), was archbishop of Mainz. He wrote many well-known hymns, including the Veni Creator.

RILKE, RAINER MARIA (1875-1927), was born in Prague, Bohemia. He lived in various countries and published Erste Gedichte, Traumgekront, Advent, and Mir Zur Feier.

RINALDO D'AQUINO (1200-1240) was a kinsman of St. Thomas Aquinas and followed the literary court of the Emperor Frederick II in the office of High Falconer.

ROCHE, JAMES JEFFREY (1847-1908), was born in Queen's County, Ireland; he emigrated early in life to Prince Edward Island and graduated from St. Dunstan's College. He was editor of The Pilot, Boston (1890-1894), and entered the consular service of the United States. His books are Songs and Satires (1887), Ballads of Blue Water (1895) and The Vase and Other Bric-a-Brac (1900).

ROCK, MADELEINE CARON.

RODENBACH, GEORGES RAYMOND CONSTANTIN (1855-1889), was born at Tournai, of French-Flemish family. His principal works are Le Regne du Silence and Les Vies Enclosés.

RODRIQUEZ DE PADRÓN (15th century), was the last of the Galician troubadours. See Pidal's Cancionero de Baena (1860) and Ticknor's History of Spanish Literature.

ROLLE, RICHARD (1290-1349), was born at Thornton Dale, educated at Oxford and early in life took to retirement, which gained for him the name of Hermit of Hampole and a reputation for sanctity. He was deeply ascetical and his numerous poems bear evidence of great mystical illumination.

ROONEY, JOHN JEROME (1866-....), was born at Binghamton, New York and graduated at Mount St. Mary's, Emmitsburg, in 1884. He became a member of the New York bar and published The Man Behind the Guns and a large collection of war poems.

ROSSETTI, CHRISTINA (1830-1894), was born in London, England, the sister of Dante Gabriel Rossetti. Her early work was published under the name of Ellen Alleyne. Her works include Goblin Market (1862), The Prince's Progress (1866), Sing-Song (1871), A Pageant and Other Poems (1881) and Time Flies (1885).

ROSSETTI, DANTE GABRIEL (1828-1882), was born in London, England, the son of an Italian exile. He was educated at King's College

School and entered the Royal Academy. He was one of the leaders of the Pre-Raphaelite school of painting and produced a series of famous paintings. His writings are: The Italian Poets (1861), Poems (1870) and Ballads and Sonnets (1881).

ROSTAND, EDMOND (1868-1918), was born at Marseilles and produced a series of brilliant plays including Les Romanesques, La Princesse Lointaine, Cyrano de Bergerac, and L'Aiglon. His lyrical poems are much admired.

RUIZ, JUAN, ARCHPRIEST OF HITA, was born near Guadalajara about the year 1283. He is a poet very similar in his work to Francois Villon, and his character has been assailed on account of his imprisonment, the cause of which is quite unknown. His chief work is El Libro de Buen Amor.

RUSSELL, MATTHEW, S.J. (1831-1912), was born at Newry, Down, Ireland, the son of Arthur Russell of Kilowen. He joined the Society of Jesus early in life and for thirty-eight years was editor of the important periodical The Irish Monthly (1873-1911).

RYAN, ABRAM J. (1839-1886), was born at Norfolk, Virginia, and, ordained to the priesthood just before the Civil War, he became a Confederate chaplain and served until the close of hostilities. With the exception of his famous poem The Conquered Banner his work is generally on religious themes. After the War he became editor of the New Orleans Catholic newspaper, The Star. His poems are published under the titles: The Conquered Banner (1880), Poems Patriotic, Religious and Miscellaneous (1880) and A Crown for Our Queen (1882).

RYAN, ANNE (1892-....), was born at Newark, New Jersey, and graduated from the College of St. Elizabeth. She has published her poems under the title Lost Hills (New York, 1925).

RYAN, KATHRYN WHITE, a contemporary poet of New York, was born at Albany, New York, and has published her work in The Golden Pheasant (1925).

SABOLY, NICOLAS (1614-1675), "The Troubadour of Bethlehem," was born at Monteux and passed his life as organist and choir-master of St. Pierre's Church in Avignon. Every year from 1658 until his death he published series of noëls which became very popular. They represent a high art in music and text. See Saboly's Noëls (Avignon, Francois Seguin, 1856).

SALVADORI, GIULIO (1862-....), was born at Monte S. Savino, Arezzo, Italy. He was an associate of Fogazzaro in his movement in North Italy that brought about the condemnation of Il Santo. Salvadori has published many poems of a mystical character and is at present professor of Italian composition in the Roman Ateneo.

SANCHEZ, LUIS ANIBAL, is a contemporary South American poet.

SANTEUIL, JEAN-BAPTISTE DE (1630-1697), was a member of the Society of Jesus and author of many devotional and liturgical hymns.

SARBIEWSKI, MATHIAS CASIMIR (1595-1649), was born at Plonsk, Masovia, and joined the Jesuits at Vilna in 1612. In 1622 he was sent to study in Rome and was ordained there in 1623. Returning to Vilna he taught in the Jesuit College (1626-1635) and became a confidant of King Wladislaw. He was remarkable as a musician and poet; his works include Silviludia and a Polish epic, Lechiados. Pope Urban VIII deputed him to revise the hymns of the Roman Breviary.

SCHAUMANN, RUTH, is a contemporary German poet.

SCHEFFLER, JOHANN (Angelus Silesius). *See* Silesius.)

SCOTT, SIR WALTER (1771-1832), was born at Edinburgh, Scotland. His education was received at the Edinburgh High School and University. In 1799 he was made sheriff of Selkirkshire. He published translations of Burger's Ballads in 1796 and Goethe's Gotz von Berlichingen (1799), The Minstrelsy of the Scottish Border (1802), The Lay of the Last Minstrel (1805), Marmion (1808), The Lady of the Lake (1810), Rokeby (1813), The Lord of the Isles (1814). With his novel Waverley (1814) he began a long series of the greatest romantic novels in the English language, the authorship of which was long concealed under the name of "The Great Unknown."

SEDULIUS, CAELIUS (5th century), according to Dr. Sigerson and Douglas Hyde (Literary History of Ireland), was a wandering Celt of the name of Shiel, who studied in Gaul and Italy and finally took up his residence in Achaia during the reigns of Theodosius the Younger and Valentinian (450-455). His principal work is the Carmen Paschale, a summary of the Old and New Testaments. The hymns A solis ortus cardine, and Hostis Herodes impie are taken from this masterpiece.

SELGAS Y CARRASCO, JOSÉ (1824-1882), was born at Lorca, Spain, and became a well-known journalist and editor in Madrid. His Obras were published in Madrid (1882).

SHAKESPEARE, WILLIAM (1564-1616), was born at Stratford-on-Avon. Very little is known of his personal history; some authorities claim that he died a Catholic and point to the marked orthodoxy revealed in much of his writing. He devoted his life to the theater with the splendid achievement of a series of historical dramas that are considered the greatest modern creations of literature. His poems are Venus and Adonis (1593), The Rape of Lucrece (1594), Sonnets (1609).

SHIRLEY, JAMES (1596-1666), was born in London and educated at Merchant Taylor's School, London, and at Oxford and Cambridge. He was the author of more than thirty plays and a

book Manductio, or a Leading of Children by the Hand through
the Principles of Grammar (1660).

SIGERSON SHORTER, DORA (1872-1918), was born in Dublin, Ireland,
the daughter of Dr. George Sigerson. She identified herself
with the Irish literary renascence and in 1896 was married to
Clement K. Shorter. Her works include Verses (1894), The
Fairy Changeling (1897), Ballads and Poems (1899), The Father
Confessor (1900), The Woman Who Went to Hell (1902), The
Country House Party (1905), Through Wintry Terrors (1907),
Collected Poems (1909) and Madge Lindsley (1913).

SILVA, JOSÉ ASUNCIÓN (1865-1896), was a native of Bogotá, Colombia, where he committed suicide in a sudden fit of depression. He
modeled his style on the poetry of Edgar Allan Poe and is considered one of the founders of the modernist school of Spanish
poetry.

SOUTHWELL, VENERABLE ROBERT (1561-1595), was born at Horsham
St. Faith's, Norfolk, England. He studied under Lessius at
Douai and joining the Jesuits in Rome he was ordained in 1594.
He passed six years hidden in Catholic houses in England. He
was captured in 1592 and subjected to torture thirteen times
before he was executed by hanging at Tyburn. His writings
were greatly admired by his contemporaries. His poems are to
be found in editions of 1595 which have become very rare among
collectors.

SPEE, FRIEDERICK VON LANGENFELD, S.J. (1591-1635), was born at
Kaiserwerth and died at Trier. He was the author of Goldenes
Treigenbuck and Trutznachtigal and Cautio Criminalis, which
virtually brought trials for witchcraft to an end.

SPENCER, LILIAN WHITE, was born at Albany, New York, and resides
at Denver, Colorado. She has written some superior sonnets.

SPENSER, EDMUND (1553-1598), was born in London and educated
at Merchant Taylor's School and Pembroke College, Cambridge.
His political activities in Ireland, where he was awarded large
grants of land, made him very unpopular among the Irish, who
burned his castle over his head and drove him back to London
where he died shortly after. His works are The Faery Queen
(1590), The Shepherd's Calendar (1579), Epithalamium (1595)
and Astrophel (1596).

STEPHEN THE SABAITE, SAINT (725-794).

STERLING, GEORGE (1869-1926), was born at Sag Harbor, Long
Island, New York, and educated at St. Charles College, Mary-
land. He resided during most of his life in San Francisco, Cali-
fornia. He published The Testimony of the Suns (1903), A
Wine of Wizardry (1908), The Caged Eagle (1916), and Selected
Poems (1923).

STODDARD, CHARLES WARREN (1843-1909), was born at Rochester,

New York, passed his youth in Boston and New York City and rejoined his parents who had settled in San Francisco in 1859. He failed to succeed as an actor and took up journalism. In 1864 he traversed the South Seas and composed his famous South Sea Idyls from the letters he had sent to a friend. His four other trips to the South Seas resulted in Lazy Letters from Low Latitudes and The Island of Tranquil Delights. In 1867 he entered the Catholic Church, explaining his course in A Troubled Heart and How it was Comforted. For five years after 1873 he traveled as special correspondent for the San Franciscan Chronicle. He then became professor of English literature at Notre Dame University and later at the Catholic University, Washington. Resigning these posts, he retired to Cambridge, Massachusets, and published his favorite book, Exits and Entrances, and shortly after his one novel, For the Pleasure of His Company. In 1905 he returned to California and died there in 1909. His other works are Summer Cruising in the South Seas (1874), Marshallah, a Flight into Egypt (1885), A Trip to Hawaii (1885), In the Footprints of the Padres (1892), Hawaiian Life (1896), The Wonder-Worker of Padua (1896) and Hither and Yon (1907).

STRAHAN, SPEER (1898-....), was born at Fife Lake, Michigan. He was educated at Notre Dame University and received Holy Orders in 1925. He is on the teaching staff of English in the Catholic University of America.

STRODTMANN, ADOLF (1829-1879), was born at Flenzburg and published Lied vom Spulen (1852) and Ein Hoheslied der Liebe (1858).

STUART, HENRY LONGAN (1875-....), was born in London of Irish family. He was educated in Ratcliffe College and served as Captain of Royal Field Artillery (1915-1919). His chief works are Weeping Cross, Fenella, and Civilization in the United States of which he was co-author. He resides in the United States.

SWINBURNE, ALGERNON CHARLES (1837-1909), was born in London, educated in France, Eton and Oxford. He was early remarked for his high metrical inventiveness. His principal poetical works are Atalanta in Calydon (1864), Laus Veneris (1866) and Tristam in Lyonesse (1882).

SYNESIUS (378-430) was born of an ancient family of Cyrene and came to be regarded with distinction among the Neo-Platonic philosophers. He pursued his studies in Alexandria where he followed the teachings of the famous Hypatia. He was made bishop of Ptolemais in 409 and consecrated by Theophilus, bishop of Alexandria. His works include De Providentia and Calvitii Encomium; there are ten of his hymns extant.

TABB, JOHN BANISTER (1845-1909), was born near Richmond, Virginia, and on the failure of his sight devoted himself to music. In the Civil War he enlisted under the Confederacy and was taken prisoner in 1864 and confined at Point Lookout where he formed a close friendship with the poet Sidney Lanier. He became a Catholic in 1872; entered St. Charles College, Maryland, and was ordained priest in 1884. He continued to teach there until his death. His works in poetry, collected from the magazines, appeared under titles of Poems, Lyrics, Child Verse, Later Lyrics, and Sonnets.

TALLANTE, MOSSEN JUAN (close of 15th century), was a native of Aragon, Spain, whose devotional poems are to be found in the Cancionero General.

TASSIS, JUAN DE (1582-1622), Count de Villamediana, was born in Lisbon. He was assassinated at the court of Isabel de Bourbon, wife of Philip IV. See El Conde de Villamediana (Madrid, 1886).

TASSO, TORQUATO (1554-1595), was born at Sorrento, Italy, the son of the writer Bernardo Tasso. He was educated at the court of the Dukes of Urbino and at the University of Pavia. He traveled extensively in Italy and France in the train of nobles and prelates. His Aminta was published in 1573. In 1581 appeared the revised edition of the Jerusalem Delivered. Tasso had developed manias of persecution, which resulted in his confinement for years. He died after Pope Clement VIII had offered him a refuge in Rome and prepared to grant him the laureate's crown.

TEJADA, JUAN MANUEL GARCIA, S.J. (1774-1845), was a member of the Society of Jesus in Colombia, South America.

TENNYSON, ALFRED LORD (1809-1892), was born at Somersby, Lincolnshire, England, and studied at Trinity College, Cambridge. He succeeded Wordsworth as poet laureate in 1850 and was raised to the peerage in 1884. His life was passed in seclusion at Aldsworth, Sussex and Farringford, Isle of Wight. His works are numerous; he is best known for his Idylls of the King (1859-1885).

TERESA OF AVILA, SAINT (1515-1582), was born Teresa de Cepeda y Ahumada, at Avila, Spain. In 1534 she joined the Carmelite Order and began her series of reforms and foundations. She was canonized in 1612 and declared co-patron of Spain with Santiago. Her poems are among the greatest gems of mystical literature.

THAYER, MARY DIXON (1897-....), was born at Philadelphia, Pennsylvania, and educated at Eden Hall Convent. She has published Songs of Youth (New York 1925) and a novel, Foam (1926).

THEODORE OF THE STUDIUM, SAINT (759-826), was of distinguished family, his brother becoming archbishop of Thessalonica. He was a monk of the monastery of Saccudion where his uncle

Plato was abbot, and he was ordained in 787. In 794 he himself became the abbot. In 799 he became head of the monastery of the Studium in Constantinople and he laid down the exact rules which still govern the Greek and Russian monasteries. In fiery feeling and elegance of language he is considered among the greatest hymnologists.

THÉRÈSE OF THE CHILD JESUS, SAINT (1873-1897), was born at Alençon, France, the daughter of Louis Martin, five of whose children entered the Visitation Order and four the Carmelite Order. She was educated by the Benedictines and when fifteen years old entered the Convent of Lisieux where her whole life was passed in extraordinary piety. Her Autobiography was published after her death and appeared in English in 1901. She was canonized by Benedict XI in 1925. There is a fine rendering of her Poems in English by the Carmelites of Santa Clara, California.

THOMAS À KEMPIS (1380-1471), was born at Kempen, near Cologne, of modest parentage. As a boy he was sent to Deventer and Windesheim, the schools of the Canons Regular. He became attached to the movement of the Brothers and Sisters of the Common Life, advocating lives of poverty, chastity and obedience without declared vows. They lived in community and were self-supporting. He was ordained priest in 1413 and became superior and novice master. The authorship of the Imitation of Christ is now generally accorded to him. There are other very beautiful works from his pen: The Chronicle of the Canons Regular of Mount St. Agnes (London, 1906), Life of Saint Lydwine Virgin (London, 1911); in English also we have the Soliloquy of the Soul, the Discipline of the Cloister, and the Manuale Parvulorum. There are fine editions under the imprint of Burns Oates and Kegan Paul of London. Thomas à Kempis' father's name was Haemerken.

THOMAS AQUINAS, SAINT (1225-1274), was born at Rocca Secca in the kingdom of Naples. His father was Count of Aquino and his mother Countess of Teano; he was related to the imperial family and to the kings of Spain and France. In 1236 he was sent to the University of Naples where he soon surpassed his masters Martini and Peter of Ireland. About 1240 he received the habit of the Dominicans who sent him to Rome. He was carried off by his family and kept prisoner for two years in a vain attempt to break his vocation, when his mother relented and he was able to return to the Dominicans. In 1245 he accompanied Albert Magnus to Paris and in 1248 went with him to Cologne. He returned to Paris where his degree of the Doctorate was involved in the long dispute between the professors and the friars of St. Dominic and St. Francis. It was conferred in 1257. His writings consist of some sixty works, chief of which is his Summa

Theologica, of which a complete translation is now in process of publication by the Fathers of the English Dominican Province (Vol. I, London and New York, 1911). His hymns, Sacris Solemnis, Pange Lingua, Verbum Supernum, and Lauda Sion, are found in his Office of Corpus Christi. There is an English edition of his Catena Aurea by John Henry Newman (Oxford, 1841-1845).

THOMPSON, FRANCIS (1860-1907), was born at Preston, Lancashire, of Catholic parents. He was educated at Ushaw College and later sent to study medicine, his father's profession, at Owens College. He neglected his professional studies for literature and ran off to London where he encountered great hardships before he was rescued by Wilfred Meynell, the editor of Merry England. He was entered as a boarder at the Premonstratensian Monastery, Storrington, Sussex, and when cured of his opium habits, he began to write his finest poetry. Between 1889 and 1896 he published Poems, Sister-Songs, and New Poems. He also published a remarkable essay on Shelley and volumes on the Life of Saint Ignatius and Health and Holiness.

TOULET, JEAN-PAUL (1867-1920), was a poet of Creole blood who settled in Paris in 1898. He passed some years in Algeria and Spain.

TOWNE, CHARLES HANSON (1877-....), was born at Louisville, Kentucky, and educated privately and in the College of the City of New York. He engaged (1915-1926) in editorial work on the Smart Set, The Designer, McClure's Magazine, and Harper's Bazaar. He has published his poems in Ave Maria (1898), The Quiet Singer (1908), Manhattan (1909), Youth (1911), Beyond the Stars, Today and Tomorrow, and Selected Poems (1925).

TRUEBA, ANTONIO DE (1820-1889) was a regional poet and story-teller of the Basque countries. He published Libro de los Cantares (1852) and Libro de las Montañas.

UNDERHILL, EVELYN (Mrs. Stuart Moore) (1875-....), was educated in King's College for Women, London. She has published A Barlamb's Ballad Book, The Grey World, The Miracles of Our Lady St. Mary, The Lost Word, Mysticism, Immanence, Practical Mysticism, Ruysbroeck, Theophanies, and Jacopone da Todi.

VALDEZ, GABRIEL DE LA CONCEPCIÓN (1809-1844), was born in Cuba, the son of a mulatto, and took his name from the asylum in which he was reared. He developed a great love of liberty and managed to obtain an excellent education. His Prayer to God was recited on his way to execution for rebellion. His Poesias were published at Palma de Mallorca, 1847.

VALDIVIELSO, JOSÉ DE (1560-1638), was born in Toledo, Spain, and won popular esteem for his devotional lyrics. His widespread Romancero Espiritual was first published in Madrid, 1612, and there was another edition in 1880. He was the author of excellent Autos and comedies and a highly esteemed Life of St. Joseph.

VALENCIA, GUILLERMO (1873-....), was born at Popayán, Cauca, Colombia. A short experience in politics has been followed by retirement to literary life in his native city. His work may be found in Poesías (Bogotá, 1898) and Mejores Poemas (Madrid, 1919).

VALÉRY, PAUL AMBROISE (1871-....), was born at Cette, Herault, France. His works include Charmes, Eupalinos, and Une Soirée avec M. Teste.

VAUGHAN, HENRY ("The Silurist") (1621-1693), was born at Skethiog-on-Usk, Brecknockshire, Wales. He studied at Oxford and practiced medicine. His works include Poems (1646), Olor Iscanus (1651) and Silex Scintillans (1650-1655).

VAUQUELIN DE LA FRESNAYE (1536-1606) was born near Falaise, Calvados, France. He was a poet of the Horatian school and author of an Art Poetique.

VEGA CARPIO, LOPE FELIX DE (1562-1635), was born in Madrid, joined in the expedition of the Armada and led a dissipated life before and after taking Orders in 1614. He is said to have written 1800 plays and 400 Autos characterized by unsurpassed fluency. Editions of his works are numerous.

VERDAGUER, JACINTO (1845-1902), was born at Riudeperas, Barcelona, and was ordained priest in 1870. In 1877 he published La Atlantida, a Catalan epic, which was translated into the principal languages. This was followed by Canigó and Idilis y Cants Mistichs (1879), Cansons de Montserat (1880), Jesus Infant (1890) and Santa Eularia (1898).

VERGILIUS, PUBLIUS MARO (70-19 B.C.), was born near Mantua, Cisalpine Gaul, and studied at Cremona, Mediolanum, Neapolis and Rome. He enjoyed the patronage of Asinius Pollio, Maecenas and the Emperor Augustus. He was intimate with the poet Horace. His chief works are the Bucolics and Georgics (42-30 B.C.) and the Aeneid. The first printed edition of the latter appeared in Rome, 1469.

VERHAEREN, EMILE (1855-1916), was born at Saint-Amand, near Antwerp. He studied at the University of Louvain and was admitted to the bar. He published Flamandes (1883), Les Contes de Minuit, Les Moines, Les Soirs, Les Debacles, Les Flambeaux Noirs, Les Apparus dans mes Chemins, Les Campagnes Hallucinées, and Les Villages Illusoires.

VERLAINE, PAUL (1844-1896), was born at Metz, France. He identified himself at first with the Parnassians and later with the Symbolists and the Decadents. He used his misfortunes as themes for his poetry. He lectured in England in 1893. His chief works are Poèmes Saturniens (1865), Sagesse (1881), Jadis et Naguere

(1885), Romances sans Paroles (1887), Bonheur (1891) and Mes Hospitaux (1891).

VERSTEGAN, RICHARD (1548-1636), was born in London of Dutch for-bears who had taken the name of Rowlands. He found he could not graduate from Oxford as he was a Catholic and returning to Antwerp he resumed his proper name. He wrote Cruelties of Contemporary Heretics (Paris, 1583 and 1588). He became a publisher of the first English catechisms and prayerbooks and wrote Odes in Imitation of the Seven Penitential Psalms (1605).

VICENTE, GIL (1470-1540), a Portuguese poet who left works in Spanish as well as his native idiom. His dramas are much ad-mired for the songs they introduce. See Menendez y Pelayo's Antologia (Vol. VIII).

VIDA, MARCO GIROLAMO (1480-1566), was born at Cremona, Italy, and was educated at the universities of Padua and Bologna. He became a canon of St. John Lateran and won the favor of Leo X for his exquisite Latin. He was made prior of St. Silvester in Tusculum (Frascati) and later under Pope Clement VIII was created bishop of Alba. He took part in the Council of Trent. His works include Christiados—an epic in twelve books (1535), De Arte Poetica (1537), De Bombycibus—On Silkworms (1527), and De Ludo Schaccorum—On Chess (1527).

VILLON, FRANCOIS (1431-1484), was born in Paris, France, of humble extraction. He gave himself to Bohemian disorders and was tried three times in court on serious charges. He wrote Le Petit Testa-ment (1456) and Le Grand Testament (1461). He served sev-eral terms in prison, was condemned to death, but released by King Louis XI he disappeared from sight.

VIOLANTE DO CEO, SISTER (1601-1693), was born in Lisbon and passed sixty years in the Dominican Convent there. She was famous as a musician as well as poet. Her Rythmas Varias were pub-lished in Rouen (1646).

VITORELLI, JACOPO (1749-1835), was born at Bassano, Italy. His principal work is the Anacreontiche ad Irene. His Rime e Pos-tume were published in 1851.

VONDEL, JOOST VAN DEN (1587-1679), was born at Cologne of a fam-ily from Antwerp, which removed early in his life to Amsterdam. He married in 1610 and published his classical Jerusalem De-stroyed in 1620. He became a Catholic in 1641, after which he published Peter en Pauwels (1641), The Mysteries of the Altar (1646) and his masterpiece Lucifer (1654). He is considered the greatest poet of the Netherlands.

WALSH, THOMAS (1875-....), was born in Brooklyn, New York, and educated in Georgetown University and Columbia University. He is the author of The Prison Ships (1909), The Pilgrim Kings

(1915), Gardens Overseas (1918), Don Folquet (1920), and editor of The Hispanic Anthology (1920).

WARD, LEO (1890-....), is the son of the late Wilfrid Ward, editor of the Dublin Review.

WILDE, OSCAR (1854-1900), was born in Dublin, Ireland, and educated at Trinity College and Magdalen College, Oxford. His Poems appeared in 1881. He undertook to introduce reforms in dress and house decorations and also became a playright of successful pieces. After suffering imprisonment for two years for moral offenses, he retired to Paris where he died, after a reconciliation with the Church.

WILHELM OF SWEDEN, PRINCE (1884-....), was born at Tullgarn, Sweden, the second son of King Oscar Gustav V. He received the title of Duke of Södermanland and was educated at Uppsala University. His writings include Slackta Fyrar, Svart och Vitt, Selene (1922), Kinangozi (1924) and a version of James Elroy Flecker's Hassan (1923).

WILKINSON, MARGUERITE (1883-....), was born at Halifax, Nova Scotia, and educated at Evanston High School and Northwestern University. Her works include In Vivid Gardens (1911), New Voices (1919) and Citadels (1926).

WILLIAM OF SHOREHAM (latter half of the 12th century) was born at Shoreham in Kent, England. In 1313 he was vicar of Chart Sutton, Kent. The fact that the translation of the Psalter attributed to him is in the Mercian and not the Kentish dialect has led to some doubt regarding the authorship of the works generally believed to be from his pen.

WIPO (died about 1048) was the Burgundian chaplain of the Emperor Conrad II.

WORDSWORTH, WILLIAM (1770-1850), was born at Cockermouth, Cumberland, England. He was educated at Hawkshead and graduated at Cambridge in 1791. He varied his residences between France and England until 1811, when he settled at Grasmere in the Lake District of England. He was made poet laureate in 1843. His chief works are An Evening Walk (1793), Descriptive Sketches (1793), Lyrical Ballads (containing Coleridge's the Ancient Mariner) (1798), The Excursion (1814), Peter Bell (1819), Yarrow Revisited (1835), Sonnets (1838) and The Prelude (1850).

ZEREA, JACOB, was emperor of Abyssinia (fifteenth century). He was a Christian and sent an embassy to the Council of Florence.

ZORILLA, JOSÉ (1817-1893), was born at Valladolid, Spain, and early achieved a reputation as a poet. He accompanied the Archduke Maximilian to Mexico and after his execution returned to face a life of poverty and literary success in Spain. His chief merit is in descriptive charm. His Don Juan Tenorio is one of the Spanish dramatic classics.

INDEX OF AUTHORS

533

INDEX OF TITLES

P

Q

R

S